A Soviet Credo: Shostakovich's Fourth Symphony

For Mum, Chris and Ellie

A Soviet Credo: Shostakovich's Fourth Symphony

Pauline Fairclough

ASHGATE

Published by
Ashgate Publishing Limited
Gower House
Croft Road
Aldershot
Hants GU11 3HR
England

Ashgate Publishing Company
Suite 420
101 Cherry Street
Burlington
Vermont, 05401–4405
USA

Ashgate website: http://www.ashgate.com

British Library Cataloguing in Publication Data
Fairclough, Pauline, 1970–
A Soviet Credo: Shostakovich's Fourth Symphony
1. Shostakovich, Dmitrii Dmitrievich, 1906–1975. Symphonies, no 4. I. Title
784.2'092

US Library of Congress Cataloging in Publication Data
Fairclough, Pauline, 1970–
A Soviet Credo: Shostakovich's Fourth Symphony / Pauline Fairclough.
p. cm.
Includes bibliographical references and index.
1. Shostakovich, Dmitrii Dmitrievich, 1906–1975, Symphonies, no.4, op. 43.
2. Symphonies – Analysis, appreciation. I. Title.
MT130.S4F35 2006
784.2'184–dc22

2005011868

ISBN 0 7546 5016 2

This book is printed on acid free paper.

Typeset by Bournemouth Colour Press, Parkstone, Poole.

Printed and bound in Great Britain by MPG Books, Bodmin, Cornwall.

Contents

Permissions

The following Shostakovich examples are reproduced by permission of Boosey and Hawkes Music Publishers Ltd:

Symphony No. 1 in F minor Op. 10 © Copyright Boosey and Hawkes Music Publishers Ltd.

Symphony No. 4 in C minor Op. 43 © Copyright Boosey and Hawkes Music Publishers Ltd.

Symphony No. 5 in D minor Op. 47 © Copyright Boosey and Hawkes Music Publishers Ltd.

Symphony No. 14 Op. 135 © Copyright Boosey and Hawkes Music Publishers Ltd.

Cello Concerto No. 2 © Copyright 1968 by Boosey and Hawkes Music Publishers Ltd.

Lady Macbeth of the Mtsensk District Op. 29 © Copyright Boosey and Hawkes Music Publishers Ltd.

The Age of Gold Op. 22 © Copyright 1993 by DSCH, Moscow. Sole publisher for the UK, British Commonwealth (ex. Canada) and Eire: Boosey and Hawkes Music Publishers Ltd.

All other extracts, except where indicated, are reproduced by permission of Boosey and Hawkes Music Publishers Ltd.

Stravinsky: *Petrushka* © Copyright 1912 by Hawkes & Son (London) Ltd.

Stravinsky: *Oedipus rex* © Copyright 1927 by Hawkes & Son (London) Ltd. Revised version: © Copyright 1949, 1950 by Hawkes & Son (London) Ltd. US Copyright renewed.

Extract from Irving Berlin, 'Always' reproduced by permission of International Music Publishers Ltd. Words and music Irving Berlin. © 1925 Irving Berlin Inc., USA. Francis Day & Hunter Ltd., London.

Kabalevsky: Symphony No. 1. Copyright 1932 by Boosey and Hawkes Music Publishers Ltd.

Khrennikov: Symphony No. 1. Copyright by Boosey and Hawkes Music Publishers Ltd.

Myaskovksy: Symphony No. 12. Copyright by Universal Edition.

Myaskovsky: Symphony No. 15. Copyright by Boosey and Hawkes Music Publishers Ltd.

Myaskovsky: Symphony No. 16. Copyright by Boosey and Hawkes Music Publishers Ltd.

Shebalin: Symphony No. 3. Copyright 1946 by Boosey and Hawkes Music Publishers Ltd.

Shostakovich: Fourth Symphony, piano draft, New Collected Works vol. 4, DSCH Publishers, Moscow, p. 318, 15a. Reproduced by kind permission of Centre Chostakovich, Paris and the Shostakovich Family Archive, Moscow.

Extracts from Pauline Fairclough, 'The "Perestroyka" of Soviet Symphonism: Shostakovich in 1935', *Music and Letters*, 83/2, 2002, 259–73, and 'Mahler Reconstructed: Sollertinsky and the Soviet Symphony', *The Musical Quarterly*, 85/2, 2001, 367–90, by permission of Oxford University Press.

List of Tables

Foreword

This book began life as a PhD thesis in 1995. Since then, the world of Shostakovich scholarship has advanced dramatically, as has that of Soviet music and culture in general. Although archival research is still difficult for many Western scholars, there is a wealth of published information now available that paints a far brighter picture of Shostakovich than the embittered figure of Solomon Volkov's 1979 *Testimony*. Elizabeth Wilson's engaging collection of reminiscences was the first Western publication (1994) to give Western readers glimpses of the Shostakovich already familiar to many Russians: brilliant, caustically witty, warm-hearted and deeply loved by those close to him. The Russian publication of his letters to Isaak Glikman in 1993 provided a more intimate view of a composer who was famously guarded in public; its translation into English in 2001 made this invaluable documentary study accessible to a wider readership. Laurel Fay's 2000 biography, based on exhaustive archival research, provided a desperately needed reliable source of information about the composer's life. In the same year, Irina Bobïkina's collection of Shostakovich's letters to various friends throughout his life was published in Russia, providing yet more insights into the 'real' Shostakovich: neither a Soviet stooge nor a conveniently blank canvas upon whom any writer can impose his or her ideological and political prejudices. Though Fay's statement, made in 2000, that Shostakovich scholarship is still in its infancy holds true in the sense that much archival material has yet to be uncovered and his manuscripts examined, the figure of Shostakovich the man is becoming clearer all the time. We no longer need to search for an elusive 'real' figure: he springs to life from the pages of these books. In looking for an anti-Soviet hero – the Shostakovich of *Testimony* and *Testimony*-inspired writings – we miss the deeper heroism of a figure who was, in the most positive sense, 'apolitical': not anti-Communist (and hence pro-capitalist, as Cold War rhetoric used to dictate), but broadly humanitarian. It is that very quality in his music that thousands of listeners have sensed and responded to, whatever their own political views. To reduce its expressive breadth and depth to a set of political messages as some commentators have done is to impoverish its meaning indeed. The longer we cling to the view of a 'dissident' Shostakovich, the longer we miss out on the richness of his role within his own society and culture. The infinite number of variables in this relationship and the infinite number of personal responses his music provokes are all part of this paradoxical reality: it was Soviet society itself that shaped this compelling music. Shostakovich was a child of his time, albeit one whose stature allows him, with the passing of time, to transcend it.

As numerous revisionist and post-revisionist studies of Soviet culture and society have demonstrated, the old Western notion of a Soviet artist engaged in perpetual struggle against the State vastly simplifies – not to say romanticizes – the complex nature of relations between art and politics in the Soviet Union. It flatters still-cherished assumptions that only in the 'free' West can artists truly express themselves. And yet popular perceptions of Shostakovich still struggle to break free of its influence. The notion that great art was created in the Soviet Union in spite of, rather than in any sense because of, the socio-political structures that supported it flourishes to this day in schools, universities and the mass media, 16 years after Reagan shook hands with Gorbachev and revoked his famous 'evil empire' speech.

The Fourth Symphony was composed on the cusp of massive changes in Soviet society. It teetered precariously on the brink of a new age: behind it lay the brief years of *perestroyka* that began in 1932 and the assassination of Sergey Kirov. Ahead lay the most terrifying years of Stalin's purges, while in the middle of its composition Shostakovich himself was singled out for unprecedented official criticism. Its musical language was completely unlike that of any contemporary Soviet symphony. One of the foremost conductors of the period is alleged to have been unable to comprehend it, though he was familiar with all Mahler's symphonies and had performed some of the most advanced Soviet works of the time. Mystery surrounds the circumstances of its withdrawal from rehearsal to this day. For me, at least, the Fourth Symphony seems to encapsulate the hope, idealism, fear and sheer insanity of those years more compellingly than does any other contemporary Soviet musical work. This study can do no more than scratch the surface of its enigmatic subject. It does not aim to 'explain' its meaning; no single writer could presume to do that. Like all analyses, it is an interpretation, not a prescription for listening. Though the symphony communicates 'something' with immense urgency, in the end, to quote Adorno on Mahler, it is a 'narrative that relates nothing'. I have not tried to put that 'nothing' into words. Instead, I have suggested ways of describing the process of its narrative in a way that does not tie the symphony to specific events or ideas; readers are free to do so if they wish.

A complete source study of the Fourth Symphony would have to include discussion of the various sketch materials that preceded work on the symphony as we know it. These include the Five Fragments for orchestra Op. 42, four piano drafts and a rejected, unfinished but fully orchestrated fragment marked Adagio – Allegro non troppo. This last was first recorded by Gennadi Rozhdestvensky on Melodiya (A10 00319 000) in 1988, along with the four piano drafts; the Adagio fragment has been recorded by Oleg Caetani (Arts 47703–2, 2004) and Mstislav Rostropovich (Andante AN4090, 2004). Volume 3 of the new DSCH collected works edition includes facsimiles of these fragments, and volume 4 (the new edition of the Fourth Symphony) includes facsimiles of substantial piano drafts of the symphony in its near-final form, as follows: first movement: bars 1–98; second movement: bars 1–394; third movement: bars 1–936. Combined with the Five

Fragments, the piano drafts provide a fascinating insight into Shostakovich's creative processes; while the second movement differs only slightly from the finished version, he made more substantial changes to the finale.

As I was not in a position to undertake a comprehensive source study while researching my PhD, I decided to restrict my research to an analytical survey of the finished score and (then) published materials, and this has remained the focus of the present study, though I have made minor changes to my discussion of the finale to take into account the most significant findings regarding the date of its composition.

Bristol, 2004

Acknowledgements

Many people have helped in the preparation of this book. My thanks go first to David Fanning, who first encouraged me to consider postgraduate study and ended up being my supervisor for seven long years. I would never have embarked upon an academic career without his support and guidance. Similarly invaluable were, and still are, David Fallows and Michael Talbot; I would also like to thank Jan Smaczny and Barry Cooper for their meticulous correction of various errors at PhD stage. Will Peters's kind assistance in translating some awkward Russian phrases was greatly appreciated. Finally, I wish to thank Richard for putting up with over a decade of Shostakovich-related ramblings, not minding my still being an impoverished student long after all our friends had proper jobs, and generally being blissfully disinterested in musicology.

I am happy to be able to acknowledge the generous assistance of the Music and Letters Trust for kindly covering my copyright charges. I am also indebed to Heidi May at Ashgate for supporting this project from the start, and to Fiona Little, whom I was fortunate enough to have as a copy-editor. I am indebted to her for her attentive and thoughtful scrutiny of the text, including over 200 music examples. Any errors that escaped her eagle eyes are, of course, entirely my own responsibility.

Mum, Chris and Ellie, to whom this book is dedicated, are in no way expected to read it – I would simply like to thank them all for their love and support.

Introduction

Composition, Context and Reception

Shostakovich's Fourth Symphony had the most extraordinary performance history of any of his major works. Written in 1935–36 after several false starts (the first of which dated back at least as far as November 1934[1]), it was, Shostakovich declared in 1935, to be 'the credo of my creative work'[2] – his 'new way' as a symphonist after the experimental Second and Third symphonies of 1927 and 1930.[3] It was abruptly withdrawn from rehearsal on the eve of its Leningrad première on 11 December 1936, in a performance scheduled to be conducted by the distinguished Austrian émigré Fritz Stiedry. Aside from a two-piano performance by Shostakovich and Moisey Vainberg in the Composers' Union in 1945, it remained unperformed until 1961.[4] The première finally took place in the Great Hall of the Moscow Conservatoire on 30 December 1961, conducted by Kirill Kondrashin. Although the original orchestral score had been lost during the war, allegedly by the conductor Aleksandr Gauk, the orchestral parts remained in the library of the Leningrad Philharmonic and were found in 1960.[5] Derek Hulme, following Dmitri

1 Shostakovich first referred to the Fourth Symphony in the article 'Schastiye poznaniye' [The joy of knowledge], *Sovetskoye iskusstvo*, 5 November 1934, where he says that he has begun the symphony but put it aside for the time being. Quoted in the collected works, vol. 2, Moscow: Muzïka, 1982, editor's note, n. 7.

2 Shostakovich described it as such in 1935. See 'Moy tvorcheskiy put' [My creative path], *Izvestiya*, 3 April 1935, 4.

3 The Beethovenian associations of the term 'new way' are well established. Michael Koball also uses the term (in quotation marks) to describe Shostakovich's Fourth Symphony in Koball, *Pathos und Groteske: Die deutsche Tradition im symphonischen Schaffen von Dmitri Schostakowitsch*, Berlin: Verlag Ernst Kuhn, 1997, 105.

4 Derek C. Hulme, *Dmitri Shostakovich: A Catalogue, Bibliography and Discography*. Second edition, Oxford: Clarendon Press, 1991, 114; and Laurel Fay, Shostakovich: *A Life*, Oxford: Oxford University Press, 2000, 97. There must also have been a single piano score dating from 1936 that Shostakovich used in these preview performances. The two-piano version may also originally date from 1936: in a letter to the cellist Viktor Kubatskiy dated 27 April 1936, Shostakovich declared his intention to make a two-piano reduction of the Fourth Symphony, which he had just finished. See Irina Bobïkina, ed., *Dmitriy Shostakovich v pis'makh i dokumentakh* [Dmitriy Shostakovich through letters and documents], Moscow: Glinka State Central Museum of Musical Culture, 2000, 161.

5 Though it seems to be accepted fact that Gauk lost the score, his published memoirs, dated 1962, claim that 'in recent years I have often looked through the score'. See Khentova, *Shostakovich: zhizn' i tvorchestvo* [Shostakovich: life and works], Leningrad:

and Lyudmila Sollertinsky, state that it was the librarian at the time, Boris Shalman, who found the parts and carried out the reconstruction work from them.[6] Most Russian-language sources state that it was Shostakovich's friend Lev Atovmyan who found the parts and made the new score together with a new four-hand transcription. However, Manashir Yakubov was claimed that it was indeed Shalman who reconstructed the score 'on the initiative of Levon Atovmian'.[7]

Several musicians and writers have offered opinions on why the symphony acquired such pariah status, as will be seen. But it is worth stating straight away that there is no single entirely reliable source that can fully account for the circumstances that led to its dramatic withdrawal. Some have suggested that going ahead with the première at that particular moment in Soviet history would have put Shostakovich's life in danger.[8] But such statements do not square with the little we do know about the generous circulation of the symphony ahead of the première. Shostakovich played his new symphony several times to friends and colleagues, including Myaskovsky and Khachaturian; Shostakovich's Soviet biographer Sofiya Khentova notes that the score was 'widely known among Moscow musicians'.[9] Moreover, Shostakovich's late-night performance for Ivan Sollertinsky, Isaak Glikman and Otto Klemperer records high levels of praise for the new work and describes Klemperer's (unrealized) plan to perform the symphony in a forthcoming South American tour.[10] But notwithstanding these positive accounts, the new work attracted its share of criticism; when Myaskovsky heard of the première's cancellation, he noted in his diary that 'Shostakovich was so persecuted by the discussions that he withdrew his new (Fourth) symphony from performance – monumental and dazzling. What a disgrace for us – his

---

Sovetskiy Kompozitor, 1985, 440. However, no copy of the score from 1936 has been found despite the best efforts of Russian archivists. Laurel Fay believes that there must have been at least one copyist's score (used by Stiedry), but no such score has so far come to light (personal communication, 24 June 2002).

6 See Hulme, *Dmitri Shostakovich: A Catalogue*, 114 and Dmitri and Lyudmila Sollertinskiy, *Pages from the Life of Dmitri Shostakovich*, trans. G. Hobbs and C. Midgley, London: Robert Hale, 1981, 154–55.

7 Manashir Yakubov editorial commentary to the Fourth Symphony, Moscow: DSCH, 2003, 242. Both Gauk and Kondrashin claim that it was Atovm'yan who reconstructed the score. See Khentova, *Shostakovich: zhizn' i tvorchestvo*, 440, and V. Razhnikov, *Kirill Kondrashin rasskazïvaet o muzïke i zhizni* [Kirill Kondrashin talks about music and life], Moscow: Sovetskiy Kompozitor, 1989, 182.

8 One of the most outspoken proponents of the view that the Fourth was 'un' socialist realist is Sollertinsky's daughter-in-law Lyudmila Mikheyeva. She claims that its première would have endangered Shostakovich because it was 'full of tragedy, not remotely responding to the canons of socialist realism'. See Mikheyeva, *Zhizn' Dmitriya Shostakovicha* [Life of Dmitriy Shostakovich], Moscow: 'Terra', 1997, 197.

9 See Khentova, *Shostakovich: zhizn' i tvorchestvo*, 440.

10 Isaak Glikman, trans. Anthony Phillips, *Story of a Friendship*, London: Faber, 2001, xxii.

contemporaries.'[11] During the more relaxed cultural climate of the war years, Shostakovich's friends considered the possibility of a belated première. Laurel Fay reports that after Shostakovich and Vainberg's private performance in 1945, Shostakovich even briefly toyed with the idea of making it his 'official' Ninth Symphony.[12] Yet despite Shostakovich's post-war stature as the Soviet Union's leading composer after the international success of his Seventh Symphony, the Fourth Symphony had to wait another 16 years to be heard. In 1948, following the so-called *Zhdanovshchina*, when the Soviet musical world was subjected to renewed attacks for 'formalism' and lack of social relevance or popular appeal, the composer Marian Koval, formerly of the RAPM (Russian Association of Proletarian Musicians) singled out the fugato from its first movement as an especially pernicious example of Shostakovich's 'formalist' crimes,[13] and Tikhon Khrennikov cited the 1946 publication of Shostakovich's two-piano arrangement as evidence of lack of zeal in the ranks of the Composers' Union.[14]

Of all the published reminiscences concerning the cancellation of the première, by far the most contentious is found in Solomon Volkov's *Testimony*, where Volkov elaborates on what was by then a familiar story: Shostakovich's withdrawal of the symphony after judging Stiedry's rehearsals to have been disastrous. *Testimony* claims that Stiedry deliberately made a hash of rehearsals in order to distance himself from Shostakovich in the aftermath of his mauling in the infamous editorials 'Sumbur vmesto muzïki' [Muddle instead of music] and 'Baletnaya fal'sh' [Balletic falsity] in *Pravda* earlier that year: 'Stidri didn't know or understand the score, and he expressed no desire to grapple with it. He said so straight out. And why be shy? The composer was an exposed formalist, so why bother digging around in his score?'[15] As will be discussed in the following

---

11 The date of Myaskovsky's diary entry is 11 December 1936. See O.P. Lamm, *Stranitsï tvorcheskoy biographii Myaskovskogo* [Pages from Myaskovsky's creative diary], Moscow: Sovetskiy Kompozitor, 1989, 255–6.

12 Fay, *Shostakovich*, 96–7.

13 For Koval's comments on the Fourth Symphony, see Koval, 'Tvorcheskiy put' D Shostakovicha' [The creative path of D. Shostakovich] (part 2), *Sovetskaya muzïka*, 1948/3, 31–43, especially 37–42. For an English translation of part of Koval's attack on the symphony, see Nicolas Slonimsky, *Lexicon of Musical Invective: Critical Assaults on Composers since Beethoven's Time*, New York: Coleman-Moss Company Inc., 1953, 177.

14 It was published in a short print-run of 300 copies. See Fay, Shostakovich, 307, n. 45. It is now vol. 19 of the new collected works, ed. Manashir Yakubov, Moscow: DSCH, 2000. For Khrennikov's remarks, see Khrennikov, 'Za tvorchestvo, dostoynoe sovetskogo naroda' [For a creativity worthy of the Soviet people], *Sovetskaya muzïka*, 1948/1, 54–62, especially 61.

15 Solomon Volkov, *Testimony: The Memoirs of Dimitri Shostakovich as Related to and Edited by Solomon Volkov*, London: Faber, 1981, 90–91. That this book cannot be viewed as Shostakovich's authentic memoirs is now beyond doubt; for the most detailed account of its plagiarized pages and other facts relating to its dishonest presentation, see Laurel Fay, 'Volkov's *Testimony* Reconsidered' and 'A Side-by-Side Comparison of Texts from

chapter, this basic version of events – bar the unpleasant inference of deliberate sabotage – has been repeated frequently in Soviet memoirs, though Glikman's more recent account paints a very different picture, as will be seen.[16]

Shostakovich himself later encouraged speculation that he had withdrawn the symphony owing to problems with the work itself rather than to anything to do with Stiedry's rehearsals or his delicate political situation. In a blandly diffident autobiographical article for *Sovetskaya muzïka* in 1956 Shostakovich dismissed the symphony, claiming that it was 'formally imperfect and overly drawn out and suffers, I would say, from "mania grandiosa"'.[17] That these words were not sincere could be inferred from Shostakovich's letter to Glikman written only two years after this article was published, where Shostakovich – bored in hospital – tells Glikman that he has been thinking about *Lady Macbeth* and the Fourth Symphony: 'I should so like to hear both of these works performed. I cannot say that I would expect much joy from the opera. ... But the Fourth could perhaps be done. Actually, I don't have very high hopes of either work being performed, but I indulge myself by imagining them in my inner ear.'[18] What is more, it is plain that in the years immediately following the symphony's withdrawal, Shostakovich regarded it as one of his most important works. In a forceful letter to his friend Boleslav Yavorsky dated June 1938, he all but demanded that he visit in order to hear a private performance of the Fourth Symphony, together with a handful of other (then) unpublished and unperformed works: the Five Fragments for Orchestra (1935) and the Four Romances on texts by Pushkin (1936); his Six

Testimony with their Original Sources', in Malcolm Hamrick Brown, ed., *A Shostakovich Casebook*, Bloomington and Indianapolis: Indiana University Press, 2004, 22–79. The first *Pravda* editorial, 'Sumbur vmesto muzïki', was published in *Pravda* on 28 January 1936; the second, 'Baletnaya fal'sh', on 6 February. Both editorials were reprinted in *Sovetskaya muzïka*, 1936/2, 4–8. For a translation, see Leo Treitler et al., eds, *Strunk's Source Readings in Music History*, New York: Norton, 1997, 1397–99. They were subsequently discussed at length in the following issue: see *Sovetskaya muzïka*, 1936/3, 16–60 for transcripts of the discussions in the Moscow Composers' Union. For full but contrasting discussions of their likely authorship, see Leonid Maksimenkov, *Sumbur vmesto muzïki: Stalinskaya kul'turnaya revolutsiya 1936–1938* [Muddle instead of music: the Stalinist cultural revolution 1936–1938], Moscow: Yuridicheskaya Kniga, 1997, and Solomon Volkov, *Shostakovich and Stalin*, London: Little, Brown, 2004, 132–42. Joseph Darby's suggestion that Stiedry may have been forced to conduct the Fourth Symphony – a work expected to be controversial – as an excuse to fire him does not seem plausible. Although Sof'ya Khentova claims that the Philharmonic directorate were planning to fire Stiedry (see Joseph E. Darby, 'Dmitri Shostakovich's Second, Third and Fourth Symphonies: Problems of Context, Analysis and Interpretation', PhD diss., City University of New York, 1999, 341), they would hardly have expected to escape unscathed from such a scandal.

16 Glikman, *Story of a Friendship*, xxii–xxiii.

17 Shostakovich, 'Dumï o proydennom puti' [Thoughts about paths I have taken], *Sovetskaya muzïka*, 1956/9, 14.

18 Glikman, *Story of a Friendship*, 78–9. The letter is dated 19 September 1958.

Japanese Romances were added in a postscript. Shostakovich's wholehearted recommendation of these works could hardly be more categorical: 'to get the full picture [of my creative work] I regard it as essential that you hear them'. The only note of caution he offers is that Yavorsky's visit would not be a short one, as the symphony would last longer than one-and-a-half hours.[19] When Shostakovich looked over the score prior to the symphony's première in 1961, he found he did not want to change a single note. Kondrashin describes how Shostakovich asked him for his own copy of the score to check over, saying that he had forgotten much of it: 'The next day he rang me. "Kirill Petrovich, I'd be very happy for you to perform the symphony. No changes need to be made. The piece is very dear to me as it is."'[20]

Another part of the mythology surrounding the Fourth Symphony concerns the nature of the work itself. Shostakovich had begun work on it at a high point in his career; he completed it two months after the second *Pravda* attack in February 1936 – one of the lowest points in his life. Given that the Fourth Symphony was not destined to be Shostakovich's 'rehabilitation' piece as the Fifth Symphony was, the differences between them invite speculation. Was the Fifth really so obviously 'acceptable' and the Fourth 'unacceptable'? Looking back at Soviet calls for a new type of 'socialist realist' symphonism during the mid- to late 1930s, it could be argued that in several respects the Fourth Symphony was a shining example of precisely the kind of new Soviet symphonism that composers and musicologists might have welcomed.[21] As will be seen, the dictats of socialist realism as applied to music in particular were vague and open to broad interpretation. Moreover, to assume that a particular style was in or out of favour at any given time (apart from, perhaps, the years immediately following the *Zhdanovshchina* of 1948) is tempting but dangerous; those who have asserted the clear 'unsuitability' of the Fourth Symphony for its time and place overestimate the extent to which musical language, structure and dramaturgy was preordained. The key question here is the notion of State imposition; Slavist scholars now widely agree that the old Western view that artists were 'forced' to create in a particular style after the 1932 Resolution relies on an over-simplified paradigm of imposition and resistance (for discussion of the Resolution, see Chapter One, p.

19 See Shostakovich's letter to Yavorsky dated 26 June 1938 in Bobikïna, *Dmitriy Shostakovich*, 124–5. Shostakovich's timing of the symphony is curious; in all recordings I have been able to consult – including Rostropovich's live 1998 performance (Andante SC-AN-4090, 2004), which frequently drops below the indicated tempi – the symphony lasts just over an hour.

20 See Razhnikov, *Kirill Kondrashin rasskazïvaet*, 183 and Elizabeth Wilson, *Shostakovich: A Life Remembered*, London: Faber, 1994, 348.

21 I have already made this point elsewhere: see Pauline Fairclough, 'Mahler Reconstructed: Sollertinsky and the Soviet Symphony', *The Musical Quarterly*, 85/2, 2001, 367–90 and 'The "Perestroyka" of Soviet Symphonism: Shostakovich in 1935', *Music and Letters*, 83/2, 2002, 259–73.

11–12).[22] If anyone created a style that later came to be regarded as socialist realist, it was surely the artists themselves, as Katerina Clark has argued throughout her study of the socialist realist novel.[23] The reality is that the development of the socialist realist symphony – insofar as such a thing can be said to exist at all – was guided by composers rather than critics or politicians.[24] Even Shostakovich's own massively successful Fifth Symphony of 1937 hardly conformed to a supposed socialist realist stereotype, with jolly popular themes and a happy ending.[25] Nor

---

22 Though such views have circulated widely in historical and literary Slavic studies since the 1980s, musicology has been slow to catch up; Boris Schwarz's magisterial survey *Music and Musical Life in Soviet Russia 1917–1981* (Bloomington: Indiana University Press, 1983) has remained the chief source for Soviet music studies, and his contention that the 1932 Resolution saw a change from 'multiformity to conformity' has only begun to be challenged. Similar claims relating to the death of the Soviet avant-garde have been vigorously contested by literary and visual art scholarship; see for example Thomas Lahusen and Evgeny Dobrenko, *Socialist Realism without Shores*, Durham, North Carolina, and London: Duke University Press, 1997. For a recent post-revisionist historical view of Soviet society and culture influenced by Michel Foucault's work on power relations between State and society, see Stephen Kotkin, *Magnetic Mountain: Stalinism as a Civilisation*, Berkeley: University of California Press, 1995.

23 Katerina Clark, *The Soviet Novel: History as Ritual*, Chicago and London: University of Chicago Press, 1981.

24 The label 'socialist realist' is a notoriously slippery one, and nearly impossible to apply to music. The widely held assumption that socialist realism is equatable with bland gaiety is not without foundation but it should be remembered that 'optimism' in art was not a stated aim in the early socialist realist period, and certainly not in the war years. It is simply not the case that, in order to be successful, all art had to be blandly optimistic; a classic Soviet novel such as Mikhail Sholokhov's *Tikhiy Don* [Quiet Don] has a bleak ending, and another staple of officially approved literary diet, Gorky's *Mat'* [The mother], is anything but cheerful. For a good account of the censorship Sholokhov's novel underwent, however, see Herman Ermolaev, *Censorship in Soviet Literature 1917–1991*, Lanham, Maryland: Rowman & Littlefield Publishers, Inc., 1997. Still, Ivan Dzerzhinsky's opera *Tikhiy Don* ends with a safe option: a quiet, minor-key marching chorus. Incidentally, the ending of this opera bears a striking resemblance to that of Shostakovich's contemporaneous, though hardly State-approved, *Lady Macbeth*; Shostakovich is, moreover, the dedicatee of Dzerzhinsky's opera. In particular, Shostakovich's stunning closing *coup de théâtre*– a final F minor chord marked *ppp–ffff* – is blatantly copied by Dzerzhinsky. Khrennikov's much later (1962) opera of Gorky's novel *Mat'* ends far more artificially with a bombastic E♭ major chorus. While it would be misguided to expect all operas and symphonies of the 1930s to end with rousing major-key endings, opting for a cheery tone was certainly a relatively safe option, and one that was undeniably over-exploited. This, together with Stalin's famous slogan of 1935 'Life has become better; life has become more joyful', formed the background against which much of the art we perceive as typically socialist realist was created.

25 The Sixth Symphony, however, has one of the most uncomplicated happy endings in all of Shostakovich's output. Despite critical voices complaining about the gulf between the long, lamenting opening movement and the uproarious scherzo finale, it was extremely well

was the call for socialist realism *per se* as loudly insistent within the Composers' Union as it was in the Writers' Union. In fact, considering Shostakovich's stature in the Soviet Union after the Fifth Symphony, it would seem that musical quality – however randomly measured – was regarded as important over and above supposed 'ideological' content even during the Stalin years. As the Fifth Symphony (1937) was written at an even more critical point in Soviet history than the Fourth – just as Stalin's purges were extending their reach into the general populace – the oft-cited claim that the Fourth was obviously 'unsuitable', while the Fifth, an unremittingly dark, tragic work which turns incongruously (and, to several Soviet critics present at the première, unconvincingly) to a major-key peroration at the end, was 'suitable', is problematic to say the least.[26] Moreover, as reports from the Composers' Union 1935 conference 'Discussion about Soviet Symphonism' reveal, the notion that symphonies had to be socialist realist at all – whatever that might mean in practice – was far from self-evident.

One of the aims of this study will be to demonstrate that, at the time when Shostakovich composed the Fourth Symphony (he was composing the finale when the *Pravda* articles appeared, but how far into it he had got is not known[27]), he had good cause to believe that it actually fulfilled – rather than defied – a significant number of his colleagues' suggestions as to what a Soviet symphony in the age of socialist realism should be. There is no reason to suggest that he was acting in defiance of Party or Composers' Union guidelines: in the first place, there had been no guidelines agreed or offered, and in the second place, there is considerable evidence to suggest that there was actually substantial aesthetic and ideological justification for the symphony's blend of heightened expressivity, theatricality and Mahlerian musical 'democracy'.

The notion of 'democratic' symphonism was suggested by Shostakovich's

---

received at its première. See Fay, *Shostakovich*, 115. For the reaction of perceptive Soviet critics to the celebrated 'forced rejoicing' of the Fifth's coda, see Richard Taruskin, 'Shostakovich and the Inhuman', in Taruskin, *Defining Russia Musically*, Princeton: Princeton University Press, 1997, 524–8.

26 For Georgiy Khubov's detailed review of the Fifth Symphony, see *Sovetskaya muzïka*, 1938/1, 14–28.

27 In a letter to Shebalin dated 17 April 1936, Shostakovich reported that 'it seems to me that I will soon have finished my symphony. I'm now orchestrating the finale.' Quoted in Mikheyeva, *Zhizn' Dmitriya Shostakovicha*, 194. As noted in n. 4 above, Shostakovich had written on 27 April to the cellist Kubatskiy with the news that he had just finished the orchestration. The official date for the symphony's completion, however, is 20 May 1936. A seven-bar fragment of the finale draft is dated 16 II 1936 – only ten days after the second *Pravda* attack – and presented in the new collected works score (p. 318, 15a). Despite Yakubov's view that this is the earliest of all the finale drafts, the fragment – which bears no relation to anything in the published score – is plainly not meant to be the finale's opening, and if anything seems to relate more to the later part of the finale, between 230 and 233. See Chapter Five, pp. 225–6 for a fuller discussion.

friend Ivan Sollertinsky, whose work on Mahler in 1932 provided Shostakovich with precisely the kind of aesthetic and ideological grounding he needed if he was ever called upon to explain (to cite just one potential problem) the proliferation of light music idioms in his Fourth Symphony.[28] Nor was Sollertinsky acting alone in trying to formulate a broad-based, liberal aesthetics of art. In terms both of contemporary political and cultural developments, the period 1932–36 has been described as a *perestroyka* in Soviet history: a time when moderate influences seemed to wrench control back from the excesses of the late 1920s and early 1930s.[29] This *perestroyka* can be seen, as I will argue, in both political events and literary and musical critical discourse. By analysing the twin processes of political and cultural *perestroyka* – as demonstrated in the appearance of political liberalization, the 1934 Writers' Congress and the 1935 Composers' Union symphonism conference – and placing them alongside Sollertinsky's work on Mahler and symphonism, it can be shown that Shostakovich had good reason to believe that his contemporaries would be sympathetic to the kind of re-creation of symphonism he had in mind. Though it balanced precariously on the cusp of a dramatic change in Soviet cultural history (a change which we of course perceive only in hindsight), Shostakovich's Fourth Symphony can be viewed not as a rebellious work, but as a brilliant example of what the new, 'socially relevant' – if not actually socialist realist – Soviet symphonism could be.

One other crucial aspect of the Fourth Symphony's context is that of contemporary Soviet symphonism, which has received almost no attention in Western musicology.[30] As will be seen, the Fourth Symphony was radically different from its contemporaries in its innovative approach both to formal principles and to musical materials. By using fixed musical types, such as march, waltz and arioso, Shostakovich tapped into a powerful vein of popular culture that was vastly different from the stilted, conventional language used by his contemporaries. In addition, his attitude to 'normal' Soviet symphonic dramaturgy – in particular to the expectations associated with the finale and coda – looks strikingly critical alongside mainstream Soviet symphonic repertoire. In conceiving the symphony as a new way forward for the symphonic genre in Soviet Russia – one that was both technically assured and comprehensible to a wide audience – Shostakovich arguably intended it not only to mark the start of his vocation as a symphonist, but also to serve as a model for other composers. As will be seen, the Soviet Union's front-rank symphonists were failing to rise to the challenge of creating symphonies with 'content' without resorting to texts, subtitles, programmes or crude musical imagery. Shostakovich's Fourth

28 Ivan I. Sollertinskiy, *Gustav Maler*, Leningrad: Muzgiz, 1932.

29 See principally Taruskin, 'Shostakovich and the Inhuman', 511–16, and Fairclough, 'The "Perestroyka" of Soviet Symphonism'.

30 A rare exception is David Fanning's essay 'The Soviet Symphony', in Robert Layton, ed., *A Companion to the Symphony*, London: Simon and Schuster, 1993, 292–326.

Symphony can be seen as a monumental attempt to rise to that challenge; in that context, its formal eccentricity and theatrical language can be seen as making symphonic language contemporary and therefore 'relevant', communicating with Soviet audiences in a clear yet sophisticated musical language.

Shostakovich needed models for the forging of his new symphonic language, and chief among these was Mahler.[31] But, as will be seen, Shostakovich's adoption of a Mahlerian tone was not merely a matter of stylistic borrowing, but was rooted in the aesthetic principles of 'democratic' symphonism as espoused by Sollertinsky. In challenging the norms of Soviet symphonic discourse, and by widening the scope of musical materials to include popular, light idioms, Shostakovich created a symphonic style that was not only 'democratic' but also profoundly critical. In many places, his employment of light music idioms is overtly nostalgic, and in other places grotesque. They are very rarely presented directly, tending to be 'estranged' by quirks of harmony or context. Waltzes in particular often sound incongruous, which has the effect of highlighting their quality of nostalgic, other-worldly ambivalence; polkas can be crude and disturbingly banal; triumphal themes are grotesquely over-stated; and so on.

Shostakovich's radical engagement with Soviet symphonic practice – namely the Conservatoire tradition of gently moulding older musical forms to accommodate a conventional, vaguely nationalistic style – also provoked a violent relationship between 'form' and 'content'. The discussion of these two indivisible dimensions of artistic creation in terms of their separate qualities was a typically Soviet preoccupation: form alone could not signify meaning, and art that could not be interpreted easily was therefore viewed as being socially irrelevant. Music, as an abstract art form, was peculiarly vulnerable to the charge of 'formalism',[32] and there was clear dissatisfaction among composers with regard to their failure to bind together the demands of form (implying technical mastery) and content (implying that 'meaning' of some sort could be discerned). Although the need to find concrete meaning in Shostakovich's music has been, if anything, more of an obsession among Western journalists than among Soviet critics and musicologists, composers did take the issue of musical meaning seriously, and, as will be seen, were increasingly dissatisfied with short-cuts to 'content' such as the song-symphony or use of programmes and subtitles. Shostakovich's strategy in the

---

31 Shostakovich's assistant I.B. Finkel'shtein recalled that, while he was composing the Fourth Symphony, the score of Mahler's Seventh Symphony invariably stood on Shostakovich's piano, and that he talked a lot about it. See Mikheyeva, *Zhizn' Dmitriya Shostakovicha*, 198. Fay notes that a page of extracts from Mahler's Third Symphony showing 'rare cases in orchestration' copied by Shostakovich is thought to date from this period. See Fay, *Shostakovich*, 306.

32 'Formalism' was a general pejorative term in Soviet art criticism in the 1930s and 1940s. It was allied to the concept of 'art for art's sake' as opposed to art that displayed obvious engagement with social issues. Though the term had its origins in the Russian literary Formalist movement, it was widely used as a general term of abuse.

Fourth Symphony was multi-faceted: he would pit form against content in a dramatic struggle for dominance in the first movement, while drawing on more direct means of communication such as allusion and paraphrase in the second and third movements. 'Intrinsic' elements in the musical fabric – tonality, thematic transformation, instrumentation – thus form as crucial a part of the symphony's dramatic structure as do the more obvious 'extrinsic' elements. The manner in which all these techniques interact in the Fourth Symphony – and how to discuss them in analysis – is the central concern of this study.

Problems of Reception and Analysis

There can be few composers whose intentions have been the subject of so much supposition as Shostakovich. However, Shostakovich himself seems to have maintained a flexible attitude to the notion of content and intention. Most of his major works have no programme or subtitle, and he avoided any attempt to justify them verbally, leaving supporters and detractors alike to wrangle over their supposed meaning. The work which most famously departs from this principle is the 'autobiographical' Eighth Quartet, a work that takes as its main theme Shostakovich's musical monogram DSCH and contains numerous allusions to earlier works (notably the Second Piano Trio and *Lady Macbeth of the Mtsensk District*), a revolutionary song, Beethoven and Wagner. According to the composer himself, in a letter to his friend and confidant Isaak Glikman, he dedicated the quartet to his own memory, and confessed (in characteristically ironic terms) that he wept while composing it:

> If some day I die, it's hardly likely that someone will write a work in memory of me, so I had better write one myself. The title page could carry the dedication: To the memory of the composer of this quartet'. .... It is a pseudo-tragic quartet, so much so that while I was composing it I shed the same amount of tears as I would have to pee after drinking half-a-dozen beers.[33]

Overlying this 'hidden' meaning was the published dedication 'To the Victims of Fascism and War' following the composer's visit to post-war Dresden. To commentators who recognize the prevalence of the DSCH motif throughout the quartet, this 'official' dedication looks temptingly artificial. However, it is dangerous to argue, as Lawrence Kramer has done, that the published dedication was merely a 'sham' and an obvious one at that. Kramer takes at face value Shostakovich's ironic reference to the quartet's 'pseudo-tragedy' to make the following assertion: 'The work … is a kind of meditation on shamming,

[33] Glikman, *Story of a Friendship*, 91. For the original Russian text, see Isaak Glikman, ed., *Pis'ma k drugu: Dmitriy Shostakovich–Isaaku Glikmanu* [Letters to a friend: Dmitriy Shostakovich to Isaak Glikman], Moscow: DSCH and St Petersburg: Kompozitor, 1993, 137.

understood as a means of personal and aesthetic survival in a totalitarian state. … In form and expression, the quartet intimates a tragedy, which Shostakovich – this time verifiably – would also identify as a sham, though an affecting one.'[34]

In conclusion, Kramer interprets the 'overabundance of self-citation and allusion' as signs of the anxiety felt by an oppressed individual, and views the quartet's tight thematic structure as indicative of its ultimate emptiness: 'Denied an ordinary life … the self secures its boundaries against colonization by an oppressive state only by collapsing into a wild marionette-theater of former identities and alter egos.'[35] I do not wish to argue in detail against Kramer's analysis here. But it is worth observing that his interpretation takes as its cue a determinedly literal reading of a letter written to a close friend, viewing Shostakovich's tone of ironic detachment (surely a mixture of his desire to confide and his embarrassment at the private nature of what he was confiding) as evidence of pretence on both levels: the 'hidden' dedication being as empty as the published one. Even to a leading figure in analytical hermeneutics, the trail of 'evidence' concerning intention and content in Shostakovich's music proves dangerously seductive. The assumption that nothing Shostakovich said can be taken seriously is as flawed as the (now thoroughly rejected) view that every statement was reliable. And while Kramer's conclusion has the appeal of analytical and hermeneutic congruence, its dependence on his own personal interpretation of documentary evidence means that his premises are unreliable. Without taking Shostakovich's irony at face value, Kramer's argument that the quartet's tragedy lies not in its musical substance but in its *lack* of substance – in its material frailty and hollow self-referentiality – would collapse like the house of cards he supposes the Eighth Quartet to be.

The caution with which all documentary evidence pertaining to intention should be treated does not preclude the general desirability of an interaction between hermeneutic criticism and analysis in a study of Shostakovich's music.[36] But analyses which actually rely on such evidence for their basic premises cannot avoid the traps laid by Soviet artists and critics well versed in the language of doublespeak, to say nothing of the unreliability of that evidence, sometimes discovered to be false years after being widely accepted as fact. However, the unreliability of Soviet sources is not the real issue here. As Richard Taruskin has argued, the multitude of claims as to the 'real' meaning of Shostakovich's music all have one thing in common: they seek to 'possess' musical meaning: to defend, sometimes with a moving sense of moral purpose, personal experiences of music

34 Lawrence Kramer, *Musical Meaning: Toward a Critical History*, Berkeley: University of California Press, 2002, 232–3.

35 Ibid., 240.

36 Such an interaction is persuasively demonstrated in Kramer, 'Haydn's Chaos, Schenker's Order; or, Hermeneutics and Musical Analysis: Can they Mix?', *19th-Century Music*, 16/1, 1992, 3–17.

which for some of Shostakovich's compatriots meant more than Western listeners can comprehend. That desire to lay claim to a particular interpretation is, as Taruskin observes, a peculiarly Soviet habit, born of decades of looking for covert meaning as vigorously as others sought to establish overt meaning. But equally, Taruskin adds,

> Whether viewed internally or externally, whether in terms of their content or in light of their context, Shostakovich's works are fraught with horrific subtexts that can never be ignored. That is why his music has always been, and will always be, the object of furious and manifold contention. We can never merely receive its messages; we are always implicated in their making, and therefore we can never be indifferent to them. It is never just Shostakovich. It is always Shostakovich and us.[37]

That Shostakovich's music has been the target of sometimes startlingly aggressive programmatic interpretation by Western devotees is not surprising. The most widely cited of these has been Ian MacDonald's 1990 biography, which, though not a work of scholarship, has been so widely cited that some discussion of it is unavoidable.[38] Some of the many problems with MacDonald's readings will be briefly discussed in the following analytical chapters, though his general approach to discussing Shostakovich's music has by now been too widely discredited to bear repetition here.[39] Though his insistence that musicologists should be historically well informed is a wholly redundant statement of the obvious, his demand that discussions of, and responses to, Shostakovich's music be shaped *primarily* by knowledge of historical events is deeply problematic. It is a presumption that still requires addressing, particularly in the domain of music journalism, but occasionally in the concert hall too.[40] Such knowledge cannot be a prime focus for an analyst; nor does it usually dominate the simple act of listening. In short, although knowledge of historical context does take on a sense of moral imperative for any scholar of Soviet culture, and though it undoubtedly enriches and informs discussion of Shostakovich's music, that knowledge is not a prime factor in our *musical* experience; it becomes so only when we allow our imagination to roam beyond the music to thoughts about Shostakovich himself: to the suffering of the

37 Taruskin, 'Shostakovich and the Inhuman', 476–7.

38 Ian MacDonald, *The New Shostakovich*, Oxford: Oxford University Press, 1990.

39 For a damning critique of MacDonald, see Taruskin, 'Shostakovich and the Inhuman', 480–89. For a Russian view (also critical), see Levon Hakobian, *Music of the Soviet Age, 1917–1987*, Stockholm: Melos, 1998, 59–62.

40 A not untypical example of forcing political messages onto an audience before performing Shostakovich's music occurred at a BBC Philharmonic concert in Manchester on 27 October 2001. The offending conductor, Andrew Litton, went so far as to urge the audience to bear in mind those who died in the 11 September hijacks as well as those who died in Red Square in 1905. However this doubtless well-intentioned sentiment may strike us, I would challenge anyone to listen to the Eleventh Symphony with such thoughts exclusively in their minds.

Russian people and to the terrible climate of fear in which he worked. Those thoughts may then form part of our aesthetic experience at any given moment in a performance, but they are 'extrinsic' to the musical experience itself: added on, a product of our imagination. We may allow for the validity of such thoughts, but we cannot demand them of the listener, nor claim that they should shape our 'intrinsic' experience of the music.

But what of Taruskin's assertion that 'internally or externally ... Shostakovich's works are fraught with horrific subtexts that can never be ignored'? Can we speak of 'intrinsic' subtexts: indications within the score itself that the surface of the music is not all it seems to be? As my analysis of the Fourth Symphony will illustrate, 'intrinsic' subtexts can be found up to a point, though these are nearly always associated with, or dependent on, allusions to other works, often texted or programmatic. The first movement of the Fourth Symphony, for example, suggests an 'intrinsic' subtext (or 'narrative') through a highly dramatized subversion of a 'normal' sonata form dramaturgy that is declared far more self-consciously than is usual for contemporary Soviet symphonies. In terms of deeper musical processes, there is an 'intrinsic' level of association between keys (or pitch centres), themes and intonations, though in this respect too, any 'subtext' or 'content' is dependent on Shostakovich's use of musical forms and archetypes such as marches, dances, scherzi and so on, which can then be presented in exaggerated or distorted ways.

If, as I believe was the case, Shostakovich regarded the symphonist's role as vocational, then it seems certain that, for him, a vital part of that vocation was to communicate – sometimes very directly, sometimes in a coded way – meaning of some sort to Soviet audiences. The form that Shostakovich's 'messages' took in the Fourth Symphony is extremely varied, ranging from a theatrical treatment of sonata form in the first movement to inter-textual relationships in the second and third movements. These relate not only to extensive references to Mahler's 'Resurrection' Symphony (suggesting, as Richard Longman has plausibly suggested, an 'anti-Resurrection' symphony[41]), but also to texted or subtitled works by Stravinsky and Chaikovsky, both in a highly suggestive manner.

Shostakovich's 'new way' as a symphonist was implicitly connected with his search for a new, contemporary symphonic language both modern and accessible, combining the most stringent formal techniques with the simplest intonations of song and dance, all constructed in a manner which pressed both musical form and expressive content to their maximum potential. My aim is to present an analysis which avoids drawing direct (and potentially unreliable) associations between historical events and music, but which is nevertheless shaped and informed by awareness of historical context, using Adorno's work on Mahler, some aspects of Russian literary criticism and contemporary Soviet cultural practice (principally

[41] Longman, *Expression and Structure: Processes of Integration in the Large-Scale Instrumental Music of Dmitri Shostakovich*, London: Garland Publishing Inc., 1989, 23.

symphonic music and theatre) as a theoretical basis for discussing the music's structure, language and inter-textual or 'extroversive' references.

Problems of Formal Analysis

One of the oldest Western criticisms of the Fourth Symphony has been the accusation that it lacks a coherent structure. Boris Schwarz described it as a 'titanic failure', in which Shostakovich 'deliberately rejects form in favour of a free-flowing stream of music', and argued that the first movement 'resists all attempts at formal analysis',[42] a view which was wholly or partially shared by British critics such as Tim Souster, Robert Dearling and Hugh Ottaway.[43] Dearling, echoing Schwarz, claims that the symphony benefits no more from analysis than would a ballet score,[44] while Souster more perceptively sees a basic sonata form outline in the first movement but judges Shostakovich's dramatization of it to have been a failure owing to its overabundance of 'eccentricity'. Comparing the Fourth Symphony unfavourably with the Fifth, Souster argues that the more balanced proportions and structure of the Fifth reflect 'the expression of socialistic aims with which Shostakovich was clearly deeply concerned, such as "the stabilisation of a personality".'[45] Criticizing the Fourth Symphony for being eccentric now, from our vantage point of revisionist and post-revisionist theorising, seems comparable to rating Mahler's symphonies less highly than Brahms's; Shostakovich's eccentricity – suggestive of a heightened level of 'extrinsic' meaning – has become something to value rather than to deplore.

Later Western analysts such as Edmund Stetina, Klaus Körner, Karen Kopp, Michael Koball, Eric Roseberry and Longman have attempted to discuss the symphony from a less entrenched viewpoint, accepting its eccentricities as an essential part of its symphonic dramaturgy rather than as flaws.[46] Although of these

---

42 Schwarz, *Music and Musical Life*, 170–71.

43 Tim Souster, 'Shostakovich at the Crossroads', *Tempo*, 78, 1966, 2–9; Hugh Ottaway, 'Looking Again at Shostakovich 4', *Tempo*, 115, 1975, 14–24; Robert Dearling, 'The First Twelve Symphonies: Portrait of the Artist as Citizen-Composer', in Christopher Norris, ed., *Shostakovich: The Man and his Music*, London: Lawrence and Wishart, 1982, 47–80.

44 Dearling, 'The First Twelve Symphonies', 56.

45 Souster, 'Shostakovich', 5.

46 Edmund Stetina, *Die Vierte Symphonie von Dmitrij Šostakovič: Ein zurückbehaltenes Bekenntnis*, Aachen, Shaker-Verlag, 1997; Klaus Körner, 'Schostakowitschs Vierte Sinfonie', *Archiv für Musikwissenschaft*, 31/2–3, 1974, 116–36, 214–36; Karen Kopp, *Form und Gehalt der Symphonien des Dmitrij Schostakowitsch*, Bonn: Verlag für Systematische Musikwissenschaft, 1990, 153–84; Koball, *Pathos und Groteske*, 130–20; Eric Roseberry, *Ideology, Style, Content and Thematic Process in the Symphonies, Cello Concertos and String Quartets of Dmitri Shostakovich*, New York and London: Garland Publishing Inc., 1989, 135–45 and 392–424; Longman, *Expression and Structure*, 4–25.

analyses only those of Roseberry and Koball seriously attempt to address hermeneutic issues, all accept the basic sonata form outline of the first movement without criticizing it for deviating from an expected path. It could be argued that, in his desire to discuss the Fourth Symphony purely from a formal point of view, Körner's analysis avoids interpretative discussion a little too rigorously, though his concern to rehabilitate the symphony's formal credentials after years of Western non-comprehension was a bold step.[47] The analyses by Stetina, Roseberry, Longman and Koball, however, indicate the start of a tentative convergence between the descriptive accounts of sympathetic Soviet critics such as Viktor Bobrovsky and Marina Sabinina[48] and the analytical preoccupations of Western analysts who have focused chiefly on tonal and motivic coherence. Soviet musicologists and critics have felt noticeably more at ease with the theatrical style of symphonic dramaturgy in the Fourth Symphony than their Western counterparts, but have tended to downplay structural discussion, while Western analysts have tended to prioritize structure at the expense of descriptive critical discussion. Indeed, from the very first Soviet review of the symphony in 1961, it is clear that the apparent lack of a clear structure in the finale, at least, gave not the slightest cause for concern; rather, the reviewer discusses its theatricality and vivid characterization with colourful enthusiasm:

> Often some characters of the drama take the stage from others at the very moment when one does not expect this. The noble hero gives way to the ironic moraliser, the guffawing crowd drives away the melancholic dreamer, the funeral procession encounters carnival dancing. This is all mingled into a unified dramatic flow and leads to the *dénouement*, where behind the theatrical masks are revealed living people with their experiences and feelings, their fears and their hopes.[49]

---

47 Körner's main approach to his discussion is to focus on motivic connections between the movements, not all of which are convincing. He says nothing about tonality, and offers very little in the way of structural analysis either. Kopp's discussion of the Fourth Symphony follows Körner's in its broad outline, but is essentially more of a description of the music than an analysis. She almost completely avoids interpretative discussion except in a very superficial sense, and is far less inclined to comment on issues such as thematic transformation than any of the other writers cited here. Körner, too, though acknowledging the potential for taking a more hermeneutic approach, chooses not to do so himself ('Schostakowitschs Vierte Sinfonie', 224).

48 Viktor Bobrovskiy, 'O nekotorïkh printsipakh temo- i formoobrazovaniya v simfonicheskoy i kamerno-instrumental'noy muzïke Shostakovicha' [On some principles of thematic and formal structure in the symphonic and chamber music of Shostakovich] and 'Posle pervogo ispolneniya Chetvërtoy' [After the first performance of the Fourth], in Ye.R. Skurko and Ye.I. Chigareva, *V.P. Bobrovskiy: stat'i, issledovaniya* [V.P. Bobrovskiy: articles and works], Moscow: Sovetskiy Kompozitor, 1990, 159–205, 262–70; and Marina Sabinina, *Shostakovich-simfonist. Dramaturgiya, estetika, stil'* [Shostakovich-symphonist. Dramaturgy, aesthetics, style], Moscow: Muzïka, 1976.

49 Aleksey Nikolayev, 'Prem'era Chetvërtoy' [The première of the Fourth], *Sovetskaya muzïka*, 1962/3,119.

Sabinina's analysis takes a similar, if vastly expanded view, as will be seen. Her awareness and acceptance of the symphony's theatricality produces an analysis very different from those even by later Western commentators. Bobrovsky, on the other hand, while fully accepting the finale's theatricality, is more concerned to demonstrate that it (like the symphony overall) is carefully structured on 'symmetrical' principles, though he does not go into any substantial analytical detail. My aim is to fuse Western and Soviet approaches to the analysis of Shostakovich's music, combining relatively close analysis of the score with acceptance of its unorthodox dramaturgy, thereby embedding Shostakovich's music in as broad a musicological context as possible.

Owing to Shostakovich's marginal status in Western academic circles until after the collapse of the Soviet Union in 1991, the study of his music is still regarded as a specialist branch of Western musicology, owing to a reluctance to take on board the weight of historical context (with all the restraints that places on analysts and commentators), combined with an uncomfortable awareness that Shostakovich's music has for a long time been regarded in the West as the province of the concert-goer rather than the serious scholar. The grounding of my own blend of 'extroversive' and 'introversive' discussion in both Russian and Western theory is an attempt both to demonstrate the possibility of hermeneutically engaged analysis (in the broadest sense) of Shostakovich's music and to give equal consideration to the values of both Western and Soviet/Russian scholarship. I also aim to demonstrate the sophistication of Shostakovich's innovative attempt to rejuvenate the Soviet symphonic tradition along Mahlerian lines. In essence, this means that Shostakovich – like Mahler – used contemporary musical idioms without cheapening his symphonic language or lowering his technical standards, entering into a critical dialogue with formal conventions in a way that enriched, rather than abandoned, symphonic form.

Methodology

The theoretical grounding for my analysis draws upon the ideas of such sociologically orientated figures as Theodor W. Adorno, Mikhail Bakhtin, the Russian Formalists and the theatre director Vsevolod Meyerhold. They all believed that art was, by its very nature, 'cultural practice', existing in dialogue with its own *milieu*; most believed that it was also open to a multitude of interpretations according to the infinite number of differences in the responses of each interpreter. Their theories provide an armoury of terms and concepts flexible and adaptable enough to enable the analyst to respond subjectively to musical events without allying that response to social factors. There are potential problems with such an approach, of course: Adorno's study of Mahler, for example, which has continued to attract scholars nearly half a century after its publication,[50] is founded on the firm premise that the music reflects aspects of Austro-German capitalist society, to which Mahler (naturally) responded negatively. The sophistication of Adorno's prose does much to make palatable assertions that, expressed more directly, would sound uncomfortably like Sollertinsky, whose 1932 Mahler study was perceived by later Soviet critics as marred by 'vulgar sociology'.[51] One of the greatest achievements of Adorno's study of Mahler is the skill and subtlety with which he balances his socio-political premises with penetrating musical observation and intuitive flashes of insight. This balancing-act produces a conceptual vocabulary that, it could be argued, simply cannot function when divorced from the (possibly less appealing) ideological apparatus underpinning it. The potency, for example, of such concepts as *Durchbruch, Erfüllung* and *Suspension* [breakthrough, fulfilment and suspension] might well be reduced when applied to musical language and dramaturgy in a sociologically 'neutral' analysis. This is where another balancing-act must come into play: that between using theory simply as material, divorced from its original ideological context, and using it in a way that imposes ideological meaning upon the music. My aim is to steer a path between these two extremes, using theoretical concepts (such as 'collapse' or 'fulfilment') in a manner that permits hermeneutic engagement without committing the music to any ideological programme.

The Fourth's Symphony's musical language poses some peculiar problems for the analyst looking for functional harmony and conventional voice-leading processes in the sense that tonal analysis (especially of the kind informed by Schenkerian precepts) has had to offer.[52] By comparison with, for example, David Fanning's study of the Tenth Symphony, my analysis of the Fourth will show far less in the way of harmonic structure, though Shostakovich's diatonic-modal language is a key element in both works. Discussions of thematic relationships and transformation take the foreground here, with questions of harmonic process often playing a secondary role. I have nevertheless spent some time illustrating tonal and linear processes, for the simple reason that they are of intrinsic interest and demonstrate that, though Shostakovich's use of tonality is certainly not

50 Theodor W. Adorno, *Mahler: A Musical Physiognomy*, trans. Edmund Jephcott, Chicago and London: University of Chicago Press, 1992. Originally published as *Mahler: Eine musikalische Physiognomik*, Frankfurt am Main: Suhrkamp Verlag, 1971.

51 See for example E. Bronfin, 'Sollertinskiy – muzïkal'nïy uchënïy' [Sollertinskiy – music scholar] in Lyudmila Mikheyeva, *Pamyati I.I. Sollertinskogo: vospominaniya, materialï, issledovaniya* [In memory of I.I. Sollertinskiy: reminiscences, materials, works], Leningrad: Sovetskiy Kompozitor, 1974, 70.

52 I am thinking here of analyses of major 20th-century symphonies such as James Hepokoski, *Sibelius: Symphony No. 5*, Cambridge: Cambridge University Press, 1993, David Fanning, *Nielsen: Symphony No. 5*, Cambridge: Cambridge University Press, 1997, and Fanning, *The Breath of the Symphonist: Shostakovich's Tenth*, London: Royal Musical Association, 1988.

'functional' in the conventional sense, there is internal musical evidence that it was nevertheless carefully worked out and planned. In some cases, such as the fugato in the first movement, harmonic analysis can show that there is a greater underlying coherence than its surface complexity might imply. In others, such as the allying of particular musical characters (such as aggressive, 'negative' scherzi, triumphal, 'positive' themes, other-worldly waltzes) to keys or at least tonal centres, Shostakovich's treatment of tonality appears to be planned according to intonational, or dramaturgical, principles rather than conventionally functional processes. Throughout the symphony, Shostakovich's use of modality and diatonicism, linear and vertical textures, and even figuration (scalic, triadic, etc.) interacts with these characters and with their framing dramaturgy in a way which suggests a 'symbolic' use of tonality. An examination of the internal workings of the music demonstrates that Shostakovich had found a way to integrate processes of thematic transformation, use of musical 'types' such as march and waltz, and even allusions to other works in a loose, but nevertheless perceptible, tonal and dramaturgical framework. This in turn shows that his theatrical dramatization of symphonic convention, and his use of 'extrinsic' material by way of paraphrase and allusion, were not simply an extra layer placed on top of a neutral structure, but were woven into the fabric of the music itself.

Note on Transliteration

In the interests of combining familiarity and phonetic accuracy, I have used the following system throughout:

Adjectival endings and paired vowels:

ий = iy
ый = ïy
ай = ay
ой = oy
ии = ii
ые = ïye
ие = iye
ое = oye
ее = eye
ая = aya
ия = iya
ую = uyu
ию = iyu

Single vowels:

ё = ë
ы = ï

I have omitted the soft sign, usually rendered as an apostrophe, in the main text, but retained it in the bibliography and footnotes. I have used the familiar spellings of Russian surnames in the main text (Chaikovsky, Sollertinsky rather than Chaykovskiy, Sollertinskiy), but all names and adjectival endings in the bibliography and footnotes keep to the transliteration system above. The consonant 'x' is transliterated as 'h' in Meyerhold for the sake of familiarity, but appears as 'kh' elsewhere.

Note on Sources

The original 1962 Sovetskiy Kompozitor score is the one reprinted by most music publishers, including the Sikorski edition that I have used as my main source. The 1982 Muzïka collected works score was based on the revised 1976 Sovetskiy Kompozitor edition, as is the new collected works edition (vol. 4, DSCH, Moscow: 2003). A list of significant differences between the two-piano version of the score (first published by Muzfond USSR, Moscow, 1946 and now re-published as volume 19 of the new collected works (DSCH, Moscow: 2000)), the 1962 and 1976 Sovetskiy Kompozitor scores and the 1982 Muzika score is given by the archivist of the Shostakovich Family Archive in Moscow and editor of the new collected works, Manashir Yakubov, in the Commentary to the Fourth Symphony, pp. 243–4. Where discrepancies exist between the Sikorski score and both collected works scores, I have indicated them in footnotes, though I have not replicated Yakubov's findings with regard to unusual metronome marks in the two-piano score.

Note on References to the Score

Rehearsal figures are in square boxes, with superscript numbers denoting the numbers of bars before or after the rehearsal figure. Symphony numbers are presented in Roman numerals, with movement numbers shown in Arabic numerals, so IV/1: [38]$^{1–4}$ means: Fourth Symphony, first movement, bars 1–4 after rehearsal figure 38.

Note on Notation

I have used a modified version of Helmholtz notation throughout, where C below middle c = C (then C^1, C^2 etc.) and middle C = c, then c^1, c^2 etc.

CHAPTER ONE

The Soviet Symphony in the 1930s: Political and Aesthetic Background

Cultural Revolution: The First Five-Year Plan

The period of the First Five-Year Plan (1928–32) was one of the darkest in Soviet history. It was intended to lay the foundations for massive rationalisation of agriculture and industry, and was executed with merciless cruelty. Yet during the time when mass collectivization was forced onto the rural populace with devastating results (deaths from the ensuing starvation as a result of famine and exile have been estimated at 5,000,000 for the year 1933 alone[1]), *Pravda* published a statement promising to 'raise the cultural level of the worker-peasant masses'.[2] Though it would be reasonable to suppose that the Soviet state had more pressing matters to attend to, as Sheila Fitzpatrick has shown, the drive against so-called 'rightists' (liberals) was a crucial part of a general whipping-up of class war. As a result, the human cost of collectivisation was kept as quiet as possible in the cities, while – as an antidote to its possible discovery – militant proletarian factions were allowed hitherto unprecedented control over the arts.[3]

The period of the First Five-Year Plan ended with Soviet musical culture in a state of crisis. Although the RAPM and Proletkult were not affiliated to the Party and never served as direct spokesmen for official cultural policy, Party support was tacitly expressed through the absence of measures taken to curb their increasingly aggressive domination of the cultural scene.[4] RAPM had assumed

1 See Ronald Hingley, *Russia: A Concise History*, revised ed., London: Thames and Hudson, 1991, 17–2.

2 *Pravda*, 30 November 1927, 1. Quoted in Sheila Fitzpatrick, *The Cultural Front: Power and Culture in Revolutionary Russia*, New York: Cornell University Press, 1992, 116.

3 See Fitzpatrick, *The Cultural Front*, Chapter 6, 'Cultural Revolution as Class War', 115–48.

4 As Neil Edmunds points out, the Russian Association of Proletarian Writers (RAPP) did receive considerable official criticism in the years immediately preceding the 1932 Resolution that ordered the liquidation of all proletarian cultural factions. The fact that RAPM did not probably had more to do with a general perception of music as less important than literature, an attitude which, apart from the attacks on Shostakovich and others in 1936, protected Soviet composers from the worst excesses of the purges of 1937–39: see Edmunds, *The Soviet Proletarian Music Movement*, Bern: Peter Lang, 2000, 289–92. For further discussion of RAPM, see Darby, 'Problems of Context', 86–90, 180–92.

control of all musical publications, with the last of the independent music journals, *Sovremennaya muzïka*, folding in 1929. Its influence had seeped into every corner of musical life, and the conservatoires were increasingly crippled by its militant control. In January 1930 the Moscow Conservatoire was renamed the Feliks Kon Higher Music School, and some of its oldest and most respected teachers, including Nikolay Myaskovsky, Reinhold Glière and Mikhail Gnesin, were harried from office, returning only once the 1932 Resolution had been passed. In addition to the stranglehold on the conservatoires, RAPM targeted the airwaves: their supporters began to take over jobs as presenters, editors and lecturers. As a result, there was a complete ban on the broadcasting of light music from 1930 and a marked increase in performances of the music of RAPM composers, complete with introductory lectures. Perceived as decadent, ideologically damaging and – worst of all – more popular with the proletariat than the edifying mass songs that RAPM composers produced specifically for their consumption, jazz and light music were especially vulnerable targets. Between 1929 and 1932, Western jazz bands were banned from visiting the Soviet Union, the popular Soviet jazz musician Leopold Teplitsky was sent into exile, and all performances of music in any way connected with jazz (including Křenek's *Jonny spielt auf*) were cancelled; even playing jazz records could lead to a fine. Publishing outlets for light music were closed down, and the light music division of the State Press's Music Section stopped publishing light music in 1930.[5] The Association for Contemporary Music (ASM), formed in 1923 as a forum for the dissemination and discussion of new trends in Western European music, was, unsurprisingly, engaged in constant polemics with RAPM, who finally succeeded in hounding it out of existence: the ASM was formally disbanded in 1931.[6]

---

5 Edmunds, *The Soviet Proletarian Music Movement*, 24. For a full account of the chequered history of Soviet jazz, see S. Frederick Starr, *Red and Hot: The Fate of Jazz in the Soviet Union 1917–1980*, Oxford: Oxford University Press, 1985. For a concise account of RAPM's attacks on light music, see Amy Nelson, *Music for the Revolution: Musicians and Power in Early Soviet Russia*, University Park, Pennysylvania: Pennysylvania State University Press, 2004, 222–8. For a summary of the paranoia with which the dissemination of potentially harmful gramophone records, and radio repertoire was monitored by GLAVLIT (Administration for Literary and Publishing Affairs), see Arlen V. Blium, *Sovetskaya tsenzura v epokhu total'nogo terrora 1929–1953* [Soviet censorship in the epoch of totalitarian terror 1929–1953], St Petersburg: Akademicheskiy Proyekt, 2000, 243–51.

6 For a fuller discussion of ASM, its membership and its activities, see Hakobian, *Music of the Soviet Age*, 46–9, Edmunds, *The Soviet Proletarian Music Movement*, 79–84, and Schwarz, *Music and Musical Life*, 49–54.

Proletarian Symphonism

Although the favoured genres of RAPM tended to be vocal, with explicitly ideological texts – mass songs, cantatas, song-symphonies, operas and so on – some of its most prominent composers also wrote chamber music, symphonies and concertos. But despite RAPM approval of past 'revolutionary' figures such as Beethoven, their suspicion of the abstract symphonic genre was deeply enough rooted to provoke calls for a new kind of 'proletarian' symphonism based on mass song. Shostakovich's own response was mixed; during the 1920s he juggled affiliations with both the Leningrad branch of the ASM (LASM) and proletarian organizations such as TRAM (Teatr Rabochikh Molodëzh [Theatre of Working-Class Youth]).[7] His Second and Third Symphonies (1927 and 1930), respectively subtitled 'To October' and 'The First of May', attempted to fuse the ideals of technical progress (in the form of dense linear counterpoint, free-flowing musical material with no thematic repetition, and the rejection of any conventional formal structure) with the demand for 'concrete' ideological content (in the form of rousing choruses with texts by the proletarian poets Aleksandr Bezïmensky and Semën Kirsanov). Shostakovich's friend and colleague Vissarion Shebalin also wrote a choral ('Lenin') Symphony in 1931, a work which, though light years away from Shostakovich's Second and Third in quality, similarly tries to maintain technical standards in the face of ideological expectations, here in the form of an excessive, rather dry use of contrapuntal techniques such as passacaglia and fugue. Shebalin was criticized – not without reason – for being over-academic; his 'Lenin' Symphony was withdrawn from the repertoire a year after its première in 1933 and was not performed again in the Soviet Union until 1960.[8] But Shostakovich's symphonies were well received: the influential ASM critic Boris Asafiev hailed the Third Symphony as marking the Soviet symphony's rebirth 'out of the dynamism of revolutionary oratory'.[9]

Composers and critics affiliated to RAPM were not alone in recognising the potential for a new kind of Soviet symphonism to emerge from the (perceived) ashes of the Western symphonic tradition. This was to become the favourite theme of both Asafiev and Sollertinsky, Shostakovich's close friend and musical ally since 1927. But neither Asafiev nor Sollertinsky saw the choral symphony or song-symphony as the way forward. Both critics were products of the liberal, intellectual branch of Marxist aesthetics, which favoured an evolutionary rather

7 For details about Shostakovich's brief relationship with LASM, see Lyudmila Kovnatskaya, 'Shostakovich and the LASM', *Tempo*, 206, September 1998, 2–6, and Fay, 'Shostakovich, LASM, and Asafiev', in Rosamund Bartlett, ed., *Shostakovich in Context*, Oxford: Oxford University Press, 2000, 51–66. For details of Shostakovich's collaborations with TRAM, see Fay, *Shostakovich*, 57–8.

8 Hakobian, *Music of the Soviet Age*, 118.

9 Schwarz, *Music and Musical Life*, 80.

than revolutionary approach to artistic development. Neither openly subscribed to the view that art was inherently non-political or ideological, whatever they may privately have thought; and both went to considerable lengths to develop an aesthetic framework for Soviet symphonism which would take pressure off composers to demonstrate political engagement, chiefly by arguing that the quality of 'symphonism' itself was inherently democratic by its foundations in the spirit of 'dialectic' and hence (so the reasoning went) of revolution. Those arguments were moderately successful, as will be seen, though it was arguably the success of a single 'abstract' symphony (Shostakovich's Fifth of 1937) that most effectively secured the genre's survival.

Asafiev's concept of symphonism shared some common ground with RAPM. Like them, he regarded Beethoven's symphonies as models of dialectical argument, infused with the intonations of revolutionary song and therefore a true reflection of the heroic spirit of their age. His earliest writings on symphonism (dating from 1917) were relatively apolitical, inspired above all by Henri Bergson's theory of *élan vital* and *durée*. To have 'symphonic' quality was to be in a state of perpetual growth, development and tension; as David Haas notes, although Asafiev never directly used Bergson's terminology, his references to a 'basic impulse of musical motion' and 'living musical fabric' are clearly related to Bergson's intuitive concept of time.[10] Throughout the 1920s Asafiev's language became increasingly politicized. In 1918 he had described symphonism in rather esoteric philosophical language as 'an unbroken stream of musical consciousness, when no element is either conceived or perceived as independent among the remaining multitude, but an integral creative entity in motion emerges by means of intutitive contemplation'. But by 1928 that language had become absurdly convoluted in his attempt to justify symphonism on ideological grounds:

> The issue of musical motion and the logic of musical thought reveal themselves more clearly and consequentially in symphonic forms than in other musical manifestations. The dialectic nature of the process of musical formation in symphonic forms allows the very concept of symphonism to emerge from the dialectic of musical consciousness, since any truly symphonic work is a dynamic process organised by consciousness embracing one or another type of life phenomena through the dialectically lawful progress of the musical idea in its successive phases of development.[11]

The implicit parallels with Marxist-Leninist jargon are clear: merely by emphasizing certain terms such as 'dialectic' and 'consciousness', 'life phenomena' (implying that the musical material itself was socially 'relevant') and the imposing 'dialectically lawful progress', in Asafiev's definition symphonism begins to look like the quintessential musical embodiment of dialectical materialism.

---

10 See David Haas, 'Boris Asaf'ev and Soviet Symphonic Theory', *The Musical Quarterly*, 76/3, 1992, 414.

11 Quoted in ibid., 427.

Whatever Asafiev's personal commitment to that line of reasoning, his strategy of defending 'symphonic' music on pseudo-ideological grounds was taken up by Sollertinsky, whose 1929 article 'The Problem of Symphonism' was an analogous attempt to provide ideological justification for the symphony. Here, following Asafiev, Sollertinsky draws a distinction between symphonism as a genre and symphonism as a 'creative principle'. He describes symphonism as an inherently collective phenomenon based on contemporary themes, which arises in response to sociological factors: 'True symphonism always reappears, like heroism, at the time of the youth of a class embarking on the creation of an entire culture; such was the case with Beethoven.'[12] This may sound crude, but the implications of Sollertinsky's claims are considerable. If a work could be described as symphonic, then – assuming Sollertinsky's claims were accepted – no other apologia would be necessary. Music which was 'symphonic' would be inherently relevant to Soviet society, in spite of its supposedly abstract language.

Sollertinsky claims that the social relevance of the symphony is embodied in the musical fabric itself, as a 'musical collectivisation of feelings'. Also of significance is his assertion that Soviet symphonism would be 'built on the working out of new musical thematic and songful material'. Symphonic language, though abstract, was to be recognizably 'contemporary' in its assimilation of popular idioms:

> Symphonism as a method (not as the canonization of a genre) in its basis is collectivist; it draws its material not from 'tradition' but from living everyday music, from songs of the street, rejecting on principle refinement, or any *recherché* quality of musical material (again the same principles as with Beethoven and Mahler; ironically it was his historical fate that Mahler was only upbraided for what they praised … in Beethoven).
>
> And now the question poses itself: is symphonism any use to us? The answer, I think, is pre-determined; of course, it is precisely our epoch, with its huge gamut of feelings, with its quantity of collectivizing ideas, that is able to continue the development of the symphonic idea as a method of collectivising experiences. Music is capable of solving this problem like nothing else.[13]

It is easy to see why, despite the acclaim Shostakovich received for his Second and Third Symphonies, Sollertinsky, although regarding the Third Symphony highly, did not consider it truly 'symphonic' but a rather formulaic 'symphony-cantata with compulsory concluding chorus on revolutionary poetic texts'.[14] Far from following the organic, developmental ideal of Beethoven held up by Asafiev, Shostakovich's two experimental symphonies were hybrids, combining (in Asafiev's and Sollertinsky's terms) 'real' symphonic qualities (a stream-of-

12 Ivan Sollertinskiy, 'Problema simfonizma v sovetskoy muzïke' [The problem of symphonism in Soviet music], *Zhizn' iskusstva* [Life of art], 46, 1929, 2 (translation by David Fanning).

13 Ibid.

14 Ibid., 1.

consciousness style of perpetual thematic flux and tension) with a pasted-on choral apotheosis. Sollertinsky, who regarded Mahler's symphonies as the chief archetypes of what he called 'democratic symphonism', evidently had in mind rather a work which embraced urban popular idioms as a vital part of its musical language – a bold suggestion to make in the face of growing RAPM opposition to light music. As will be discussed, this was a key element in Sollertinsky's design for the Soviet symphony, and one which Shostakovich embraced, albeit cryptically, in his Fourth Symphony. In those last years of RAPM power, despite the chaos of musical life in Russia, Asafiev, Sollertinsky and Shostakovich were re-grouping, working out a way to beat RAPM at their own game (by challenging them on theoretical grounds, basing their own position firmly on Marxist-Leninist principles) and, in Shostakovich's case, putting further experimentation in the symphonic genre on hold. Other Soviet composers who continued to write symphonies throughout this period did not fare so well, and, as discussed below, many prominent composers fell into the traps of dry academicism, jaunty mass-song banality and formulaic dramaturgy.

Until the unprecedented success of Shostakovich's Fifth Symphony in 1937, Myaskovsky was widely regarded as the Soviet Union's foremost symphonist. By 1932 he had composed twelve symphonies, of which only one (the Sixth) has a text; the rest of them, with the possible exception of the Tenth (subtitled 'The Bronze Horseman'), the Twelfth (subtitled 'Kolkhoz' [Collective Farm]) and the Sixteenth (see n. 94 below), are completely abstract. The Twelfth Symphony is not radically different from its predecessors in structure or style: it has a three-movement format, with a dramatic first movement opening after a long, slow introduction, followed by two themes, developed separately as is normal for Myaskovsky. However, the second movement, after a conventional scherzo beginning, contains a dramatic, declamatory *Invocando* section, which semi-quotes from the first movement of the Eleventh Symphony (XI/1: [15]), and the finale subsequently refers to the first movement's Adagio severo and scherzo. Though such cyclic reminiscences – even quotations – were not unusual for Myaskovsky,[15] the narrative function of those in the Twelfth Symphony is notable; in the composer's own words, the symphony was intended to show the collective farm 'before and during the struggle for a new life, and finally, the new village'.[16] The symphony ends on a decidedly forced note, with an uncharacteristically bombastic, major-key ending (both the Eleventh and Thirteenth Symphonies end in the minor, and Myaskovsky often chose to end on a unison tonic, thereby avoiding the potentially banal effect of a final major chord). Compared with the much darker and more modernistic single-movement Tenth Symphony of 1927,

15 His Sixth Symphony of 1923 quotes the 'Carmagnole' and 'Ça ira' as well as the old Russian chant 'The parting of soul and body' and 'Dies irae' in the finale and ends elegiacally. See Fanning, 'The Soviet Symphony', 295–6.

16 Quoted in Schwarz, *Music and Musical Life*, 167.

the Twelfth – and, to some extent, the Eleventh as well – shows how far-reaching RAPM's influence on the musical establishment was. Although the looser structure of the Twelfth produced a more obvious narrative-style 'dramaturgy' than was usual for Myaskovsky, both the Eleventh and Twelfth Symphonies are marred by their overblown finales, with main themes more typical of 1930s Soviet socialist realist film scores than of symphonies.

An especially sad casualty of the RAPM years was the innovative and influential composer and pedagogue Vladimir Shcherbachëv. His Second Symphony of 1926 – a massive choral work setting poems by the distinguished symbolist poet Aleksandr Blok – is one of the most important works to emerge from the relatively liberal period of experimentation before 1928.[17] But his Third Symphony of 1931 is strikingly conventional by comparison (in tone if not in structure), with crudely diatonic themes of a mass-song character only partially salvaged by the parallel fourths and sevenths that spice up their otherwise bland presentation. Like Myaskovsky's Twelfth Symphony, Shcherbachëv's Third makes extensive use of cyclic recall, though in a more gradual, evolutionary way; the first movement serves as the source of all the thematic material (with the exception of that of the slow fourth movement), which is subjected to continuous transformation throughout the course of the symphony. In its colourful orchestration, rejection of schematic formulas and tight-knit motivic development, Shcherbachëv's symphony retains hallmarks of his 'progressive' style; only the gaudy, film-score character of its themes betrays the influence of RAPM.

Shostakovich became a target for RAPM through his penchant for writing light music and specifically his use of 'decadent' Western dances in his 1930 ballet *The Golden Age*. He quickly responded to their criticism, asserting his own contempt for light music and sternly advocating its banishment from Soviet musical culture.[18] But in 1931, at the Plenum of the Union of All-Russian Comedy and Drama Workers, Shostakovich spoke out boldly against the decline of musical composition, describing the music of one prominent RAPM composer, Marian Koval, as 'pitiful': 'It is necessary to criticise RAPM sharply for these helpless, illiterate things. ... RAPM must be answerable to the production of its members and not put out light pulp. ... I do not see progress among proletarian composers in their creativity.'[19] By 1935 Shostakovich was staunchly defending his (resumed) use of light music, even advocating it as suitable material for symphonic composition, as will be seen; with the benefit of hindsight, his rejection of it in 1930 looks transparently opportune. That he felt able in 1931 to criticize RAPM

17 The Second Symphony is discussed at length in David Haas, *Leningrad's Modernists: Studies in Composition and Musical Thought, 1917–1932*, New York: Peter Lang, 1998, 123–54.

18 For a translation of Shostakovich's letter to *Proletarskiy muzïkant*, see Darby, 'Problems of Context', 185–7.

19 Quoted ibid., 198. For a general discussion of the Plenum, see ibid., 194–9.

so openly testifies not only to his confidence in his own position as one of Leningrad's leading composers, with a string of commissions and plaudits behind him, but also to the growing sense that RAPM had over-reached themselves. In the same year, a large number of composers formed a group independent of either the ASM or RAPM, which sought to find a 'third way', mediating between the overt modernism of ASM and the extremism of RAPM. This group, comprising so-called 'fellow travellers' such as Myaskovsky, Mikhail Gnesin and Levon Atovmyan, could not be ignored, partly because of the stature of individual members and partly because the political climate with regard to 'fellow travellers' was changing in favour of a more tolerant, conciliatory view. Moreover, the Association of Proletarian Writers (RAPP) was subjected to severe official criticism in 1931, which implicitly weakened RAPM's position.

Sollertinsky on Mahler: 1932

Sollertinsky may have exaggerated Mahler's stance towards popular music and 'collective' symphonism in his 1929 article. But the extent to which he manipulated the details of Mahler's life and work to present him in the best possible ideological light is even more striking in his 1932 monograph.[20] In his portrayal of Mahler's symphonies as engaging with collective consciousness, Sollertinsky draws on Paul Bekker's books *Die Sinfonie von Beethoven bis Mahler* and *Gustav Mahlers Sinfonien*.[21] He had already credited Bekker in his 1929 article with the idea that the post-Beethovenian symphony was inherently collectivist in orientation; this assumption then formed the basis of his conclusion that the Soviet Union provided the most fertile soil for the revival of true symphonism. Sollertinsky's book plainly aims to present Mahler's works as ideologically acceptable. By extension, then, Mahler's symphonism could be a viable model for Soviet composers.

Sollertinsky repeatedly asserts Mahler's own political orientation as humanitarian; like Rolland's Jean-Cristophe, he argues, Mahler was a 'protesting petit-bourgeois humanist and utopianist'[22] trying to combat a corrupt social order with his own sense of morality. Such moral motivation was, Sollertinsky claims, of utmost relevance for his music, since for Mahler, music was 'inseparable from the social-aesthetic world-view problems which confront every person'.[23] Already his premise is slippery; its general truth does not lead to the assumption that

20 Sollertinskiy, *Gustav Maler*, Leningrad: State Music Publishers, 1932.

21 Bekker, *Gustav Mahlers Sinfonien*, Berlin: Schuster und Loeffler, 1921. Sollertinskiy quotes the Russian translation of *Die Sinfonie von Beethoven bis Mahler*, *Sinfoniya ot Betkhovena do Malera*, trans. R. Gruber, Leningrad: Triton, 1926, in his bibliography.

22 Sollertinskiy, *Gustav Maler*, 25.

23 Ibid., 13.

Mahler was actively engaged in social protest. Sollertinsky crucially blurs the all-important dividing line between passive (but honest and effective) reflection, as approved by Marx, and active participation in the class struggle, as demanded by Marxism-Leninism.

After establishing this dubious starting-point, Sollertinsky goes on to make equally contentious claims for Mahler's much-vaunted adoption of popular idioms. Mahler, he claims, wrote not for 'connoisseurs or aristocrats', but for 'the people', embracing their musical culture from soldiers' songs to Viennese waltzes and operetta refrains.[24] Significantly, Sollertinsky maintains that Mahler's treatment of this material was not ironic or intended to produce an 'estranged' effect; nor was it exploitative, borrowing it for its novel popular colour. Rather, so he claims, these idioms receive the most sophisticated technical transformations and are stripped of their 'trivial nature'. This is clearly unsatisfactory. If Mahler wrote for 'the people', using their language, then why would he feel it necessary to strip this language of its 'trivial nature'? Sollertinsky is making a self-contradictory claim: that Mahler adopted these popular idioms with respect, since he had a genuine love for them and a genuine sympathy with the working classes, but that Mahler's music was at the same time too sophisticated to permit 'trivial' music to retain its identity.

This level of sophistry was an inevitable by-product of Stalinist culture. Artists had to think big: large-scale Romantic genres reflected the grandiose pretensions of the Stalin administration. Though a prominent feature of the 1930s was the wholesale abandonment of the proletarian cause, this could not be acknowledged, and so the rhetoric of collectivity remained potent. So Sollertinsky had to juggle demands for social relevance, technical sophistication and moral integrity. One assumption running through all discussions of the Soviet symphony's future development, during both the proletarian period and afterwards, was that it should be able to rank alongside the greatest works of Romantic bourgeois culture. For Sollertinsky to advocate expanding the symphonic vocabulary with unmediated 'trivial' music would have been self-defeating. A hybrid half-art, half-entertainment genre was out of the question. So Sollertinsky contrives to have it both ways. He argues that popular idioms in Mahler's music are not patronized, since he wants to portray Mahler as in tune with the proletariat and opposed to bourgeois class divisions. But he must also claim that Mahler's use of such idioms by no means led to a degradation of symphonic language. There is a glaring paradox here that Sollertinsky never acknowledges. Instead, he extends his argument to claim that Mahler's 'democratization' of his musical language was a premeditated and socially motivated step:

> The so-called 'banality' in Mahler's *melos* is the result of a conscious aim to 'democratize' musical language; banality is used as a protest against impressionist refinement, salon artistry and aristocratic individualism. Here

24 Ibid., 30–1.

> Mahler exceeds the limits of Romantic music, overcoming individualistic Romanticism, the culmination of which was marked by Wagner's *Tristan*. Cherishing the dream of the utopian idea of 'collective symphonism', Mahler was first and foremost orientated towards song.[25]

Sollertinsky's all-important claim that Mahler's 'democratisation' of language was 'conscious' emphasizes the dominance of will over intuition in artistic creation. It was a vital ingredient in his depiction of Mahler as an active, not passive, opponent of his social environment.

Another issue raised in this extract is the notion of Mahler's 'anti-individualistic' stance, one of the most suspicious aspects of Sollertinsky's argument. 'Individualism' carried a serious political, as well as creative, stigma in the Soviet Union. It implied indifference to the proletariat and a lack of social engagement. It is therefore not surprising that Sollertinsky should seek to clear Mahler of such a charge, nor that he should exaggerate the extent of Mahler's own sense of social responsibility. It is certain that Sollertinsky was well aware of the at times almost autobiographical nature of Mahler's music; Richard Specht's revised 1925 book on Mahler, which contains details of Mahler's annotations to the 'Purgatorio' movement of the Tenth Symphony, appears in his bibliography.[26] Sollertinsky refers in passing to Křenek's 1924 edition of the Tenth Symphony and mentions its five-movement plan, but not much else. All the same, this admittedly suspicious aspect of Sollertinsky's argument should not be over-stressed. The importance he attaches to Mahler's orchestration throughout his book suggests that the incomplete nature of the Tenth Symphony manuscript may well have been a factor in the decision not to include it in his main discussion. And while it is undeniable that Sollertinsky plays down the connections between Mahler's life and works, it is nevertheless surely true that the scope of Mahler's symphonies – not just the Second, Third and Eighth – is universal over and above any personal identification Mahler himself might have felt with them. Sollertinsky overstates, but does not invent, Mahler's 'collective' vision.

Concluding his book with more logical sleight-of-hand, Sollertinsky baldly asserts that Mahler could not possibly be regarded as any sort of a model for Soviet composers, but then proceeds to list his most pertinent qualities for precisely that purpose:

> It would be naive to declare the creative method of Mahler a basis on which to rebuild Soviet symphonism, with his Romantic utopianism, his convulsive intensity, leading to paroxysms, in reviving the Beethovenian spirit and repeating his 'Ode to Joy', his idealistic relationship to folk songs (peasants', craftsmen's, soldiers'), and finally, the pessimism in his last years – all this reveals the world-view of a left-petit-bourgeois *intelligent*, and shows the crisis of the capitalist world, but does not point to any solution apart from social utopianism. …

25 Ibid., 32–3.

26 Richard Specht, *Gustav Mahler* (Stuttgart and Berlin: Deutsche Verlags-Anstalt, 1925.

> Regarding the creation of a new Soviet symphonism, Mahler is closer to us than Debussy or Stravinsky, Strauss or Hindemith. His symphonies have the most important artistic-ideological quality more or less absent from the leaders of musical impressionism and constructivism:
>
> – a great philosophical-aesthetic pathos
> – the rebuilding of symphonism on the basis of song
> – a striving for expression … stemming from a tendency to embrace the greatest possible collective of listeners
> – a mastery of the orchestral apparatus and the human voice.[27]

Sollertinsky plainly considered Mahler's symphonies to be ideal models for Soviet composers, but it would have been self-defeating to declare this openly. The idea that European symphonism was in catastrophic and irreversible decline at the turn of the century was treated as a well-established fact in Soviet musicology of the 1930s. How then could Mahler, whose supposed acknowledgement of this fact was a primary component of his own alienated symphonic language, be regarded as a model for composers in the brave new world of socialism? Perhaps Sollertinsky's caveats were merely intended to deflect possible criticism; perhaps they contained a grain of something more sincere. Deflection seems the more likely strategy. 'Utopianism' and 'pessimism' had extremely negative connotations in Soviet critical discourse of this period. The building of socialism could hardly be openly described as a 'utopian' project; all commentators were aware that their attitude to this event ought to be one of certainty rather than hope. 'Pessimism' was outlawed for the same reason. Sollertinsky's vague list of approved Mahlerian qualities speaks for itself. Having trumpeted Mahler's employment of urban popular idioms in the previous chapters, it is noteworthy that he omits to mention it in his conclusion. Instead, like any prudent Soviet critic, Sollertinsky keeps his terms as broad as possible, and says nothing that could be regarded as controversial or that might undermine his plan to have Mahler admitted into the pantheon of unassailable historical figures.

Perestroyka: The Resolution of 1932

In 1932 a new era in Soviet culture began. The Party Resolution of 23 April 1932, entitled 'On the Reconstruction [*perestroyka*] of Literary and Artistic Organizations', effectively ended the power of the proletarian factions. Their demise preceded the end of the First Five-Year Plan by a year. But it was nevertheless part and parcel of the series of reforms that characterized the *perestroyka* years between 1932 and 1936. Schwarz's contention that the Resolution 'signified the end of an era of flexibility and inaugurated one of regimentation',[28] transforming Soviet art from a state of 'multiformity to

27 Sollertinskiy, *Gustav Maler*, 65–6.
28 Schwarz, *Music and Musical Life*, 110.

conformity', seems paradoxical at first glance: if anything, many artists welcomed the Resolution with open arms precisely because they imagined it would signal the end of RAPM's aggressive demands for conformity. But, speaking with the benefit of 40 years' hindsight, Schwarz sagely noted, 'Little did they realise that they exchanged the dictatorship of a small clique for the control of a super-power – the Soviet government and the bureaucratic machinery of the Party.'[29] Artistic groups were re-formed into unions, with strictly controlled membership – expulsion effectively meant the end of a career – and with a single journal, in the case of the Composers' Union, *Sovetskaya muzïka*. Schwarz's observation that the advance of socialist realism as the chief guide of artistic creation around this time meant that 'advanced composers turned conventional, and conventional composers became commonplace'[30] presupposes a great deal, not least that socialist realism was so well defined and so powerfully enforced that composers had no choice but to toe the line. A glance through symphonies composed in the years immediately following its official unveiling would seem at first glance to justify Schwarz's claim, but this is chiefly because the influence of the 1920s mass-song genre cemented its influence on Soviet symphonies only during the 1930s. Kabalevsky's First and Second Symphonies (1932 and 1934), following Myaskovsky's earlier example, attempt to infuse symphonic language with the jaunty diatonic platitudes of mass songs, orchestrated in a sickly, string-dominated film-score style. But those works are stale by-products of the RAPM years, when Kabalevsky was still Myaskovsky's student. Though they are not isolated examples, they do represent a branch of Soviet symphonism that was to be challenged in the years following the Resolution, most vociferously by Shostakovich, Sollertinsky and those close to them such as the composers Gavriil Popov, Valeryan Bogdanov-Berezovsky and others. It should also be remembered that the 1930s saw a swing away from experimental modernism across Europe and America as economic crisis, mass unemployment and, not least, the spread of fascism from Italy to Germany, marked the beginning of a decade of relative musical conservatism, characterised by a return to traditional genres and tonal idioms. While the parallels between Soviet and fascist art of the 1930s are widely recognized, their colourful depictions of joyful peasants, heroic political leaders and re-inventing of their national heritage and psyche have equally striking parallels with the meteoric rise of American consumer culture and Hollywood. What was overt political propaganda in Europe and the Soviet Union differed from capitalist 'propaganda' (advertising, public education broadcasts, the portrayal of heroic pioneers in literature and film) primarily in the nature of the message being delivered rather than in its delivery. If Soviet composers became 'conventional', they were not alone: the 1930s had become the decade of Art for the People across the Western world.[31]

29 Ibid.

30 Ibid., 115.

31 For a concise discussion of the cultural similarities between socialist realism and

The Writers' Congress of 1934

After the havoc wreaked on Soviet society by the First Five-Year Plan and the widespread unrest that ensued, Stalin, faced with dissent in the Politburo itself, was forced to take conciliatory measures. In addition to cultural reform, the 1930s saw two major social changes: first, an apparent move towards democratic reform (supported by moderates in the Party such as Nikolay Bukharin and Sergey Kirov), and second, the rise of socialist realism and Stalin's 'cult of personality'. The two were in fact inextricably linked. The Stalin Constitution – unveiled in 1936, and marking the reinstatement of economic and political links with Europe – trumpeted the ideal of democracy in theory, but in practice public order was maintained not through improved rights and pay but through fear and control. There was a massive rise in Party propaganda, dividing Soviet society into those 'for' and those 'against' the Party through sustained media campaigns against so-called 'enemies of the People', starting with popular Party figures such as Bukharin, who was arrested in 1937, tried, and executed in 1938.[32] The Party purges began with Kirov's assassination in December 1934: by 1937 they had spread to the public at large, with the arrests of millions of innocent Soviet citizens: an unimaginably horrific period now widely referred to as the 'Great Terror'.[33] However, the early years of this *perestroyka* period – roughly between 1932 and 1935 – were characterized by, if not unanimous, then certainly widespread, optimism; few, if any, could have foreseen the horrors that were to come. In what seemed an unexpectedly conciliatory move, Stalin commissioned none other than Bukharin, together with his fellow Old Bolshevik Karl Radek, to write the new Constitution, which aimed at establishing multi-candidate elections, secret balloting and civil rights.

National Socialism, see Igor Golomstock, 'Problems in the Study of Stalinist Culture', in Hans Günther, ed., *The Culture of the Stalin Period*, London: Macmillan, 1990, 110–21.

32 The purges in the party began as early as 1934, when half a million members were expelled. See Geoffrey Hosking, *A History of the Soviet Union 1917–1991*, final ed., London: Fontana, 1992, 187. For an account of Bukharin's relationship with Stalin and fall from grace see Stephen F. Cohen, *Bukharin and the Bolshevik Revolution: A Political Biography 1888–1938*, London: Wildwood House, 1974, especially 270–336. Sarah Davies's *Popular Opinion in Stalin's Russia: Terror, Propaganda and Dissent, 1934–1941*, Cambridge: Cambridge University Press, 1997, makes it clear that the statutes of the Constitution were flagrantly ignored, and that many workers reacted angrily to the trumpeting of their supposed civil rights when they lacked basic necessities of life (see especially pp. 102–12).

33 Robert Conquest coined the term in the title of his book *The Great Terror*, London: Macmillan, 1968. He reports that in 1928 the prison camp population was 30,000; by 1935–36 it had risen to six million. Conquest puts the total figure for further arrests between 1937–38 at between seven and nine million (pp. 526–7). For further comment on the estimated figures for Stalin's purges and some official statistics from the Soviet archives, see Véronique Garros, Natalia Korenevskaya and Thomas Lahusen, eds, *Intimacy and Terror: Soviet Diaries of the 1930s*, New York: The New Press, 1995, xii.

After temporarily breaking with Stalin over collectivization in 1928, Bukharin's political comeback had begun with an invitation to address the Seventeenth Party Congress in January 1934, the first he had spoken at since 1927. This in itself looked promising for the moderates, who interpreted Bukharin's reinstatement as evidence of Stalin's recognition that social reform was urgently needed. Following this event, he was presented with editorship of *Izvestiya* and commissioned to draft the Constitution. Later the same year, he and Radek found themselves joining the writer Maxim Gorky and the newly appointed Minister of Culture Andrey Zhdanov as keynote speakers at the Writers' Congress: a major international two-week event, covered exhaustively in *Pravda* and serving as the platform from which socialist realism was first properly launched.

The official definition of socialist realism was printed in *Pravda* before discussion even started: 'Socialist realism, the basic method of Soviet artistic literature and literary criticism, demands truthfulness from the artist and an historically concrete portrayal of reality in its revolutionary development.'[34] As a coherent aesthetic, socialist realism has long been discredited, and justly so. It was essentially a demand for art to function as propaganda, justified by the assertion that such art would play a vital role in bringing about the socialist utopia allegedly under construction. Even at the Writers' Congress its validity was questioned by the very people chosen to proclaim it. Radek's passionate critique of National Socialist demands for optimistic art, for example, looks suspiciously 'Aesopian'. Arguing that world literature was essentially split into two camps, the pro-fascist and the anti-fascist (i.e. sympathetic to the proletariat), he went on to claim boldly that the 'fellow travellers' castigated in the old days of proletarian militancy should be encouraged rather than reviled. The gist of Radek's argument ran thus: if writers are honest, especially those who are living and writing in fascist regimes, they will reflect the suffering of the people. Thus a fundamental humanitarianism combined with artistic integrity should be enough to produce 'socialist realist' literature in a broad sense. There are phrases in Radek's speech which seem to contradict this, just as there are obligatory adulatory references to Stalin and confessions to having been a former 'Trotskyite'. But the basic message of his address was pure Marx: integrity is all one can demand of an artist; history will see to the rest.[35] Bukharin, too, challenged Zhdanov's demand for tendentious literature, calling for art to reflect life in all its complexity and multiplicity:

---

34 Jeffrey Brooks, 'Socialist Realism in *Pravda*: Read All About It!', *Slavic Review*, 53, 1994, 977.

35 Radek's speech 'Contemporary World Literature and the Tasks of Proletarian Art' is printed in translation with those of Zhdanov, Gorky and Bukharin in H.G. Scott, ed., *Problems of Soviet Literature*, Westport, Connecticut: Greenwood Press, 1979, after the offical 1935 translation (Moscow: Cooperative Publishing Society of Foreign Workers in the USSR), 73–162. For a discussion of the Congress in English, see John and Carol Garrard, *Inside the Soviet Writers' Union*, London: The Free Press, 1990, 34–43.

> Unity does not mean we should all sing the same song at the same time. … Unity consists in a single aspect – that of building socialism. All the richness of life, all tragedies and conflicts, vacillations and defeats, struggle of conflicting tendencies – all this must become the material for poetic creation. The better we are able to show the diversity of this life … the better and higher will be the standing of our literature and our poetry. … If we do not do this … there is a very grave danger of this kind of art ceasing to be art.[36]

This was fighting talk, standing as directly in opposition to the official line presented by Zhdanov as was possible. Though it was not the case that Bukharin's speech impressed all (or even most) of his literary compatriots, at least one source reported that, following Bukharin's address, delegates embraced each other in joy and relief.[37] Like Radek, Bukharin went through a certain amount of ritual breast-beating as a way of attempting to secure his own uncertain political position: rescinding on his earlier argument with Stalin against collectivisation, for example, Bukharin now claimed that he had not fully understood the reasons behind it. Nevertheless, the aesthetic premises of both his and Radek's speeches were deeply founded in the liberal Marxist view on art. Marx's and Engels's famous letter to Ferdinand Lassalle urging the writer to be less tendentious and to 'Shakespeare-ize more' was published in Russian in 1932 and was seized upon by those who sought to deflect Soviet aesthetics from the path of uniformity to one which allowed for the existence, and thus portrayal, of life in all its diversity. As will be seen, this was an important element in Sollertinsky's musical arguments, and at least one of his colleagues attributed Sollertinsky's idea of 'Shakespeare-izing in music' to the belated discovery that Marx and Engels – in direct contravention of Zhdanov's strictures at the Writers' Congress – actually disapproved of tendentious literature.[38]

---

36 Bukharin, 'Poetry, Poetics and the Problems of Poetry in the USSR', in Scott, ed, *Problems of Soviet Literature*, 246–7.

37 Cohen, *Bukharin*, 356. Volkov reports that Bukharin was terrified by the ovation his speech received, knowing that Stalin – always a jealous rival and already deeply suspicious of him – would be closely monitoring the proceedings. Volkov claims that NKVD reports demonstrate that the Congress was indeed positively buzzing with praise for Bukharin. See Volkov, *Shostakovich and Stalin*, 108–9. However, see Andrey Artizov and Oleg Naumov, eds, *Vlast' i khudozhestvennaya intelligentsiya 1917–1953 gg*. [The regime and the artistic intelligentsia 1917–1953], Moscow: 'Demokratiya', 1999, 232–50 for details of secret NKVD reports to Stalin from the Writers' Congress. While reports of foreign delegates note that Bukharin's speech provoked lively discussion (p. 235), there was harsh criticism of Bukharin (and Gorky) from Soviet delegates as well as praise; see especially pp. 235–6. In fact, there was so much criticism of Bukharin that one writer (P. Sletov) defended him, claiming that the importance of his speech had not been understood. A few other writers (S. Budantsev, V. Sovsun) praised him; Sovsun (said to be expressing the mood of the whole group) thought that Bukharin had been too afraid to stray far from the Party line (p. 245). This hardly points to unanimous praise for Bukharin, who was evidently seen first and foremost as a politician interfering in literary affairs.

38 Marx's and Engels's letter to Lassalle was printed in *Literaturnoe nasledstvo*,

'Discussion about Soviet Symphonism': 1935

Just as writers were encouraged to produce epic novels and poems in the interests of 'building socialism', composers were expected to produce symphonies and operas. These seemed the genres best suited to the kind of collective marketing of Soviet propaganda that Stalin's programme of mass brain-washing depended on. But in reality, the situation for all creative artists was extremely complicated. In the first place, the new unions had the power to veto performances and publication, and works deemed – for often random and unpredictable reasons – to have fallen short of the standard expected by the upper echelons of the unions could be subjected to extremely harsh criticism. Also, the vagueness of socialist realist precepts meant that, even assuming that composers accepted it as the sole officially sanctioned method of artistic creation, they, in common with other Soviet artists, had no way of knowing what that might actually involve.[39] As late as 1935, the arguments raging around what should and should not be models for the Soviet symphony focused more on technical quality than on prescriptions for the uplifting, mass-song tone to which composers had previously retreated in response to RAPM pressure. Although most of those present at the 1935 conference 'Discussion about Soviet Symphonism' avoided the topic of socialist realism, those who did not were forced to rely on abstruse jargon to mask their own uncertainty about what it really involved.[40] One of the keynote speakers, Aleksandr Ostretsov, fell straight into the trap when he proclaimed that 'The symphony must contain within itself maximum concentrated strength, ideological depth and clarity in the transmission of definite, vital content.'[41] Neither he nor anyone else present could have withstood an honest debate about the possible meaning of those words. What is more, there were those who were able to laugh at his exhortations at the time and place of their delivery. Vissarion Shebalin, the courageous, outspoken colleague and friend of Shostakovich, mocked Ostretsov openly at the conference, comparing the obtuseness of his attempts to define musical socialist realism to a particularly unflattering literary model:

1932/3, 18–22. See Abram Gozenpud, 'Khudozhnik i uchëniy' [Artist and scholar], in Mikheyeva, *Pamyati*, 32.

39 It would not be accurate to say that socialist realism was ever really the only officially approved 'method'. The official explanation was that it should be the 'basis' [*osnovoy*] for creative work; this could in theory be used to justify almost anything. It is worth noting that in the post-war artistic crackdown of the *Zhdanovshchina*, the desirability of socialist realism as a creative method for composers is rarely mooted; criticisms tend rather to centre on the old charge of 'formalism'.

40 The conference was held on 4–6 February. Incomplete stenographic reports were printed in *Sovetskaya muzïka*, the house journal of the Composers' Union. The order of speeches is given in *Sovetskaya muzïka*, 1935/3, 101–3. It is discussed in Schwarz, *Music and Musical Life*, 157–63.

41 *Sovetskaya muzïka*, 1935/4, 3. Ostretsov (1903–64) was a musicologist and critic.

> Unfortunately I heard only the end [of Ostretsov's address], but from that it was possible to conclude that it was similar, I would say, to Khlestakov's letter from the most famous of all Gogol's plays, *The Government Inspector*. In this letter it is written that the Mayor is as stupid as a mule, that the postmaster, though a good fellow, drinks terribly, Zemlyanika is like a sow in a nightcap and so on. However, I would conclude that the definitions given by the Gogolesque hero are significantly more clear and concrete than those given in Comrade Ostretsov's address.[42]

If even Ostretsov's contemporaries could poke fun at the vague heroics of the new socialist realist-speak, then it would seem fair to speculate that socialist realism and its attendant concerns (social relevance, the formulation of a new 'form' and 'content', the conscious re-forming of aesthetics to embrace new ideology) were perceived by all intelligent composers and musicologists as laughable from the start. But the target of Shebalin's sarcasm was not the notion that music should fulfil a social function, nor even that it might convey ideology; it was actually the absence of concrete demands and explanations that either amused or irritated him. It is worth noting that four speakers – Shebalin, Sollertinsky, Genrikh Litinsky and Georgiy Khubov – were united in their criticism of Ostretsov's vagueness; Litinsky even cited one of Ostretsov's published analyses – of Shebalin's 'Lenin' Symphony – as an example of over-simplification and vulgarization of musical concepts. Clearly, Ostretsov was not then widely regarded as a man to be reckoned with.

Sollertinsky tried to draw attention away from some of the more imponderable issues – such as how best to 'transmit definite vital content' – and to focus on practical ones, such as how best to renew symphonic language with specific models in mind. This he set about doing, on the face of it, very circumspectly; though as his first paper was omitted from the collection printed in *Sovetskaya muzïka*, it is impossible to gauge the real extent of his overall caution at the conference. However, recurring themes in Sollertinsky's writings from the 1930s and 1940s are present here, mixed in, as always, with the standard (and distinctly Slavophile) cliché of those years: as inheritors of the socialism that was the implicit goal of the last 100 years (if not more) of Western culture, the Soviets were ideally placed to take over from the West as world leaders in artistic culture. Alongside these more conformist notions, Sollertinsky argued for the 'democratizing' of musical language after Mahler's example, advocated better knowledge of the works of the allegedly 'decadent' Schoenberg and Berg, insisted that Soviet composers must look for 'new intonations', and urged composers to avoid the pitfalls of crude programmaticism and its related aesthetic paradigms. His words were more than casual exhortation; they were a crucial part of his wider vision for the Soviet symphony, which emerges most clearly from his writings on Mahler and symphonism dating from several years before the conference, as discussed above.

---

42 *Sovetskaya muzïka*, 1935/5, 41.

Sollertinsky's perceptible frustration over the neglect of his favourite composer at the symphonism conference probably stemmed from the fact that, in contrast to almost every other conference speaker, he had his own quite specific aesthetics of Soviet symphonism already formulated, founded on key aspects of Mahler's symphonies. As is apparent from his 1932 monograph on Mahler and his 1929 article 'The Problem of Symphonism in Soviet Music', Sollertinsky evidently hoped that a number of these aspects – namely a supposedly 'democratic' approach to musical material and an underpinning humanitarian world-view – might be compatible with certain prominent socio-philosophical ideas of the time. At the symphonism conference, Sollertinsky enlarged on his hypothesis:

> Much that is interesting and instructive may be said about the symphonism of Mahler. We have up till now underestimated this composer. We have recognized him as a petit-bourgeois fellow traveller and let it rest at that. … Mahler – a unique composer – tried to resolve the problem of the Beethovenian symphony … tried to solve the problem of bringing elements of folklore into the symphony … tried to address the problem of a democratic musical language.
>
> I say from the heart that if I have a profound faith in Soviet symphonism, then it stems from the other side: being exhaustively occupied with modern Western symphonism, I can see that there are no premises for its development. We have all the preconditions. … there is no great collective idea, no symphonic idea in the West, and, of course, can never be. … There is an immoral atmosphere; ideology has rotted [culture] through and through – in these conditions symphonic art cannot exist.[43]

Beethoven was still one of the few historical figures beyond criticism. His symphonies had been held up even by RAPM as an example of all that abstract music could and should be.[44] The Soviets' appropriation of Beethoven never extended to a full recognition and acceptance of his creativity; it tended rather towards a generalized rhetorical lauding of his supposedly heroic tone and humanitarian ethos. All the same, a connection between Beethoven and Mahler provided Sollertinsky with a strong ideological basis for the aesthetics of symphonism he had in mind. In 1935, Beethoven was still very safe territory, for the functionary critic Ostretsov and Sollertinsky alike. Ostretsov's description of Beethoven's symphonies is a classic example of Soviet jargon, drowning the object of either praise or derision in a sea of meaningless rhetoric:

> In his own time, the great Beethoven gave immortal images of the revolutionary struggle of individual people of his own time in the context of the struggling masses. … The iron logic of the thoroughly motivic movement

43 *Sovetskaya muzïka*, 1935/6, 30 and 32.

44 One of RAPM's leading writers, Yuriy Keldïsh, advised young RAPM composers to take the symphonies of Beethoven and Chaikovsky as models: see Edmunds, *The Soviet Proletarian Musical Movement*, 38. For an account of the Beethoven centenary celebrations in Russia, see Nelson, *Music for the Revolution*, 185–205.

> of those symphonies and their conflict stems from Beethoven's basis of profound understanding of the concrete facts of history.[45]

No composer could reasonably be expected to take this language seriously: it was (presumably) intentionally abstruse, and those who used it were merely trying to avoid saying anything that might compromise them at a later date. But the fact that critics like Ostretsov – who was after all a keynote speaker at the conference – felt that they were on safe ground with Beethoven, referring sweepingly to his heroic tone and revolutionary sympathies without saying anything that might be construed as specific, shows all the more clearly why Sollertinsky went to such pains to ground his symphonic aesthetics in the Beethovenian tradition, and why he could reasonably have expected to receive a sympathetic hearing.

However, another strand of Sollertinsky's argument – that of symphonism as a 'democratic' and 'contemporary' genre – was more problematic. Despite the demise of the proletarian factions in 1932, disapproval of popular music – an essential ingredient in Sollertinsky's brand of 'democratic' symphonism – was ingrained in many minds. It is evident from the conference that Shostakovich and Sollertinsky hoped to take advantage of the increased scope for discussion to challenge this particular prejudice. Nevertheless, Sollertinsky's approval of Mahler's 'democratic' use of urban popular idioms was on the very borders of political respectability in 1932 when his short book on Mahler was published, and it remained so by 1935. Shostakovich's advocacy of these idioms as viable material for the Soviet symphony prompts the hypothesis that Shostakovich's evolving symphonic 'credo' had much in common with Sollertinsky's views:

> Soviet listeners … demand that musical art should simply give them pleasure. Perhaps I am expressing it crudely. But it is true. I am afraid that we at times forget this. We say that our symphonies must excite them, recount heroic deeds, and stigmatize and discredit the vacillating personality, of which Ostretsov spoke. But I have not heard one person say that our Soviet symphonism should give pleasure. This is a serious problem which cannot be ignored. … When the public, during a performance, laugh or simply smile, then that gives me pleasure.
>
> When I wrote *Lady Macbeth*, or, as it is known in Moscow, *Katerina Izmaylova*, everyone began to say that, finally, Shostakovich has shown humanity. But I would be interested to know: what did I do that was inhumane? Was it writing light music? I did write light music and will continue to do so. … I consider it necessary for all Soviet composers not to forget this music, which can give the Soviet listener pleasure and healthy diversion.[46]

The fact that Shostakovich could assert his intention to continue writing light music, despite the criticism he had already received with regard to his 1931 ballet score *The Bolt*, suggests that he believed that such music could still find a basis for official acceptance. The absorption into symphonic language of 'street' music

45 *Sovetskaya muzïka*, 1935/4, 8.

46 *Sovetskaya muzïka*, 1935/5, 33.

[*ulichnaya muzïka*] 'refusing on principle any refinement or recherché quality of material' – in Sollertinsky's words – had a nominal claim to 'democratic' respectability, even as both composer and musicologist would surely have recognized its subversive overtones. Just how precarious this respectability was, however, is evident from Iosif Rïzhkin's conference speech:

> In order for the [symphonic] genre to develop, composers must work very hard at a democratic musical language. It is well known that, in the renewal of language, a large role should be played by the everyday [*bïtovoy*] songs and dances of the peoples of our Soviet Union. There are, however, dangers inherent in these attempts to devise an aesthetic musical language and to speak in the 'language of the masses'. Soviet composers, wishing to break down the gap created by the landowners and bourgeoisie between 'real music' and 'music for the masses', must not go along the path of least resistance, along with the prejudices of the masses. The problem cannot be solved in terms of the vulgar phrases of petit-bourgeois songs and dances. ... Shostakovich offers a dubious example in his suite *The Bolt*, which presents third-rate musical material with immense musical mastery.[47]

Kabalevsky joined in the debate, taking issue with Shostakovich's claim that 'street songs and gypsy romances are all wellsprings for the creation of a new musical language', and offering his opinion that the composer must exercise more discrimination in his choice of materials, Shostakovich's acceptance of such urban vulgarity being in his view 'excessively liberal'.[48] In this context it is not hard to see that Shostakovich's defence (provocatively overstated) of music for pleasure went against the prevailing notion of music as edifying social function.

One of the greatest obstacles for composers to negotiate was the perceived problem of 'form and content'. The political necessity of 'content' in art raised severe formal problems, which some musicologists, not without considerable contortions of semantics and logic, tried to address. One of the best attempts was made by Rïzhkin at the 1935 conference. He tried to argue – building on the line of thought offered by Asafiev and Sollertinsky in the late 1920s – that the forms of the Classical symphony *per se* were democratic, breaking away from courtly rituals towards free expression, struggle and expression of *bït*. This term, meaning the 'everyday', provided Rïzhkin with the key to a complicated defence of pure symphonism which ultimately paralleled the concept of *bïtovost'* (having the quality of everyday-ness, or *bït*) with obedience to laws of rational development within the confines of symphonic architectonics. Rïzhkin arrived at this conclusion by means of an obscure alignment between dialectical materialism and the symphony's supposedly inherent *bïtovost'* and *massovost'* (having the quality of mass consciousness), arguing that 'the question of a creative solution for the

47 *Sovetskaya muzïka*, 1935/6, 7. Rïzhkin was a Moscow-based musicologist and author of articles on music theory, including Boleslav Yavorsky's theory of modal rhythm.

48 *Sovetskaya muzïka*, 1935/4, 38.

development of Soviet symphonism is also the question of the reflection of fundamental aspects of Soviet reality in its revolutionary development'.[49]

Rïzhkin's speech was in essence a defence of abstract symphonism at a time when composers were experiencing dissatisfaction with the song-symphony genre (itself an attempt to adapt to the ideological climate of the early 1930s) and trying to agree on methods of constructing a new form of pure [*chistïy*] symphonism that could match past Western achievements. By focusing less on tone (the generalized 'heroism' of Beethoven's 'Eroica' or Fifth Symphony, as vaunted by Ostretsov, for example) and more on form, Rïzhkin probably hoped to foster acceptance of formal experimentation and to draw attention away from the appearance of content to a more traditionally Marxist view of art: acknowledgement that any product of a society, whether it be material or cultural, reflects that society in some way, and that to force a social message onto a work of art impoverishes and demeans it.

The aesthetic tortures thrust upon Soviet composers by simultaneous demands to communicate concrete images and ideas to the whole spectrum of Soviet listeners, while departing from old, familiar intonations, took aesthetic arguments over the relative value of abstract instrumental music over very familiar eighteenth- and nineteenth-century ground, as Sollertinsky himself observed.[50] The concept of *syuzhetnost'* (having 'content' or subject-matter in art) was especially problematic, since the importance of this element was not open to question. Even those, like Rïzhkin, who tried to argue that the very process of symphonic development was, in its logic and 'rationality', akin to *bït*, and hence to *syuzhetnost'*, had to acknowledge the absolute dominance of the requirement for 'content'. The flexibility of the concept lay in the extent to which content had to be concrete and identifiable; the easy way out offered by political subtitles, tagged-on programmes and insertion of the odd revolutionary song – even a whole texted cantata-style section – was aggressively targeted at the conference. Lev Knipper, the maligned composer of mass-song symphonies (his Fourth, 'Poem about the Komsomol Fighter' of 1933, was much discussed at the conference), was singled out by Shostakovich for criticism, and others agreed: Knipper's Fourth was 'vulgar', 'trite', but worst of all 'inorganic'. As Rïzhkin noted, 'In Knipper's Fourth Symphony, we are given impressions of musical characters (especially the partisan song), but in a congealed, immovable state. The musical images of conflict (in the first movement) have a theatrical quality and do not lead to internal transformations, to the emergence of a new quality.'[51]

Rïzhkin's remarks have an obvious resonance with Asafiev's concept of highly

49 *Sovetskaya muzïka*, 1935/6, 7.

50 For a concise account of eighteenth- and nineteenth-century musical aesthetics, and especially the views of Kant, Schopenhauer and Hegel, see Carl Dahlhaus, *Esthetics of Music*, trans. William Austin, Cambridge: Cambridge University Press, 1982, especially 16–31. For Sollertinskiy's remarks, see *Sovetskaya muzïka*, 1935/6, 29.

51 *Sovetskaya muzïka*, 1935/6, 21.

developmental, 'dialectical' symphonism. The demand that a symphony should be 'organic' may have been a vague one, but it was suggestive of certain standards: merely inserting a mass song into a symphony was perceived as a debasement of symphonic form. The ideological resonances of the term were likewise positive, and it was vague enough to be infinitely pliable in persuasive hands. Admittedly, its use at the conference was rooted in less appealing preoccupations: hostility towards 'intuitivism' (a composer's right to compose according to his or her own creative instincts) and an oppressive emphasis on 'rationality' that went hand in hand with the imperative for 'content'. Both these obsessions can be seen only too clearly at the conference: Knipper, Shebalin and Kabalevsky were among those upbraided for their alleged failure to 'review their ideological baggage' and their propensity to 'fall back on intuition'.[52] Whilst such criticism was unhelpfully obscure, a particular perpetrator of 'intuition' – Myaskovsky – was openly criticized by the ex-RAPM composer Viktor Beliy for dwelling too lingeringly on visions of the pre-Soviet era in his Twelfth Symphony.[53] A subtitle, then, was no guarantee of immunity. Sollertinsky added his own voice to criticisms of composers' reluctance to break with the old style and format of Romantic symphonism, extending his comments to musicologists' stubborn preoccupation with Romantic aesthetics:

> I must talk about one tendency which seems to me dangerous and which slipped into Ostretsov's and Rïzhkin's talks. Much was said on the subject of the fabula-type, programmatic symphonic music. In addressing this issue, I felt that the talks had a tendency to revive the old theory that music with a subject is music with content. ... There is a vast range of discussion about the subject-based and fabula-based style that hangs on the fear of writing a piece of pure symphonic music. ... Of course, we need programme symphonies. But we should not focus on them alone.[54]

The key word here is clearly 'fear'. It was as difficult to construct a viable aesthetics of music as it was to compose an abstract symphony and get away with it, even a year before the notorious *Pravda* attacks on Shostakovich in early 1936 changed the Soviet cultural scene for ever. Suggestions for ways around this difficulty ranged from the audacious to the laughable; the composer Konstantin Kuznetsov earnestly offered the following programme for a single-movement symphony:

> The first section presents tension, setting up an opposition to the second section, which has a more lyrical, emotional tone. There follows an intermezzo, repeating with sharp irony the material just expounded. The reprise provides a background for the material of the satirical intermezzo and this demolishes the positive impression that may be gained from the exposition. The symphony concludes in a depressed, slow vein.[55]

52 Ibid., 35.

53 *Sovetskaya muzïka*, 1935/5, 36.

54 *Sovetskaya muzïka*, 1935/6, 29.

55 *Sovetskaya muzïka*, 1935/5, 27.

That Kuznetsov also advocated ending his symphony with, as he put it, 'the weariness and subdued quality of Chaikovsky's symphonism' demonstrates that for some, at least, the compulsory happy endings of socialist realism we are familiar with today did not seem the inevitable way forward in 1935. Shostakovich's own Fourth Symphony (1936) ends *morendo*, in C minor. Myaskovsky's Thirteenth (1933) and Tikhon Khrennikov's First (1935) likewise end in the minor. Optimism does not seem to have been a key issue here; rather, composers were primarily concerned with how to communicate feelings or ideas in music, without relying on 'primitive' methods. Arseni Gladkovsky, for example, brought up the problems he had experienced when composing his 1925 opera *Red Petrograd*:

> I represented the Reds with the 'Internationale' and the Whites with Preobrazhensky's march; both motifs then came together and merged into one. … I tried just about everything to represent the class enemies. We have the workers, I thought to myself, and gave them a theme, and we have the enemies; this opposition persecuted me and obsessed me in my work. … For example, I used a poem commemorating the 26 Baku Commissars, which contained the line: 'There the white hand of the Menshevik softly spreads the bed, but it is a hard bed to sleep on' – the harmony then actually 'hardened' and became rather rough on the ear. … When representing the English interventionists I could not think how to portray an English officer other than by inserting 'Rule, Britannia'.[56]

Gladkovsky was honest enough to see that he had become trapped in a fallacy that assumed that to convey images and ideas in music required a crude schematicism that even the most passive listener could follow. The result was a debasement of the concept of leitmotif (another much-debated concept at the time) to a cartoon-like caricature. Texts, popular songs, subtitles and programmes all carried their own pitfalls and problems for the symphonist, and there was something approaching a consensus at the conference that these methods had not yet proved fruitful. Of course, there was no unequivocal conclusion drawn from this; but the fact that no-one had any answers to the problems composers described at the conference does at least put Sollertinsky's ideas in context. It is significant that Popov's First Symphony – which ends in an explosive C major apotheosis – was banned after its première at the end of March 1935, for reasons only vaguely hinted at. Aleksandr Ossovsky, then professor of music history at the Leningrad Conservatoire and artistic director of the Leningrad Philharmonic, perceived it as 'reflecting the ideology of hostile classes':[57] a remark probably born of old-fashioned conservatism as much as of his awareness that Popov's luxuriant idiom might seem inappropriately self-indulgent in the puritanical climate of the 1930s.

---

56 Ibid., 29.

57 Quoted in Zarui A. Apetyan, Gavriil Popov: iz literaturnogo nalsediya: Stranitsï biografii [Gavriil Popov: from a literary legacy. Pages from a biography], Moscow: Sovetskiy Kompozitor, 1986, 260–61.

The ban on Popov's symphony was lifted only a month after it was instigated, but the work never received another public performance in the composer's lifetime.[58]

Although Kabalevsky's and Rïzhkin's remarks show that both Sollertinsky and Shostakovich were treading on fairly thin ice in their support of Mahler and *ulichnïy* intonations, no-one had anything more constructive to offer, and they must have hoped that their ideas had potential for acceptance if presented with an appropriate veneer of political correctness. Sollertinsky's recommendation that composers take a closer look at Mahler's symphonies had at least superficial claims to ideological respectability. By implying that Mahler intentionally, and for socio-political reasons, undermined the hegemony of bourgeois intonations with his urban and folk idioms, Sollertinsky aimed to render him as unquestionable a source as possible. Though he discussed Mahler only briefly at the conference, Sollertinsky's 1932 monograph makes his position clearer: Mahler was to be the model for Soviet composers, and – it may safely be guessed – Shostakovich was to be a pioneer in the new 'democratic' symphonism.

On the Eve of the Great Terror: 1935–1936

Shostakovich had already begun work on his Fourth Symphony at the time of the symphonism conference. In an article for *Literaturnaya gazeta* in late 1934, he declared his intention to focus his creative energies on his new symphony, which was to be 'a monumental programme composition of expansive thought and immense passion'. He referred to earlier drafts and plans that he intended to scrap, and remarked that he was going to begin again from scratch.[59] Interestingly, Shostakovich revealed that he had 'nurtured' the project for 'many years', but was still struggling to find the right 'form and technique'. This might suggest that following his Third Symphony of 1930 Shostakovich, perhaps under the influence of Sollertinsky, was carefully assessing his composer's vocation, consciously deciding to take on the mantle of a symphonist and thus spending several years pondering the future direction of Soviet symphonism. But in 1931 he had written a 'Deklaratsia' to the proletarian journal *Rabochiy i teatr* [Workers and the theatre], in which he stated his intention to cancel all his theatrical commissions in order to concentrate on a new symphony, 'dedicated to the 15th anniversary of the October Revolution'.[60] Shostakovich was referring to the symphonic poem 'From Karl Marx to our Own Days', of which the first of five sections was completed

58 It was next performed in 1989 in Moscow.

59 Shostakovich, 'We will be Trumpeters of a Great Era', *Literaturnaya gazeta*, 28 December 1934. Quoted in Manashir Yakubov, 'The "Original" Fourth Symphony', *DSCH Journal*, 15, 2001, 60.

60 *Rabochiy i teatr* [Workers and the theatre], 1931/31, 6. A full transcript is given in Darby, 'Problems of Context', 369, and a translation on 190–92.

before he abandoned the work in February 1932. Despite Shostakovich's detailed description of this work in the press – stating his intention to finish it by September 1932 and mentioning its anticipated première by the Leningrad Philharmonic conducted by Gauk – no traces of it have survived.[61] But the fact of its existence suggests that the 'many years' Shostakovich supposedly devoted to mulling over the form of his Fourth Symphony as we know it could not have been much more than two.

More references to the Fourth Symphony trickled out over the next year: Sollertinsky referred to it in passing at the symphonism conference as being in an 'embryonic state'.[62] More false starts plagued Shostakovich: in April 1935 he again mentioned his dissatisfaction with the drafts he had made and announced that he was beginning again 'from scratch'. The extent to which Shostakovich was agonizing over the symphony can be judged from his own remarks: 'I cannot say anything definite about this next symphony, about its nature or subject matter. I have rejected all the drafts I had for this work.'[63] Shostakovich began work on the Fourth Symphony in its present form in September 1935, and completed it in April 1936. Mid-way through its composition, *Pravda* published damning attacks on Shostakovich's opera *Lady Macbeth of the Mtsensk District* and his ballet *The Limpid Stream*.[64]

The impact of those editorials has been well documented; Shostakovich was subjected to vitriolic criticism in the press and in the Composers' Union, while those who were associated with him – notably Sollertinsky – were eventually forced to repent of their own 'formalist' leanings.[65] Nevertheless, Shostakovich himself did not attend any of the Composers' Union meetings arranged to discuss his music and made no promises to change his ways. In 1974, marking the 38th anniversary of the infamous 'Muddle instead of Music' article with Glikman,

---

61 See Fay, *Shostakovich*, 65 and 71. Shostakovich recalled the work in a 1973 interview: see Khentova, *V mire Shostakovicha* [In Shostakovich's world], Moscow: Kompozitor, 1996, 35.

62 *Sovetskaya muzïka*, 1935/6, 31.

63 Shostakovich, 'Ballet and music', *Vechernyaya Moskva* [Evening Moscow], 11 April 1935, quoted in Yakubov, 'The "Original" Fourth Symphony', 60.

64 In a letter to Atovm'yan dated 15 February 1936 (just over a week after the second *Pravda* attack), Shostakovich reports that under the circumstances he was feeling cheerful, playing the piano and composing the third movement of his Fourth Symphony. However, he adds that he is upset about Heinrich Neuhaus's opportunistic criticisms of him in the Moscow discussions immediately following the *Pravda* attacks and that he is staying at home most of the time and not meeting anyone; he signs off with a request to write 'at length and often'. See Bobïkina, *Dmitriy Shostakovich*, 229. For the Moscow discussions in which Neuhaus spoke against Shostakovich, see *Sovetskaya muzïka*, 1936/3, 16–60; for Neuhaus's speech see 27–8.

65 See principally Glikman, *Story of a Friendship*, 213–24, Hakobian, *Music of the Soviet Age*, 127–31, Fay, *Shostakovich*, 87–92 and Fitzpatrick, *The Cultural Front*, 183–215.

Shostakovich – with a touch of pride – recalled how 'the authorities tried everything they knew to get me to repent and expiate my sin. But I refused. I was young then, and had my physical strength. Instead of repenting, I wrote my Fourth Symphony.'[66]

Although there can be no doubt that the whole affair was intensely stressful for Shostakovich, he could have drawn some comfort from the fact that the Leningrad branch of the Composers' Union did not express unanimous approval of the *Pravda* editorials, and there were several prominent voices raised in his defence. As Fitzpatrick observes, Leningrad composers reacted defensively to the *Pravda* criticisms, since these implied that they 'had been asleep at the wheel and failed to recognise the formalist danger'.[67] And although there was more hostility in the Moscow branch – in particular from ex-RAPM composers such as Lev Lebedinsky and the critic Boris Shteynpress – it was moderated by the opprobrium that their extreme criticisms subsequently received. Even *Pravda* rebuked Lebedinsky and Shteynpress for their opportunistic attempts to revive RAPM composers at the expense of Shostakovich.[68] The fact that so many of Shostakovich's colleagues felt able to speak in his defence suggests that although with hindsight the *Lady Macbeth* affair signalled the start of terrifying cultural purges – to which many distinguished figures were to fall victim – the extent of those purges was not anticipated in the musical community. Added to that, the fact that Shostakovich went on to complete his symphony, confident that the performance would take place and – presumably – believing that the quality of his work would overcome any hostile criticism, strongly suggests that, at least by September 1936, Shostakovich's situation had recovered sufficiently for the première of his new symphony to be potentially a success. As noted in the Introduction, Shostakovich's preview performance of the symphony to Sollertinsky, Glikman and Klemperer had been extremely well received.[69] Meyerhold, too, had written to Shostakovich in the autumn of 1936 to encourage him about the forthcoming première: 'Stiedry tells me that soon your new symphony will be performed in Leningrad. I will make every effort to be in Leningrad for this concert. I am sure that when you hear your new work you will once more throw yourself into new, monumental music, and that you will find strength in that work.'[70]

Not surprisingly, earlier that year Shostakovich had urgently needed encouragement. In April that year he had written to Shebalin: 'I am now orchestrating the finale (the third movement). When it's finished, maybe I could

---

66 Glikman, *Story of a Friendship*, 194.

67 Fitzpatrick, *The Cultural Front*, 203.

68 Ibid. For further criticism of Lebedinsky and Shteynpress, see *Sovetskaya muzïka*, 1937/5, 10–15.

69 See Glikman, *Story of a Friendship*, xxii.

70 Mikheyeva, *Zhizn' Dmitriya Shostakovicha*, 193–4.

come to Moscow to show you. ... I am in a sour mood. I don't know how things will turn out. So I'm putting off finishing the symphony. If I had other commitments I could finish it in five days. But since I'm not working much it will take me 10–15 days.'[71]

It is possible – though obviously not certain – that Shostakovich's bad mood was caused by feelings of anxiety over the likely reception of his new symphony. Given the near-complete banishment of his name from the musical press since the attacks on him in *Pravda* and within the Composers' Union, and the massive significance attached to the success of his Fifth Symphony in 1937, it is reasonable to suppose that he must have felt under intense pressure as his Fourth Symphony neared completion. When rehearsals began, the signs seemed bad. According to Glikman, there was a general mood of apprehension in Leningrad's musical circles as the rehearsals got underway, owing, Glikman recalls, to the symphony's 'diabolical complexity' and 'formalist tendencies'. Its withdrawal from rehearsal, according to Glikman's account, was prompted by direct pressure on Shostakovich from Vladimir Iokhelson, then secretary of the Composers' Union, and an unnamed Party official. Musing on these events many years later, Glikman exonerated Stiedry completely and laid the blame for the symphony's withdrawal squarely at the door of faceless Soviet officialdom:

> A mythology has grown up around the withdrawal of the Fourth Symphony, a mythology to which writings about Shostakovich have unfortunately lent quasi-scriptural status. The essence of the legend is that the composer, persuaded that Fritz Stiedry was inadequate to meet the demands of the symphony, had made the decision to cancel the performance. It would be hard to imagine anything more absurd.[72]

As discussed in the Introduction, the version of events Glikman rejects here was more or less the officially accepted story in the Soviet Union. Both Gauk and Kondrashin were happy to go on record during the 1960s blaming Stiedry for conducting rehearsals poorly; Kondrashin, in conversation with Sofiya Khentova in 1963, spread the blame a little wider to take in the Philharmonic directorate and 'conservative' orchestral musicians. According to Kondrashin, the fate of the Fourth Symphony could be attributed to several factors: 'lack of understanding on Stiedry's part, the cowardice of the Philharmonic director I. Renzin and the protests of conservative orchestral musicians who didn't understand the style of the symphony. He [Shostakovich] could not take the risk.'[73] Gauk's account, which

---

71 A.M. Shebalina, ed., *Pamyati V.Ya. Shebalina: vospominaniya, materiali* [In memory of V.Ya. Shebalin: reminiscences, materials]. Moscow: Sovetskiy Kompozitor, 1984, 222.

72 Glikman, *Story of a Friendship*, xxiii.

73 Khentova, *V mire Shostakovicha*, 1996, 196. Kondrashin, who discussed the symphony with Shostakovich before the première, may have heard this version of events from the composer himself; alternatively, he may have been repeating the story that had circulated in musical circles for the last 25 years. In conversation with V. Razhnikov, Kondrashin briefly alludes to the symphony's withdrawal, speculating that Shostakovich

dates from 1962, tells a similar story. He had attended rehearsals in 1936 and reported that Stiedry did not understand the music and that the orchestra played terribly; in consequence, Shostakovich was forced to withdraw the symphony.[74] More recently, Lyudmila Mikheyeva has presented yet another slant on this story, this time offered by the conductor and composer Gavriil Yudin, who wrote to Mikheyeva in 1987:

> The remarkable, inspired conductor Stiedry was not able easily to enter into the world of a symphony that was more or less alien to him. In the same way, for example, he wasn't able to give a satisfactory performance of Glazunov's Eighth Symphony. And all the time with Shostakovich's Fourth Symphony he seemed to be a 'guest' rather than 'at home' in the work; he couldn't enter into its world. I spoke about this with my friends from the orchestra, who by no means blamed Stiedry but simply confirmed this as fact. And D.D. [Shostakovich] himself felt uncertain about the successful outcome of the proposed public showing of this symphony, if even Stiedry himself was having doubts [about it]. It is also important that in the committee of the Communist Party there was a wise, well-intentioned man; I can't recall what he did, but anyway he held a responsible post. He phoned Shostakovich and invited him to come to Smolniy to discuss [things] with him. There he asked Shostakovich if it wouldn't be better not to risk anything so soon after the publication of that remarkable article 'Sumbur vmesto muzïka' so as not to invite more trouble and appear to be 'incorrigible'. This was said purely from the heart, and D.D. [Shostakovich] listened to him. He came straight from Smolniy to the Philharmonic and withdrew the symphony from performance himself; it was absolutely not 'cancelled'.[75]

Though Glikman's version offers the most appealing scenario – exonerating a musician and blaming interfering officials – these stories cannot easily be dismissed. Though it seems extraordinary to accuse Stiedry of finding the Fourth Symphony too complex – he had after all given the première of Popov's ultra-complex First Symphony only the previous season – it is nevertheless true that, of the two works, Shostakovich's is by far the more unpredictable and volatile, and the finale alone, with its medley of popular references, is famously daunting. Noting the symphony's challenging character, Khentova herself modified the harsher judgements of her interviewees in her 1985 biography:

> He [Shostakovich] realised that the affair was not merely to do with the conductor, orchestra or the Philharmonic directorate. There was a far deeper reason: the style of symphonic presentation, the sharp intensity of disclosures of feeling, was as yet unusual for the composer himself. Having moved far ahead in this symphony, he now needed time to mull over such a leap.[76]

Mikheyeva herself offers a more direct opinion: 'it was impossible to give a

---

had taken the decision, probably on the advice of Sollertinsky. See Razhnikov, *Kirill Kondrashin rasskazïvaet*, 182.

74 See Khentova, *Shostakovich: zhizn' i tvorchestvo*, 440.

75 Mikheyeva, *Zhizn' Dmitriya Shostakovicha*, 196.

76 Khentova, *Shostakovich: zhizn' i tvorchestvo*, 440.

public performance [of the Fourth Symphony]: it was too outspoken. … Its time had not yet come.'[77] Volkov's recent interpretation of events differs sharply from that offered in *Testimony* and attributed to Shostakovich. Following the officially accepted assumption that Shostakovich himself took the decision to withdraw the symphony, Volkov then suggests that this was due not to problems with conductor or orchestra, nor to pressure from above, but to Shostakovich's own timely awareness of its obvious and deliberate 'seditious' nature.[78] He even goes so far as to suggest that Shostakovich feared that Asafiev, no less, would expose the presence of all its carefully scattered allusions (Volkov cites the finale's parodic allusion to Stravinsky's *Oedipus rex*, Mahler's 'Die zwei blauen Augen' and an apparent (unspecified) quotation from the finale of *The Firebird*), arguing that this fear accounted for Shostakovich's hostility to the musicologist after 1936.[79] Reflecting on the nature of Shostakovich's growing long-distance relationship with Stalin, Volkov claims that withdrawing the symphony was intended as an act of both self-preservation and apparent self-sacrifice: abandoning a 'formalist' work for 'useful' work on film scores.[80]

Clearly, trying to second-guess the reasons for events of which there is no authoritative account is a futile exercise. Still, Volkov's suggestion is by far the least plausible. Asafiev was not the only one who might have recognized some of those allusions – the finale's opening evocation of Mahler is hardly an esoteric reference, and most of the cellos and basses in the Leningrad Philharmonic would probably have associated the throbbing ending with Chaikovsky's 'Pathétique'. In any case, no amount of inter-textual association can really add to the unmistakeably tragic tone of the finale's coda; it could even be claimed that these allusions were not intended to be covert but were simply 'intonations' in the richest sense of Asafiev's term: their half-recognizable familiarity is what communicates most powerfully. In the end, we are left with a series of anecdotes

---

77 Mikheyeva, *Zhizn' Dmitriya Shostakovicha*, 199–200.

78 This is also the view of Sofia Moshevich in *Dmitri Shostakovich, Pianist*, Montreal & Kingston, McGill-Queen's University Press, 2004, 89.

79 In fact, Shostakovich's mistrust and dislike of Asaf'ev went back to 1926, as his letter to Sergey Protopopov of 13 May that year makes clear. In it Shostakovich complains bitterly of Asaf'ev's failure to support him before the première of his First Symphony by coming to a preview performance. Stung by this snub from Leningrad's chief music critic and suspecting him of petty intrigues, Shostakovich accuses Asaf'ev of not attending 'on principle' because the performance occurred under the auspices of LASM and its leader Yulia Veisberg, from whom Asaf'ev had broken to form his Circle for New Music. See Bobïkina, ed., *Dmitriy Shostakovich*, 135. However, this does not mean that the relationship between Asaf'ev and Shostakovich was permanently soured; Fay notes that Shostakovich biographers have regarded their relationship as cordial and fruitful. On the other hand, the counter-caution could be made that no Soviet biographer would have been keen to portray Soviet Russia's most original musical philosopher in such a negative light.

80 Volkov, *Shostakovich and Stalin*, 167–71.

similar in nature (by Gauk, Kondrashin, Yudin) versus Glikman's account. Although Glikman hints that the Philharmonic directorate were under pressure from higher officials, he does not take speculation any further than that; to try to pin down a specific reason for such events would be to presuppose a rationale behind the countless arbitrary and senseless decisions made during the insane, terrified climate of the 1930s. For this reason, I feel that to assert, as Mikheyeva does, that the Fourth Symphony could not have been performed because it failed to conform to the 'canons of socialist realism' (see Introduction, n. 8) assumes too much. If it is the case that Shostakovich withdrew his symphony primarily because either he or the Philharmonic directorate feared reprisals should the première have gone ahead, then it seems likely that their anxiety stemmed not primarily from the symphony's dark tone but from its 'formalistic' complexity; perhaps even from its similarity with the style of *Lady Macbeth*. It is worth bearing in mind at this point the substance of *Pravda*'s criticisms of Shostakovich's opera *Lady Macbeth* and his ballet *The Limpid Stream*. Shostakovich was criticised not for his pessimism but for the complexity of his musical language; it was the stigma of 'formalism' that hung over him in the wake of the *Pravda* attacks, which memorably described *Lady Macbeth* as 'fidgety, screaming, neurotic music'.[81] According to Laurel Fay:

> Given the political and aesthetic climate of the time, there seems very little doubt that even in a flawless performance the massive, 'Mahlerian' work would have been construed as the epitome of formalism, an act in arrogant defiance of the Party's benevolent guidance. Indeed, the more intriguing question is not why it was withdrawn but how it came as close to public performance as it did. The symphony had been conceived on an ambitious scale, as the artistic 'credo' of an enlightened modernist; the final movement, written after the launching of the *Pravda* campaign, made no conspicuous acknowledgement of or concession to the critical furor.[82]

Fay is surely correct in guessing that the reason for disquiet over the Fourth Symphony stemmed from its complexity in the wake of *Pravda*'s accusations of formalism. Nevertheless, the symphony's cancellation came as a shock to Shostakovich and his friends. However obvious it may appear with the benefit of hindsight, it seems that his friends and colleagues expected the première to go ahead. Shostakovich had put his best creative energies into his new symphony; he may have been anxious about its official reception but he was proud enough of it to have invited Moscow's two leading lights, Shebalin and Myaskovsky, to the première. Nevertheless, before the anticipated première Shostakovich confessed to his close friend Lev Atovmyan, 'As you can probably guess, I'm trembling with fright [*Ya drozhu ot strakha*]', though whether this was a result of the general atmosphere of apprehension Glikman describes or of his fear of official censure owing to the complex or gloomy content of the symphony remains uncertain.[83]

---

81 Treitler et al., eds, *Strunk's Source Readings in Music History*, 1399.

82 Fay, *Shostakovich*, 96.

83 The letter to Atovm'yan is dated 23 September 1936, two months before rehearsals

When Atovmyan recalled the events more than 30 years later, however, he remembered Shostakovich's attitude to the authorities as belligerently self-confident: 'I don't write for the newspaper *Pravda*, but for myself'.[84]

Shostakovich's confidence was not unjustified. Though the path of Popov's own equally 'modernist' symphony had not been smooth – it had been cancelled two months after its première, but reinstated after the intervention of Shostakovich, Sollertinsky and others – it had at least been performed and discussed without too much hostility.[85] Sollertinsky, whose career suffered a surprisingly brief setback after the vicious attacks on him during the 'Muddle instead of Music' debacle, was still an active critic in Leningrad, and Shostakovich could reasonably have expected his new symphony to restore his own status. 'Mahlerian' it certainly was; but Sollertinsky's efforts to portray Mahler as a 'fellow traveller', while not meeting with conspicuous success, had not met with criticism either. For Sollertinsky, Mahlerian symphonism meant not merely large-scale symphonism; it meant a symphonic language infused with the intonations of urban popular music and a work that engaged with philosophical issues through its dramaturgy. It was, in short, anything but the traditional brand of Soviet symphonism that could potentially be dubbed 'formalist'. Although the tight-knit motivic structure and contrapuntal virtuosity of Shostakovich's first movement might have made it vulnerable to the charge of formalism, the finale – with its sequence of funeral march, divertimento embracing various popular genres from manic polka to Keystone Kops chase music to popular song, and massive C major apotheosis – ought to have been immune. What is more, it stood on the shoulders of a number of earlier successful Soviet symphonic finales, borrowing their frames of reference (popular music, dance idioms and funeral march) and even paraphrasing them in the first C major coda, as will be discussed.

Shostakovich's finale was new and original, but its use of popular idioms and funeral march was not entirely unprecedented. What was striking was the directness of their presentation: Popov's finale alludes far more obliquely to popular music, reflecting it through an Ivesian cloud of realistic street chaos rather than treating it as 'proper' thematic material. Shostakovich's symphony went far

---

began. Fay suggests that the letter was misdated, and that it was probably written on 23 November (Fay, *Shostakovich*, 95 and n. 34), and if Shostakovich used roman numerals for months then it is certainly possible that he had written IX instead of XI. The possible confusion over the date of the letter only adds to the uncertainty of the story. Shostakovich makes no reference to the rehearsals having already begun, and his brief confession 'Ya drozhu ot strakha' is almost the only personal remark in the letter, which is otherwise characteristically factual, briefly describing recent concerts and rates of pay. See Levon Atovm'yan, 'Iz vospominaniy' [From a reminiscence], *Muzïkal'naya akademiya*, 1997/4, 75–6. For Shostakovich's letter, see Bobïkina,ed., *Dmitriy Shostakovich*, 237–8.

84 Fay, *Shostakovich*, 306.

85 For events surrounding the banning and reinstatement of Popov's First Symphony, see Apetyan, *Gavriil Popov*, 260–61.

beyond its predecessors, but could also have sheltered behind them. Although the scale and complexity of the Fourth Symphony might have provoked accusations of formalism, in other respects it was fulfilling current demands for a new type of Soviet symphonism. Criticisms (not directed at Shostakovich) voiced at the 1935 conference drew attention to *raznostilnost* [polystylism] and 'inorganic' symphonism (Knipper), over-dependence on formal schemes or 'workshop mentality' (Shebalin and Popov), a 'shallow photographic portrayal of reality',[86] a reluctance to 'bid farewell to the past'[87] (Shaporin and Popov) and – crucially – technical incompetence. Though Shostakovich was criticized for his undeniably over-the-top use of popular idioms in the ballet *The Bolt*, he had defended his use of light music, even to the point of asserting its suitability for symphonic use. Other criticisms aimed at Shostakovich during the 1935 symphonism conference had centred on his tendency to employ a dry, inexpressive 'constructivism'.[88] No-one could have reasonably levelled this accusation at him after hearing the Fourth Symphony; dry and inexpressive it was most definitely not.

Although there was no consensus at the conference over the form the new symphonism should take (few composers would have welcomed such prescription), composers were called to the task of 'reflecting reality' and creating a new Soviet symphonic language. Kabalevsky called for 'an attentive attitude to all creative phenomena of our rich musical reality'[89] (though he was also one of the severest critics of Shostakovich's use of light music), and Sollertinsky argued that 'it is necessary to look for new intonations … [that] will at first provoke misunderstanding and even dislike';[90] Sollertinsky, Shebalin and Shostakovich called for greater awareness of contemporary Western music; the heavyweight ex-RAPM critic Khubov demanded that symphonists 'confront the question of big ideas, forms and philosophical depths' and called for a revival of the programme symphony (the use of leitmotif in works by Liszt, Berlioz and Wagner was broached as a possible aid to contemporary Soviet symphonists by a number of speakers). He also criticized Knipper, Shebalin and Kabalevsky for continuing 'along a well-trodden path … Soviet composers still fall back on intuition and don't review their ideological baggage … they will never try to find new forms and principles of development.'[91] Ogolevtsev's description of the 'composer-chronicler' detailed the composer's responsibility to write in a clear, expressive (but not simplistic) musical language 'intelligible to audiences of workers'.[92]

From the mass of vague pontificating about the form Soviet symphonism

---

86 *Sovetskaya muzïka*, 1935/4, 18.
87 *Sovetskaya muzïka*, 1935/5, 28.
88 *Sovetskaya muzïka*, 1935/5, 36.
89 *Sovetskaya muzïka*, 1935/4, 38.
90 *Sovetskaya muzïka*, 1935/6, 32.
91 *Sovetskaya muzïka*, 1935/6, 35.
92 *Sovetskaya muzïka*, 1935/6, 38.

should take, then, several key elements can be drawn. Its musical language should be both technically sophisticated and comprehensible to everyone. It should be conceived on an epic philosophical scale, perhaps using leitmotif or a programme as an aid to narrative, but it should not fall into the trap of sound effects or glib musical images (cf. the excerpt from Gladkovsky's paper quoted on p. 23 above). It should set itself the task of chronicling Soviet reality, making use of a wide range of modern intonations, and not keep using the same traditional intonations and styles. Add to that calls (unchallenged) for Soviet composers to become better acquainted with Western music, and what emerges is entirely compatible not only with Shostakovich's Fourth Symphony but also with Sollertinsky's vision, published six years earlier, for a reconstruction of epic symphonism based on Mahler's use of popular idioms. The residue of Asafiev's influence is perceptible in a general concern that a symphony should be 'organic', but this too is perfectly compatible with the Fourth Symphony, at least with its first movement. Shostakovich might well have expected criticism for portraying Soviet reality in dark colours, but he would not – or at least should not – have been accused of empty formalism, philosophical shallowness, reluctance to break with past traditions or composing incomprehensible music.

One criticism that might nevertheless have been voiced is that the Fourth Symphony lacks a coherent narrative structure. Unlike the Fifth Symphony, which was belatedly interpreted as a *Bildungsroman*-style epic (the novelist Alexei Tolstoy called it 'the formation of a personality') and which could hence be read as a cousin – albeit a problematic one – of the *per aspera ad astra* darkness-to-light symphony, the Fourth has no comparable overall narrative strategy. Unlike many of its contemporaries, it bears no dedication to the Revolution or to Lenin, and Shostakovich wrote no programme for it: it is thus a completely abstract symphony. There is not even a slow movement to denote an expressive subject or an evocation of a Russian folk-idyll (both typical of contemporary Soviet symphonies), and there are no cyclic elements tying the structure together that might suggest a 'summation' of some kind. However, in other respects – especially to modern Western musicological ears – it does have narrative features: the first movement uses sonata form as a 'normal' template from which it then sharply deviates, and thematic transformation is taken to extremes which blatantly invite hermeneutic reading, even if they ultimately resist it. Even the finale, which follows no formal scheme at all, uses quotation and paraphrase in a highly suggestive manner that could be construed as narrative, even if not 'novelistic' in the sense of character development. As Fanning has suggested, there is no reason why Shostakovich could not have argued, had he felt the need, that the funeral march which opens and closes the finale was a tribute to Sergey Kirov, murdered (probably on Stalin's orders) in December 1934.[93] There were plenty of such

93 See David Fanning, 'Shostakovich: "The Present-Day Master of the C-major Key"', *Acta Musicologica*, 73, 2001, 128.

tribute symphonies, and the funeral march archetype had the most respectable of forebears in Beethoven's 'Eroica'.[94] Such strong musical images certainly constitute 'content', but, as with all musical images, the exact nature of that content is conveniently open to dispute. In short, the Fourth Symphony was abstract, but not unsalvageably so; a plausible programme could easily have been attached to it if needed.

The Fourth Symphony was almost certainly intended to be a milestone in the development of Soviet symphonism. It differed from every other Soviet symphony that had preceded it in several key areas: in the extreme 'simplicity' of much of its material, including a movement almost entirely composed of stylisations of light music genres; in the overtly dramatized nature of thematic conflict and development in the first movement and the strong presence of an expressive subject therein; in the entirely episodic, non-developmental form of the finale; and in its exceptional range of references to other works: to Mahler's First and Second Symphonies, Stravinsky's *Oedipus rex*, Chaikovsky's 'Pathétique' and even that most impeccable of role-models – Beethoven's 'Eroica'.

A Typology of Soviet Symphonism

First Movements: Themes

Comparatively few Soviet symphonies from the 1930s have first movements in the tidy sonata form mould that might be expected from the 'heroic classicism' that Taruskin has defined as the Soviets' prime musical response to socialist realism.[95] Exceptions include those of Myaskovsky's Sixteenth (1935–36), Kabalevsky's Second (1934) and Khrennikov's First (1933–35), all of which have fairly short allegro first movements. The more usual type of long, complex opening movements behave a little like truncated sonata forms in that they have two or three themes which are subsequently developed, both immediately following presentation (developmental expositions are standard) and in a further development section, which is then typically rounded off with a coda. It is uncommon for themes to interact, even in development sections, and dramatic thematic transformation is also rare. That may explain why so few of these first movements have real recapitulations: since themes are commonly subjected to

94 Vano Muradeli's First Symphony (1938) was dedicated to Kirov's memory, and there were numerous other tribute works written for him and his fellow Politburo victim Sergey Ordzhonikidze, who killed himself in early 1937. Myaskovsky's Sixteenth Symphony (1934) has a tragic third movement that supposedly reflects upon the death of the pilot of the airship *Maxim Gorky*; Khubov's glowing review of the work draws specific parallels with Beethoven and the 'Eroica' (*Sovetskaya muzïka*, 1937/1, 25).

95 Taruskin, 'Shostakovich and the Inhuman', 517.

'developing variation' treatment in expositions, and are then re-stated, often with some contrapuntal development, in development sections, further repetition in a recapitulation is not required. And with no 'conflict' in the bland development processes, a 'resolution' would be completely incongruous. One notable exception to this is Popov's remarkable First Symphony (1928–32), the first movement of which has a formal recapitulation and long coda.

Robust allegro themes are predictably common: typical examples are found in Myaskovsky's Twelfth, Fifteenth and Sixteenth Symphonies and Shebalin's Third (Example 1.1). Lyrical themes may be presented soloistically (Myaskovsky XII, Shebalin III) or with lavish string colouring (Myaskovsky XVI, Kabalevsky I) (Example 1.2). While thematic interaction in Soviet symphonic developments or recapitulations is minimal, the recapitulation of Shebalin III/1 alters the presentation of its first and second themes so that the introductory bars of theme A lead instead into an A-coloured variant of theme B, and the introduction of B leads to an augmented variant of A (Example 1.1d and 1.3). The Shebalin example is particularly interesting in view of Shostakovich's similar alterations of his first and second themes in the recapitulation of IV/1, as will be seen. But this is a rather isolated case; dramatic conflict and thematic interaction was simply not a feature of 1930s Soviet symphonism.

Example 1.1

a Myaskovsky XII/1: [12]$^{1-6}$

Allegro giocoso

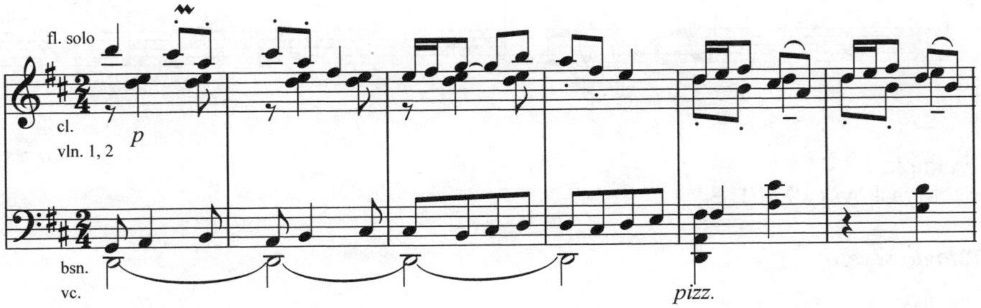

b Myaskovsky XV/1: [1]$^{1-4}$

Allegro appassionato

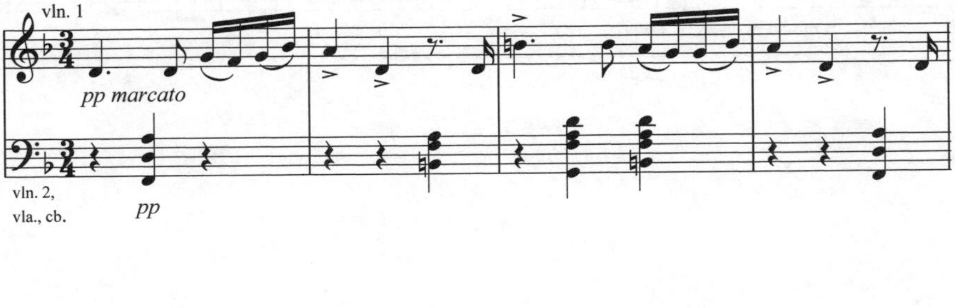

c Myaskovsky XVI/1: 6–2[1]

Allegro vivace

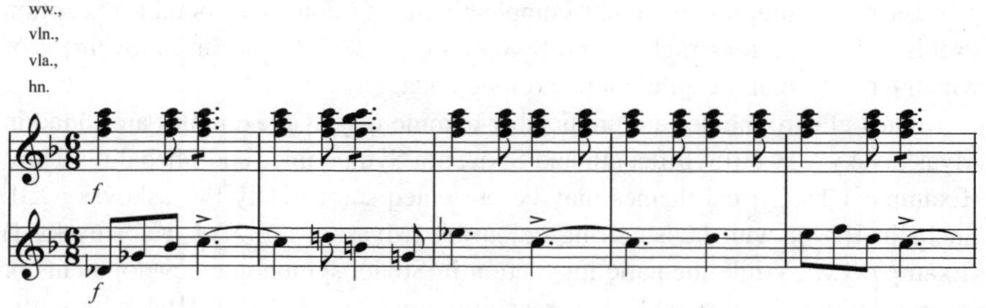

d Shebalin III/1: [2]1–10

Allegro assai

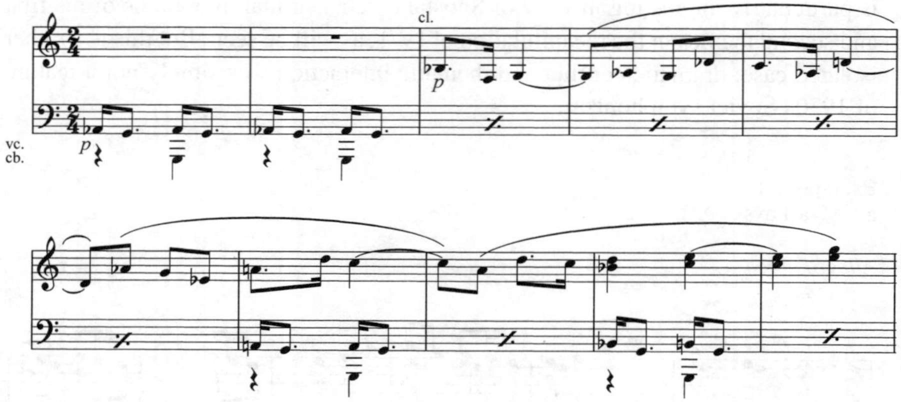

Example 1.2
a Myaskovsky XII/1: [3]1–8

Adagio severo

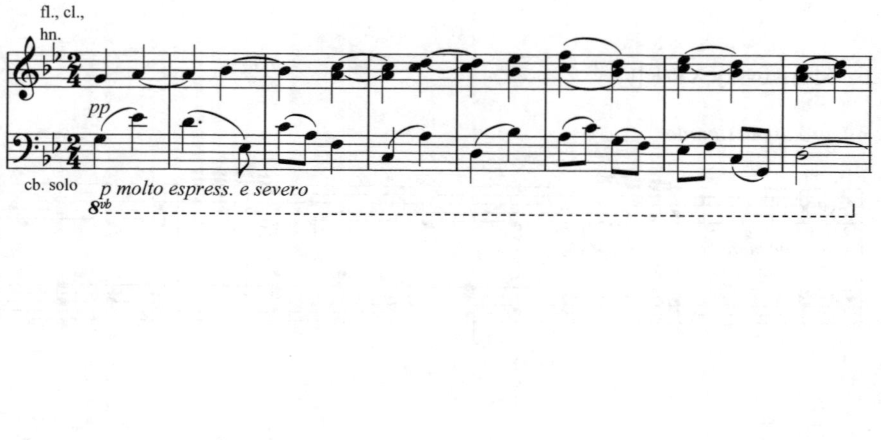

b Shebalin III/1: 7$^{1-14}$

Allegro assai

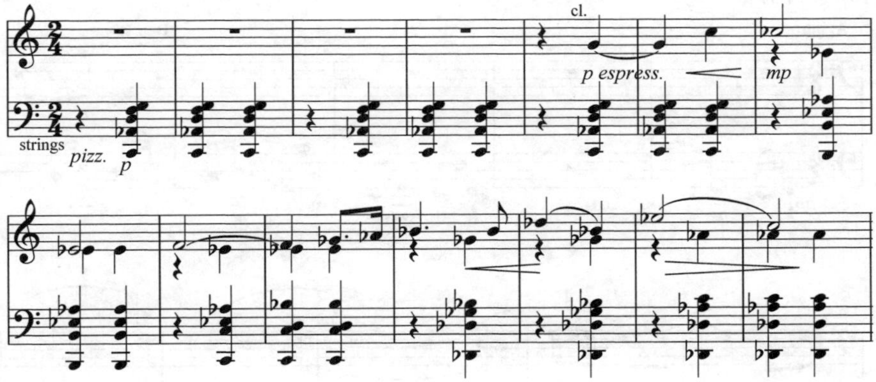

c Myaskovsky XVI/1: 9$^{1-8}$

Meno vivo

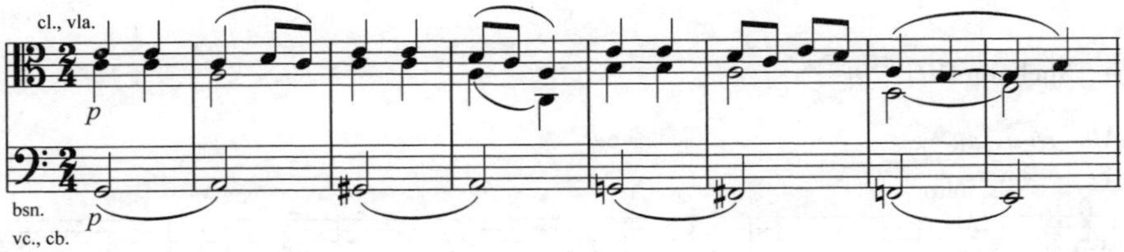

d Kabalevsky I/1: bb. 1–8

Andante molto sostenuto con moto

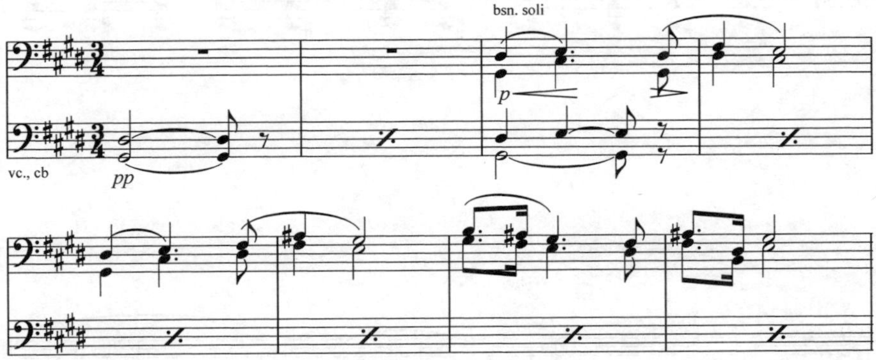

Example 1.3

a Shebalin III/1: [25]1–10

Allegro assai

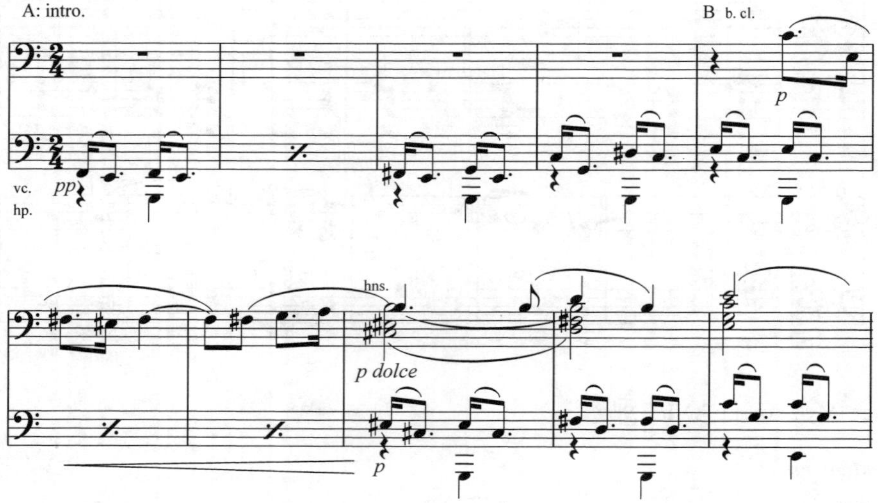

b Shebalin III/1: [29]1–18

Allegro assai

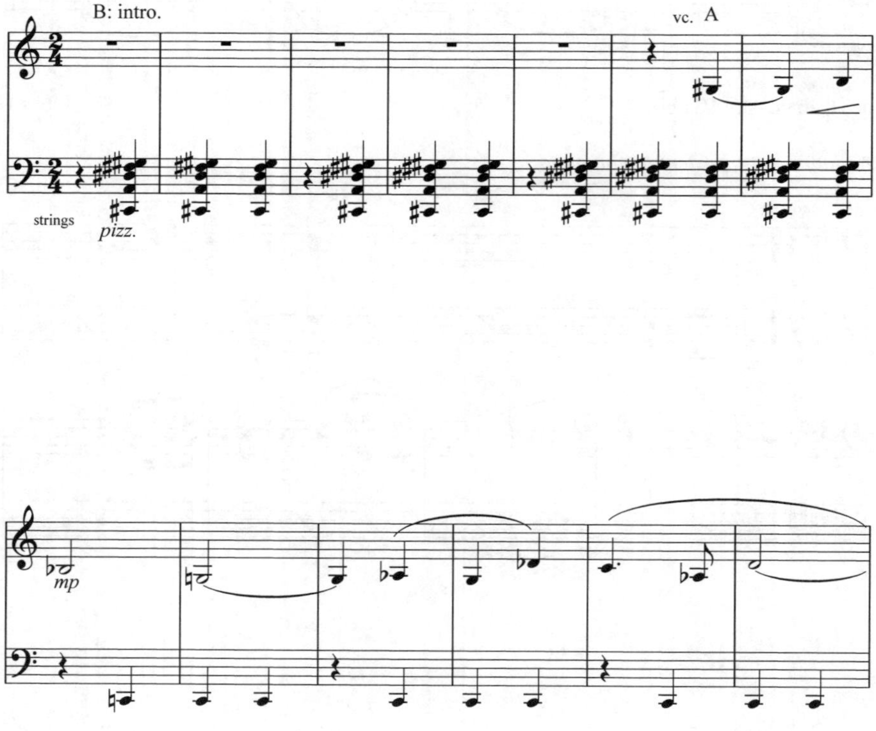

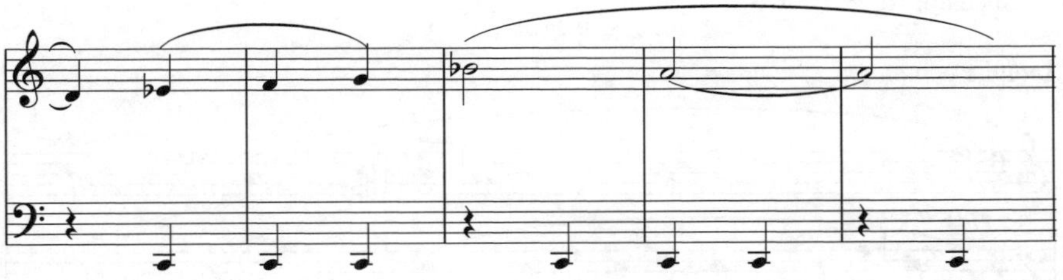

Middle Movements

Middle movements could be more experimental. Where Myaskovsky XII/1, for example, is extremely routine, the second movement is one of his most theatrical, with a declamatory *Invocando* section containing a near-quotation from the Eleventh Symphony (compare XI/1: $\boxed{15}^{1-7}$ with XII/2 $^{3}\boxed{17}$ – $\boxed{17}^{3}$), which completely overshadows the insignificant march theme following it. Khrennikov I/2 takes variant technique to new lengths, with no fewer than six variants of the 'unstable' first theme anchored by a 'stable' second theme. But again, these are exceptions: even where middle movements do not obviously conform to a stable structural formula such as ABA, slow movement themes are invariably either gently folk-like or more conventionally lyrical (Myaskovsky XVI/2, Shebalin III/2) while scherzo themes are typically scurrying (Khrennikov I/3, Shebalin III/3) (see Example 1.4).

Finales

Surprisingly few Soviet symphonies from the early 1930s have four movements; three- and even two-movement symphonies are more common. The Khrennikov

Example 1.4
a Myaskovsky XVI/2: $^{11-4}\boxed{1}$

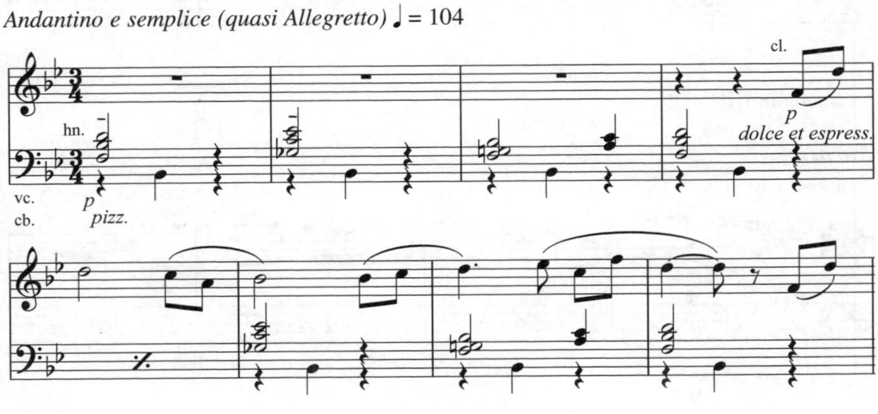

b Shebalin III/2: [2]$^{1-4}$

Andante con moto

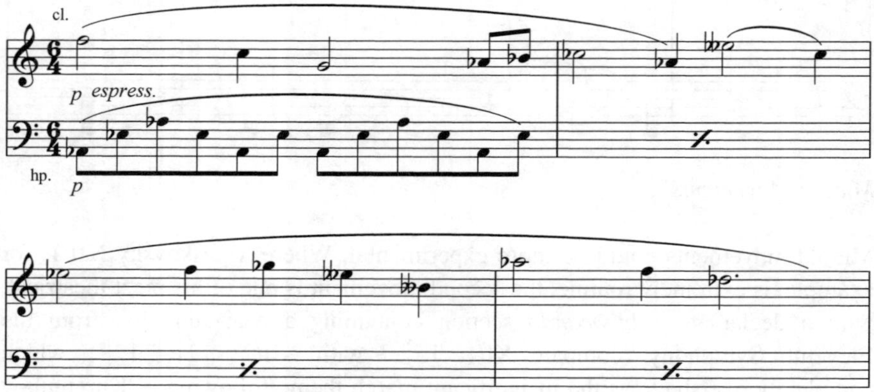

c Khrennikov I/3: bb. 1–9

Allegro molto

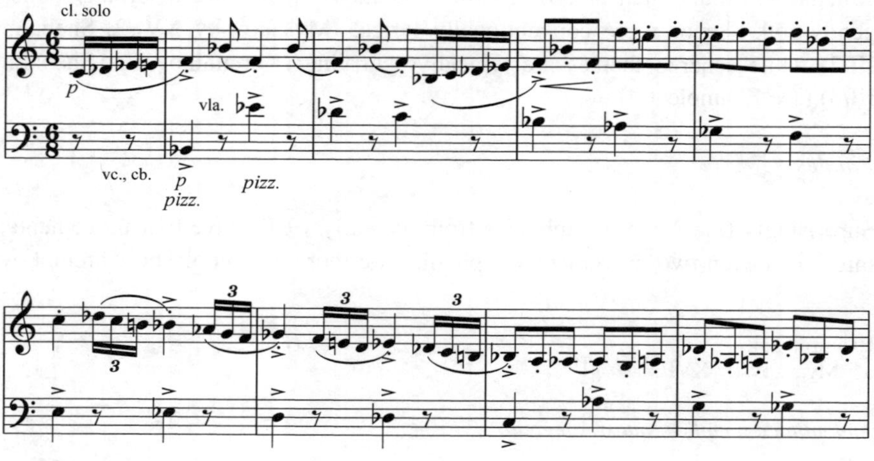

d Shebalin III/3: [2]$^{1-7}$

Vivo assai

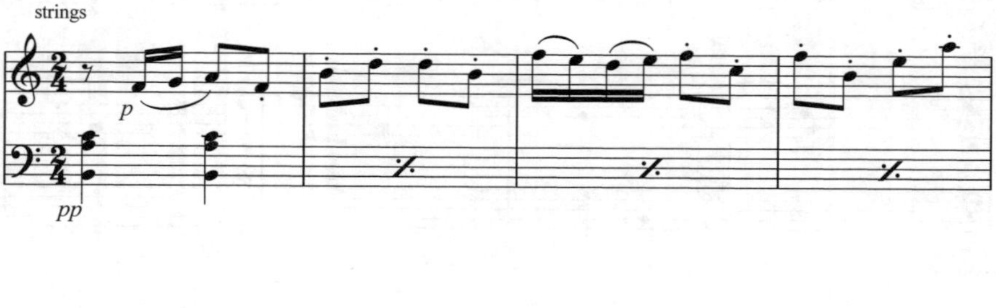

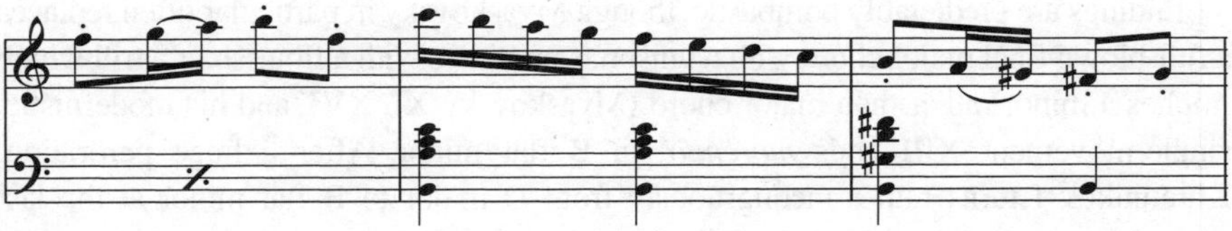

scherzo quoted in Example 1.4c is actually a scherzo-finale, as are Kabalevsky I/2 and II/3 and Popov I/3. They can be long and fairly complex: Kabalevsky I/2 has four main themes, all in different tempi, and both this finale and that of II/3 quote from the first movement – a typically Myaskovskian technique. Most feature the kind of jaunty, mass-song-like themes typically associated with socialist realism (Kabalevsky I/2, II/3, Myaskovsky XII/3; see Example 1.5).

Example 1.5

a Kabalevsky I/2: [70] 1–8

Gajo (Presto) 𝅗𝅥 = 160–168

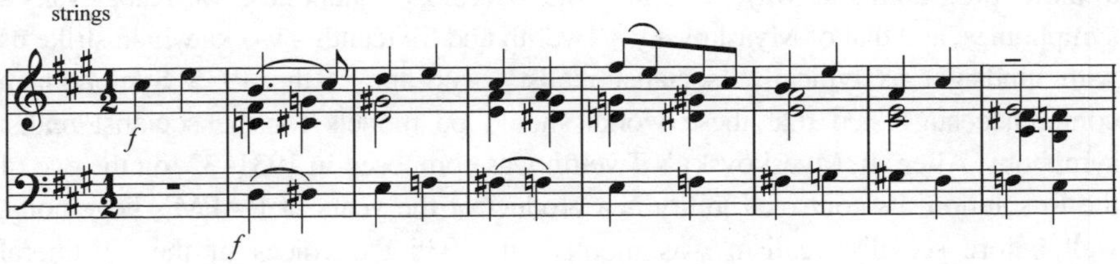

b Kabalevsky II/3: [30] 1–5

Molto agitato 𝅗𝅥. = 72–76

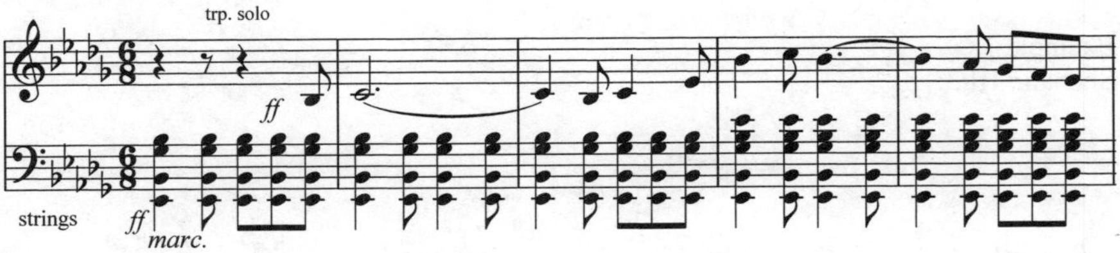

c Myaskovsky XII/3: [1] 1–4

Allegro festivo e maestoso

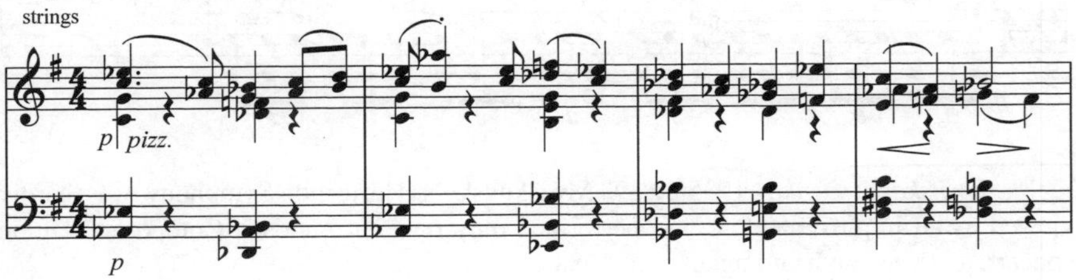

Endings are predictably bombastic, though Myaskovsky in particular often replaces a full-blown final major chord with a unison, sometimes with a flourish or a trill which implies a minor rather than major chord (Myaskovsky XI, XV), and his modernistic, single-movement XIII ends *morendo*, in B flat minor. After a huge peroration, Khrennikov I turns rather incongruously from D major to B flat minor at the last moment, more in the spirit of playfully thwarting expectations than in true seriousness. Most interestingly from the point of view of possible models for Shostakovich IV/3 is the ending of Shebalin III, in which a prolonged coda on a C pedal features the very same pulsating rhythm found in Shostakovich's coda (Example 1.6). While total uniformity was neither possible nor desirable, all the symphonies discussed above – with the exception of Myaskovsky XIII and Shebalin III – feature straightforward 'positive' themes, both fast and slow, generally developed separately, and 'positive' major-key finales. However, it was not the case that the more conventional the materials and form, the better the symphony would be received; at the symphonism conference Kabalevsky cited Myaskovsky's Twelfth Symphony as an example of deterioration in technical and musical quality resulting from an attempt to compose in a more programmatic way.[96] Despite the overblown jauntiness of Kabalevsky's symphonies, and that of Myaskovsky's Twelfth and Sixteenth – works which strike us with hindsight as typically 'socialist realist' – no-one at the 1935 Symphonism conference suggested that these works should be models for the socialist realist symphony. After all, Myaskovsky's Twelfth was composed in 1931–32, on the eve of the Resolution; its contrived jollity is a product of the years of RAPM's hegemony, well before socialist realism was mooted. In 1935 the voices of the left-liberal *intelligentsia* (Shostakovich, Shebalin, Sollertinsky and others) were still powerful, and as discussed, even in the post-'Muddle instead of Music' confusion, *Pravda* itself threw its weight behind squashing any suggestion of a re-ascendency of RAPM.

Example 1.6
Shebalin III/3: 23 1–3

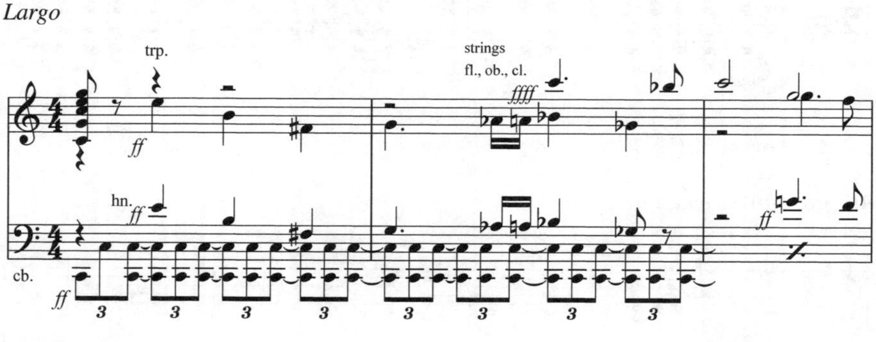

96 *Sovetskaya muzïka*, 1935/5, 39. Myaskovsky's Thirteenth Symphony was hardly viewed as an improvement: it was performed only once, at a closed Composers' Union concert, and was not heard again until 1988.

Popov: First Symphony

Popov's First Symphony merits some discussion, since it is the only 1930s symphony pre-dating Shostakovich's Fourth which is at all comparable in scale, complexity and quality. It was composed between 1928 and 1932 but not orchestrated until 1934, and premièred in March 1935. As discussed above, it was banned immediately afterwards in typically vague terms ('reflects the ideology of hostile classes'), but the ban was lifted by the end of April following the intervention of Sollertinsky, Shostakovich and others. By August 1935 Popov was planning an adventurous Second Symphony, which was to be a 'spring into the future' with no concessions to comprehensibility.[97]

The most striking feature of Popov's first movment is the absence of a 'normal' theme: after an explosive introduction, a toccata-like repeated-note pulsation underpins the cellos' disjointed, searching phrases. After an immense fugal build-up and climax there is a *lunga pausa* before a new theme begins, initially sounding like a funeral march but turning into an expressive yearning theme of Mahlerian intensity. After some contrapuntal development, there is a massive climax, the most memorable and significant of the symphony, based on a sequential theme initially unrelated to either of the two main themes, but subsequently loosely connected with the second. The development which follows begins indistinctly with abstract motivic development: there is no clearly recognizable theme between [31] and [51]. After that, first and second themes take turns to be developed, with no conflict or interaction. A surprisingly formal recapitulation precedes a long coda, ending in C♯ minor, *ppppp*.

Although there is no record of Shostakovich's response to the first (or second) movement,[98] he may well have been struck by the power of its main climax, and by the fact that neither of the two main themes played a conspicuous part in it. This, in fact, was to be one of the distinguishing features of his own first movement and the one that, as will be discussed in the following chapter, most persuasively indicates an authorial 'subject' situated outside the main body of the movement.

After a more conventional second movement, Popov's finale 'Scherzo e coda' features an almost Ivesian celebration of street music. Overlapping entries of the main march theme are supported by a dominant–tonic bass pedal, topped by military-band-style clarinet and flute flourishes between [7] and [12] (Example 1.7). Though structurally this is worlds away from Shostakovich's rigidly episodic divertimento, the intonational frame of reference here (military band) clearly evokes an urban sound-scape. Finally, an immense coda moves from a grotesque march ([34]) to a prolonged peroration: the final crescendo begins at [37] and continues for another 191 bars, effecting a shift from C♯ to C, with a full orchestral

97 See Apetyan, *Gavriil Popov*, 261.

98 In February 1932 Popov played through his symphony for Shostakovich, who apparently liked the finale but made no comment on the rest: ibid., 245.

Example 1.7
Popov I/3: 9[1–4]

Prestissimo

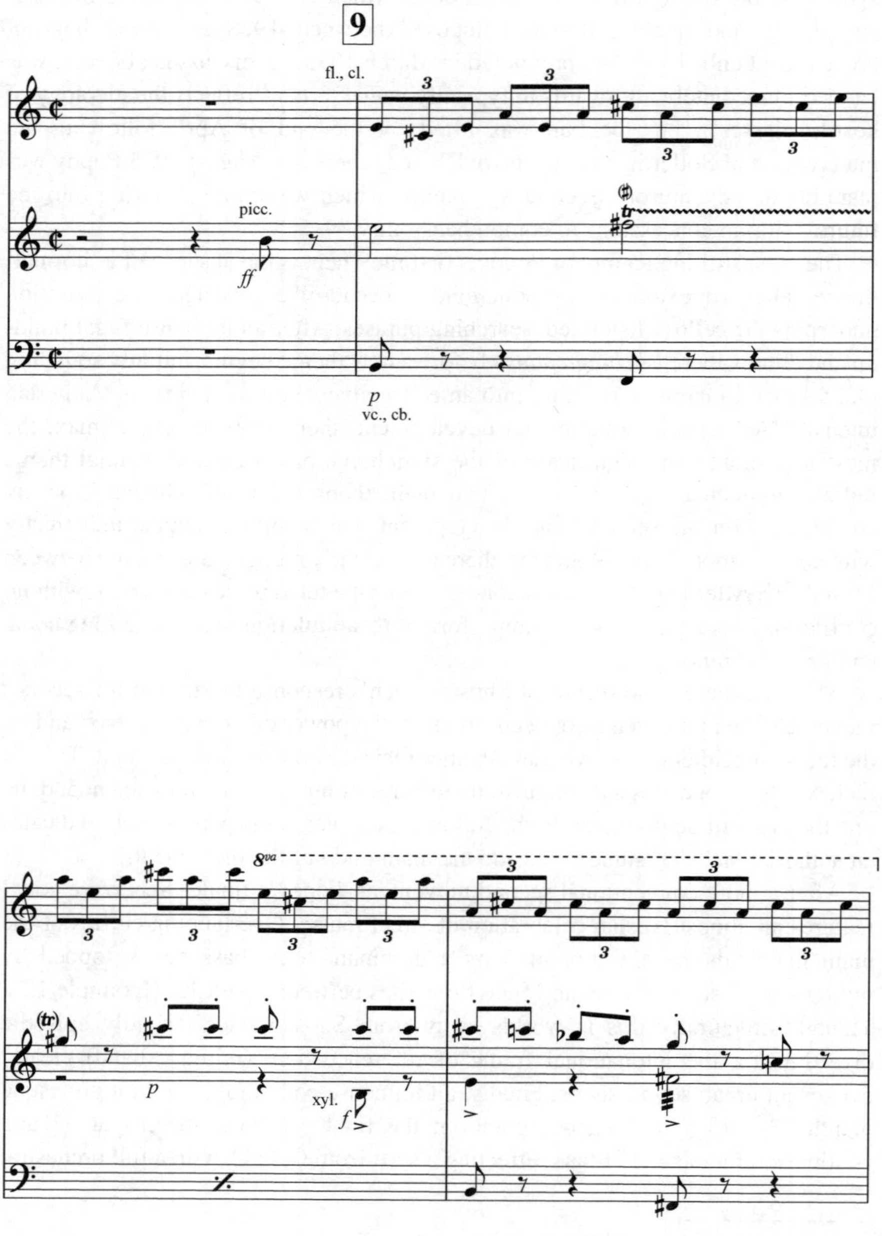

tutti including eight horns (all instructed to play with lifted bells) and full percussion complete with tubular bells.

Although Shostakovich's own finale coda ultimately takes a very different direction, Popov's chaotic representation of urban street music in the finale may well have inspired Shostakovich's own highly original 'street' sequence: this movement was the only one which elicited a favourable comment from Shostakovich when Popov played his symphony through on the piano for him in 1932. But the key point here is not really one of influence but rather one of reception. If Popov's symphony could be deemed officially acceptable (albeit after a struggle and, as it turned out, only briefly) in April 1935, in the uneasy post-*Lady Macbeth*-debacle atmosphere of the Composers' Union, then the chances of Shostakovich's new symphony receiving a sympathetic hearing must surely have seemed reasonably high. As noted earlier, Shostakovich's symphony was far less 'difficult' and complex than Popov's; its themes were clearer, and its dramaturgy more richly suggestive for anyone looking for 'content'. But in its ambition and scale, and in its potential for dismissal on grounds of 'formalism', Popov's symphony is a clear precedent. It scraped through 1935 – just. Shostakovich's Fourth would not be so lucky.

CHAPTER TWO

Analytical Approaches to the Fourth Symphony

Adorno and Sollertinsky on Mahler

The Fourth is widely acknowledged to be the most 'Mahlerian' of Shostakovich's symphonies. Its debt to Mahler is most apparent in the third movement's striking paraphrasing of his 'Resurrection' Symphony and the 'Bruder Martin' funeral march of the First Symphony. But the extent of Shostakovich's apparent affinity with Mahler goes far deeper than thematic allusion. It is at the more fundamental level of structure and dramaturgy that the parallels between them are most suggestive. Marina Sabinina views Mahler's symphonism as not merely the model for Shostakovich's approach to symphonic form and language, but as the basis for his symphonic ethos: at the centre of Mahler's *Weltanschauung*, she argues, was 'the approach to … individuality and the outside world … striving to open up the vital conflicts that torture the author'. Translated into musical terms, this resulted in 'peculiarities of language (acutely expressive intonations of harmony and timbre) and composition – surprise, apparently illogical contrasts, ruptures between the inner world of the artist-humanist and his aggressive banal surroundings'.[1]

The debt to Sollertinsky in such remarks is clear enough: his 1932 monograph on Mahler, together with the translation into Russian in 1926 of Paul Bekker's 1918 *Gustav Mahlers Sinfonien*, laid foundations for a flourishing tradition of Russian Mahler scholarship. More striking to the Western reader is the affinity with Adorno's study *Mahler: Eine musikalische Physiognomik*, which continues to attract the attention of hermeneutically orientated musicology from semiotics to narrative theory.[2] Adorno's concept of Mahler's symphonism, where 'formal categories are overlaid with material ones' in a way which he suggests could lead to a new way of analysing music through a 'material theory of form',[3] has obvious potential for analysis of Shostakovich's music. Certain features of Adorno's

1 Sabinina, *Shostakovich-simfonist*, 99.

2 Recent examples include Robert Samuels, *Mahler's Sixth Symphony: A Study in Musical Semiotics*, Cambridge: Cambridge University Press, 1995, James Buhler, '"Breakthrough" as Critique of Form: The Finale of Mahler's First Symphony', *19th-Century Music*, 20/2, 1996–97, 125–43, and Vera Micznik, 'Music and Narrative Revisited: Degrees of Narrativity in Beethoven and Mahler', *Journal of the Royal Musical Association*, 126/2, 2001, 193–249.

3 Adorno, *Mahler*, 44.

discussion overlap with a number of significant analytical concerns in the analyses by Sabinina, Koball[4] and Roseberry[5] of the Fourth Symphony's first movement: namely, his extensive discussion of rupture and disintegration; his argument that Mahler gravitates towards an epic, even 'documentary' approach to symphonic form which overrides normal structural principles; and his emphasis on thematic, or motivic, transformation processes.

In a less politically restrictive climate, Soviet discussions of Shostakovich's music might have developed along similar lines to Adorno's. The most fundamental assumptions of early Soviet art criticism were based on the same Marxist principles embraced by the Frankfurt School. Chief among these assumptions was the belief that both the formal structure and the expressive content of any work of art were shaped by the social and economic climate of its time. With Bekker as their shared starting-point, Adorno's and Sollertinsky's discussions of Mahler take as read the notion that his fractured symphonic language and structures reflect the death of Enlightenment idealism, the demise of the Habsburg Empire and Mahler's own critical stance towards the social injustices of his time. Although the Soviets' discussions about symphonism in the 1930s seem obsessively ideological in retrospect, their aesthetic stance towards classical forms was, at heart, shaped by the same principles underpinning Adorno's musical philosophy. For example, as some Soviet critics (such as Rïzhkin) argued, sonata form was a musical microcosm of the philosophical privileging of dialectical process during the Enlightenment; by extension, its breakdown in Mahler's symphonies was presented by Sollertinsky as symptomatic of a loss of faith in that dialectic. And while Sollertinsky was blatant in his attempt to align Mahler's aesthetic stance with his political and social conscience, Adorno is only slightly more circumspect:

> The emerging antagonism between music and its language reveals a rift within society. The irreconcilability of the inward and the outward can no longer be harmonized spiritually, as in the classical age. This induces in Mahler the unhappy consciousness that that age believed overcome.[6]

> The Mahlerian subject is less a soul that bears witness to itself than a political will unconscious of itself, which makes the aesthetic object a metaphor of that which it cannot induce real people to espouse.[7]

Hence what was for Sollertinsky a matter of intention – Mahler's conscious engagement with social injustice – was for Adorno a matter of subconscious reflection. The Marxist premises of both, however, are unequivocal.

Sabinina's reading of Shostakovich's Fourth Symphony is clearly influenced by the sociological interpretation of Mahler's symphonism begun by Sollertinsky 30

4 Koball, *Pathos und Groteske*, 113–20 .

5 Roseberry, *Ideology*, 135–45 and 392–424.

6 Adorno, *Mahler*, 16.

7 Ibid., 130.

years earlier, and by Bekker before him. The cracks and fissures in Shostakovich's symphonic edifice are explained in terms of Mahler's own 'ruptured' form and language. In particular, the concept of 'rupture' forms a central part of her discussion of the first movement. Her concluding remarks observe that 'Rupture is not a compositional error on the composer's part, but a reflection of the *idea* of rupture, of the glaring disharmony of life, of struggle and of the polyphony of opposing premises.'[8] Of equal importance in Sabinina's analysis is her assumption of a level of narrative not normally associated with non-programmatic symphonism. Observing that the 'lyric' subject in the Fourth Symphony finds itself threatened by sudden, harsh gestures, she observes:

> It will be noted that such 'negation' as witnessed by the fanfare signals, chord-bursts or blows, serves as a singularly important semantic element of the dramaturgy of the Fourth and especially the first movement. They provoke turns of narrative, displacing it from one schema to another. Their expressive function may be compared only with their functions in later works, in the programmatic Thirteenth Symphony and *The Execution of Stepan Razin*; clearly, in the Fourth there is a strong influence of programmatic-theatrical logic, perhaps even a secret programme.[9]

The presence of narrative in some form or other was also a key assumption for Adorno, though he never went so far as to suggest that Mahler's symphonies were programmatic. In fact, he went out of his way to stress that the peculiar expressivity in Mahler's music stemmed not from its wholesale programmatic character, but from the dynamic between the forces of narrative – of direct, 'poetic' expression which disrupts normal structural processes – and conventional formal demands. Nevertheless, his observation that Mahler's symphonies are 'documentary' in nature is central to Adorno's argument; the aesthetic premises for his discussion of thematic mobility and structural collapse are built into such a view: 'Mahler tends towards the documentary as Proust's novel does toward autobiography; this results finally from the will of art to transcend itself. The structure of meanings that assimilates every element coexists with disintegration, with the loosening of the aesthetic spell by material communicated without illusion.'[10]

The idea of a 'structure of meanings that assimilates every element' is dependent on the overarching presence of a narrative strategy, however non-specific. The resulting 'disintegration' of normal symphonic dramaturgy fractures the unity between the whole (formal structure and conventional symphonic dramaturgy) and the parts (use of orchestral timbre, themes). In this, Mahler's orchestration is, for Adorno as for Sollertinsky, a key element. Together with eccentricities of structure and language, Mahler's use of the orchestra was coloured, so Adorno claims, by awareness of life's multiplicity and conflict. His

8 Sabinina, *Shostakovich-simfonist*, 105.
9 Ibid.
10 Adorno, *Mahler*, 147–8.

sound 'strives away from the spherical acoustic form' towards distinctness: 'the sound that honestly shows everything … is akin to disintegration. The more sharply the elements of composition are distinguished, the more resolutely they renounce a primary identity.'[11] Hence the 'parts' of Mahler's symphonism – extremes of orchestral timbre, fissures in 'normal' symphonic dramaturgy, and popular idioms – assert themselves over the symphonic 'totality' in a way which leads to formal disintegration. Where Mahler attempts to bring about reconciliation between those parts (as, for example, in the finale of the Seventh Symphony), the effect for Adorno is contrived: 'fruitlessness itself speaks from it'.[12] Adorno argues that, whether the sense of incongruity is intended or not, it is essential to confront it honestly, since it is in such 'stigmata of contrivance' that the 'truth' Mahler speaks can be perceived: 'It says that human beings want to be redeemed and are not.'[13]

Adorno's distinction between 'part' and 'totality' is the linchpin of his theory of material form. If, before Mahler, 'the specific life of the composition was trimmed willy-nilly to fit the prescribed categories' or, on the contrary, the specific elements asserted themselves over the form, using it only as a 'vehicle', then Mahler was unique in 'restoring the reciprocity'.[14] In particular for Adorno, Mahler's questioning of the accepted formulas of recapitulation and closure brings into sharp relief his aesthetic challenge to the Beethovenian concept of dynamic evolution. The function of the recapitulation and coda in Beethoven is equated by Adorno with 'complicity with the guilt of the great idealistic systems … In the recapitulation, music … remained, like the society in which it is, and which is in it, enslaved to mythical unfreedom'.[15] Mahler's treatment of sonata form gravitates more strongly towards narrative: expositions are 'presentations of *dramatis personae*, whose story is then told'.[16]

For Adorno, Mahler's approach to musical material – comprising form, instrumentation, technique and the themes themselves – refuted both formal and narrative self-containment, capitulating neither to structural demands nor to a programmatic, narrative method which usurps form altogether. The dynamic between the two is what interests him, which is why he pursues the idea of establishing 'material' categories to describe musical phenomena that seem to reach beyond their symphonic confines to another state of being. The often-cited categories of *Durchbruch*, *Suspension* and *Erfüllung*, for example, are 'essential genres in his [Mahler's] idea of form'.[17]

---

11 Ibid., 124.
12 Ibid., 128.
13 Ibid., 129.
14 Ibid., 92.
15 Ibid., 94.
16 Ibid., 95.
17 Ibid., 41.

The rich potential of Adorno's categories for analysing Shostakovich's music, particularly the symphonies, remains unexplored. Although, as will be seen, it is impossible to find instances of *Durchbruch* and *Erfüllung* occurring in Shostakovich's music in the generally positive sense that Adorno originally intended, it is possible to identify instances of 'reversed' *Erfüllung* which seem deliberate enough to suggest a conscious, if subverted, reference to a Mahlerian model. The most obvious examples of that can be seen in Shostakovich's use of overstatement, notably in the finale codas of the Fourth and Fifth Symphonies. *Suspension*, too, is certainly an important 'material' category in Shostakovich's symphonies. Again, both the Fourth and Fifth Symphonies contain passages that have a suspended, 'out of body' effect, as will be discussed in due course.

Adorno's two further categories – disintegration and negativity – have, however, been fairly commonplace in discussions of Shostakovich's music dating back at least as far as Sabinina's 1976 analysis. Disintegration for Adorno is produced by the strain placed on the 'totality' by the 'parts': invasive use of instrumental colour and characterization; 'shocks' such as sudden changes of tempi and dynamics; and the undermining of the concept of a thematic or tonal 'first principle' or 'centre of gravity'.[18] Shostakovich's highly theatrical approach to dramaturgy meant that his music is often dominated by just such disintegrative techniques, and the Fourth Symphony is a particularly extreme example.

For Adorno, negativity in Mahler's music arises from the estranged nature of much of his thematic material ('the banal that declares itself banal … sentimentality that tears the mask from its own wretchedness'[19]), and through Mahler's exposure of 'catastrophe', to be found in the first movement of the Ninth Symphony and the finale of the Sixth Symphony. The disrupted coda of the Sixth Symphony's first movement (VI/1: 37 – end) is for Adorno such a negative event; the music 'says no to itself'[20] in the face of conventional closure. Such events are clearly not intended to be heard at face value – as unmusical or crude – but are actually meant to be perceived as negative. Similarly, certain attempts to bring about *Erfüllung* without a real *Durchbruch* – Adorno particularly dislikes the finale of the Seventh – may ring false and so qualify as a 'negative' moment in Mahler's music, regardless of the composer's intentions: 'Mahler was a poor yea-sayer. His voice cracks, like Nietzsche's, when he proclaims values … and makes music as if joy were already in the world.'[21]

To label a given passage as 'negative' is clearly a highly subjective decision, for which there may not always be musical justification. Adorno's discomfort over Mahler's 'positive' endings went far beyond the Seventh Symphony's finale; he also disliked those of the Second and Fifth Symphonies and thoroughly despised

18 Ibid., 124.
19 Ibid., 125.
20 Ibid.
21 Ibid., 137.

the Eighth Symphony in its entirety. Nevertheless, negativity as a 'material category' is an extremely useful conceptual tool for Shostakovich analysis, partly because it enables us to 'explain' passages which seem banal or crude, and partly because it suggests by implication the presence of an alternative: in other words, it raises the possibility of a critical engagement with an earlier model in much the same way as does his 'reversed' *Erfüllung*, to which it is closely related.

There is a further relationship between Adorno's understanding of what constitutes negativity in music and Sollertinsky's writings. In the 1941 lecture 'Historical Types of Symphonic Dramaturgy', Sollertinsky accounts for Mahler's ambivalent tone thus:

> The method of the straight lyric (which is more or less realised in the final Adagio of the Third Symphony, in the last movement of the Song of the Earth, and above all in the first movement of his Ninth Symphony …) begins to be combined with the method of indirect or eccentric lyric, in which the lyrical is distorted by grotesque intonation. The lyric, darkened by the grotesque, the lyric made eccentric, a profoundly humane feeling disguised by the self-protective mask of buffoonery – Mahler gave birth to all of this, together with another important artist in the West, Charlie Chaplin.[22]

Sollertinsky's examples of Mahler's 'indirect lyric' include, naturally enough, the 'Funeral March in the Manner of Callot' from the First Symphony, the scherzo of the Second, the finale of the Fourth and the second movement and Rondo Burleske of the Ninth. He stresses the serious nature of Mahler's 'indirect lyric', both to distance it from the colder 'urban' grotesqueries of Stravinsky or Křenek and to draw comparisons between Mahler and Shostakovich. Sollertinsky argues that Shostakovich's Sixth Symphony – which, appearing to bypass a first movement, begins with a long slow movement, followed by two scherzi – serves to contrast the 'deeply philosophical, direct lyric (the first movement) with the indirect lyric (the last two movements)',[23] but he stops short of drawing further conclusions as to what this contrast actually signifies. The very fact that Sollertinsky chose this work, however, throws light on what he may have meant by 'indirect lyric'. The finale of the Sixth Symphony is the only instance in Shostakovich's symphonic output where a light music style is employed apparently entirely without ambivalence. Its tone is consistent; its ending is not violently overstated in a manner comparable to the Fifth Symphony's coda, but is an uproarious circus galop; the sharpness of its contrast to the first movement is even mitigated by the preceding scherzo. Nothing in Mahler bears any resemblance to it. But Sollertinsky is prepared to see whole movements – not just moments of grotesquerie – as operating within this 'indirect' sphere, as though playing a part. It is no accident that all Sollertinsky's cited instances of Mahler's indirect lyric relate to movements with either a folk-rustic or a light music frame of reference:

---

22 Sollertinskiy, 'Historical Types of Symphonic Dramaturgy'; translation taken from Roseberry, *Ideology*, 513.

23 Ibid., 533.

a ländler undercut by over-exertion and collapse; a folk tune transformed into a sinister march; heavenly life seen through the eyes of a starving child;[24] and the violent Strauss parodies of the Rondo Burleske.[25] In this light, Sollertinsky's interpretation of Shostakovich's adoption of a frivolous circus-like tone in his scherzo finale as an 'indirect lyric' makes sense. Both Mahler and Shostakovich are using recognizable popular idioms in a far from innocent manner. Those idioms do not need to be framed in such a way as to belie their innocence (although they frequently are elsewhere in both Mahler's and Shostakovich's symphonies); it is their historical and social context, as well as their context within the symphonic genre, that makes them double-edged. In the case of Shostakovich's finale, that context is the period after the Fifth Symphony and at the height of Stalin's purges. Its hilarity is, in the final analysis, acutely ambivalent, largely because it is a mask presented consistently and convincingly in Shostakovich's finest light music style. It is not a parody of that idiom, but a shining example of it; it is the contemporary circumstances and the tragic tone of the first movement that reveal it as a mask. The Fourth Symphony is an especially knotty example of Shostakovich's earliest adoption of this mask-like ambivalence. Popular idioms abound in the finale, frequently with precisely the kind of apparent innocence displayed in the Sixth Symphony. Sollertinsky's notion of direct and indirect lyrics, however, provides an additional lens through which to view those idioms, and sits easily alongside Adorno's definition of negativity when the same kind of socio-historical context is brought to bear on them.

Given their shared aesthetic and philosophical foundations, a degree of congruence between Adorno's view of Mahler and that of earlier Soviet writers is only natural. And, in a general sense, the proposal to bring Adornian concepts into a discussion of Shostakovich's music does not promise anything particularly surprising. Commentators have long noted Shostakovich's use of banal, even malignant, themes to obviously negative effect, his theatrical instinct for shock effects, and his overblown perorations that question their validity as loudly as they seem to proclaim it. But Adorno's work does offer an unusually rich body of aesthetic and analytical discussion which can fruitfully be used – in combination with discussions of dramatic structure, narrative and issues of musical influence – to build on the insights of Russian and Western Shostakovich scholarship in a way which takes account of, and balances, both analytical and socio-historical parameters.

24 This was Sollertinskiy's interpretation. See Sollertinskiy, *Gustav Maler*, 41.

25 See Mahler IX/3, bb. 526–30 (woodwind, horns) and bb. 634–7 (woodwind, violin 1) for the moments where the Rondo's biting parody of Johann Strauss's *Radetsky March* is most categorical.

Adorno: Variant Form

Again, it is Adorno who provides the richest source for a discussion of thematic relationships. Adorno's premise that Mahler's symphonism is novelistic, even documentary, in nature has considerable implications for his discussion of thematic construction. Although both Koball and Sabinina refer to Shostakovich's themes as characters, Adorno goes into far greater depth than either in establishing the theoretical framework to justify that label. For example, Mahler's habit of introducing new themes unrelated to any of his main characters is cited by Adorno as especially novelistic: 'as if, unexpectedly, a previously unregarded person now entered the scene to assist development'.[26] Striving to escape the inexorability of symphonic logic, Mahler's themes 'crave the open air'; they function like characters in a novel, who 'retain their essence unchanged'. Nevertheless, like people, his themes go through certain processes and events; they 'shrink, expand, even age'.[27]

The issue of how such novelistic themes can interact in a formal process is addressed in the chapter 'Variant-Form'. Unlike other composers, who used *variation*, Mahler used the *variant*: 'The Mahler variant is the technical formula for the epic and novelistic element of the always different yet identical figures.'[28] Mahler's themes have a primary identity; they are *Gestalten*. Their inner motivic structure may be deconstructed, but their outlines always remain recognisable. In the process of such blurring of motivic identities, thematic outlines are subtly reformed, so that the technique of variant exerts a tectonic influence on the original theme. Thus themes are *Gestalten* but 'with mobile motivic content'.[29] One of the most fascinating aspects of Adorno's discussion of Mahler's variant technique is his observation that the very concept of a 'theme' is questioned, since Mahler's themes are not 'givens' but exist in a process of continuous variation. His claim that they are 'relatively stable' may appear to contradict this remark, as his claim that they are 'not initially expounded either' may appear to contradict his earlier observation that Mahler's expositions are presentations of '*dramatis personae*'. Indeed, Adorno's switch from finding the outlines of a theme intact, but noting that the activity of its inner motifs can somehow transform their surrounding thematic contours, to noting that the thematic 'nucleus' undergoes a narrative-style, gradual transformation, appears similarly confusing. However, this may be explained by interpreting Adorno's concept of the thematic nucleus or outline as a form of 'essence' which may be manifest in a number of ways: in broad melodic contour, in a basic motivic principle, even in tone; in short, what it seems to *represent*. This nucleus may be elusive:

26 Adorno, *Mahler*, 71.
27 Ibid., 72.
28 Ibid., 86.
29 Ibid., 88.

> The firm, identical core, which nevertheless exists, is difficult to pin down, as if it shunned mensural notation. No theme is positively, unambiguously there, none is ever quite definitive; they submerge in and re-emerge from the time continuum, which is itself constituted equally by their indefinite nature and the rigor of their deviations.[30]

The 'time continuum', or surrounding musical material, is dependent on thematic content for its existence. It feeds on the elusiveness of its thematic content, dislocating our sense of thematic identity, then feeds themes back to us, mutated or intensified. In this sense, Adorno continues, the variant is a counterforce to fulfilment, which can come about only through a 'positive manifestation of what the theme has not yet become'.[31] Where there are true themes, Adorno claims that they feel out of place in the musical process; he quotes Bekker's observation that the Andante theme of Mahler's Sixth Symphony, with its closed structure, 'seems to strive to be forgotten' in the rest of the work. Such themes cannot be dynamic; they are 'reified' and 'congealed'.[32]

The parallels with Shostakovich are rather shaky here. Adorno's remarks on developing variation do not square with Shostakovich's penchant for strong themes. The opening theme of his Fourth Symphony is certainly far more four-square and 'unambiguously there' than anything Adorno had in mind. But not all Shostakovich's themes are as unequivocal as that opening; the second subject group (B1 and B2) of the first movement fits Adorno's description, as does the elusive first movement climax theme, which is fully presented only in the recapitulation. In any case, Adorno is not claiming that all of Mahler's themes fall into the category he is describing; his theory of variant form is only one aspect of his analysis of Mahler's technique.

But there is another problem with transferring Adorno's ideas to Shostakovich's music. Thematic transformation is a far more potent element of Shostakovich's symphonic dramaturgy than it is of Mahler's, and by its very nature such a dramatized treatment of themes presupposes precisely the kind of strong thematic primary identity that Adorno claims much of Mahler's themes do not possess. There are relatively few instances of transformation in Mahler's music of comparable force to the role-reversals in the recapitulation of Shostakovich's Fourth Symphony's first movement, and those that could be cited – the transformations of the slow movement theme in the finale of Mahler's Fifth Symphony and those of the Ninth Symphony's finale and Rondo Burleske – are less calculated to shock and confuse the listener than to place an ironic question mark over their 'true' identity. The importance of thematic transformation in the first movement of Shostakovich's Fourth Symphony cannot be discussed in the context of 'developing variation' alone; it needs a more inclusive approach that

30 Ibid.

31 Ibid.

32 Ibid., 89.

takes into account deeper analytical structures as well as historical context. Nevertheless, Adorno's notions of 'congealed' and dynamic themes are useful for discussing Shostakovich's music, especially where popular idioms are used in an incongruous manner. One such case might be the D♭ major waltz transformation of the first movement's second subject in the development (at [84]), which sounds strangely self-contained in the context of the movement's overall dramaturgy, and therefore registers as artificial. Another might be the finale's divertimento sequence ([191] – [235]), where a series of popular idioms is presented in a strikingly unproblematic way. Again, it is the incongruity of their presentation which unmasks these themes as 'congealed' and hence – in Sollertinsky's terminology – 'indirect' lyrics.

In a wider dramaturgical context, Adorno's theory of variant form is a theory of resistance: it opposes easy fulfilment and thematic complacency. The distinction between 'congealed' and 'dynamic' themes is of particular interest as it overlaps with the broader remit of his theory of material form. 'Congealed' themes are perceived to be suspect and potentially negative, while 'dynamic' themes are the basic stuff of Mahler's symphonic structures, controlled by, but giving substance to, the 'material form' of the overarching dramaturgy. Paradoxically, though, in the Fourth Symphony's first movement, Shostakovich's most aggressive and four-square themes – seemingly 'congealed' in tone – are highly 'active', generating extensive motivic development, while the more 'personal', soloistic ones tend to have a much looser phrase structure and are far less motivically 'active'. If anything, it is these lyrical themes that are 'congealed'. But this in itself is significant: if the 'direct lyric' implied by the soloistic character of the first movement's second subject is comparatively passive, that passivity plays a part in both highlighting the aggressive, dominating force of the first subject and also in surreptitiously bringing about the climax theme, which evolves within the sphere of the second subject group but is not actually stated until the climax itself ([47]). Thus, despite the considerable differences between Mahler's symphonism and Shostakovich's, Adorno's concepts can fruitfully, if selectively, be transferred from one to the other.

Syuzhet, *Fabula* and Material Form

Adorno's concept of material form seems at face value to presuppose form as something relatively stable, and 'material' – or 'content' – as the variable element. But this is not really the case; Adorno regarded the relationship between the two elements as dialectical, each influencing the other. In his polemical *Philosophy of Modern Music*, he identifies the middle-period works of Beethoven as marking the high point of that dialectical process, achieving an ideal weighting of rational and mimetic impulses. For him, Mahler's symphonies constituted another landmark in that process, but also reflected the disintegration of that social idealism which

Adorno claimed underpinned – indeed brought about – Beethoven's rational/mimetic balance. As already discussed, Adorno was not alone in reflecting upon the dialectical relationship between form and content, nor in viewing it as bound to social and economic factors. In Russia, Boris Asafiev was the strongest advocate of what he called 'musical form as a process': a theory which argued that the dynamic, evolutionary aspect of musical 'intonations' – motivated chiefly by the musical instincts of the mass listening public – kept form in a permanent state of flux. In spite of Asafiev's views, however, Soviet musical aesthetics during the 1930s degraded the conceptual distinction between form and content to a level that became ultimately meaningless.[33]

Yet in the early Soviet period, the literary group known as the Formalists were grappling with this very issue. They initially sidelined the question of 'content' – the 'meaning' of a text, the biography of the writer, its socio-political significance – in favour of a purely structural approach to textual analysis. Extreme statements from those years include Viktor Shklovsky's claim (made in 1921) that 'A work of literature is the sum total of all the stylistic devices employed in it'.[34] A less hard-line attitude quickly replaced this polemical position, and Shklovsky, together with Boris Eikhenbaum, Boris Tomashevsky and Yury Tynianov, began to consider seriously the question of meaning in a text. The assumption that the structure of a text and its content were, though interdependent, essentially separate was already in place; they needed to find a way of analysing the nature of that interdependence. This they did by differentiating between a novel's *syuzhet* – its plot – and *fabula* – its story, or basic material.

The Formalists' distinction between plot and story combined awareness of textual formulas – the 'stable' element – with a recognition of the complexity and richness of meaning that played through those formulas. Neither the concept of plot (or 'device' as it was sometimes called) nor that of materials was rigorously formulated; there was disagreement over what the actual substance of 'material' was. It could be pure verbal texture, in the same way as 'material' for an artist is colour and for a composer notes; or it could be the writer's emotions and ideas. Both these positions seem rather crude today, in our post-Bakhtin, post-Structuralist, post-Deconstructionist age. But there was some fruitful mediation between them, as illustrated in Tomashevsky's essay 'Thematics' of 1925.[35]

'Thematics' is an attempt to formulate a coherent system of literary analysis

---

33 For a discussion of the form/content debate, see Marina Frolova-Walker, 'National in Form, Socialist in Content', *Journal of the American Musicological Society*, 51/2, 1998, 331–71.

34 Shklovsky, quoted in Victor Erlich, *Russian Formalism: History-Doctrine*, New Haven and London: Yale University Press, 1965, 70.

35 A translation of 'Thematics' is given in Lee T. Lemon and Marion J. Reis, *Russian Formalist Criticism*, Lincoln: Four Essays, Nebraska: University of Nebraska Press, 1965, 61–95.

that takes equal account of the 'extrinsic' and 'intrinsic' elements in a text. Motifs – repeated phrases, images, essential parts of a story, scenery and so on – constitute the structural fabric of a text, while the story is presented through a manipulation of those motifs, guiding the reader as the author wishes. All these motifs are classified as static, dynamic, bound (essential to storyline) and free (essential to plot). They are controlled by a further system of 'motivation', relating both to aesthetics (choice and frequency of motifs) and to meaning (manipulating the reader). Although the plot, or system of literary devices, is flexible, various conventions can become stale in any given period: Tomashevsky cites marriage at the end of a comedy, and death at the end of a tragedy as instances of plot devices too stereotyped to retain any narrative force.

Tomashevsky's pragmatic approach might have marked the beginning of a new era in Soviet literary criticism. But only five years after 'Thematics' was published, Shklovsky – the Formalists' chief spokesman – was forced to 'admit' that 'in the last analysis, it is the economic process which determines and re-organizes the … literary system'.[36] It was impossible for Formalism to continue as a viable literary movement in an increasingly repressive climate; the very word 'Formalist' was even used as a catch-all term of abuse in the 1930s and 1940s to stigmatize anyone who was perceived to deviate from the current Party line. Nevertheless, the Formalists' influence was extremely widespread, not only in Europe, where Roman Jakobson carried the Formalist torch into the new age of Structuralism, but also in Russia, primarily though the theatrical innovations of Meyerhold, which are discussed below.

Asafiev's theory of *intonatsia* also bears the imprint of Formalist thought: clear parallels can be seen between Tomashevsky's description of the evolutionary cycle of structural devices and Asafiev's notion of 'intonations'. Both are subject to the same process of natural selection: both literary and musical 'devices' retain their vitality for a time, then become clichés and fall out of use. As Tomashevsky's devices embraced a wide range of textual elements, from fashionable descriptions of characters (glittering eyes, pale faces, tiny waists and so on) to actual storylines (expectations of sad or happy ending), musical intonations could be anything from the character and tone of a theme (urgent, lyrical), to particular chords (the diminished seventh was one of Asafiev's favourite examples of a chord whose original flavour degenerated into cliché) or intervals, rhythms and so on. The changing lexicon of literary and musical devices meant that form itself was in a constant process of evolution, shaped by the changing perceptions and preoccupations of the time.

The more deeply Formalist theory probed into this question, the closer it moved to linguistic analysis and the conclusion that each 'utterance' conveyed an infinite number of meanings according to the intentions of the speaker and the inclinations of the listener, both of which were in a process of constant change themselves.

36 Quoted in Erlich, *Russian Formalism*, 116.

This, of course, became a major preoccupation of European 20th-century linguistic theory, but Russian Formalism itself (though it continued to be influential through the Prague Linguistic Circle, of which Jakobson was a founding member) had little opportunity for developing along these lines. Nevertheless, that particular line of enquiry was taken further in Russia by the then (internally) exiled writer and philosopher Mikhail Bakhtin, whose ideas will be discussed in due course.

What Formalism, intonation theory and Adorno's concept of material form all have in common is the precept that 'content' influences 'form'. This presupposes a degree of formal self-consciousness against which the new expressive demands of a work struggle for dominance. The degree of self-consciousness is variable; but in general, works showing a high degree of conflict between formal parameters and expressive content were, for the Formalists, also the most innovative. A favourite example of such a work was Laurence Sterne's parodic novel *Tristram Shandy*, which defined two key Formalist concepts particularly well: 'defamiliarization', or 'estrangement' (*ostraneniye*), and 'baring the device'. Sterne's parody of formal norms – which included such basic elements as an author's preface, a logical time-sequence in the storyline, even the numbering of chapters – meant that his preface appears some 200 pages into the novel, inserted 'in a spare moment'; storylines are spliced to the point of absurdity, broken up by irrelevent pseudo-philosophical digressions and stream-of-consciousness gossip about characters' life histories. It was this degree of literary self-consciousness that excited the Formalists; Shklovsky's monograph on *Tristram Shandy* was even called 'Sterne's Tristram Shandy and the Theory of the Novel'.[37] Sterne's propensity for stepping outside his own narrative to reflect on his role as an author and mock the literary conventions of his time focused on, and questioned, the procedures of novelistic form to an unprecedented degree. Although Sterne's intention was to ridicule, the Formalists recognized the expressive potential of his parodic devices. Shklovsky's 1917 essay 'Art as Technique' shows why Sterne became so important to Formalist thinking:

> Art exists that one may recover the sensation of life; it exists to make one feel things, to make the stone *stony*. The purpose of art is to impart the sensation of things as they are perceived and not as they are known. The technique of art is to make objects 'unfamiliar', to make forms difficult, to increase the difficulty and length of perception because the process of perception is an aesthetic end in itself.[38]

Hence, the 'materials' of literature – speech, characters, objects, opinions, beliefs – are absolutely dependent on their relationship with a formal structure for their vitality. Art, for the Formalists, was not supposed to be a passive reflection

---

37 Shklovsky's stylistic commentary on *Tristram Shandy* is reproduced in Lemon and Reis, *Russian Formalist Criticism*, 25–57.

38 Quoted ibid., 12.

of reality; it was supposed to present that reality in a new way, to force people to question complacently held assumptions, and to experience the elements of their own lives in a fresh and challenging way. Art that had this 'defamiliarizing' quality was critical art: art that made people think and feel more intensely. The Formalists found that quality not only in Sterne, but also in the Russian classics: Tolstoy, Gogol and Chekhov. They went so far as to maintain that it was this manipulation of device and plot which effectively constituted the essence of a work's meaning; the 'story' merely provided the material. Thus, Shklovsky wrote of Pushkin's *Evgeny Onegin*: 'The plot of *Evgeny Onegin* is … not the romance of the hero with Tatyana, but the fashioning of the subject of this story as produced by the introduction of interrupting digressions.'[39] Pushkin did not merely write *Onegin*, then, to tell a story about a handful of men and women, but told that story in a particular way to convey more than the sum of its material parts and to comment on the human condition – a reading with which few acquainted with the poem today would be likely to disagree, and moreover, one which can be comfortably applied to a vast range of literature and poetry. The broad truth of Shklovsky's remarks does not, however, detract from their originality for their time, nor from the considerable impact that Formalist thinking had on the arts in Russia both before and after the Revolution.

The crucial point about the Formalists' attraction to technique – the actual processes of the plot – was that the meaning of a text lay not in the story itself, but in the *way* it was told. That view is clear in the texts they chose to analyse – Sterne's novel being the extreme example – though it is more difficult to see how that theory might be applied to a wider literary field.[40] But Formalist theory was no idle academic exercise; its purpose was overtly didactic. The gospel of *ostraneniye* was preached in the eagerly receptive environment of the St Petersburg Institute for the History of Art, where Tynianov, Eikhenbaum, Shklovsky and Viktor Vinogradov (also Asafiev and Sollertinsky) taught. As Katerina Clark has noted, the institute's Division for the History and Theory of the Theatre was

> no mere dry academic center but a major player in the movement for theater reform; plays were frequently produced there, and whenever Meyerhold's troupe visited Leningrad it was the place to which he gravitated to discuss his latest work. Additionally, the Division for the Theory and History of Music under B. Asafiev played a crucial role in introducing contemporary music to

39 Shklovsky, from 'Sterne's Tristram Shandy and the Theory of the Novel', quoted ibid., 57.

40 A connection between this aspect of Formalist thought and Harold Bloom's idea of misreading could be made here; its implication seems to be that the meaning of any text actually resides in its relationship to other texts rather than being an immanent quality of the single text itself. Both have sought to define meaning purely in terms of inter-textual relations. For an excellent digest of Bloom's theory of misreading, see Kevin Korsyn, 'Towards a New Poetics of Musical Influence', *Music Analysis*, 10/1–2, 1991, 3–72.

> Leningrad and, together with the Theater Division, working out a theory of the kind of new opera pioneered by Shostakovich.[41]

The parallels between Formalist thought and Meyerhold's theatrical innovations were hardly coincidental. Both believed that art could reveal 'truth'; it could make people see themselves and their surroundings in a new, clearer, light – in short, it could exert a positive social influence. While Meyerhold was always more engaged with the political implications of this thinking than were the Formalists, their shared roots placed them squarely in the *fin de siècle* mood of faith in 'essence' which began with the metaphysical musings of the Symbolists. Meyerhold merely breathed new life into an established assumption: that somewhere in art, as in life, there was a truth to be uncovered, and (at least in theatre) it was the performer's duty to uncover it.

Meyerhold

Meyerhold was one of the many innovators of 20th-century theatre who reacted against the extremes of the realist tradition exemplified by August Strindberg and Maurice Maeterlinck. His productions stressed the element of *spectakl'*, emphasizing the artificiality of theatre rather than trying to disguise it. From the earliest years of his career as a director, Meyerhold was fascinated by the ritualistic forms of Oriental and Ancient Greek theatre. Their preoccupation with the *idea* of a play rather than with the object of creating a realist portrayal of the events themselves was a key ingredient in his evolving theory of theatre. Hand in hand with this went his attraction to the static forms of popular theatre: puppet shows, the *commedia dell'arte*, circus spectacles and so on. Elements from all these sources found their way into Meyerhold's productions. Their purpose for him was absolutely clear: they were intended to surprise the audience, to jolt them out of their preconceived, lazy expectations of theatre, and force them to see familiar plays in a new light. In that context, the concept of individual characterization shifted from the realistic tradition to a far more stylised, even stereotypical approach. Instead of allowing each character to 'develop' in the normal way, actors adopted a set of 'masks' corresponding to a list of 'types': lover, clown, moralist, villain and so on. The masks were not usually literal face covers, but could be make-up, costume, a manner of speech, physical gestures and so on. Thus reduced to ciphers, Meyerhold's characters were able to communicate their dramatic or social 'meaning' rather than their individual psychology.

Meyerhold's production of Aleksandr Blok's *Balaganchik* [The Puppet Booth] in 1906 marked an early stage in the development of what he termed 'the

---

41 Katerina Clark, *Petersburg, Crucible of Cultural Revolution*, Cambridge, Massachusetts: Harvard University Press, 1995, 149–150.

grotesque' as a key element in his style. The artificiality of the stage – its machinery, props, special effects – was 'laid bare' for the audience to observe. And, at the critical moment of the drama, where Harlequin stands before a window and recites his paean to springtime ('Greetings world! You're with me again! / So long your soul has been close to me! / And now once more I will breathe your spring / Through your window of gold!'[42]), that artificiality achieves tragic status when he jumps ecstatically through the window only to fall into a black hole: the window was only paper after all. In his essay of 1912, 'Balagan', Meyerhold wrote of the grotesque that 'Beneath what we see of life there are vast unfathomed depths. In its search for the supernatural, the grotesque synthesises opposites, creates a picture of the inscrutable, and encourages the spectator to try to solve the riddle of the inscrutable.'[43]

As Robert Leach has observed, Meyerhold's production of *Balaganchik* was a classic exercise in theatrical defamiliarization: 'The act of expression itself is 'foregrounded' … the friction between 'fable' … and 'plot' … is obvious'.[44] This was, however, also an inherent quality in Blok's play, whose use of the *commedia dell'arte* and references to its artificiality (a clown, struck on the head by a knight, falls down shouting 'Help, I'm bleeding cranberry juice!') were intended to convey the same poignancy as Aleksandr Benois felt about Stravinsky's *Petrushka*.[45] More radical was Meyerhold's extraordinary 1924 production of Ostrovsky's classic *The Forest*, where the original sequence of acts and scenes was divided into 33 'episodes' in the manner of Eisenstein's montage technique: the dominating principle behind the construction of the episodes was that of 'collision'. One critic noted that 'Meyerhold's *Forest* isn't theatre at all but a film … Meyerhold cuts and edits his scenes like film; as in film he works through gesture'.[46] The purpose of splicing Ostrovsky's drama in this way was to change the emphasis from merely portraying a particular social class (provincial gentry) to showing class conflict. As was by then typical for Meyerhold, characterization was highly stylised, with each character's 'essence' reflected in his or her costume. The repellent, fawning character of Milonov became a parish priest attended by an army of sycophants, while the weak, tearful character of Aksyusha (the poor relation and therefore a positive character, offsetting the rich, drunken and sentimental widow Gurmuzhskaya) became a Komsomol heroine in red dress and white scarf.

42 Quoted in Edward Braun, *Meyerhold: A Revolution in Theatre*, Iowa City: University of Iowa Press, 1995, 62.

43 Quoted ibid., 68.

44 Quoted in Robert Leach, *Vsevolod Meyerhold*, London: Cambridge University Press, 1989, 128.

45 It is worth noting, however, that Benois disliked Meyerhold's ideas, and that Meyerhold actually set out to oppose Benois's 'cult of mystery' when producing *Balaganchik*. See Clark, *Petersburg*, 92.

46 Quoted in Braun, *Meyerhold*, 209.

It could not be claimed that such innovations aimed at subtlety. Meyerhold's motivation was from the outset political, and this tendency became stronger rather than weaker after the Revolution; he was one of the most ideologically committed artists of the turbulent 1920s and 1930s. His techniques (which extended far beyond those described here) played out Formalist ideas in their most blatant form, and for blatantly ideological purposes. They show not only how those ideas chimed with a general *Zeitgeist* which rejected an individualistic attitude to art in favour of art which addressed wider social issues, but also how they inspired Soviet artists in their search for new 'forms' in which the new 'content' of social relevance could be most fully expressed.

Shostakovich and Meyerhold

Shostakovich's relationship with Meyerhold has been well documented. Not only did he initially play the piano for Meyerhold's productions; he soon began to compose music for them and even performed onstage in productions of Gogol's *Revizor* [The Government Inspector].[47] One such collaboration took place in the production of Vladimir Mayakovsky's *Klop* [The Bedbug] in 1928; Shostakovich famously composed music in the style of a firemen's band, since that was apparently Mayakovsky's favourite kind of music. Mayakovsky's own programme note (actually a poem) asserted that 'Theatres / are not / stony piles / for unravelling / of miniature souls. / Let's strip such individuation / of its robes. / Make art / from all / for all!' and 'The theatre / is not a reflecting mirror / But – / a magnifying glass.'[48] Meyerhold himself could not have put it better.

Many writers have noted Meyerhold's influence in Shostakovich's stage works. Roseberry takes the analogy further to extend to his symphonies, citing the transition from the first subject group to the second between [24] and [31] of the Fourth Symphony's first movement as an example of Meyerhold's *pereklivcheniye*: a 'sudden change-over of mood, tempo and lighting' apparently used in his production of Gogol's *The Government Inspector*.[49] He also relates this passage to Shostakovich's well-known love of parody and the grotesque, noting that 'here we have a kind of devil dance, superimposed on the Brucknerian/Mahlerian repeated note transitional style'.[50] Sabinina discusses Meyerhold at greater length, noting Shostakovich's penchant for 'low' musical genres (primarily in his ballets), his rejection of 'traditionalism' and his inclination

47 Fay, *Shostakovich*, 44–45. Shostakovich's reminiscences of playing the piano in *Revizor* can be found in *Teatr*, 1974/2, 52. Quoted in Bobïkina, ed., *Dmitriy Shostakovich*, 120, n. 2.

48 Quoted in Leach, *Vsevolod Meyerhold*, 153.

49 Quoted in Roseberry, *Ideology*, 402.

50 Ibid., 403.

towards spectacle in his operas (especially *The Nose*) and works such as the revue *Conditionally Killed*. Although Meyerhold is not specifically claimed to have been an influence on the Fourth Symphony, which Sabinina sees as more Mahlerian than anything else, her approach to its analysis is overtly 'episodic', describing the effect of each section in distinctly theatrical terms. Her reference, quoted above, to the implied presence of a 'programmatic-theatrical logic' speaks for itself. More recently, Esti Sheinberg has noted similarities between Shostakovich's affinity for grotesque stylisation and Meyerhold's techniques.[51] Extending the discussion to film techniques and Eisenstein's innovations, Richard N. Burke observes that the Fourth Symphony's generic collisions could profitably be analysed 'in terms of montage' rather than of sonata form.[52] This may well be true for the episodic form of the finale; but the extent to which the first movement deliberately manipulates the norms of sonata form suggests that it is better analysed within that context. Taking Adorno's concept of material form as a starting-point for analysing Shostakovich's Fourth Symphony means that it is the dialectic between form and content which is the main focus of analysis, not merely the disjointed effect produced by their struggle for dominance.

Bakhtin: Epic and Novel

There is one other branch of literary criticism that may be helpful in establishing a conceptual framework for a hermeneutic analysis of the Fourth Symphony. Bakhtin's name has been evoked many times in relation to Shostakovich in the 1990s, usually with regard to what is perceived to be his ethical stance towards 'monological' art (or, by extension, art criticism). The 'dialogical novel' exemplified by Dostoevsky (described in Bakhtin's 1929 book *Problems of Dostoevsky's Art*), where all voices mingle in joyful 'polyphony', is a potent metaphor for ideological tolerance. In the 1990s a kind of 'fortress Bakhtin' mentality arose in Shostakovich scholarship, besieged as it briefly was by the aggressive media presence of a handful of journalists and internet pundits claiming Shostakovich's entire *oeuvre* to be explicitly anti-Soviet. Yet the trend for appropriating Bakhtin's ideas as a defence is in some respects wholly inappropriate. Shostakovich's music is hardly a model of 'polyphony' in the Bakhtinian sense; his strong authorial presence instantly disqualifies him as a composer of 'dialogical' symphonies. That presence may be ambivalent, as it is in the Fourth Symphony; but it is there nonetheless. It marks the start of a trend that, if anything, intensifies throughout his career, beginning with the famous quotation

51 See Esti Sheinberg, *Irony, Satire, Parody and the Grotesque in the Music of Shostakovich: A Theory of Musical Incongruities*, Aldershot: Ashgate, 2000, 297–309.

52 Richard N. Burke, 'Film, Narrative, and Shsotakovich's Last Quartet', *The Musical Quarterly*, 83/3, 1999, 421.

from his Pushkin Romances in the finale of the Fifth Symphony and ending with the quotations from Siegfried's funeral music in the Fifteenth.[53] The notion of an authorial voice in Shostakovich's music is, in fact, invariably assumed, even though it is rarely located or discussed.

It is not Bakhtin's early study of Dostoevsky that is potentially of most relevance to Shostakovich's treatment of symphonic form; his politically motivated ideas about dialogism and polyphony do not transfer easily to music. However, two essays written during his period of exile during the 1930s, 'Epic and Novel' and 'Forms of Time and Chronotope', develop his early theory of novelistic discourse along less extreme lines. The gist of the essay 'Epic and Novel' is that the novel is a genre perpetually in flux, characterized by a questioning attitude to its forms and language. This is contrasted with the epic style, which is more rigid in both form and attitude to material and less critical, adopting an unquestioning attitude to the past or even (notably in the socialist realist novel, though Bakhtin obviously does not mention it) the present. It is precisely the novel's engagement with the present that defines it and gives it its 'unfinished' quality: it is in a continual process of 'becoming, as an uninterrupted movement into a real future, as a unified, all-embracing and unconcluded process'. Semantic stability is also lost: 'its sense and significance are renewed and grow as the context begins to unfold'. Thus, for example, literary imagery does not provide a static database of meaning, but instead develops in relation to 'the ongoing event of current life in which we, the author and readers, are intimately participating'.[54] Bakhtin's perception that the novel, being a 'present' genre, cannot adopt the same complacent attitude to its form and language as the 'epic', has clear links with Adorno's thought as well as with Asafiev's. Asafiev focused on the contemporary nature of the symphony and its evolving intonational structures; Adorno on Mahler's critical attitude to the 'guilt of the great idealistic systems' underpinning Enlightenment symphonism.

One of the most interesting ideas broached in 'Epic and Novel' is the notion of 'authorial surplus': 'the knowledge that the author has, that which the hero does not know or does not see'.[55] That 'surplus' can then be used to manipulate the narrative. This ties together the concept of an authorial presence with that of *syuzhet*: it is the conscious will of the author that shapes the 'plot', or narrative, and thus controls the reader's response. But that authorial will has also to enter into dialogue with the 'unfinished' reality of his or her own time, and in turn with

53 For a discussion of the Pushkin quotations, see Richard Taruskin, 'Interpreting Shostakovich's Fifth Symphony', in Fanning, ed., *Shostakovich Studies*, Cambridge: Cambridge University Press, 1995, 42–5.

54 All quotations from Bakhtin, 'Epic and Novel', in Bakhtin, *The Dialogic Imagination*, ed. Michael Holquist, trans. Caryl Emerson and Michael Holquist, Austin: University of Texas Press, 1981, 30.

55 Ibid., 32.

that of the reader. Thus there can be no single revealed 'essence' as the Formalists or Meyerhold would have understood it; whatever the meaning produced, it is always subject to change. The essay 'Forms of Time and Chronotope' develops this idea further. The reader cannot help but enter into dialogue with the author; thus a text is always renewed and revitalized. Once more asserting the freedom of this dialogical principle, Bakhtin cautions:

> We must never confuse – as has been done up to now and is still often done – the represented world with the world outside the text (naive realism); nor must we confuse the author-creator of a work with the author as a human being (naive biographism); nor confuse the listener or reader of multiple or varied periods, recreating and renewing the text, with the passive listener or reader of one's own time (which leads to dogmatism in interpretation and evaluation).[56]

It is not hard to see from this passage that Bakhtin's motivation was, at least in part, motivated by the reductive and dogmatic nature of Soviet literary criticism. It is also easy to see why 21st-century Shostakovich scholarship might be grateful to Bakhtin for expressing himself so unequivocally. Here is a Russian literary philosopher, writing in exile in 1938, later to be acknowledged both in Russia and in the West as one of the most profoundly humanitarian thinkers of his time, reminding his reader that they have a part to play in re-creating the work of art: that the intention of the author is just one part of what goes to make up that work, and that the author's personality and biography are irrelevant to that dynamic author–reader relationship. We do not have a moral obligation to concur with Bakhtin in this, just as we are not obliged to take on the vast weight of ideological and biographical baggage around Shostakovich's music every time we hear it or discuss it. The point is that if we are not to investigate authorial intention or programmatic content on anything but the very broadest level, Bakhtin's ideas of intention and reception, combined with his analysis of novelistic discourse, offer a theoretical basis for musical analysis which complements Adorno and Formalist theory.

To summarize, then, both Bakhtin and the Formalists assert that the novel is an inherently contemporary – hence 'unfinished' – genre. Its materials – typical storylines, characters, descriptions – are in a state of perpetual evolution. Both introduce the idea that the author manipulates the responses of the reader through the mechanics of the plot, or *syuzhet*. Both insist that this process constitutes a work's meaning rather than its *fabula*, or story. The implications for meaning in narrative, then, are as follows:

1. Meaning does not derive from the actual story, but from the manner in which it is told.
2. The author has control over that meaning, and uses technical devices to manipulate our responses.

56 Bakhtin, 'Forms of Time and Chronotope', in Bakhtin, *The Dialogic Imagination*, 253–4.

3. How that meaning is then interpreted by each individual reader is determined not solely by the author, but is subject to an infinite process of change, depending on historical and cultural context as well as each reader's own personality.
4. Thus, the ultimate meaning of a text is undefinable. It resides in a dialectical process that takes place between the author and the reader.

Narrativity in Shostakovich?

All descriptions of Shostakovich's Fourth Symphony as theatrical, filmic or Mahlerian share a common motivation: a desire to account for the collisions, ruptures and shock effects in his music in terms of other art forms or – as in the case of Mahler – another composer's music. That approach takes us halfway: it provides a particular terminological framework for describing the surface gestures of the music but stops short of combining those 'immediate' observations with structural analysis.

Where music, particularly abstract symphonic music, seems to suggest narrativity – through diverging from 'normal' procedure and tone, or by striking thematic transformations – it is all too easy to 'interpret' them according to our own individual responses. That, as discussed, has been a major problem in Shostakovich commentary; but even in the wider musiological community, forming literal interpretations from analysis has found cautious acceptance.[57] Still, musicological discussions of narrative have, in the main, favoured relatively abstract propositions. They have addressed the issue of narrative shape (as with Anthony Newcomb's discussion of a *Bildungsroman* plot in Schumann's Second Symphony[58]) and sought to define what it is about certain pieces that prompt the listener to think along 'narrative' lines. As Jean-Jacques Nattiez has observed, musical narrative is an essentially 'immanent' phenomenon; it cannot aspire to the syntactical clarity of a textual narrative. When writers have described a 'narrative impulse' in music, it is because on the level of the strictly musical discourse … [they] recognize returns, expectations, and resolutions, but of what … [they] do not know … [Music] is, to take up Adorno's paradoxical comment referring to Mahler, "a narrative which relates nothing".'[59]

Vera Micznik's 2001 article on narrativity in Beethoven and Mahler ends by concluding that, while music cannot 'be' narrative in the sense of actually telling

57 For one startling example of literal hermeneutics, see Timothy L. Jackson, *Tchaikovsky: Symphony No. 6 (Pathétique)*, Cambridge: Cambridge University Press, 1999.

58 Anthony Newcomb, 'Once More "Between Absolute and Program Music"': Schumann's Second Symphony', *19th-Century Music*, 7/3, 1984, 233–48.

59 Jean-Jacques Nattiez, 'Can One Speak of Narrativity in Music?', *Journal of the Royal Musical Association*, 115/2, 1990, 245.

a story, it can 'present semblances of situations analogous to those presented in stories'.[60] By this she means primarily instances where a piece of music deviates from what is expected of it, and therefore contains some element of surprise. Our field of knowledge which produces such expectations thus functions as 'narrational knowledge'; the 'projection of a 'possible story' (a concept clearly linked to Bakhtin's notion of 'authorial surplus' and hence to the author's potential to manipulate a reader's response). Citing Gerald Prince's definition of narrativity, in which the 'degree of narrativity ... depends partly on the extent to which that narrative fulfils a receiver's desire',[61] Micznik finds musical narrative in the undermining of 'causal relationships' such as the reversal of the 'normal' classical procedure of a strong 'masculine' first subject and a weaker 'feminine' second subject. Thus 'in music, the more the events and the discourse of the piece contradict an expected order and make the listener constantly wonder what unexpected situation will occur next, the more "narrative" the music will be'.[62]

Writers on Mahler from Bekker onwards have found his heavily rhetorical language hermeneutically suggestive: the idea that his alienated characters and deviations from 'normal' musical processes had as their motivation (however subliminally) an extrinsic agenda is the driving force behind Adorno's study. Carolyn Abbate's discussion of Mahler's *Todtenfeier* similarly proceeds from identifying a moment of surprise or rupture and concludes that, while not perhaps 'meaning' anything specific, such moments nevertheless 'signify' something. She suggests that the E major 'Gesang' theme of the *Todtenfeier* constitutes a 'deep sonic break' extreme enough to 'signal a singer and a song', reinforced by a 'self-reflexive' quotation from *Die Walküre*: 'By means of its peculiar and marked musical diminishment, it tells itself intrinsically as a phenomenal song and as a voice from outside.'[63] Though she does not take the discussion any further, Abbate has nevertheless included this moment as a classic example of 'voicing' in symphonic music, albeit at a relatively abstract level. There are clear parallels here with the Formalists and Bakhtin, and given the scope of their influence on modern literary criticism – and hence musical discussions of narrative – this is not surprising. The separation of *syuzhet* and *fabula*, the notion of the authorial voice and its endless dialogue with the reader, and the beginnings of formulas for discussing texts in that way, has had far-reaching consequences in both Structuralist and Post-Structuralist criticism.

The temptation to construct an analysis guided principally by the desire to justify a hermeneutic reading has been especially strong in discussions of Shostakovich's music. As Patrick McCreless has observed, it is music culturally

60 Micznik, 'Music and Narrative Revisited', 244.

61 Ibid.

62 Ibid., 246.

63 Carolyn Abbate, *Unsung Voices: Opera and Musical Narrative in the Nineteenth Century*, Princeton: Princeton University Press, 1991, 151–52.

conditioned to communicate 'extramusical meaning', which we ignore at our peril:

> the music itself clearly demands a marriage of analytical and interpretative approaches, a reckoning with both its immanent and its extrinsic meaning. For Shostakovich was, on the one hand, a sophisticated composer in a high-art tradition … on the other hand, he was also a composer who lived in a culture that passionately believed in the power of music to communicate extramusical meaning, and that relied on a well-established complex of critical conventions to gain access to and articulate that meaning.[64]

However, even McCreless's own attempt to marry intrinsic and extrinsic elements in the Piano Trio relies on biographical information that we know to be incorrect. The Trio was not, as he claims, written in response to the news of Sollertinsky's death on 11 February 1944; Shostakovich had begun work on it in late 1943, and the first movement was complete by 15 February 1944.[65] Another key prop for his extrinsic discussion is *Testimony*, a source so discredited that casual acceptance of its contents is not (or should not be) an option any more. Hence McCreless's approving citation of MacDonald's *Testimony*-derived claim that the Trio's finale was a 'directly programmatic image' of stories Shostakovich had heard about Jews in Nazi death camps being forced to dance on their own graves takes as its starting-point rumour and hearsay rather than fact.[66] Nevertheless, McCreless's analysis of the Trio is, though guided by, not actually dependent on such observations: the balance of intrinsic and extrinsic elements in his analysis is finely enough judged to withstand the rejection of some of his historical assumptions. He even goes so far as to explicitly distance his analysis from specific dependence on events, real or otherwise: 'It hardly requires explicit knowledge that Shostakovich composed the piece while coping with the shock of the death of a close friend to catch the import of the opening canon.'[67] In other words, in a sensitive analysis – even one that quotes with impunity from *Testimony* – there can be no question of dependence on a fixed, specific correlation between historical events and a listener's (or analyst's) response. We can, therefore, afford to accept that the question of Shostakovich's intention may be left alone; there is enough to say about the music without needing constantly to bolster analytical argument with historical facts that can so easily turn out to be unreliable.

Although no major published analysis of Shostakovich's Fourth Symphony attempts to extend discussion into the kind of one-dimensional hermeneutics that has dogged discussions of Shostakovich's music for decades, there is a justifiable – even desirable – element of hermeneutics in their approach. Even if Shostakovich's symphonies do not constitute evolving narrative structures, they

---

64 Patrick McCreless, 'The Cycle of Structure and the Cycle of Meaning: The Piano Trio in E minor, Op. 67', in Fanning, ed., *Shostakovich Studies*, 118–19.

65 See Fay, *Shostakovich*, 141.

66 Ibid., 126.

67 McCreless, 'The Cycle of structure', 121–2.

evoke a starker intrinsic/extrinsic dialogue than do those of his contemporaries. That very starkness can be off-putting, even perceived as a weakness, depending on the aesthetic orientation of the listener. Taruskin, for example, has sensed a 'debased level of musical discourse' in the Eighth Quartet, in which he finds 'overreliance on extroversive reference as bearer of essential meaning'.[68] That value judgement echoes Adorno's insistence upon an ideal rational/mimetic balance – a balance which had, in his view, already fallen by the wayside as early as late Beethoven. It also echoes some of the prejudices of the Formalists, whose anxiety to wrest literary criticism from the mire of sociological and biographical interpretation led them to find meaning or essence in structure rather than in the story. It suggests that musical meaning is ideally articulated through a dialectical relationship to form and not through stepping outside it.

The fact that such passages in Shostakovich can embarrass while similar ones in Mahler fascinate can be in part attributed to the easily decodable nature of some of Shostakovich's extroversive references. Those in the Eighth Quartet (and there are many) embrace principally the composer's own musical monogram DSCH, but also the well-known Russian revolutionary song 'Tormented by Grievous Bondage'. Add to that the wealth of biographical information swamping the quartet's reception history, and we have a work which, as Taruskin observes, has indeed acquired an 'overreliance on extroversive reference as bearer of essential meaning'. Whether the responsibility for that lies with the composer or with the legion of 'bearer[s] of essential meaning' who have been contentedly decoding it for years is a separate issue. Those works that contain some of the most powerful extrinsic references (the Fifth Symphony finale's Pushkin song quotation, or the Tenth Symphony third movement's ELMIRA horn call[69]) presented them in such a subtle way that few people noticed they were there at all. In other words, their impact is primarily musical rather than extramusical, and their belated decodification adds to, but does not dominate, their initial impression.

In the case of works whose historical context makes them especially inviting to programmatically inclined commentators, extroversive discussion tends to depend heavily on historical information and supposition. Although most of the extroversive baggage has amassed around works like the Fifth and Tenth Symphonies, the Fourth has not been immune. Volkov's Shostakovich began the mythologizing process thus:

> The mass treachery [experienced in the wake of the 1936 *Pravda* attacks] did not concern me personally. I managed to separate myself from other people, and in that period it was my salvation. Some of these thoughts you can find, if you wish, in my Fourth Symphony. In the last pages, it's all set out rather precisely.[70]

---

68 Taruskin, 'Interpreting Shostakovich's Fifth Symphony', 55.

69 See Nelly Kravetz, 'A New Insight into the Tenth Symphony of Dmitry Shostakovich', in Bartlett, ed., *Shostakovich in Context*, 159–74.

70 Volkov, *Testimony*, 89.

This is clearly a reference to the extraordinary double coda, where a long C major apotheosis (a paraphrase of the 'Gloria' chorus from Stravinsky's *Oedipus*) crumbles, leaving a shell-shocked evocation of Chaikovsky's 'Pathétique' coda to conclude the symphony *morendo*, in C minor. Those references are certainly extroversive enough (in the sense that they make intertextual reference to other works with either a dramatic or a programmatic basis) to invite a hermeneutic response; it would be disingenuous to pretend otherwise. But, even given the discredited status of *Testimony*, the statement quoted above actually keeps to an absolute minimum of hermeneutic interpretation. Shostakovich is allegedly describing how, in spite of the treachery of friends and colleagues, he managed to minimize personal damage by distancing himself from other people. Such a generalized claim hardly attempts to pin specific meaning on to the Fourth Symphony, regardless of the phrase 'set out rather precisely' (though as a matter of fact, the coda's reference to the 'Pathétique' does not seem to bear out the claim that Shostakovich was not personally affected by those events). Contrast that rather neutral claim with MacDonald's interpretation of the first movement's climax point:

> Taken to a choked crescendo by the strings, the vigil theme is resumed by bass clarinet until, as a quiet horn greets the dawn, a bird stirs on E flat clarinet, its drooping two-note motto uncomfortably suggesting that of a cuckoo clock. … The music's skeletal textures now begin to fill rapidly, tension rises, and the dreaded thing finally happens: the secret police arrive, audibly climbing the stairs (figures 46–7) and bursting in through the door on a triumphant crescendo. In a brilliant alienative stroke, Shostakovich switches the two-note motto around in the upper orchestra like torch-beams while the NKVD move grimly through the darkened apartment in the guise of the vigil theme.[71]

The striking thing about this interpretation is that it deals exclusively with the music's introversive qualities, subjecting them to a hermeneutic analysis based on knowledge of the symphony's historical context and on a set of interpretative codes previously established by the author. It cannot even be claimed that those introversive elements are discussed in a semantically coherent manner; MacDonald confuses themes so that, for example, the recasting of the 'vigil theme' (the second subject) in the intonational sphere of the first subject at the start of the recapitulation is mistaken for a straightforward return of the first subject. But there is a crucial 'extroversive' reference implicit in MacDonald's reading: two-note motifs represent the State (and thus oppression – hence their hardly coincidental appearance in military marches, for example) and three-note motifs represent the People (typically dance-like). This is possibly how he comes to interpret the climax as a negative, oppressive event; the return of the climax theme in the recapitulation (a particularly moving passage) receives no comment whatever, since it only serves to confuse his interpretation. Without his 'semantic'

71 MacDonald, *The New Shostakovich*, 112–13.

codes and their selective application, much of the 'analytical' hermeneutics in his book would simply disintegrate.

The desire to find extrinsic meaning in Shostakovich's music on the basis of historical context is understandable, and, in the light of numerous suggestive instances of intertextual references in his major works, it would be extreme, in Shostakovich's case, to echo Schoenberg's demand that music must be understood 'purely in terms of music'.[72] But aspects of Schoenberg's polemic are still pertinent: discussions of Shostakovich's music do still tend to assume the presence of images or a programme in a way which does not extend to the work of his contemporaries Prokofiev or Myaskovsky. Schoenberg's parting shot – reminding his readers that the work of art outlives its historical verisimilitude (or lack of it) – resounds with relevance for those aggressively political readings of Shostakovich's music which seek to ally him to a set of intentions, opinions and actions which we can never ascertain.

Adorno, Formalist theory, Bakhtin and Meyerhold offer Shostakovich studies the prospect of a relatively clean slate. Their shared focus on the dynamic relationship between form and content allows for an intrinsic/extrinsic analysis founded on generalities rather than specifics, and at the same time gives priority to demonstrating why a piece of music is effective in terms not only of its intrinsic qualities but also of its intertextual relationships. While Adorno (in his Mahler book), Meyerhold and the Formalists predicated much of their theory on the assumption of narrative manipulation, whether ironic (*Tristram Shandy*), didactic (*ostraneniya*) or alienating (Mahler), the nature of narrative itself never became the focal point of their discussions, but was taken as read: it was perhaps considered too obvious (and insufficiently interesting) to merit attention in its own right. Despite all the lengthy speculation on Shostakovich's authorial intentions, it is nonetheless possible to discuss Shostakovich's music in a way that is enriched by the ideas of his contemporaries (including Adorno) but does not attempt to formulate any one system or set of narrative principles.

The Fourth Symphony offers an unusually rich opportunity for such a project. Not only is the first movement a fascinating example of a self-conscious and critical approach to sonata form dramaturgy, but the second movement is an intriguing 'misreading'[73] of the scherzo of Mahler's 'Resurrection' Symphony, prompting a cycle of references to that work which reaches its tragic apogee in the finale. Although it is the Formalist emphasis on structure as 'bearer of essential meaning' which informs my own approach to Shostakovich's treatment of sonata

---

72 Schoenberg, 'The Relationship to the Text', in Arnold Schoenberg, *Style and Idea*, London: Faber, 1975, 141.

73 Bloom's terminology is used here, divorced from its original context, simply because it is useful to describe the kind of critical engagement with Mahler that runs through the Fourth Symphony, and for the second movement in particular. It is not intended to convey the 'anxiety of influence' associated with Bloom's original use of the term.

form and genre in this work, there can be no question of specifying that 'essential meaning' as would be possible in a text, no matter what the composer's actual intentions might have been. The fact is that we cannot know those intentions, and to speculate is, though tempting, pointless. As we have seen, the main clue we have as to the 'meaning' of the symphony – Shostakovich's supposed explanation of the coda as related in *Testimony* – seems to contradict rather than support the musical evidence. What is more, the characterization in the first movement constitutes one of the most ambivalent examples of thematic transformation found anywhere in Shostakovich's music; it is near-impossible to think of a plausible dramaturgical interpretation that fully takes account of all the transformation processes that have preceded it.

Another complication arises from the fact that it is difficult to speak of a 'normal' type of symphonic discourse or dramaturgy at the time when Shostakovich penned the Fourth Symphony. As discussed in the previous chapter, it was not even the case that a symphony – even a socialist realist one – had to end positively, in a major key. Though there was a degree of predictability in Soviet symphonies dating from five or six years before the Fourth, those features were not so entrenched that deviation from them *per se* can form the basis for the kind of narrative discussion that can so fruitfully arise from, for example, Schubert's treatment of tonality and structure in his songs or piano music.[74] If the presence of musical narrative is suggested by a work's breaking out of the patterns of 'normal' musical discourse, how may we discuss symphonies written in a culture where such 'narrativity' was encouraged so as not to sound too abstract and bourgeois? An entirely 'formal' symphony, devoid of subtitle, programme, text or extrinsic/mimetic 'content' (popular songs, sirens, whistles and so on) was a symphony which needed justification: hence the convoluted attempts made by Sollertinsky, Asafiev and Rïzhkin, among others, to define abstract symphonism as inherently collective and contemporary. Discussions of narrative in Western music, such as those of Mahler's music, are rather turned on their heads in this kind of cultural environment. Art is not just reflecting society, but is performing a grotesque balancing-act between appearing to reflect a false reality and (ideally) remaining true to the 'real' reality.

The stress laid by both Adorno and Sollertinsky on tone in Mahler's music – extended by Sollertinsky to that of Shostakovich – is of paramount importance here. Tone – or 'intonation' – is dependent on context: musical, cultural, social; and that of the listener as well as of the composer. As the context of Shostakovich's own society and culture in the 1930s is more or less inaccessible to all but those few still living, it is impossible to re-create it in terms of musical expectations.

74 The classic article of this kind is still (in my view) Edward T. Cone's 'Schubert's Promissory Note: An Exercise in Musical Hermeneutics', *19th-Century Music*, 5/3, 1982, 233-41. See also Lawrence Kramer, *Franz Schubert: Sexuality, Subjectivity, Song* (Cambridge: Cambridge University Press, 1998).

However, it is possible to judge (in a very general sense) what sounds 'normal' by the standards of contemporary Soviet symphonies, and to hear where Shostakovich is manipulating our awareness of sonata form for dramatic purposes; where he is paraphrasing other works (as he does in the finale), and whether the tone seems positive, negative or somewhere in between. A level of re-creation, then, is a useful starting-point for forming our own instincts about what, and where, the Fourth Symphony seems to signify. Using terms and concepts taken from Adorno, Sollertinsky, Formalist theory and Bakhtin has the potential to enrich the conventions of music analysis without displacing them. These are principally applied in the analysis of the first two movements, since the dramaturgy of these movements is dependent on either formal norms or earlier musical models, which are then subverted. But the finale departs so categorically from any preceding symphonic model that an assessment of tone based on convention is significantly harder. Its central divertimento sequence presents one popular idiom following the next in an apparently haphazard manner. However, the gestures of fulfilment operate here as they do elsewhere, most tellingly in the paraphrases of the dual coda, which uses intertextual references to subvert those gestures. As I hope to show, even the finale has a strong level of intrinsic/extrinsic congruence, using linear forces to emphasize intonational relationships and bringing in the full armoury of inter-textual semantics to create a devastating, but tightly constructed, whole.

CHAPTER THREE

First Movement: Allegretto poco moderato

Shostakovich's extended sonata form first movement embodies a powerful tension between structure and content. Almost entirely devoid of the inter-textual resonances which fuel the narrative of the second and third movements, the first movement's dramaturgy is sustained chiefly by a dramatized relationship between formal structure (*fabula*) and 'content' (*syuzhet*). As discussed in Chapter One, contemporary Soviet symphonies tended to avoid the classic pattern of exposition–development–recapitulation by having a developmental exposition followed by further development (usually contrapuntal) and then a coda. Thematic interaction was unusual, and any that took place was strictly confined to the development or (for example, in Shebalin III/1) recapitulation, in a spirit of co-operation and resolution. Where themes did occasionally interact, they did so comfortably and without any tension: actual conflict was non-existent.

By contrast, Shostakovich sets out to dramatize and at the same time to problematize, 'academic' sonata form, using the very template that his contemporaries avoided. Though he retains the developmental exposition and used contrapuntal techniques to extend the material into the development, Shostakovich's re-enthronement of the recapitulation makes a powerful gesture to its traditional role as the resolver of tensions, while at the same time its strategy of character exchange and gradual draining away of energy prevents actual resolution from taking place.[1] In his choice of musical materials, too, Shostakovich sets up a strikingly polarized strong–weak relationship which casts the first subject (A1) – a crude, four-square march with a well-defined diatonic character – as the aggressor, while both its gentle subsidiary theme (A2) and the second subject (B) are far more loosely phrased and tonally indistinct. The result is a dramatization of passive and active, lyrical and aggressive, strong and weak completely unprecedented in the Soviet symphonic tradition.

Shostakovich's decision to cast this movement in sonata form is an obvious gesture not only to the Rimskian conservatoire tradition in which he had been schooled, but also to nineteenth-century Austro-German symphonism as practised by composers from Beethoven to Mahler. The Fourth Symphony marks Shostakovich's rejection of single-movement, through-composed symphonism as practised in his Second and Third Symphonies, the roots of which are traceable not

[1] Körner describes the recapitulation as a 'composed-out [*auskomponiertes*] decrescendo' ('Schostakowitschs Vierte Sinfonie', 135).

only to Myaskovsky (cf. his single-movement Tenth Symphony), but also to Skryabin's symphonic poems. It does not set out to present a revolutionary concept of symphonic structure, however; both in language and overall form (Allegro – Moderato – Largo–Allegro), the structure of the Fourth Symphony is actually rather conservative considering Shostakovich's then status as the Soviet Union's *enfant terrible*. For a young composer to follow his modernist Second and Third Symphonies with a three-movement work beginning with a sonata allegro was a powerful signal – initiated entirely by Shostakovich – that his years as an experimentor and radical were over.[2]

As discussed in Chapter One, the RAPM years did encourage a certain brand of academicism among the then front rank of Soviet symphonists, and it is no surprise to find three- and four-movement symphonies of the 1930s which do not venture beyond conventional academic or film-score-style language. But added to the weight of both RAPM and conservatoire tradition was a general move away from radical modernism across Europe and America; Shostakovich's Cello Sonata of 1934 marked the beginnings of his own *rapprochement* with the Classical and Romantic tradition after a decade of modernist experimentation. And, as reports from the 1935 symphonism conference show, the survival of the symphonic genre was by that time regarded as vital for the Soviet Union's musical development and reputation. Arguments were now no longer focused exclusively on the question of music's social relevance, but encompassed discussion of technical standards, of how best to engage with Western (chiefly nineteenth-century) traditions and of how symphonic language could be rejuvenated and made meaningful to Soviet audiences. Shostakovich's enthusiasm for Mahler provided him with an ideal role-model: here was a composer who took the tradition of post-Beethovenian epic symphonism to new expressive and dramatic heights, who used popular idioms both critically and lovingly and who, as Sollertinsky had argued, did not trivialise either his popular sources or his own musical language. Mahler provided Shostakovich with both an ideological and a musical way forward: the new Soviet symphonism was to be epic and monumental, yet accessible enough in its language to communicate to a broad spectrum of listeners.

Shostakovich needed models for his concept of dramatized symphonic form. For those he turned not just to Mahler, but also to Meyerhold and his theories of *ostraneniye*, or estrangement. Just as Meyerhold had relied on the established theatrical conventions of realism and temporal continuity for the shocking effects of his anti-realistic sets, displacement of scenes and acts, and mechanized acting style to have maximum impact, so Shostakovich played on the expectations

2 However, Levon Hakobian has plausibly argued that Shostakovich was following Popov's lead in composing a large-scale symphony with a sonata form first movement. See Hakobian, *Dmitriy Shostakovich: opït fenomenologii tvorchestva* [Dmitri Shostakovich: an attempt [to analyse] the phenomenology of his creative work], St Petersburg: Dmitriy Bulanin, 2004, 148.

produced by an allegro opening movement – complete with a starkly characterized opening theme – to disconcert his audience. The estranging effects he used ranged from sudden breaks in musical progress, analogous both to the Mahlerian 'rupture' or 'collapse' and to Meyerhold's use of *pereklivcheniye*, or sudden change-over, to the interpolation of a narrative voice, a technique beloved of the Russian Formalists, who found its original source in *Tristram Shandy*. Such a 'voice' in the first movement of the Fourth Symphony can be found in a theme which occurs at two critical points: the exposition climax at [47] and the central section of the recapitulation at [98]^{3}. Though generated within the second subject group, this theme is not presented fully until the recapitulation, where the dramatic nature of its earlier incarnation, combined with its complete absence from the development, gives it an emotional force not present in any of the main themes. As will be seen, this theme is one of the most important elements in the first movement's dramaturgy. It not only ties in with Formalist (and Meyerholdian) theories of *ostraneniye*, but is also a vital ingredient in the movement's *syuzhet*; if the *fabula* of the first movement is its basic sonata form, then its *syuzhet* lies in the way Shostakovich manipulates that form.

The first movement's combination of Formalist techniques with a Mahlerian 'democratic' approach to musical materials (clear-cut marching theme, waltz and polka) was intended to breathe new life into a tired form and language. It was also intended to communicate to audiences something more than the mere sum of its formal parts, of its *fabula*. The very act of questioning symphonic form and language constituted *syuzhet*, even if its specific meaning could not be expressed in words. As with Meyerhold's theatre, the motivation behind Shostakovich's polarized characterization, ruptures and transformations was not a flippant desire to shock or to entertain, but an urge to communicate 'higher' meaning.

Exposition

^{5}[1]–[5]: *Introduction – First Subject*

Of all Shostakovich's symphonic introductions, only those of the Fifth and Eighth share the epic, declamatory tone of the Fourth Symphony's opening bars. For sheer theatricality, it is unsurpassed: the five-bar introduction is delivered in the spiky woodwind and xylophone combination familiar from Shostakovich's incidental and ballet scores (see Example 5.20 for the polka from the ballet *The Golden Age*), and plunges from there straight into a crude militaristic march. As discussed already in Chapter One, although epic introductions were common – almost mandatory – for Soviet symphonies in the 1930s, the theatrical, grotesque tone of the Fourth sets it apart from its contemporaries. Even Popov's brilliant, unconventional First Symphony shies away from anything as blatant and 'crude' as this. To use a march as a first theme is also unusual; its coarse, aggressive tone has few, if any, symphonic precedents, although the opening of Mahler's Sixth comes close (see Examples 3.1 and 3.2).

Example 3.1
Shostakovich IV/1: ^{5}[1]–[3]: introduction and A1, showing motivic structure I (Introduction): a, A1:a, b, c, d

Allegretto poco moderato ♩ = 92

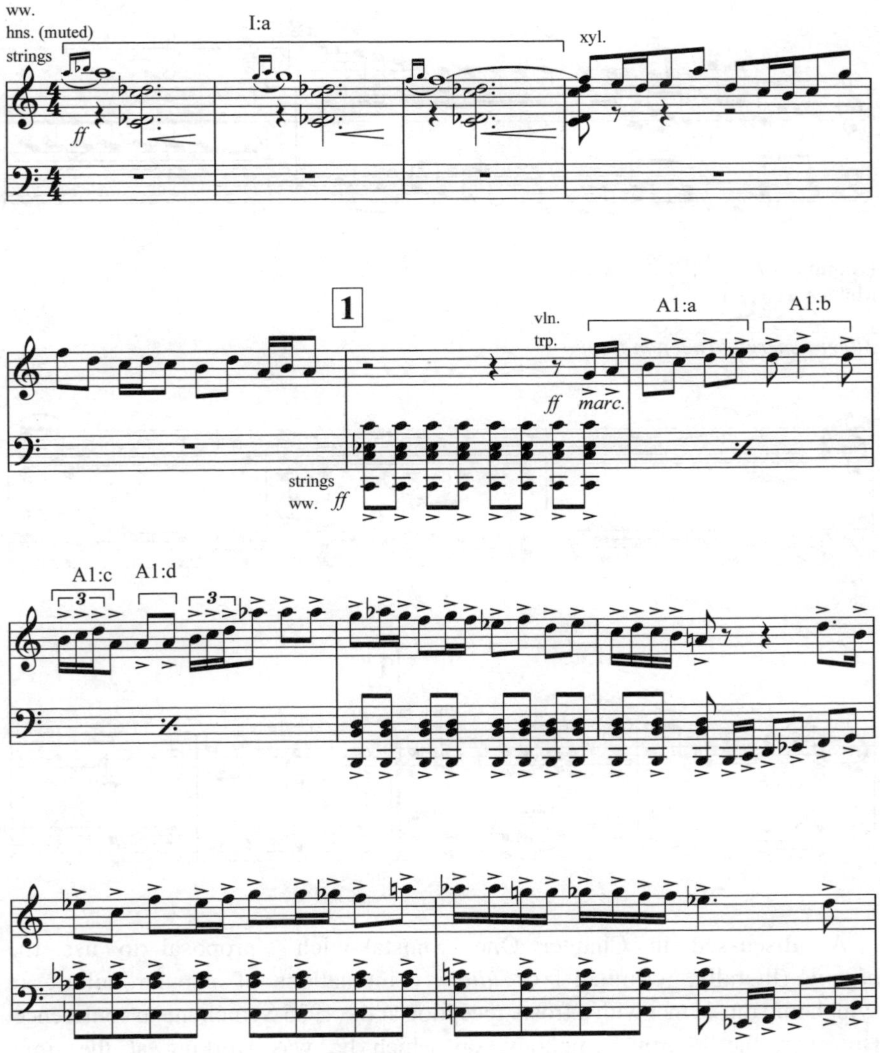

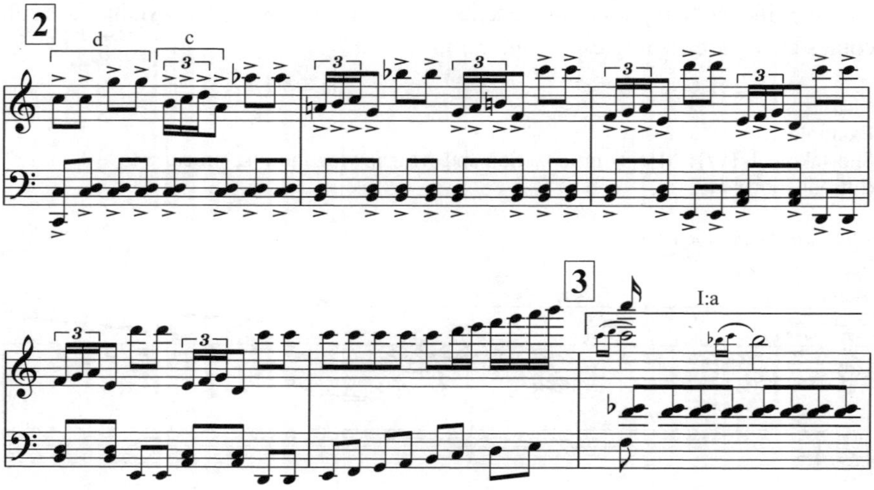

Example 3.2
Mahler VI/1: 5[1]–[1]2

Allegro energico, ma non troppo

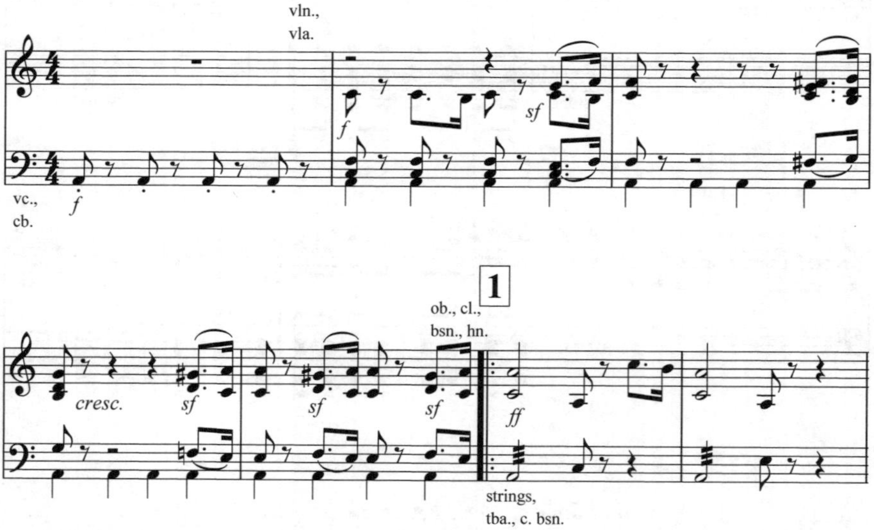

As discussed in Chapter One, Shostakovich's proposal to use the *blatniy* (literally, 'criminal') or *ulichniy* intonations of popular culture in symphonic music met with a frosty reception at the 1935 Symphonism conference. However, the Fourth Symphony, on which he was working at the time, demonstrates that his intention in using those intonations was to be anything but frivolous. This is no 'democratic' celebration of popular music, striving to please a wide audience. Instead, popular idioms are used critically, subverting both their apparently straightforward idiom and the high-minded, heroic mood expected of a Soviet symphony (see Table 3.1). The crude tone of the first theme derives in part from an unsophisticated, but strongly diatonic, harmonic presentation, with minimal bass movement. The first statement overlaps with the second at [3], which begins with a version of the introductory theme over an F/G♭ horn dissonance. The subsequent variant of A1 at [3]^{4} quickly leads to a reiterated variant of the triplet figure (A1: c) over A♭ in the bass. The move to D minor via A♮ at [4] piles flattened fifth, seventh and ninth degrees on top of the A bass (see Example 3.3, bar 24). But instead of freeing further motivic and harmonic movement, this instigates a further fixation on A1:c and d, the C minor feel of its reiterated d^{1}–c–b suggesting a possible return to the tonic. However, the

Table 3.1 Shostakovich IV/1: summary of first subject group

Figure	Theme	Tonal centre	Notes
$^{5}1$	Introduction	C	Fanfare-like introduction, with 'squeezed' horn C/D♭ chord.
1	A1	C	Aggressive marching theme with 4 main motifs a–d. A1:c reiterated from ^{2}[4], bringing A1 to crisis and collapse.
5	Transition	C–F	Introduces new A–G figure over C bass at [5]^{4}.
7^{2}	A2	F	Meandering, metrically unstable lyrical theme, a loose inversion of A1.
9	A2/A1	–	A1 motifs (esp. A1:a) begin to merge with A2, culminating in their co-statement at [19]. Leads again to crisis-point and breaks off sharply at [23].
23	Transition	A♭ pedal	Long, static section with triplet figuration. Establishes trochaic rhythm, and moves to short waltz-like passage before a sudden climax in F minor.

return to C minor, if such it is, is ambiguous. At ^{2}[5] – the climax of A1 – the bass harmony initially implies F minor, but it comes to rest on an inconclusive A/C dyad at [5]. Example 3.3 shows the way in which the reiteration of A1:c and d interacts with harmonic movement to retard motion, replacing the scalic, diatonic movement of A1 with motivic repetition and weakened tonal process; the move to D minor at [4]^{1} is unprepared, feeling more like an attempt to break free from the immobility produced by the repetition of A1:c, and even the move to F at [3] with the return of I:a is prompted by the reiteration of A1:c and d (see Example 3.1). Motifs A1: c and d are therefore used to push A1 beyond its limits and provoke crisis and collapse, here at ^{2}[5].

The collapse of A1 is brought about by the freezing of motivic development combined with weak harmonic movement; the climax point at [5] is not a fulfilment of either motivic or harmonic processes, but the result of their over-exertion and collapse. Although the martial aggression of A1 is presented in a seemingly 'active' diatonic framework, its motivic fixation and weakened diatonic movement after [4] make it sound laboured rather than mobile. Thus the strikingly 'energetic' opening theme is not only far more crude and aggressive than was normal for

Example 3.3
Shostakovich IV/1: ^{5}[1]–[5]: linear, motive and harmonic summary (oblique wavy lines denote scales)

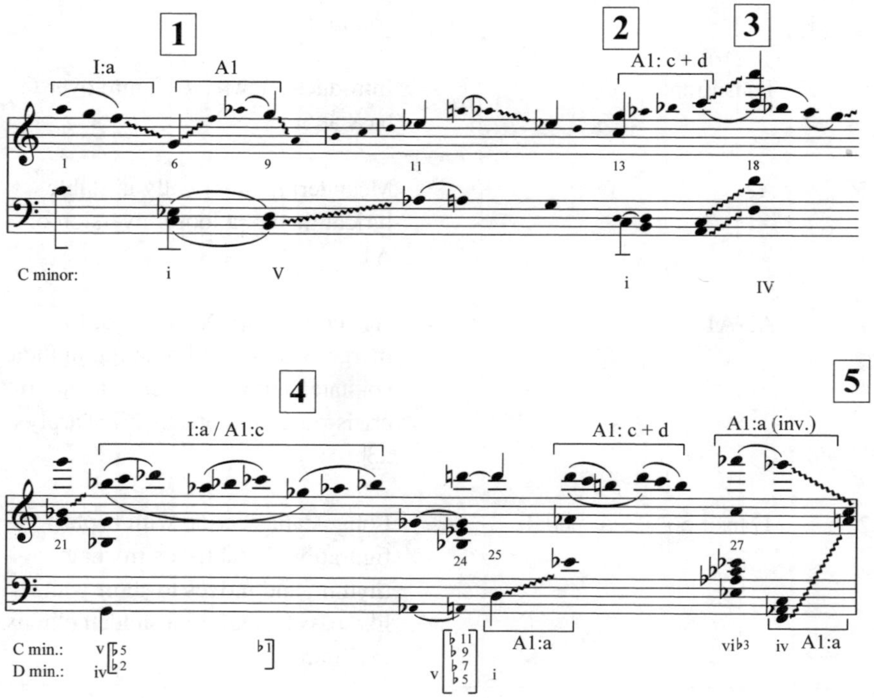

contemporary Soviet symphonies; it is also prevented from playing itself out in a conventional manner. After being artificially and precariously inflated, it is unceremoniously abandoned.

[5] – [7]^{2}: *Transition to A2*

The abrupt switch from the climax to the gentler transition passage is dramatized by a stabbing figure derived from A1:d at [5]^{1} that clears the texture and prepares for a new theme. A new, gentler tone quickly emerges on low strings: C is still the tonal centre here, though it is soon clouded by a bitonal E♭/E echo of A1 between ^{1}[6] and [7]. Although this transition takes motifs from A1 as its basic material – as well as preparing an important motif for A2 – its tone is elusive. Although it initially sounds secure with the tonic–dominant bass at [5]^{4} and the new two-note figure (to become A2's anacrusis), each apparent move to a secure footing is immediately destabilized. Elements of A1 are immediately broken down into their constituent parts: the two-note A–G oscillation on violas at [5]^{4} (bracketed in Example 3.4) is traceable to the introductory descent A–G–F (I:a), here for the first time affirming its long-range relationship with a bass C, while the scherzo-like figures from ^{1}[6] – [6]^{4} are clearly derived from A1's ascending scale (A1:a). A brief fixation on E♮ from [6]$^{4–6}$ foreshadows the role of a solitary E as a 'pause' figure in the A2 section, as will be discussed below. Its presence here plants an association between this open, 'suspended', tone and its recurrence later on in the A2 section, hinting at A2's inherent weakness before it has even started.

Example 3.4 shows how the C minor bass ascent C–D–E♭–F between bars 34 and 39 is coloured by this recurring e♮^{1}, which by bar 40 briefly immobilizes bass movement before slumping back onto e♭ at bar 44. E♮ is not presented as a leading-note to F, however: it is an entirely 'alien' pitch, used in conjunction with high-register orchestral textures to provide a contrast with the warmer string writing of [5]^{4} and A2. It does have important mid-range significance, however, as will be discussed. By subsequently flattening the E at bar 44, the move to F (major mode) for A2 at [7]^{2} registers weakly: this is a crucial part of Shostakovich's dramaturgical strategy which will see the 'passive' A2 swallowed up by the 'active' A1 in a striking process of thematic conflict and usurpation which has no parallel in any contemporary Soviet symphony.

[7]^{2} – [13] : *A2 and Development of First Subject Group*

The descending scale of A2 is a clear inversion of A1:a, as shown in Example 3.5. Its distinctive anacrusis, however, comes from the violas' two-note figure at [5]^{4}, bracketed in Example 3.4 and Example 3.5. The identification of this second, lyrical theme has caused some confusion. Roseberry and Longman label it 'A2', since its scalic derivation from A1 and eventual alignment with it at [19] suggest a degree of

Example 3.4
Shostakovich IV/1: 5 – 7 : linear summary

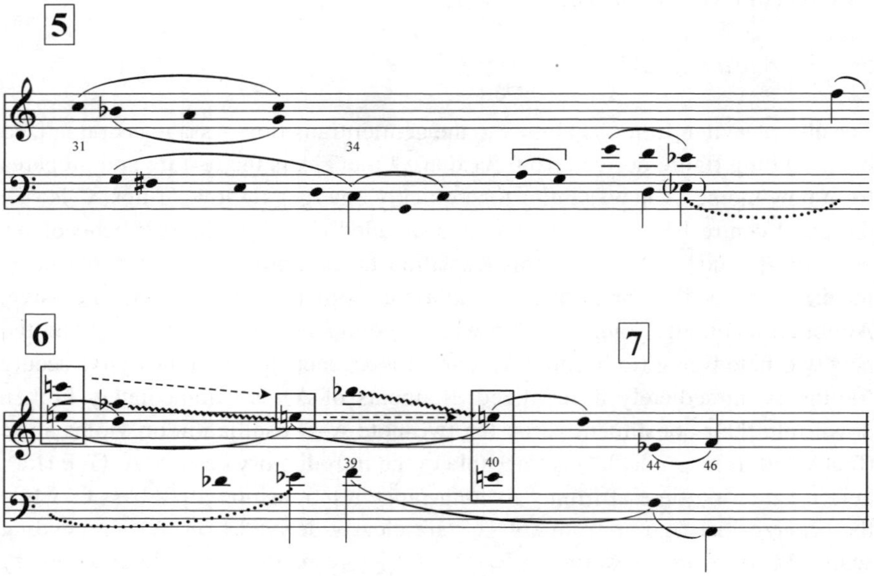

Example 3.5
Shostakovich IV/1: 7$^{2-8}$: A2, showing derivation from A1:a and two-note figure (A2:a)

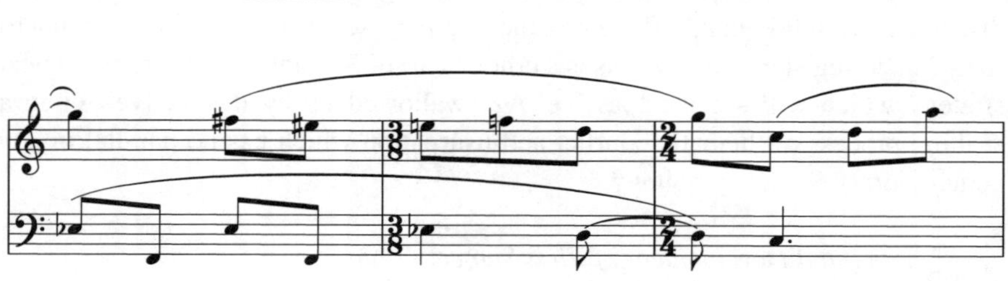

dependence on the first subject that can best be expressed by bracketing them together.[3] The presence of a distinctive third theme at 31 lends further weight to the view that the second subject group begins at this later juncture rather than here. Ottaway's 1975 analysis nevertheless identifies the A2 theme as the second subject proper, with the new theme at 31 as the third, which he views as situated not in the exposition but in the development.[4] Sabinina, taking into account A2's weak intonational character and its rapid absorption into A1, describes A2 in terms of its failure as a theme in its own right: as a 'false second subject' [*lozhnaya pobochnaya partiya*].[5]

Leaving aside for a moment the issue of exposition and development boundaries, the general view that A2 is a distinctive theme in its own right is surely appropriate. It is treated as such in the recapitulation and is initially perceived as a new voice when it first appears; it is only when A1 begins to infiltrate it that its lyrical identity crumbles and is subsumed. The confusion over the labelling of this secondary theme is in fact indicative of the peculiar dramaturgy of the whole section from 7^{2} to ^{6}24. A2 is a weakly articulated theme, metrically ambiguous and lacking a clear harmonic focus. Its initial tonal orbit is F, but it soon moves briefly to C at 8, repeating the A–G viola figure from 5^{4} and I:a. By 9, A1-derived scales begin to encroach upon its lyrical flow and to destroy any sense of a tonal centre; by 13, A2 is entirely dominated by A1, and it is not heard again in a complete form until its reincarnation in the recapitulation at 101. In this sense, Sabinina's description of A2 as a 'false' theme, rather than a normal subsidiary theme within the first subject group, is apt. It is a theme fated from the outset to be swallowed up by its more aggressive precursor, and it does not provide an adequate counter-weight to A1 in terms of either intonational clarity or dramatic impact to qualify as a proper 'second subject'.

Although A2 is not intended to be a strong character, it does have a crucial purpose. On a broad dramaturgical level, its function is to highlight the violent, encroaching nature of A1, and to be the passive vessel through which A1's aggressive development within the exposition can take place. Its non-diatonic, loose intonational sphere liberates the motivic structure of A1, which becomes generative in a way that its original presentation did not allow. The loosening effect of the A2 area thus enables development to take place. On another level, and equally importantly, A2 raises the possibility of a triple metre as the alternative to A1's relentless duple-time hegemony. Weak and unfocused at first, the triple-time bars gradually assert themselves against the scalic, duple-time infiltration of A1, a process which begins at 10 and effectively ends at 13.

A variant of the static E 'pause' figure at 6$^{4\text{-}6}$ (shown as A2:d on Example 3.6) appears first at 10, in triple time. The polarisation of this 'passive' intonation with

---

3 Koball calls this a 'subsidiary' theme (*Pathos und Groteske*, 5), as does Körner ('Schostakowitschs Vierte Sinfonie', 132). Kopp regards it as a transition theme (*Form und Gehalt*, 157).

4 Ottaway, 'Looking Again at Shostakovich 4', 20.

5 Sabinina, *Shostakovich-simfonist*, 101.

the 'active' scalic movement of A1 is more pronounced here than at $\boxed{6}^{4\text{-}6}$, with timbre and register playing an even more crucial role. Its context of fluctuating duple and triple metres and triadic figuration at $^{2}\boxed{10}$ (shown as A2:c on Example 3.6, and inverted between $\boxed{11}$ and $\boxed{12}$) further reinforces its separation from the scalic contours of A1. Scalic movement is suspended altogether for six bars (between $^{1}\boxed{10}$ and $\boxed{10}^{5}$); its resumption at $\boxed{10}^{5}$ is within the constraints of a triple metre (still distancing itself from A1) and focused around the 'static' intonational orbit of E up to $\boxed{11}$. In contrast to the earlier bass presentation of the A1 scales (starting at $\boxed{9}$), the register is higher and the timbre lighter. Scalic movement continues in bass woodwind at $\boxed{11}$, though still in triple time; at $\boxed{11}^{5}$ scales give way to flute triads, again in a high register. These also oppose the A1 encroachment and similarly suspend scalic movement. As duple-time scales begin to pick up in the bass at $^{3}\boxed{12}$, they are again arrested by triple-time, high-register figuration related to A2:c: thus the intonational spheres of the E 'pause' figure A2: d and that of A2:c are closely related. At this point, two new rising motifs appear (shown in Example 3.6 as variants (v.) of A2:b) between $\boxed{12}$ and $\boxed{13}$), suggesting a new point of departure for the triple-time passages. They are traceable to the bass movement (A2:b) between $^{1}\boxed{8}$ and $\boxed{8}^{4}$, and eventually feed into the second subject at $\boxed{31}$, thus affirming an allegiance between the triple-time aspect of A2 and its fulfilment later in the exposition with the entry of the second subject proper. In this way, before A1 begins to encroach in earnest on the A2 sphere, A2 is already associated with figuration linked with triple time (triads instead of scales), and with the idea of openness to other elements connected with either the first or the second subject. A2, then, is less a definite theme in its own right than a space in between the two main themes where the conflict between basic musical 'signs' (active, duple-time scalic movement and passive, triple-time triadic movement) are introduced. At least in the exposition, the A2 section will see A1 emerge as the stronger theme, gradually dominated by rising scales and duple metre until A2 is swallowed up completely by A1.

$\boxed{13}$ – $\boxed{19}$: *Intensification and Approach to Climax*

Now with greater rhythmic definition, A1:a-derived scalic figures predominate in the approach to climax at $\boxed{19}$. Although there is no motivating harmonic process here, E nevertheless maintains a weak presence up to $\boxed{15}$, moving to D at $\boxed{16}$. After this point, only A2's anacrusis figure is retained in a maelstrom of ascending scales in the sweep towards the merging of A1 and A2 at $\boxed{19}$. The iambic rhythm of the anacrusis figure A2: a is gradually merged with that of A1:b from $\boxed{15}$ to $\boxed{19}$, as shown in Example 3.7. A sudden return to triple metre at $\boxed{16}$ moves the intensification process up a notch. Rising chromatic scales bolster this process, which now lacks any tonal foundation: momentum is sustained by two cymbal crescendi ($^{2}\boxed{18}$ – 18 and $\boxed{18}^{4\text{–}8}$) and the start of a trochaic rhythmic propulsion at $\boxed{18}$. The approach from here to the climax at $\boxed{19}$ is punctuated by two successive bass themes, the first of which merges the intonations of A1:b and A2:a, while the second, though sharing A1's aggressive, accented tone,

Example 3.6
Shostakovich IV/1: [7]² – [13] : linear and motivic summary

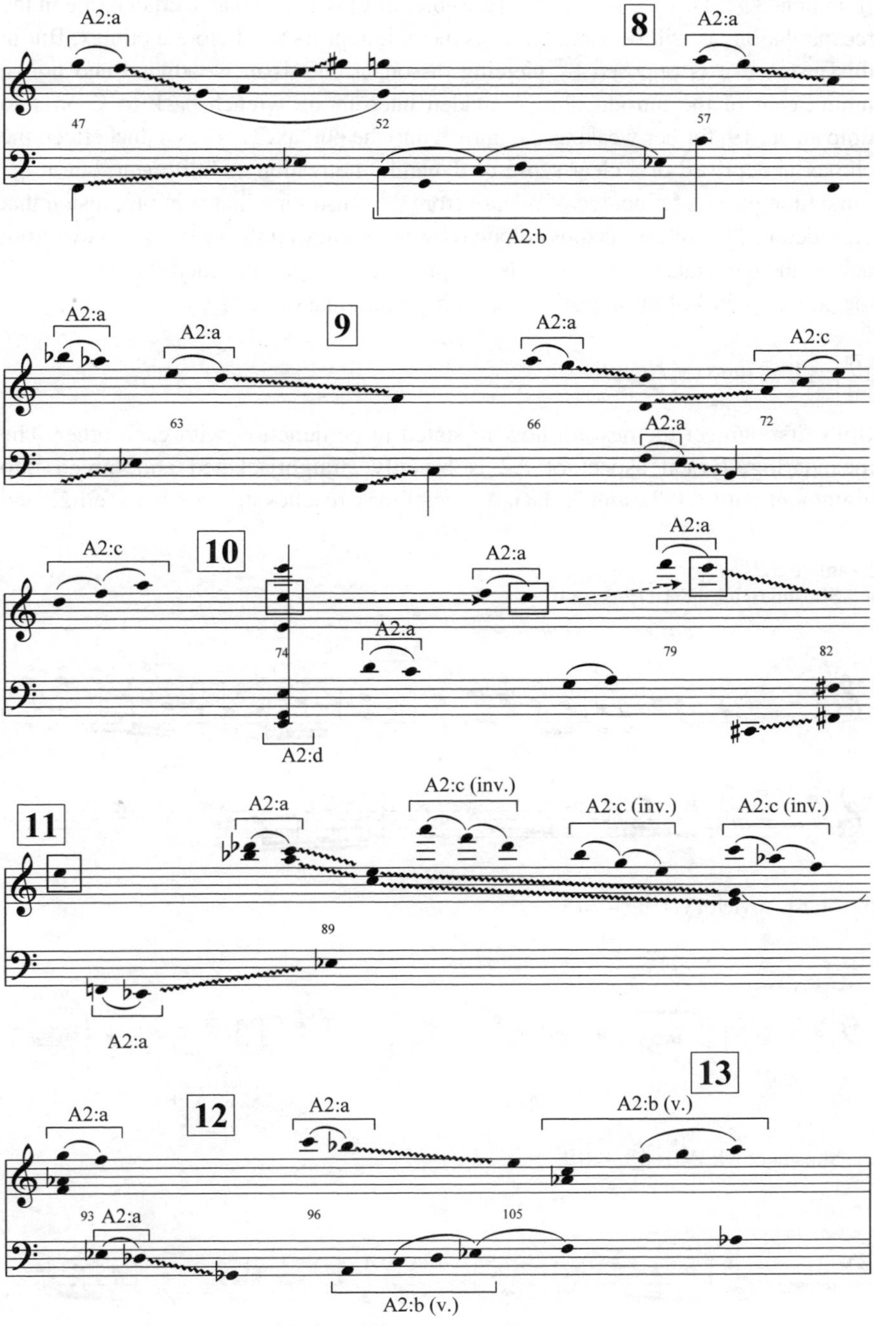

has a trochaic rhythm (a rhythmic inversion of A2:a) which will eventually gain prominence in the second subject group and exposition climax, as discussed below (Example 3.7). This second theme (Example 3.7 c) will also play a crucial role in the recapitulation, as will be seen. Here, as there, it appears just before a climax. But in this instance it is opposed by piercing dissonant chords in woodwind and horns, reminiscent of the introduction. A sudden interrupting wrench back to C on solo timpani at ^{1}[19] further weakens the onrush into the climax. This has a dual effect: the climax is deprived of a clear sense of dynamic motivation or fulfilment, but at the same time provides a degree of release from the frustrating hiatus in propulsion that preceded it. That release is thus coloured by an urgency all the more aggressive from having the wind taken out of its sails: a typical act of negation which characterizes all the climax points of the exposition apart from the final one at [47].

[19] – [23]: *Climax – Negation*

Both first subject themes are now re-stated in conjunction with each other. The meandering, lyrical aspect of A2 is brutally straightjacketed and forced into alignment with A1 (Example 3.8). As the climax reaches its apex between [22] and

Example 3.7

a Shostakovich IV/1: [1]$^{1-5}$: A1

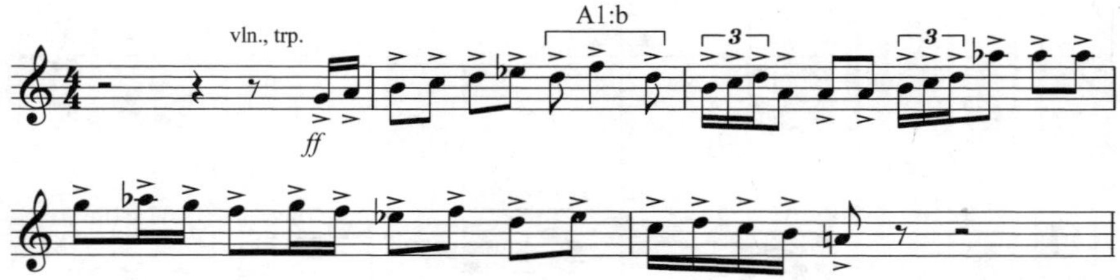

b Shostakovich IV/1: [17] – ^{1}[18]

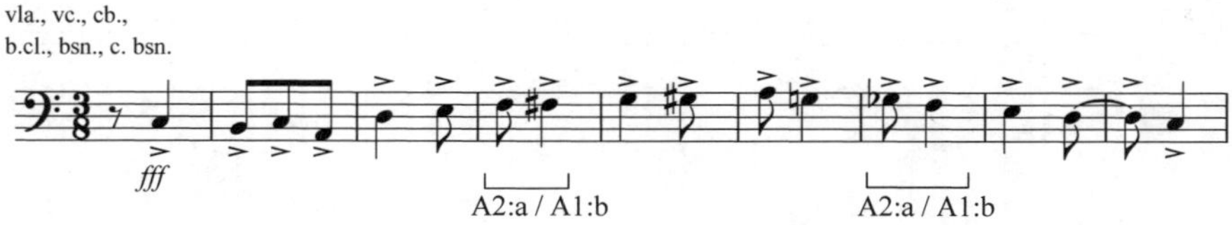

c Shostakovich IV/1: [18] – ^{1}[19]

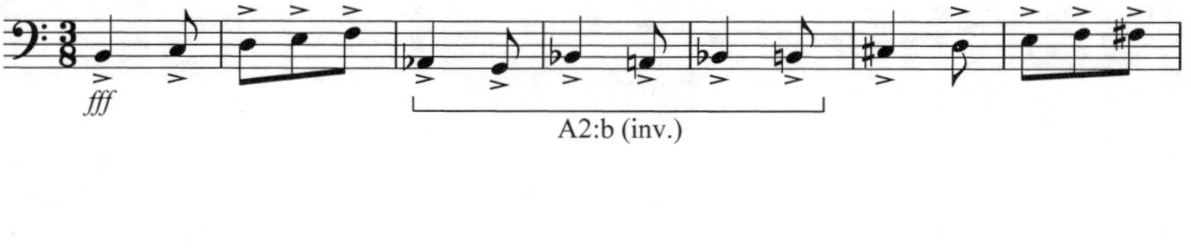

Example 3.8
Shostakovich IV/1: 19^{2} – ^{2}20

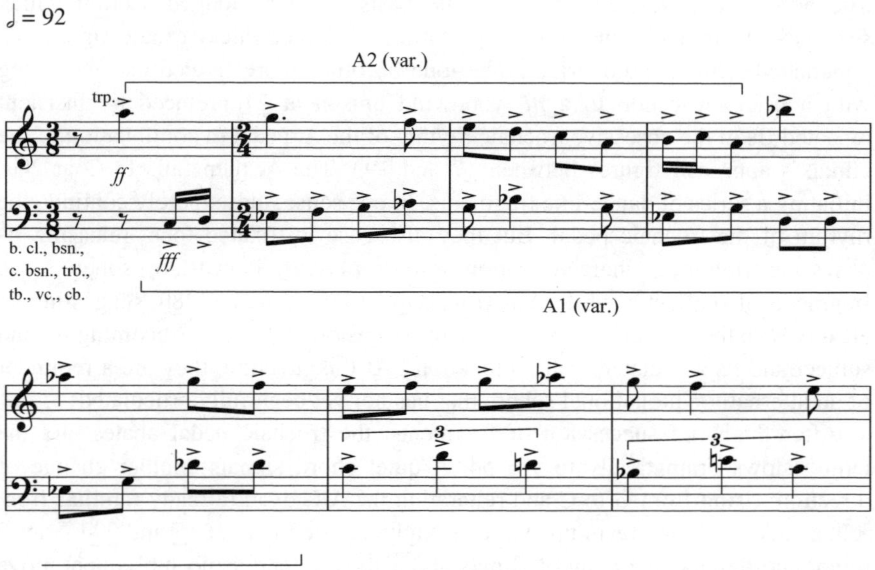

23, it falls to a weak C^6 (with no fifth), echoing the original collapse of A1 at ^{2}5 onto an A/C dyad. The jazzy syncopated rhythm that suddenly replaces the brutal reiterated quavers from 22^{5} further weakens the impact of the climax, trivializing it and bringing it to an unsatisfactory and abrupt end. As at 5^{1}, stabbing chords and descending figurations complete the disintegration process, but here the insistent A♭ in the horns seems to protest against the aborted climax, echoing its origins in the first subject's stabbing quavers (A1:d): the descending horn theme at 22 is an inversion of the D minor scale at bars 4$^{1-3}$ which heralds the original climax and breakdown of A1 (see Example 3.9).

Example 3.9
a Shostakovich IV/1: 4$^{1-3}$

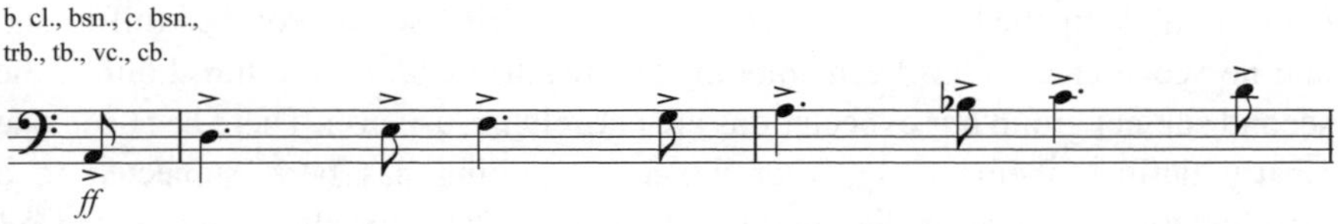

b Shostakovich IV/1: 22$^{1-5}$

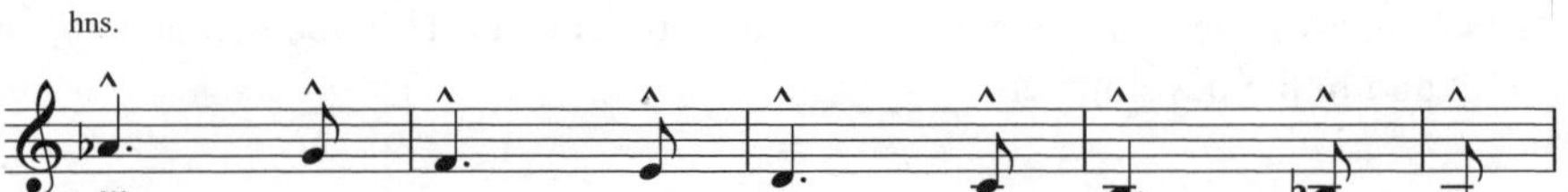

^{5}[24] – [31]: *Fixation – Climax*

The horns' A♭ pedal now becomes the basis for a prolonged section which suspends all dramatic and tonal expectations in directionless triadic figuration, punctuated with G minor triads. The tone becomes more fixated and menacing with a brief crescendo to a *fff* woodwind unison at [27] prefaced by insistent repeated Bs in the obsessive trochaic rhythm of the A♭ pedal (a continuation of the climax's approach figures between [17] and [19]). The A♭ then falls to G at [28]^{3}, initiating a series of dance-like fragments. In one sense, these merely continue the rhythm of the trochaic pedal. But they also ease its fixated tone, releasing its obsessive rhythmic characterization into a playful, dance-like sphere. The fragments also effect a subtle shift from duple to triple time (^{2}[28]), suggesting an affinity with the gentler tone of A2 and, by extension, with the forthcoming second subject and its associated waltz intonations. At this juncture, they are a reminder of an alternative intonational sphere that has not yet been fully articulated.

After this brief succession of fragments, the trochaic pedal abates and the tempo slows dramatically to ♩ = 54. A quiet chord signals another change of direction: rising from G to C and reiterating the A/C dyad (already familiar from ^{2}[5]), a sudden climax rears up. More strongly asserted than at ^{3}[5] and [22]$^{1-5}$, an F minor chord marks the point of climax at [30], though there is no subsequent move to the A/C dyad or C^{6} here. Neither is there any comparable process of negation or disintegration; the F minor tutti breaks off abruptly and is followed simply by a bar's rest. The move to A minor comes with the start of the second subject in the following bar, thereby recalling earlier tonal processes but dramatizing them further so that the second subject comes as a really new tone, in a new key. Whereas harmonic weakness is essential to Shostakovich's strategy to negate the force of the first subject group climaxes, the weak movement from F minor to A minor would spoil the impact of the second subject if it were allowed to feature more obviously here.

This constant estranging of dramaturgical norms such as climax and transition is a key feature of the first movement, and one which can plausibly be traced to Meyerhold's influence, or at least understood in those terms. In Shostakovich's exposition, no theme has reached a natural end; no climax has provided fulfilment, and no scene change has been smooth. The result is that on the threshold of the second subject group our expectations are entirely in suspense. There has been one clearly defined theme (A1), after which everything has been subjected to a disorientating process of disruption and change. The only alternative to the A1 sphere to suggest itself with any lasting force has been the triple-time figuration, which has only assumed a tangibly dance-like character between [27]^{6} and [29]. Those waltz-like intonations will assume a more crucial role in the second subject group and in the development.

31 – 51: *Second Subject Group*

Although nearly all analyses of this movement agree that the bassoon theme between 31 and 32 is the second subject of the exposition (see Example 3.10a), Ottaway's claim that it marks the start of the development is understandable. Although Ottaway acknowledged that the broad outline of the movement is sonata form, Shostakovich's deliberate subversion of familiar signposts is disorientating enough to provoke disagreement over the boundary between exposition and development. Most other commentators have drawn the boundary according to thematic rather than tonal premises (except in the case of Roseberry, as will be discussed), further adding to the potential for confusion. Nevertheless, as will become clear, there is a wide-ranging tonal scheme at work here, taking up the limited presence of treble A against bass C in the first subject group (cf. introduction, violas' two-note figure at 3 6, and the second phrase of A2 at 8) and making A now the main focus for the second subject, with C as the climax key (see Table 3.2).

Another disorientating feature of the second subject group is the unfocused, almost reticent, nature of its two main themes. Following the inital statement of the bassoon theme (B1), a new theme (B2) immediately takes its place (32). This initiates a sequence of three more themes, all of approximately the same length (10+10+11 bars) and rising to a peak of intensity before B1 returns in a series of three variations (see Table 3.2) that will bring the exposition to an end. Both B1 and B2 are too weakly articulated to play a major generative role in the second subject group, as will be seen; a stronger sense of motivic propulsion comes from the 'indirect' voices that play over the second and third variations of B1, and from the climax theme at 47, which will be discussed in due course.

31 – 36: *B1 and B2*

The soloistic presentation of B1 (see Example 3.10) prefigures Shostakovich's middle- and late-period predilection for sustained recitative-style arioso solos. Symphonic analogues are found in the wartime and Tenth symphonies, although recitatives also feature strongly in the quartets.

Both Roseberry and Sabinina note that B1 belongs to the 'personal' sphere, as opposed to the 'collective' clamour of A1. Sabinina also observes that the bassoon acquired a dual persona in Shostakovich's music, 'either melancholy or sarcastic', found in 'exhausted monologues … or in comic images'.[6] The 'comic' bassoon characterization does figure in the recapitulation, though in an extremely problematized manner, as will be seen. But the lyrical, soloistic characterization of B1 at 31 is not straightforward either: it lacks the recitative rhythms and contours of its antecedents, yet it is too metrically ambiguous at first to feel like the waltz

6 Sabinina, *Shostakovich-simfonist*, 104.

Table 3.2 Shostakovich IV/1: summary of second subject group

Figure	Theme	Tonal centre	Notes
31	B1	A	Solo bassoon. Meandering, metrically ambiguous at first. No dynamic shape: all level *p*. Oscillating harp figure recalls introductory figure (w).
32	B2	–	Viola and cello. Greater dynamic shaping: *p–ff–p*. Stronger waltz character. Harp figure absent.
33	(i)	–	First B2 outgrowth. Rises to new oscillating figure loosely based around C minor. Harp figure returns.
34	(ii)	–	Second B2 outgrowth. Oscillating figure varied. Falls to C in bass (see Example 3.13).
35	(iii)	–	Third B2 outgrowth. Oscillating figure further varied. Bass drops to A (see Example 3.13).
36	B1	B → A	First B1 variation. B1 in bass, below harp E pedal. Puppet and waltz figuration displaces B1 at [37].
38	–	–	Ghost waltz displaces B1.
40	B1	A	Second B1 variation. B1 below cuckoo-calls and more waltz figures. New theme (E♭ clarinet) leads to first stage of climax over C♯ tracing oscillating shape from [33]$^{8–9}$.
43	–	–	Beginning of 2nd stage of climax. Trumpet solos at 45 and ^{3}[47] marks approach to climax.
47	?	C	Climax of 2nd subject group based on oscillating figure from [33]$^{8–9}$.

48	B1	–	Third B1 variation, registrally compressed, below violent breakdown of climax.
51	A1	A	Development.

Example 3.10
a Shostakovich IV/1: [31] 1–23: B1

♪ = 108

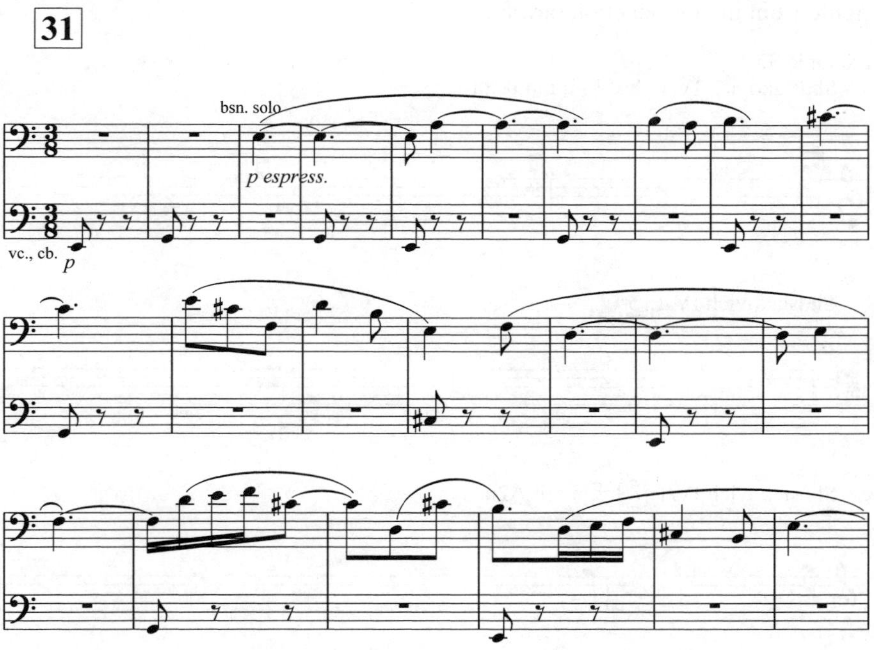

b Shostakovich IV/1: [32] 1–12: B2

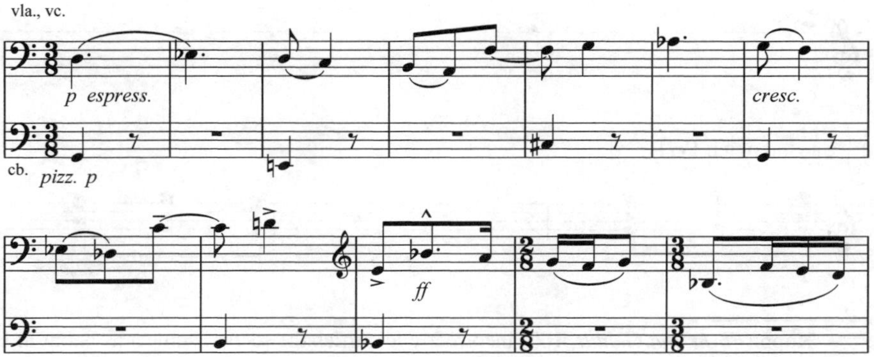

that might be expected; the absence of a stable pulse underpinning the theme, and the initial displacement of the second note from the expected downbeat to an upbeat ($\boxed{31}^{4}$), spoils its potential waltz character. It is also dynamically flat and shapeless, which adds to its numbed tone and lack of lyrical definition. An A major arpeggiation from E to e sits on top of what initially sounds like an E minor bass oscillation;[7] this subsequently turns out to be part of the diminished triad on C♯ underpinning B2 (see Example 3.12 below).

A harp figure divides B1 and B2: this echoes the A–G descent which has been such a salient feature of the first subject group, initially developed out of the introductory motif (I:a). Example 3.11 summarizes the development of this harp figure from the introduction onwards.

Example 3.11

a Shostakovich IV/1: bb. 1–3: motif I:a

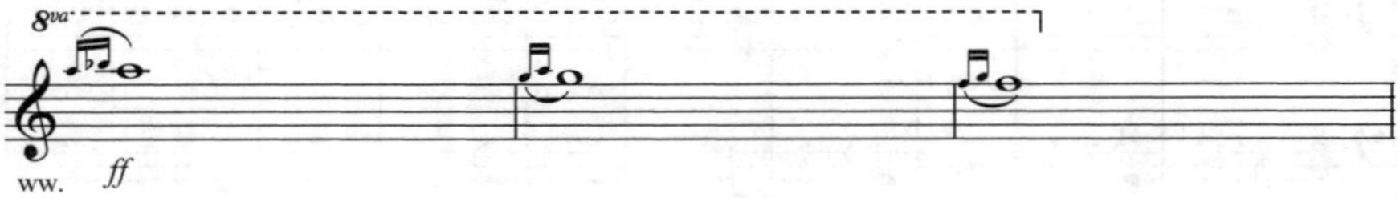

b Shostakovich IV/1: $\boxed{5}^{4}$

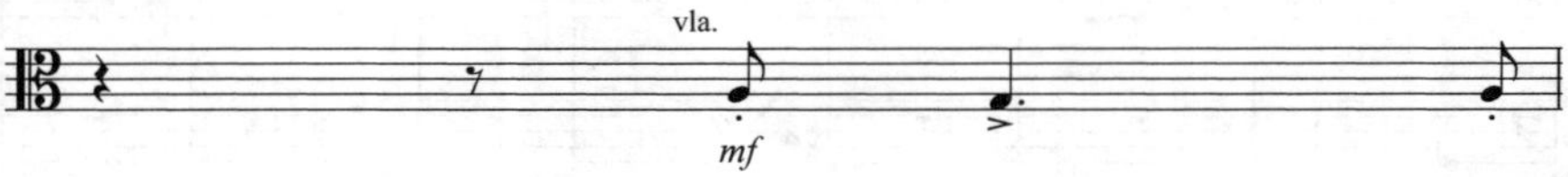

c Shostakovich IV/1: $\boxed{8}^{3-4}$: motif A2:a

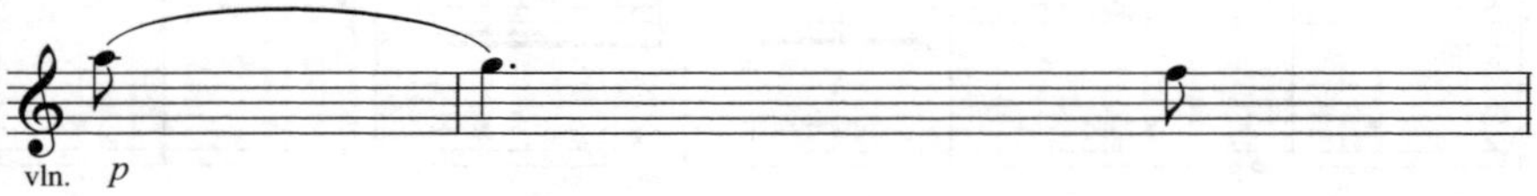

d Shostakovich IV/1: $\boxed{19}^{2-3}$

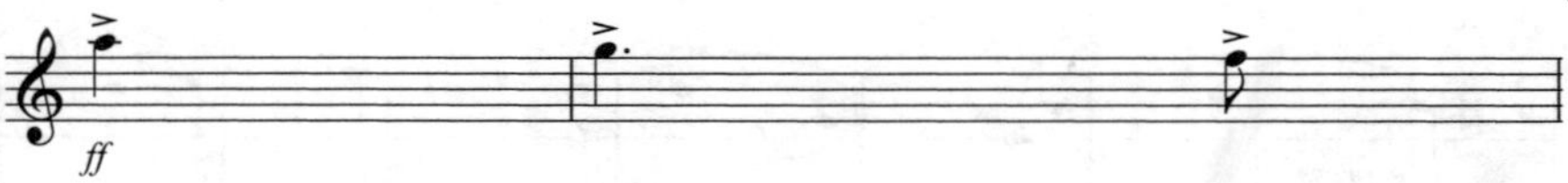

e Shostakovich IV/1: $^{3-1}\boxed{32}$

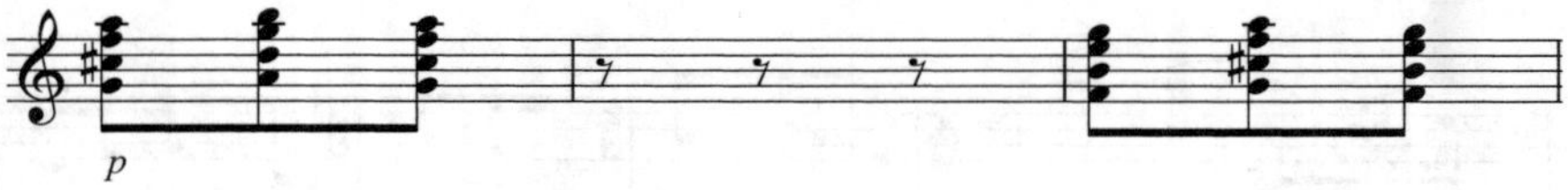

7 Kopp (*Form und Gehalt*, 160) incorrectly identifies the second subject as being in E minor.

B2 has a clearer metrical focus than B1, and its shorter phrases make it more waltz-like. It also develops more normally in terms of phrasing and dynamics, forming a clear arch shape moving from *p* to *ff* to *p*. It therefore has greater momentum than B1, which proves crucial for the ensuing sequence of peaks between [33] and [36]. B2 is less tonally defined than B1, however, moving around a diminished triad (D–F–A♭) and an F dominant seventh; its tonal orientation is thus broadly F, but the C♯ diminished bass clouds any real sense of a tonal centre (see Example 3.12).

The sequence of extensions from B2 begins at [33] with the first ascent to e♭^{2}: the oscillating figure at its apex at [33]^9 loses its distinctive shape with each subsequent ascent. The second continues to f^2 at bar 317 before rising once again to e♭^{2} at [35]. Although these three peaks form a clear sequence of rising intensity, the extent to which the initial theme is varied prevents the sequence from sounding like either a development of B2 or a new theme. Even the waltz figuration receives little attention here: apart from growing out of the B2 statement, the whole section between [33] and [36] sounds like a new departure, albeit one which soon subsides. As the recapitulation will show, this section is an extension of B1 and B2, and the oscillating 'apex' figure will assume greater significance not only there but also at the climax of the second subject group at [47].

Example 12 shows that, like B1 and B2, the themes between [33] and [36] outline a series of triads. The bass constantly gravitates towards C: the first melodic peak occurs over a strong bass pull to A minor (see bars 308–9: V^7–$i^6{}_3$); the second occurs over another dominant pull to C (bars 317–19), while the third is prolonged by the continuation of the ascending octatonic to chromatic scale from bar 317, ending with a bass A/treble A♭ below a treble G major triad at bar 329 before returning to C minor. Shostakovich thus signposts this oscillating figure as one associated with the tensions of cadential drive in a way that will soon bear fruit.

[36] – [48]: *Variation and Climax*

The first of the three B1 variations now begins at [36], still presented in the bass and retaining its association with the harp, here a pedal-point over the theme. B1 itself remains more or less intact in each of the three variations; only its presentation changes according to what is placed above it. Here, only the first half of B1 is stated, outlining a B rather than an A major arpeggio (from F♯^{1} to F♯), though the harp's descent from e^2 to c♯^{2} at [36]$^{7–8}$ suggests that A is still a force here. In fact, the B arpeggio has a secondary dominant function, continuing to E and so back to A at [40] (see Example 3.13). This gives a very broad harmonic focus to what otherwise appears to be a loosely constructed fantasy on waltz and puppet-like fragments.

It is only at [37] that the waltz intonations are revived, starting with a tiny fragment at [37]$^{3–5}$ over which the puppet-like piccolo figuration plays, suspending

Example 3.12
Shostakovich IV/1: 31 – 36: linear summary of B1 and B2

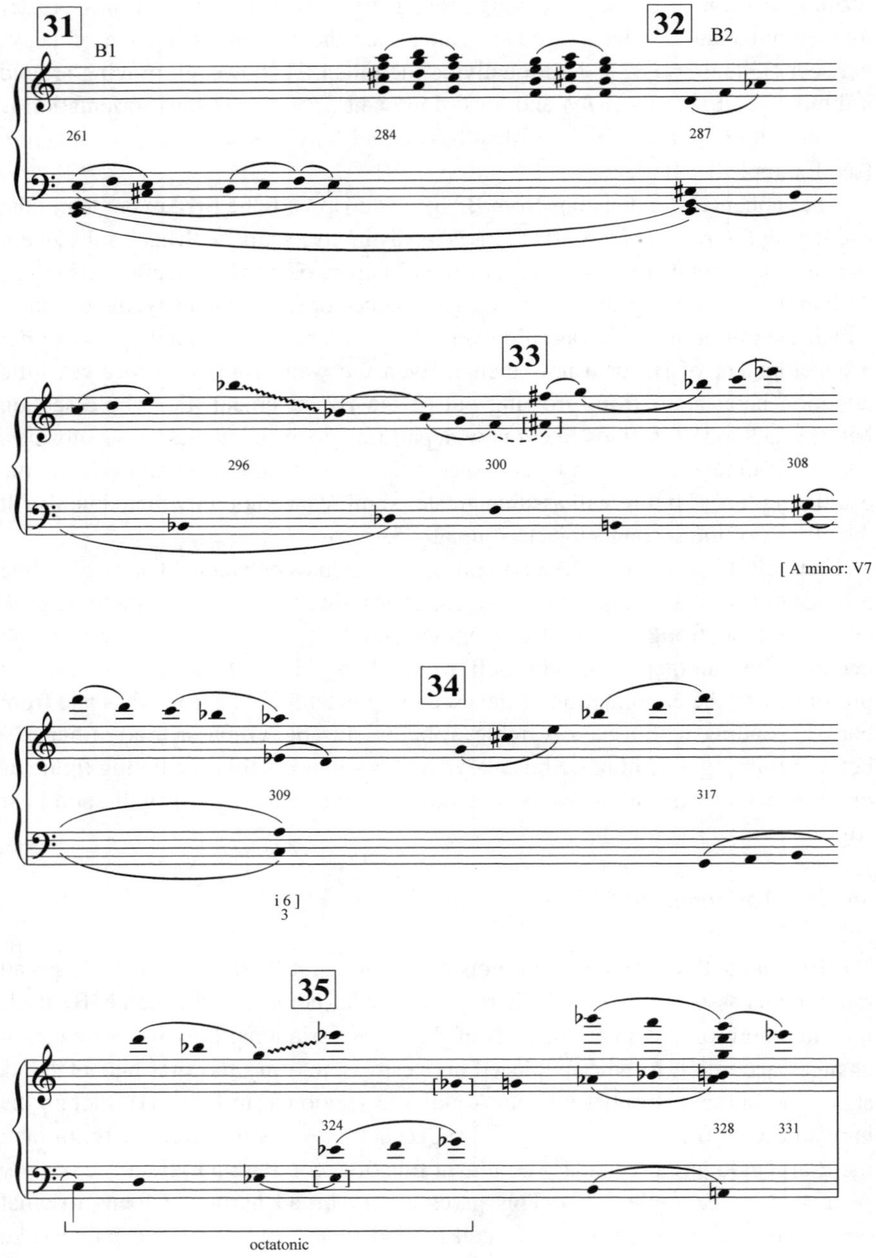

Example 3.13
Shostakovich IV/1: 36 – 40 linear and harmonic summary

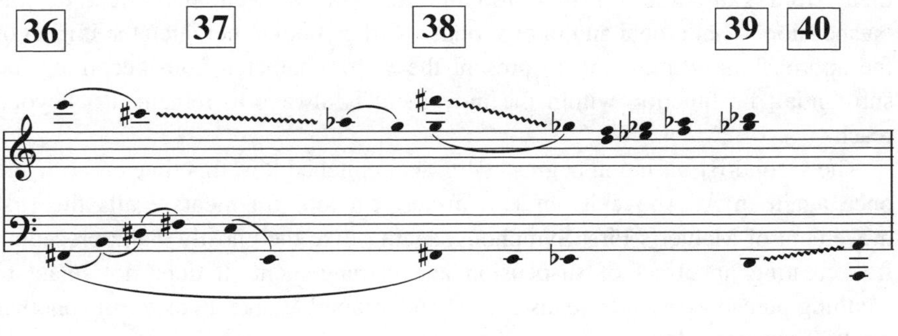

further progress of B1 (see Example 3.14), and continuing through to 41^{6}, having been dropped since their last appearance between 27^{6} and 29. Once again, 'normal' thematic progress is thwarted, though here in a very different manner from the immobilizing of A1 in its opening statement. The 'real' theme (B1), now beginning the first of its three variations, is presented as a background to musical characters that seem to come from 'outside' the symphonic framework and assume foreground prominence.

A ghostly waltz (see Example 3.15) picks up the cue at 38, further delaying the continuation of B1; its chromatic melodic contour and initial tritonal bass, combined with its muted string colouring, give it a shimmering, spectral quality. The waltz fades out rather than coming to a natural end; there is no cadence or

Example 3.14
Shostakovich IV/1: 37$^{3–5}$

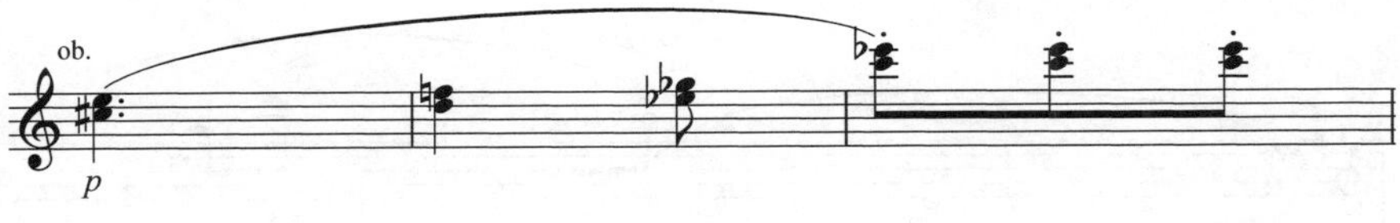

Example 3.15
Shostakovich IV/1: 38$^{1–6}$

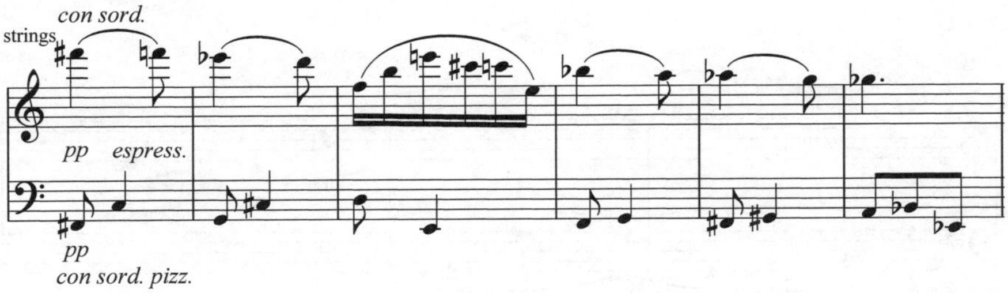

clear phrase ending. Hence the first, long-awaited 'real' waltz sounds distinctly unreal, which estranges the apparently 'positive' waltz intonations and prevents them from gaining too firm a footing. As will be seen, the effect of this 'suspension' – both tonal and intonational – will be both to heighten the impact of the approaching climax and to present the waltz character from becoming too substantial; its function within the movement is always to remain just beyond reach.

The second B1 variation begins at 40, again pitched low, this time on horn and once again in A. Above it, an E♭ clarinet 'cuckoo' fragment recalls the first movement of Mahler's First Symphony, again – like the ghostly waltz preceding it – creating an effect of suspension and estrangement. It does not relate to anything preceding it, but sounds remote and intangible, like a voice from another world (Example 3.16).

Example 3.16

a Shostakovich IV/1: 40$^{3\text{–}5}$

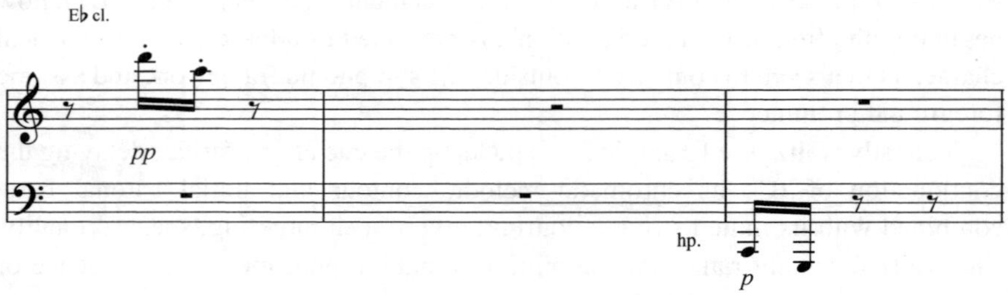

b Mahler I/1: 13$^{2\text{–}6}$

Etwas zurückhaltend

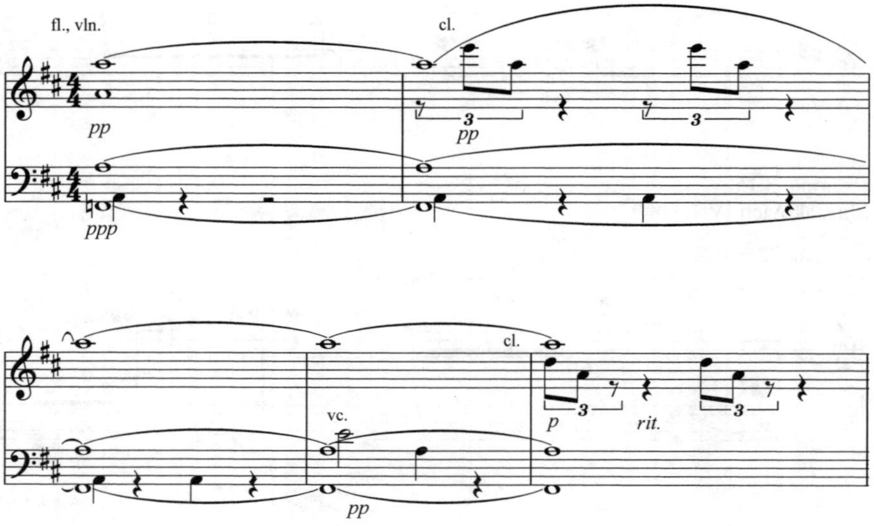

The 'cuckoo' passage plays over a fleeting waltz fragment rather than a true theme, though the violins' five-bar iambic rhythm at [41] prefaces and reinforces the two-bar bassoon fragment. This will be the last appearance of waltz intonations until late in the development, where they will receive more complete, but scarcely less complex, treatment. Their role in the exposition has been enigmatic, though they are implicitly connected with the second subject group by virtue of their shared triple metre and relatively passive tone. The dramatization of the A1/A2 duple/triple conflict has also played a part in setting up a gentler, triple-metre intonational sphere in opposition to the aggressive, encroaching march theme: hence anything which comes within the orbit of the triple-metre sphere is coloured by its counter-aggressive, and in that sense 'positive' dramaturgical role. Nonetheless, the triple-metre sphere is a weak one, characterised by incompleteness, instability and unreality. The strongest triple-time intonations are the fleeting waltz fragments of the transition section ([27]^{6} – [29]) and second subject group ([37] – [42]); but all sound other-worldly and nostalgic owing to their fragmentary nature and lack of harmonic definition. They refer outside the basic dramaturgy of the exposition to a realm that cannot find a place within its boundaries. Their function is to point to that realm and draw attention to its intangibility and remoteness, and in so doing to highlight the fact that no strong counter-weight to A1 has yet emerged. The waltz intonations refer to the existence of a possible 'positive other' but the manner of their presentation simultaneously negates that possibility. In terms of Formalist theory, they can be seen as 'free motifs': motifs not bound to the central *fabula*, but an important element in a work's *syuzhet*.[8] As will be seen in the development, that possibility is explored to highly ambivalent effect, and in the recapitulation the waltz intonations reappear in their original disembodied state. Ultimately, they do not lead anywhere in the first movement, though, as will be seen, the finale picks up the pieces and works them into something more substantial. The role of the waltz intonations within the first movement is crucial, if only in a negative sense: they offer something that they cannot themselves fulfil, yet at the same time they hold seeds of fulfilment. That, too, is a vital part of the first movement's *syuzhet*: the possibility of renewal is both referred to and denied. Its full implications will become apparent only in the recapitulation, when not only are the waltz intonations left hanging in the air, but the theme from the main exposition climax at [47] – having partially evolved throughout the exposition – is given full voice in a poignant cor anglais solo between [96] and [99].

The climax theme itself is initially motivated by the sinuous E♭ clarinet line that lies on top of the waltzy bassoon-and-strings fragment at [41]. The cuckoo-call at ^{1}[41] develops into a new 'ascent' similar to those between [33] and [36] and has clear motivic links with the first of those themes, as shown in Example 3.17

8 The idea of 'bound' and 'free' motifs in literature was Tomashevsky's; see Chapter Two, 56–7.

Example 3.17

a Shostakovich IV/1: $\boxed{42}^{4-5}$

♪ = 138

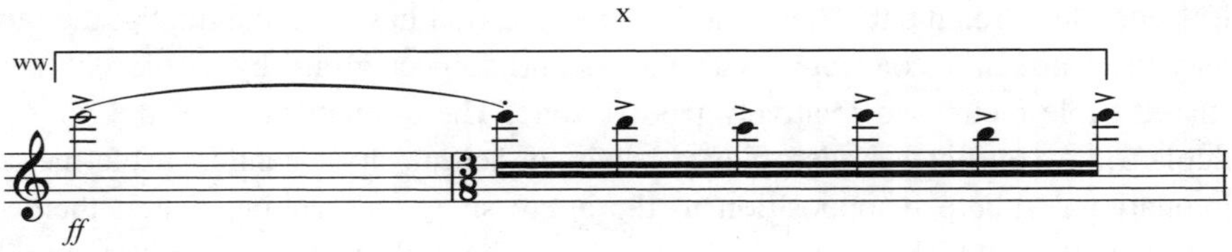

b Shostakovich IV/1: $\boxed{33}^{6-9}$

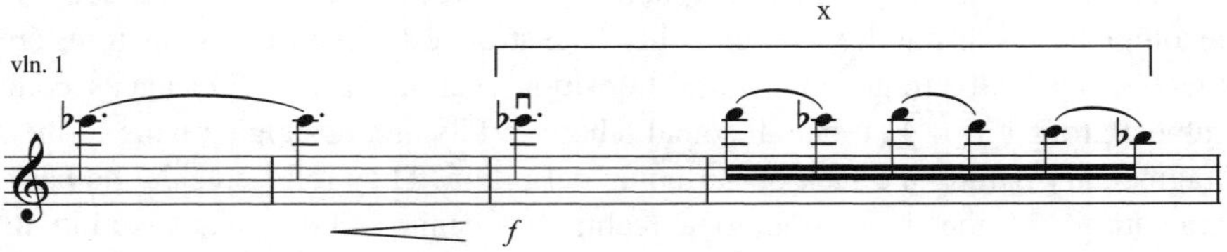

(related motifs are bracketed and labelled x). Like those earlier themes, the clarinet theme beginning at $\boxed{41}^{4}$ functions as the approach to a climax, at first to a wind unison ($\boxed{42}^{4}$) which functions as a 'plateau' stage in the approach to the real climax at $\boxed{47}$. This unison theme[9] is a clear variant of the original 'apex' motif of $\boxed{33}^{8-10}$ and, as with that earlier sequence, the apex occurs *en route* to a bass goal, here less balanced on the cusp of that goal than poised halfway through a bass descent from E to A, as shown in Example 3.18. Compared with the cadential tensions which frame the sequence of 'apex' themes between $\boxed{33}$ and $\boxed{36}$ (see Example 3.12 above), the climactic unison at $\boxed{42}^{4}$ is harmonically weak, pulling away from the stronger D major at $\boxed{42}$ and orbiting around a C♯ bass with no clear subsequent tonal orientation until the 'real' C $^{6}_{4}$ climax at $\boxed{47}$. The entry of the first climax 'herald' theme on solo trumpet at $\boxed{45}^{2}$, with the squeezed horn dissonances from the introduction (see Example 3.19a), is cut off on a C minor-ish cluster ($^{1}\boxed{46}$; not shown in Example 3.18); the second 'herald' theme (trumpet solo, $^{3}\boxed{47}$) leads straight into the main climax.

The climax theme itself derives from the oscillating 'apex' theme from $\boxed{33}^{8-10}$, now given full voice and echoed throughout the orchestra. The impact of this climax is enormous: it is the only truly convincing climax of the exposition, both properly prepared and given adequate time to subside.[10] What makes it particularly unusual is that none of the four exposition themes (A1, A2, B1, B2) are used for

9 The Sikorski score indicates ♩ = 138 at $\boxed{42}^{4}$; both old and new collected works scores have ♪ = 138, which makes more sense in view of the ♪ = ♪ marking in the following bar.

10 Despite the consistency of the metronome marking of ♪ = 60 at $\boxed{47}$ in all published editions and the autograph manuscript of the piano reduction, very few conductors observe this dramatic drop from 138 to 60; the closest I have heard is Rostropovich's 1992 Teldec recording, which hovers between 60 and 72 (Teldec 0630–17046-2).

Example 3.18
Shostakovich IV/1: 40–51: linear summary

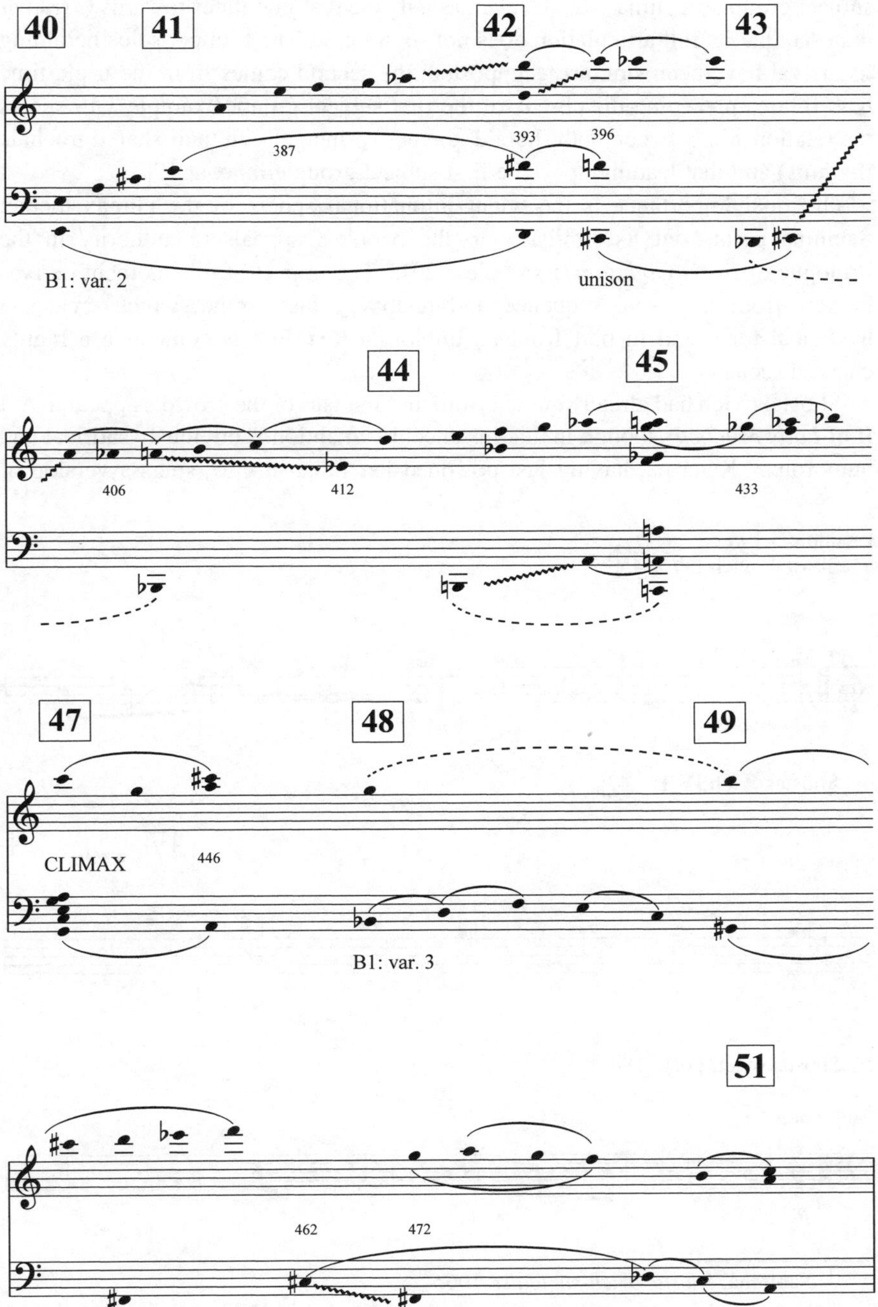

this moment; in fact, the climax theme as it appears here has never been heard before. Nevertheless, it has been so carefully signposted throughout the second subject group as a climax theme, even as a theme that gravitates towards C (rather than A), that its full articulation does not sound new. The trumpet solos heralding its arrival have been similarly signposted: the second comes from the triple-time bass figures preceding the climax of the first subject group. Example 3.19 shows the relationship between both 'herald' themes (principally in their shared trochaic rhythms) and that leading up to the first subject group climax at $\boxed{19}$.

Of equal importance is the wider intonational sphere of the climax theme: Sabinina points out its similarity to the people's appeals to authority in the Prologue of *Boris Godunov* (Example 3.20).[11] The impact of this moment derives in part from its rising sequence and relatively fast tempo, which creates a hysterical tone, and in part from its imploring text and its context in a highly charged scene.

Shostakovich had already quoted from the first part of the crowd's appeal in Act II of *Lady Macbeth*, though in that instance the intention is obviously satirical and humorous.[12] Katerina, having just poisoned her father-in-law, sings a version of

Example 3.19

a Shostakovich IV/1: $\boxed{45}^{2-5}$

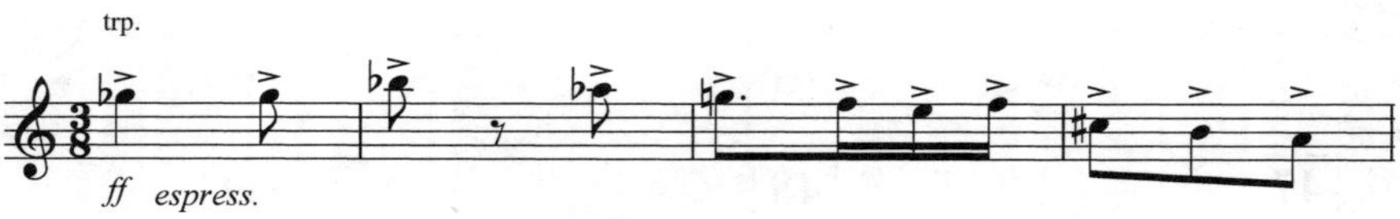

b Shostakovich IV/1: $^{3}\boxed{47}$

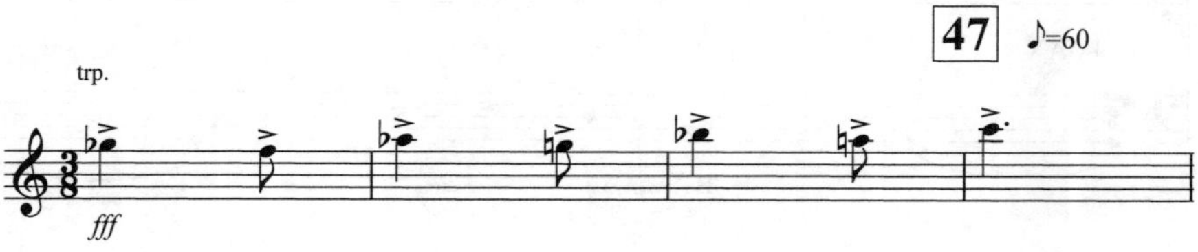

c Shostakovich IV/1: $\boxed{18}^{1-4}$

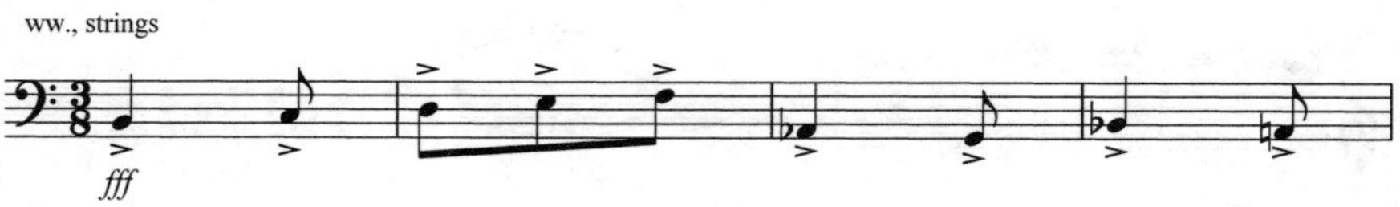

11 Sabinina, *Shostakovich-simfonist*, 106.

12 See David Fanning, 'Leitmotif in Lady Macbeth', in Fanning, ed., *Shostakovich Studies*, 148.

Example 3.20
Musorgsky: *Boris Godunov*, Prologue: 8$^{1-4}$

Poco animando

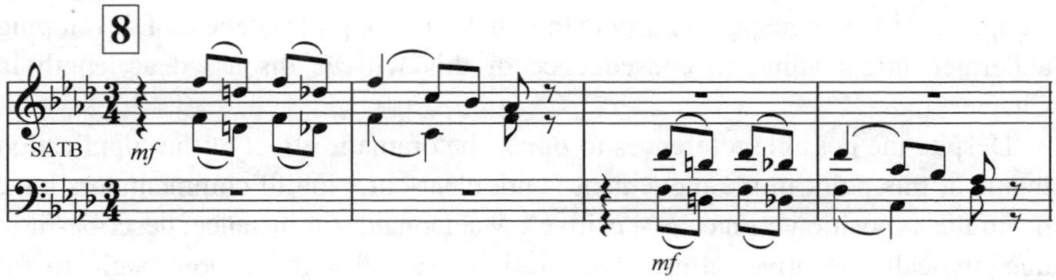

'Otyets nash! Ti kormilyets, Boyarini, smiliusya!' [Our father! You are our providers, Boyars, have mercy on us!]

Musorgsky's lament over his corpse for the benefit of the priest and the servants, considerably speeded up and in a high register (Example 3.21). This usage does indicate not only the unsurprising fact that Musorgsky's Prologue was very well known to Shostakovich (he was to orchestrate the whole opera in 1940), but also that it was familiar enough to his audience to work as satire in *Lady Macbeth*. It is reasonable, then, to suppose that the climax theme (henceforward the 'supplication' theme) of the Fourth Symphony's first movement may have been intended to be recognized as an allusion to Musorgsky's, and thus to communicate

Example 3.21
a Shostakovich *Lady Macbeth*, Act II, scene 4: 275$^{1-5}$

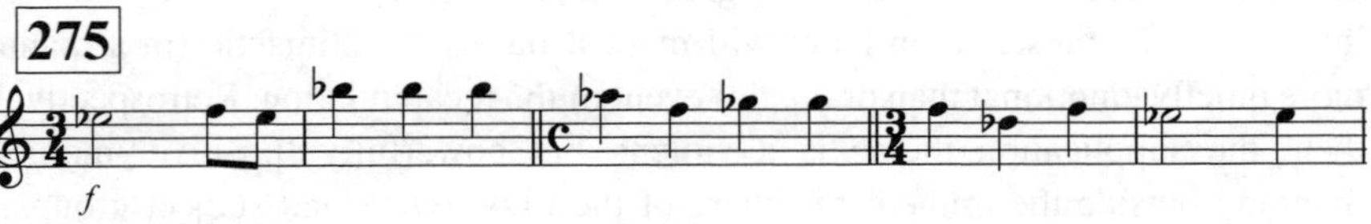

'Akh, Boris Timofeyevich, zachem tï ot nas ushël?' [Ah, Boris Timofeyevich, why have you left us?]

b Musorgsky: *Boris Godunov*, Prologue: 5$^{1-7}$

♩= 92

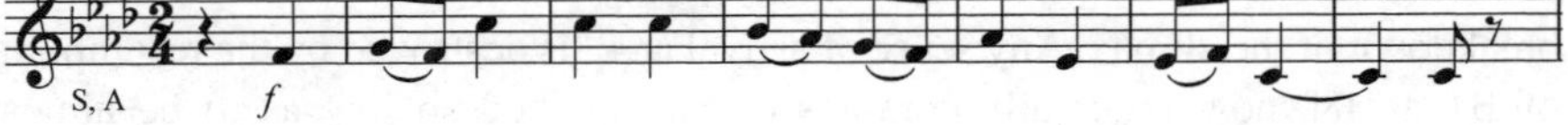

'Na kogo tï nas pokidayesh, otyets nash!' [Father, why forsake us?]

a similar supplicatory meaning to the exposition climax. That supposition does, of course, open up the possibility of 'reading' the Fourth Symphony as political protest: a process fraught with danger and, as already discussed, now in severe disrepute. As the symphony progresses, however, other equally suggestive signposts will emerge, particularly in the finale. The appropriateness of developing a hermeneutic reading in consequence of this will be discussed at length in Chapter 5.

Despite the possible references to *Boris*, the dramatic effect of the supplication theme at this point in the movement is not clear-cut. Not all commentators have heard the exposition climax as 'positive'; MacDonald, for instance, describes it in unequivocally negative terms: 'The music's skeletal textures now begin to fill rapidly, tension rises, and the dreaded thing finally happens: the secret police arrive, audibly climbing the stairs (figures 46-7) and bursting in through the door on a triumphant crescendo.'[13] Leaving aside the fact that such a literal interpretation of musical events is clearly a matter best left to the individual listener's own inclinations; it is interesting that MacDonald hears the 'supplication' climax as entirely negative. Certainly, the 'supplication' theme has yet to acquire the poignancy it achieves in the recapitulation, and my own interpretation of it is shaped retrospectively by that final presentation. At [47], the supplication theme registers chiefly as a massive climax, made all the more dramatic by the unsatisfying nature of the preceding climaxes, none of which have been so motivically prepared as this one has, nor have had so prolonged both a build-up and time to subside. Poised on a C $^{6}{}_{4}$, memorably sequential and diatonic, the 'supplication' climax is the only musical event that can rival A1 for clarity and impact. Its arrival has been signposted throughout the exposition in a process of near-subliminal subtlety that will be taken still further in the recapitulation. At that point, its impact will prove to be greater than that of A1, and the emotional intensity of its presentation there will mark it out as the climactic (in a manner more quietly emotional than dramatic) event of the recapitulation. Retrospectively, then, the supplication theme is a violent, but powerfully 'positive' moment. Standing outside the immediate sphere of the first and second subject groups, it may even be heard as an 'authorial voice': the theme which, despite the aggressive authority of A1, claims centre stage in both exposition and recapitulation, and yet which is not heard in its entirety – with all its signposts intact – until the recapitulation.

[48] – [51]: *Variation 3: Breakdown*

The cuckoo-calls from [40] are now transformed into jagged ninths in a violent breakdown of the climax. Any sense of arrival at [47] is destroyed by the resumption of B1 at [48], now registrally compressed and pitched so low as to be almost

13 MacDonald, *The New Shostakovich*, 112.

indistinct. Within this anarchic frenzy of self-destruction, there is nevertheless some semblance of continuity in terms of the C/A relationship: the G bass shudders violently back to A (^{1}48), and the bass goal is once again A at the start of the development at 51. Momentum is sustained through violence rather than being harmonically or motivically generated, and the clearest sense that the exposition is nearing its end comes only four bars before 51 – the start of the development – when a *ritenuto* through a repeated turn figure signals approaching closure.

On one level, such a violent reaction to the climactic supplication theme feels musically justified. At 47, it does not have the sequential (and hence expressive) force that it acquires in the recapitulation: here it is merely a three-bar motif repeated three times which does not 'end' but simply stops. The bass move to A coincides with the resumption of B1 in its third variation, as though trying to restore order and re-assert the viability of the second subject, but falling into chaos instead, with B1 almost unrecognizable. Interpretations of this section are predictably varied: MacDonald, continuing his theme of nocturnal arrest, has the NKVD moving 'grimly through the darkened apartment', flashing their torches (the transformed cuckoo-calls) around. His interpretation of the re-appearance of B1 at this point is that it is a 'positive' theme used in a sinister manner, as with Orwell's use of 'Oranges and Lemons' in the arrest scene in *Nineteen Eighty-Four*.[14] Sabinina has a quite different view. She describes the supplication theme's origins in *Boris*, but refers not to the ironic text that accompanies the oscillating motif in the Prologue, but to that of the starving crowd in the St Basil's scene in Act II, in which the motif does not actually figure.[15] The supplication theme sung by the peasant chorus is ambivalent from the start: it is a forced plea to authority given genuine pathos and power by its subtext: hungry peasants bullied by police and forced to pay homage to a murderous usurper. That association is already powerfully suggestive in the context of a symphony written as Stalin's personality cult was reaching major proportions. The fact that it is possible to hear the climax as negative underlines the processes of reversal at work in the Fourth Symphony: what sounds too obviously positive could prove to be a mask. An allusion as pointed and violent as this one, however, comes as a major release: a 'positive' event musically speaking but 'negative' in its anger.

14 Ibid., 113.

15 In fact, the idea of forced supplication was Musorgsky's creation; the crowd in Pushkin's poem are indifferent, but cynically (and probably far more realistically) compliant. One eyewitness source actually describes the events leading up to Boris's accepting the throne thus: 'L. Boris Pheodorowich … was most unwilling to receive the kingdome, but the people would make no other choice, nor have any other'. Quoted in Aleksandr Pushkin, *Boris Godunov*, trans. Philip L. Barbour, Westport, Connecticut: Greenwood Press, 1953, 171. The idea that it was the crowd who persuaded Boris to become Tsar seems to have become a popular myth, which Pushkin then challenged with his portrait of a murderous Boris and an indifferent populace. Musorgsky's version of Pushkin's poem goes a step further in overtly presenting the crowd as oppressed.

Sabinina then interprets the second subject (B1) as under attack but resolutely holding its ground: 'threateningly … the transformed second theme rises up on two tubas, fighting against the convulsive stabs of the orchestra.'[16] Whether the transformation of B1 denotes a 'positive' or 'negative' character is open to different interpretations. But the overall nature of this section – its lack of motivic or harmonic momentum, the suppressed characterization of a weakly articulated lyrical theme, the grotesquely inflated cuckoo-calls – surely signifies negativity, violence, destruction and the negation of fulfilment.

Development

The sectional divisions given in Table 3.3 are identical to Sabinina's, with the exception of her marking section 3 at [72] and my marking it at [71]. Although sections 2 and 3 run into each other, [71] is the point at which all the fugal entries are completed and a new, A1-derived theme (see Example 3.30 below) begins in the bass; while [72] marks a change of texture, moving from the strings-only fugue to the addition of wind and horns, its main theme has already begun at [71], and there is no change in rhythm to reinforce the textural change.

All published analyses agree broadly on the episodic nature of the development. It is clearly not a 'working-out' of thematic material in the conventional sense (that process has taken place in the exposition); nor does it necessarily subject the themes to transformation which invites a hermeneutic response (that will come in the recapitulation). And it is certainly not driven by the process of carefully directed modulation characteristic of the Classical-Romantic sonata development. For these reasons, the development section seems at first glance strangely superfluous to the dramaturgy of the first movement. It merely expands and further transforms both the main themes of both first and second subject groups (with the exception of B2, for reasons which will become apparent

Table 3.3 Shostakovich IV/1: [51] – [90]: summary of development section

Figure	Episode
51	1 (polka)
63	2 (fugato)
71	3 (march–climax)
80	4 (waltz I)
84	5 (waltz II)
90	6 (retransition)

16 Sabinina, *Shostakovich-simfonist*, 106.

in the recapitulation) without adding anything much to the processual aspects of the movement's dramaturgy. As will be seen, however, the development is crucial in its appropriation of the dance intonations of the exposition, giving them substance and definition to extremely ambivalent effect: this alone is arguably as important a part of the movement's dramaturgy as anything in the exposition. It also creates a necessary temporal distance between the 'supplication' theme at 47 and its powerful reincarnation in the recapitulation, since there is no reference to it at all in the development. In short, the development section is essential if the recapitulation is to have the necessary impact; the series of character variations makes the return to gravitas and drama in the recapitulation an unpredictable and shattering event.

Section 1: 51 – 63*: A1 and B1 as Polka*

A radical change of tone marks the start of the development: the first subject is cast as a lightweight polka for wind only.[17] Its original pungency is here smoothed over: the intervallic structure is altered so that the prominent B–F tritone of the first bar becomes a perfect fifth from e♭1 to b♭1 (see Example 3.22). At 53, a variant of B1 features in the bass, to which piccolo and E♭ clarinet respond with *Petrushka*-like scales and appoggiaturas (Example 3.22c). The wind-only scoring is very light, and the menacing tonic bass which characterized A1 is absent, counterpoint having replaced the heavy vertical texture of the opening. However, the jovial tone of the

Example 3.22
a Shostakovich IV/1: 1$^{1–3}$: A1

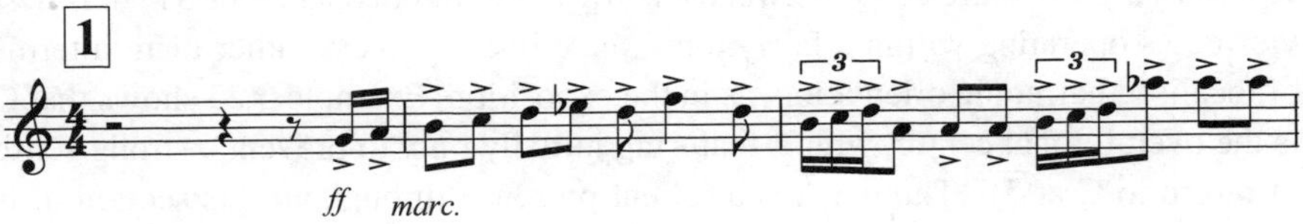

b Shostakovich IV/1: 51$^{1–4}$

♪ = 108

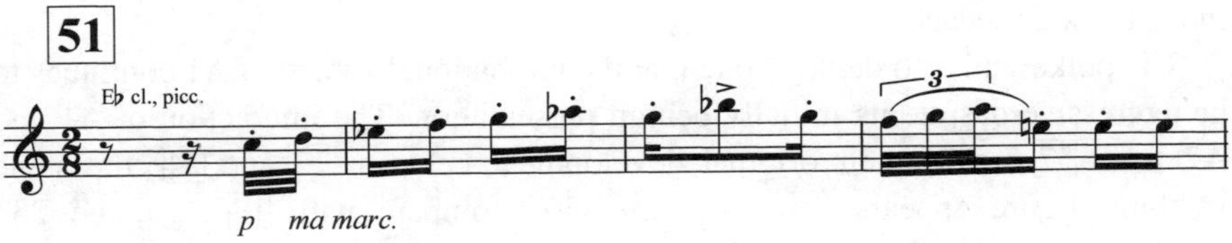

17 Viktor Bobrovskiy compared Shostakovich's adoption of thematic transformation here to Berlioz's in his *Symphonie fantastique*. See 'Posle pervogo ispolneniya Chetvërtoy' [After the first performance of the Fourth], 263.

c Shostakovich IV/1: 53–54

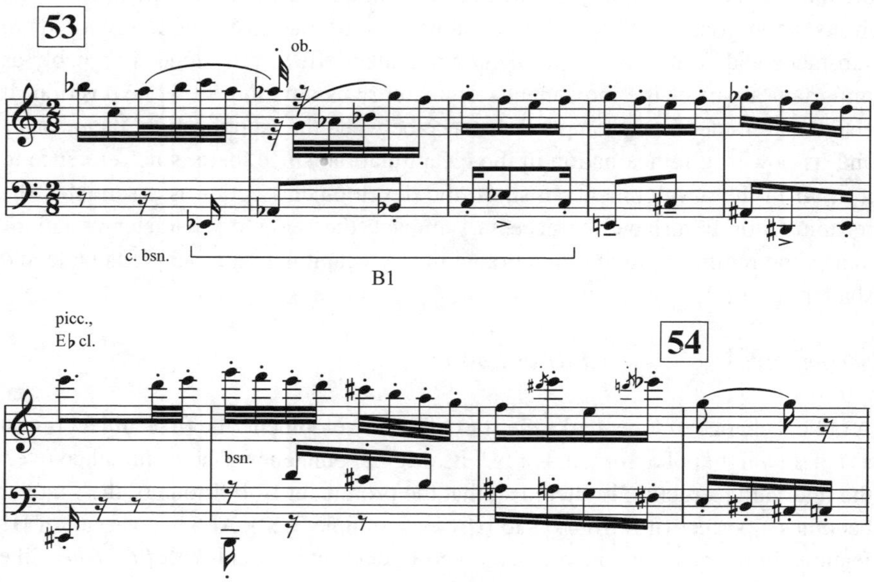

polka is slightly offset by the suspension of any strong tonal centre of gravity. Roseberry and Longman both account for the chilly tone of the first part (up to 53) by reading it as a bitonal C and A minor.[18] This is perhaps too neat an explanation: though there is a weak, but persistent, C/A axis throughout the section (continuing that of the exposition, which has seen C and A paired in the introduction, in the violas' two-note figure at ^{3}6, between 8 and 10, and implied again in B1), it is best viewed as operating within a fairly long-range linear process rather than in terms of localised harmonic orientation, as in the exposition. Example 3.23 shows that C is the overall tonal centre, with A featuring initially only to prevent a strong sense of return to C at 51. Though A is a salient presence throughout this section, it is not mooted as a tonal alternative to C, but rather, as in the earlier instances of C/A ambiguity at 5 and at the first subject climax between 22 and 23, functions as an added sixth. The tonal centre is therefore a weakened C, with moments of relative clarity, most notably in the bass between 60 and 61 when A1 regains its original intensity and menace.

The polka will also demonstrate that the intonational sphere of A1 continues to be aggressive despite its initially benign presentation. The interaction of A1 and A2 from 57 recalls their original development between 13 and 24: the same stabbing figure appears here as there (56: compare with 13^{3}, 15 and 23) heralding, as at 13^{3}, the onset of more aggressive development. As at ^{2}5, F minor

18 See Roseberry, *Ideology*, 411, Longman, *Expression and Structure*, 12.

Example 3.23
Shostakovich IV/1: [51] – [63]: linear and motivic summary

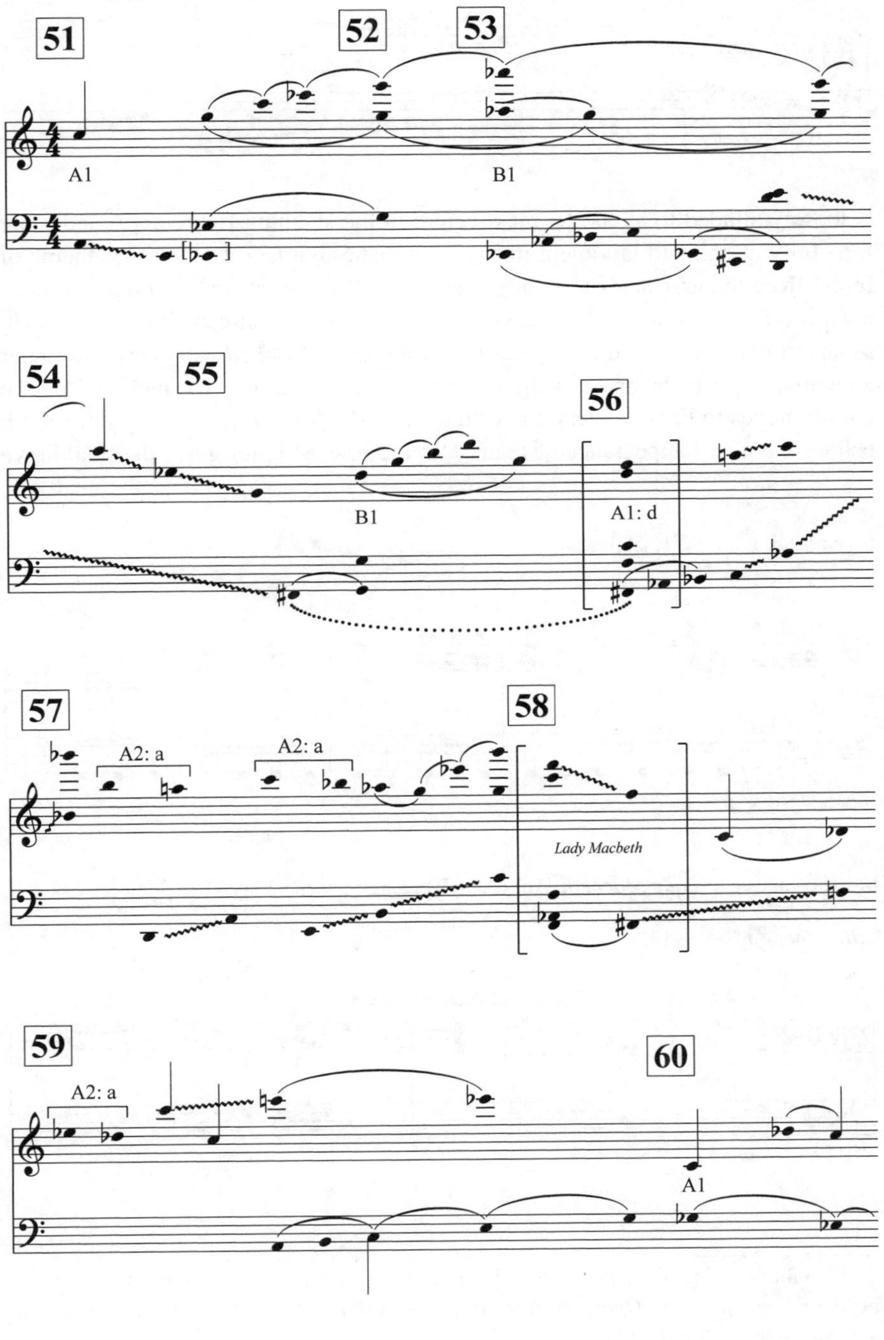

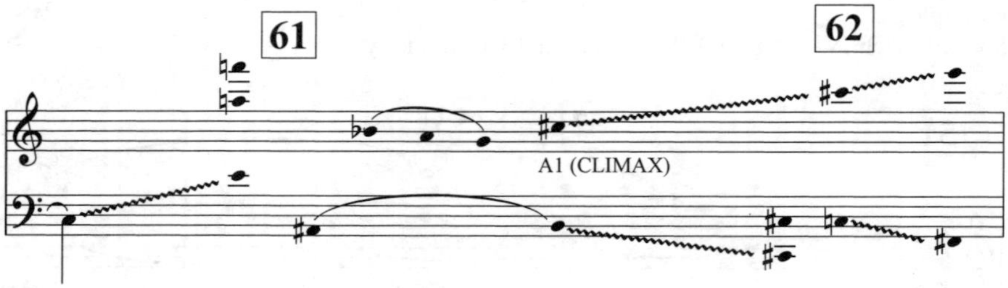

is loosely alluded to as the 'climax' centre in the stabbing figure at 56 and more forcefully at 58, with a violent interjection that Sabinina relates to the 'theme of force' from the entr'actes to scenes 3 and 7 of *Lady Macbeth*.[19] Though she does not provide an example, her reference to the 'coarse can-can' intonation at 58 seems to indicate not a direct quotation of the *Lady Macbeth* passages, but rather a paraphrase of their tone of vulgarity overlaid with menace (Example 3.24). The bass F moves to F♯ at the very end of the *Lady Macbeth* allusions (58^{5}); this both echoes the initial appearance of F♯ at 56 in the bass and prefigures the final move

Example 3.24
a Shostakovich IV/1: 58$^{1–5}$

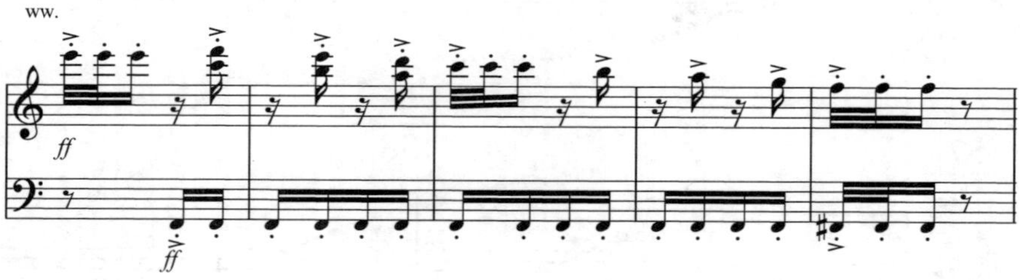

b Shostakovich: *Lady Macbeth*, Act I, entr'act acte to scene 3: 113$^{1–2}$

Allegro con brio ♩ = 132

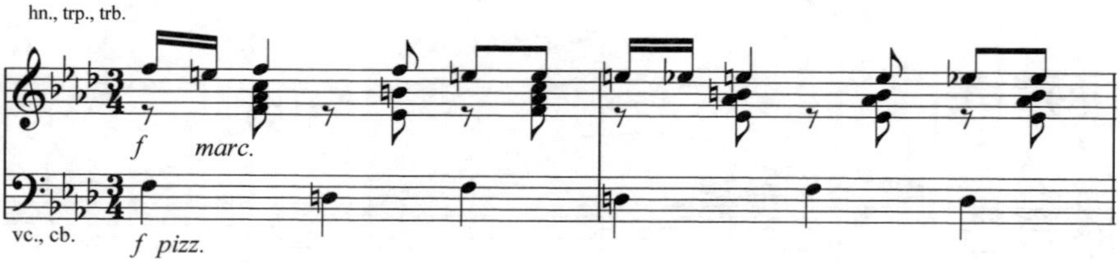

19 Sabinina is not referring here to the 'theme of force' as designated by Ekhart Kröplin in *Frühe sowjetische Oper*, Berlin: Henschelverlag, 1985, 220–21. See Sabinina, *Shostakovich-simfonist*, 106.

to F♯ at the end of the polka section. F♯ is not a functional pitch centre in the same way as is F or C; it is intended only to clash with the treble F, and so to heighten the violent tone.

With the third variant of A1 at 59^{4}, the tone becomes more menacing. As with the polka variant at 51, a perfect fifth (C–G) initially replaces the first tritone, though the second (B–E♭) is retained; the fourth variant, which forms the climactic point of the section, sharpens the tonic, omitting the upbeat and leaning on the C♯, opposing the C of the preceding entry (Example 3.25). This final variant brings the polka to breaking-point over a diminished-feeling C♯–G movement (from 61: see Example 3.23 above): it self-destructs with the transformed cuckoo-call motif which signalled the demise of the exposition between 48 and 51.

Section 2 63 – 71 : *Fugato*

This whirlwind fugato sustains a massive accumulation of energy, stretching over some 200 bars in approximately two and a half minutes. Once again, the first subject is the blueprint for the new theme, though at almost four times the speed and subjected to severe registral compression, it is barely recognizable. Example 3.26 illustrates the relationship between A1 and the fugato subject. The subject itself is 20 bars long; it comprises the initial A1-derived phrase (F:a), a related answering phrase (F:b), an inversion of (F:a) in a three-bar sequence (F:c) and, to round off, a reiteration of F:a (Example 3.27a). None of the four fugal entries proceeds with exactly the same intervallic structure, though they are similar enough, particularly for the first 12 bars, to give the impression of exact correspondence. The first major difference (shown in Example 27b) comes with the second entry, which avoids the G♭ that should come with the initial diminished fifth. Though the second tritone remains intact, the diminished fourth between A♭ and E at the start of the second bar of the fugato subject here becomes a minor

Example 3.25
a Shostakovich IV/1: 59^{4} – 60

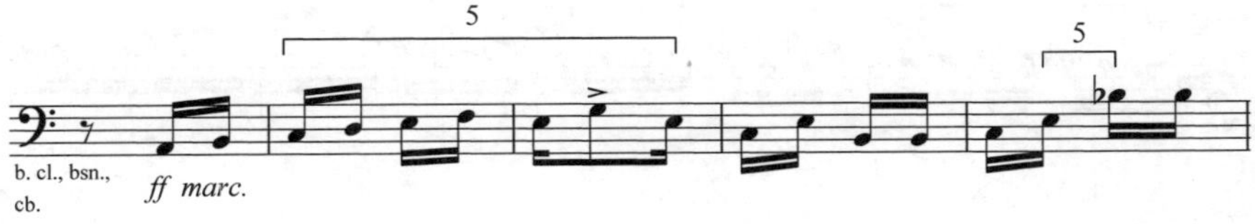

b Shostakovich IV/1: 61$^{2–6}$

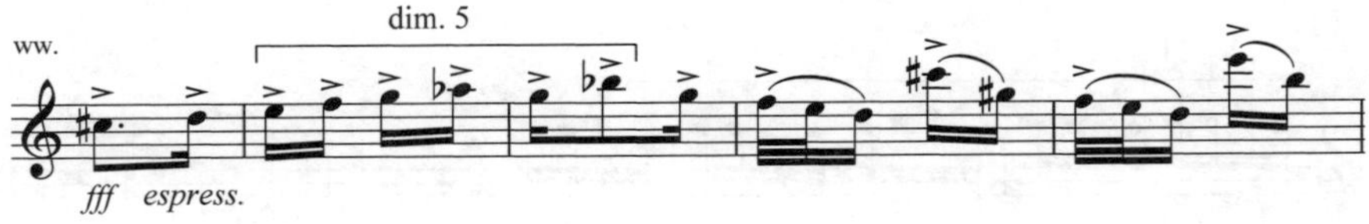

Example 3.26
a Shostakovich IV/1: [1]$^{1-3}$

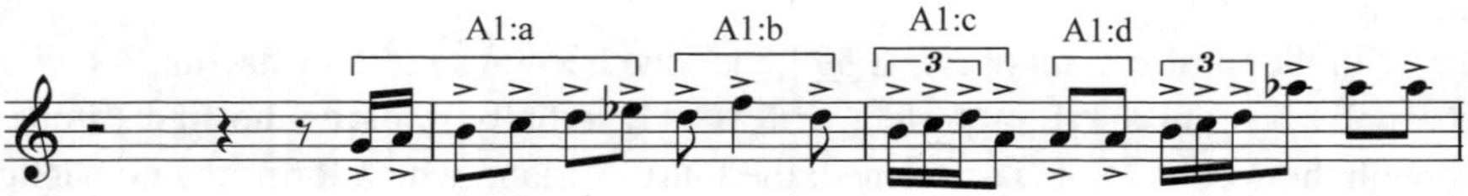

b(i) Shostakovich IV/1: [63]$^{1-3}$

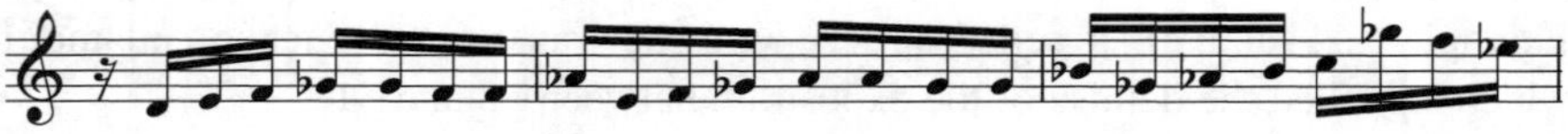

b(ii)

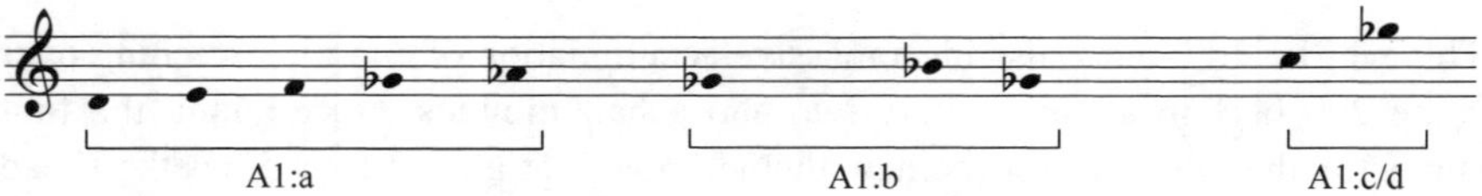

Example 3.27
a Shostakovich IV/1: [63]$^{1-19}$

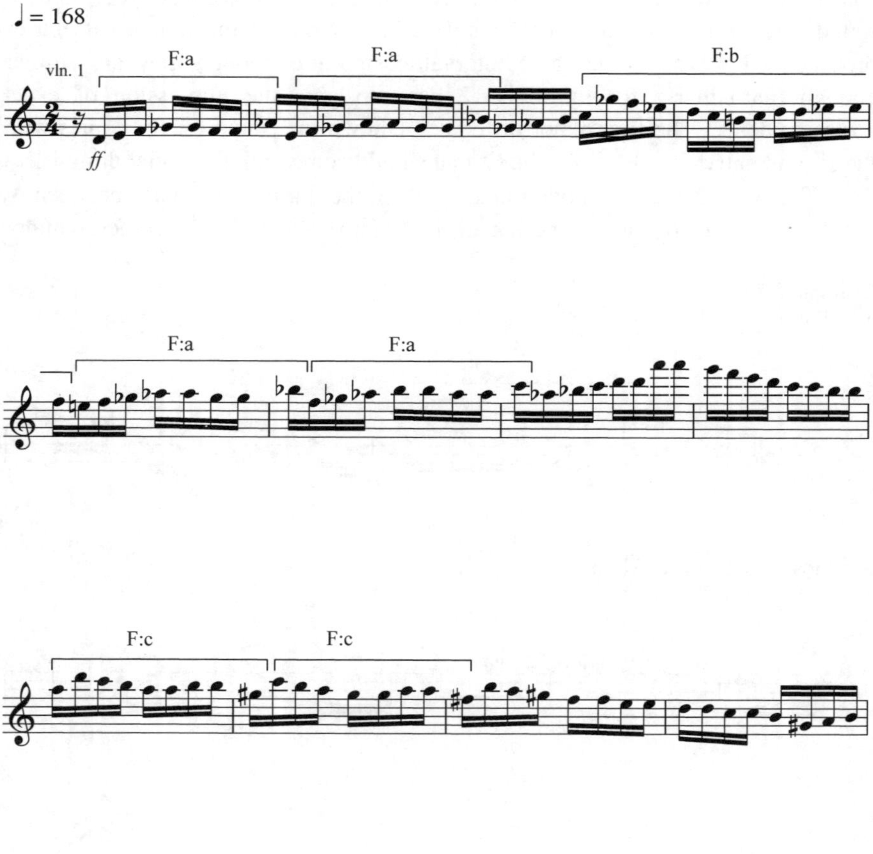

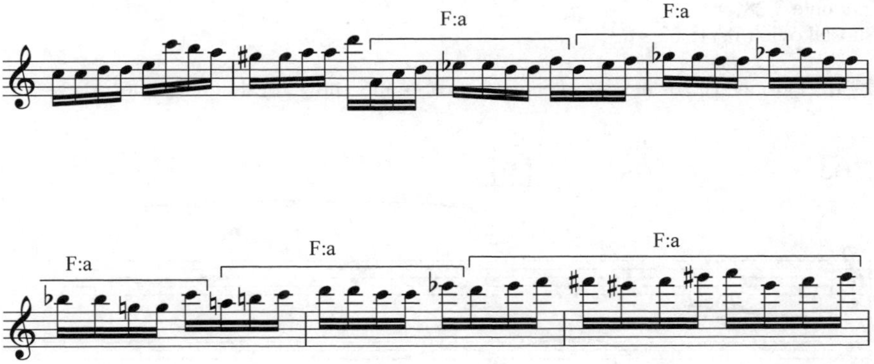

b Shostakovich IV/1: 64$^{1–7}$

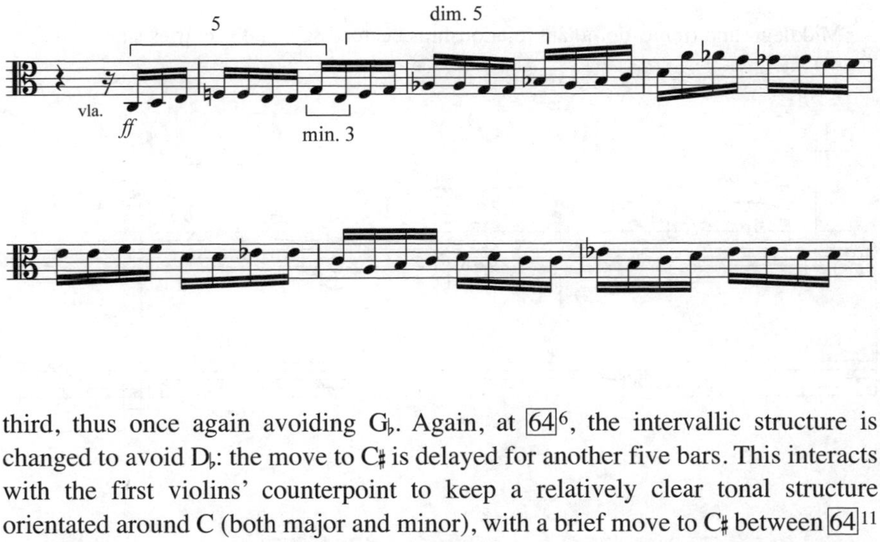

third, thus once again avoiding G♭. Again, at 64^{6}, the intervallic structure is changed to avoid D♭: the move to C♯ is delayed for another five bars. This interacts with the first violins' counterpoint to keep a relatively clear tonal structure orientated around C (both major and minor), with a brief move to C♯ between 64^{11} and 65. There is also a marked tonic/dominant axis at work in the first two entries which further clarifies the dense texture; the third entry has a weaker dominant presence, while the fourth (which, like the second, begins on C) briefly posits A♭ as an alternative to G. Example 3.28 presents three levels of salience within the overall anarchy of this fugato, with the background level showing both subject entries and dominant support where present. The middleground level shows a degree of arpeggiation that gives substance to C minor and its dominant between 64 and 65, and to A minor between 66 and 67. After the final entry at 69, the treble A is flattened, and F minor is once again loosely referred to as the 'climax' key between 71 and 72. In this way, though the surface harmonic logic of the fugato seems tenuous, the same tonal forces are at work here as in the exposition, with C as a prominent centre, flanked by A (also the dominant of the opening D),

Example 3.28
Shostakovich IV/1: 63 – 73

a Background (notes in boxes denote entries; beams show any dominant support)

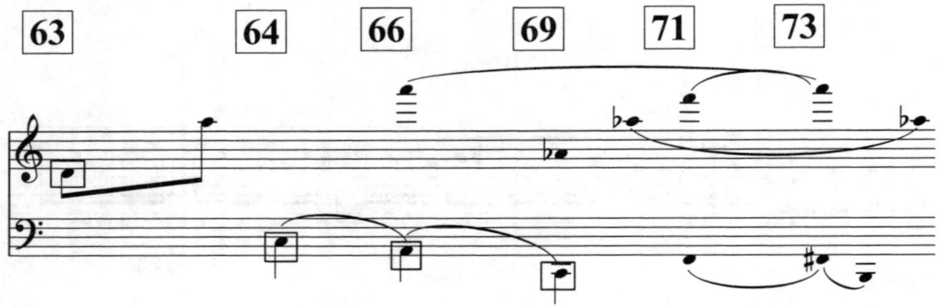

b Middleground (tonic–dominant relationships beamed separately, entries shown in boxes)

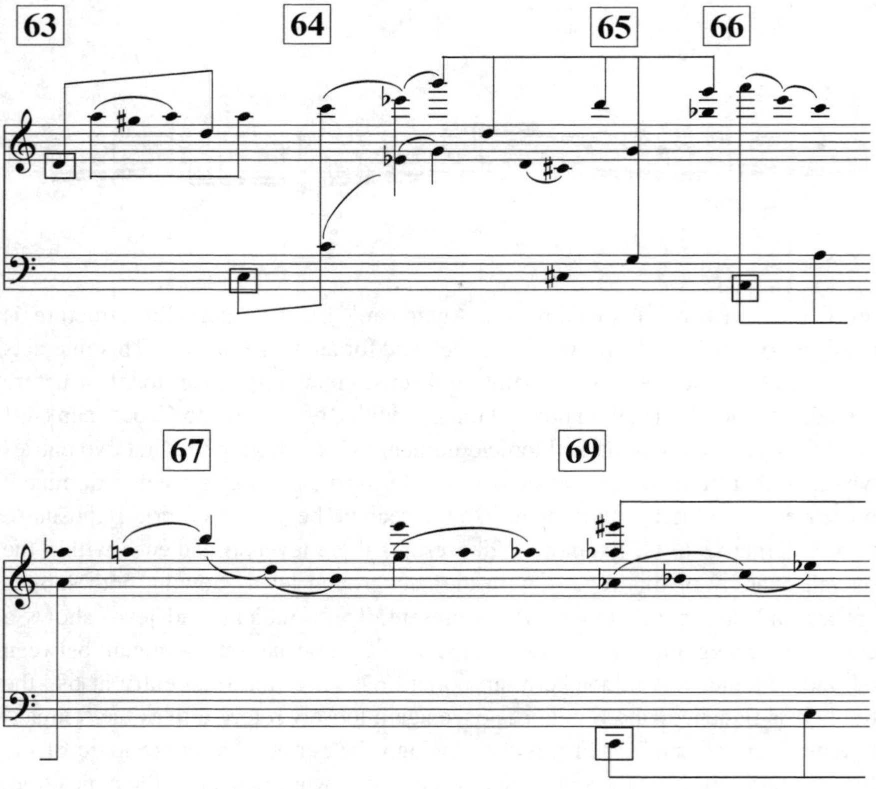

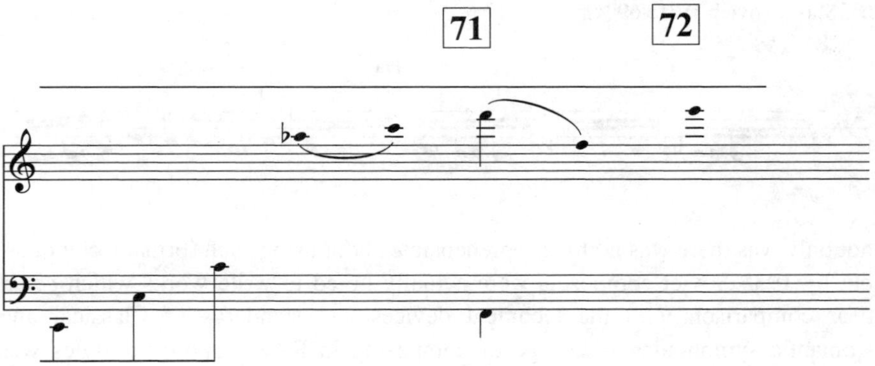

with the C bass and treble A first mooted in the introduction playing a significant part here too: as the treble A is flattened over the bass C at 69, it feeds into the F minor arpeggiation that marks the climax of the fugato at 71, and continues to be prominent at the approach to the climax at 78^{8}.

The second and third entries extend into codettas of seven and nine bars respectively. The first of these functions as a retardation of the scalic ascent initiated by the final phrase of the previous entry, spinning out a minor sixth over seven bars: an octave ascent in the first violins starting at 65 is completed (g^1–g^2), while the codetta itself spans d^1–$b\flat^1$. Momentum is thereby held fractionally in check so as to increase the impact of the third entry at 66. The second codetta, which has no comparable slowing of ascent or descent, has the opposite effect: with the fourth entry, regularity is waning, with registral compression of the fugue subject, and a marked increase in oscillating figuration (Example 3.29).

This fugato was singled out for criticism in 1948 by the ex-RAPM composer Marian Koval as a glaring example of Shostakovich's 'formalism', or unrepentantly modernistic complexity. Yet, as discussed, to use fugal techniques in a development section was common in contemporary Soviet symphonic practice;

Example 3.29
a Shostakovich IV/1: 63^{1-5}

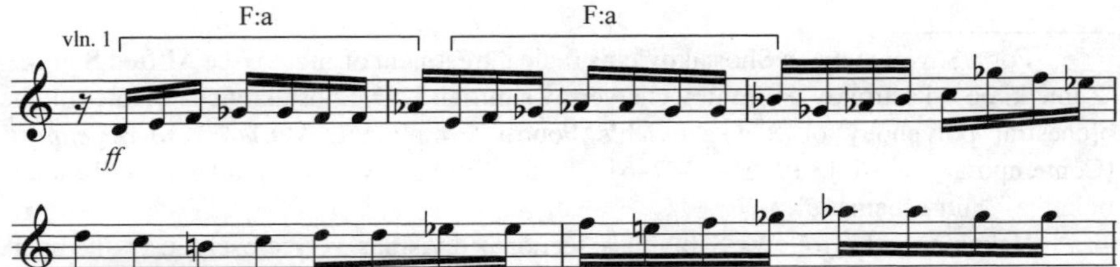

b Shostakovich IV/1: 69 1–3

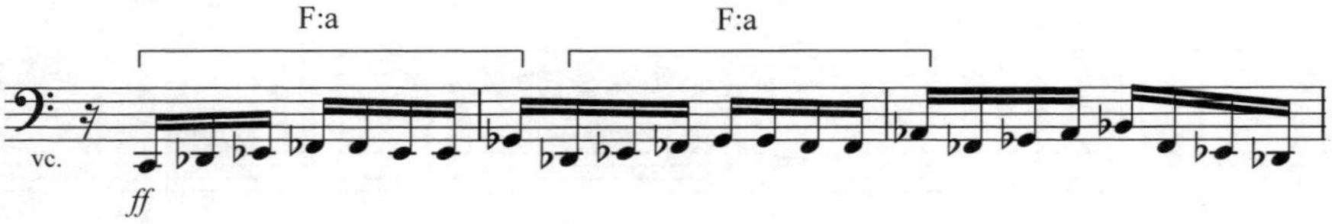

not only was there was nothing reprehensible about using such formal techniques, but by 1935 Soviet composers were actually urged to write works which *could* bear comparison with the technical devices and standards of Classical and Romantic symphonies – the age of composing in RAPM-approved styles was over. What this analysis shows is that the fugato, though apparently chaotic, is structured in such a way as to guard against the risk of losing all sense of tonal coherence, while at the same time maximizing dramatic impact though speed and textural density. If anything, Shostakovich's treatment of fugato is anything but 'formalist': that label could more fairly be applied to the academic use of contrapuntal techniques in Shebalin's or Myaskovsky's symphonies. His dramatization of an otherwise rather tired developmental technique demonstrates that the challenge for composers was not to abandon established forms, but to renew them. Therefore, though on the surface this fugato might seem gratuitously complex, it is in fact a further example of Shostakovich's intense critical engagement with sonata form convention and Soviet symphonic practice.[20]

Section 3: 71 – 80: *March and Climax*

As soon as the fourth fugal entry is complete, a new theme emerges at 71, tenuously based on the fugue subject, with its ascending scalic contour and central tritone (Example 3.30). This marks the start of an attempt to regroup and establish a stronger tonal focus, discernable in the G minor – D major triads at 72 1–5. This process is initiated by the semiquaver *Fortspinnung* at the end of the fugato at 71, only to be sabotaged by persistent contrapuntal 'entries' of the bass theme, which gradually mutate into a conflation of A1 and A2 as the section progresses (see Example 3.31). The march character of the initial bass theme prompts Sabinina's labelling of the section between 72 and 75 as 'Procession', and my own march label, as opposed to viewing it as a continuation of the fugato.[21] The fugato has

20 For a Soviet view on Shostakovich's radical treatment of fugato, see Al'fred Shnitke, 'Zametki ob orkestrovoy polifonii v chetvërtoy simfonii D.D. Shostakovicha' [Notes on the orchestral polyphony of Shostakovich's Fourth Symphony], *Muzïka i sovremennost'* [Contemporary music], 1966/4, 127–61, especially 160, where Shnitke describes this fugato as 'anti-schematic'.

21 Hakobian, who follows Sabinina's sectional divisions very closely, uses the same label here. See Hakobian, *Dmitriy Shostakovich*, 149.

Example 3.30
Shostakovich IV/1: 71$^{1-8}$

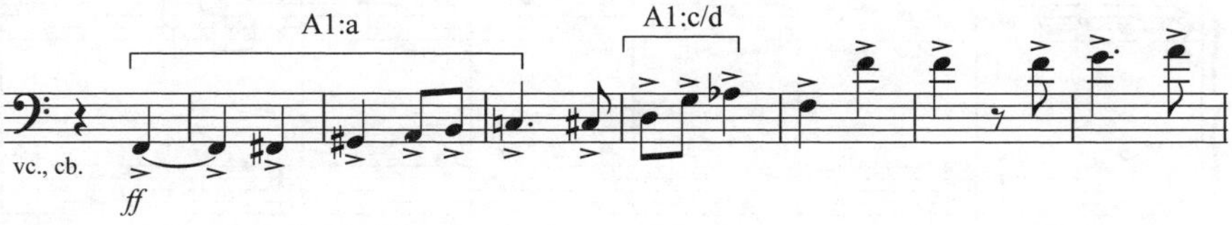

come to an end by 72, and the bass theme is distinctive enough to justify a separate generically- or intonationally-based label. However, the emergence of A1 throughout this section, and its subsequent transformation into the stretto from 75, could easily form the basis of a case against drawing dividing lines between 63 and 80, and instead for viewing the whole of sections 2 and 3 as a loose contrapuntal structure, with the fugato held in suspense in a prolonged episode between 71 and 75 before proceeding to its concluding stretto. A1 is first hinted at at 73 on trumpets, with A1 a and b clearly recognizable (see Example 3.31). Its closing phrase is

Example 3.31
a Shostakovich IV/1: 73 – 75

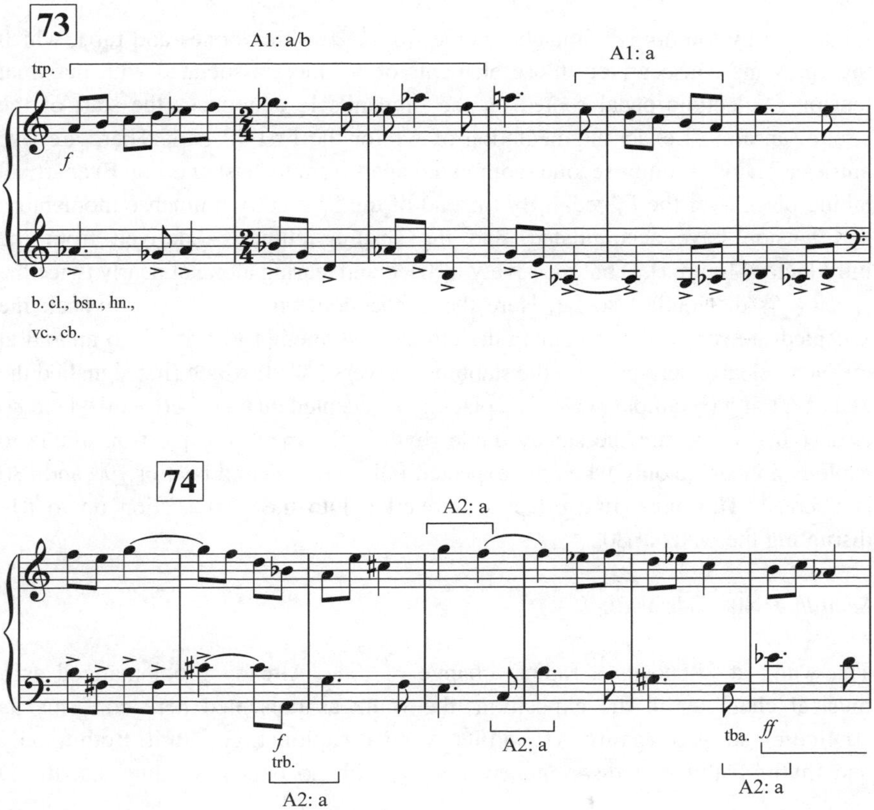

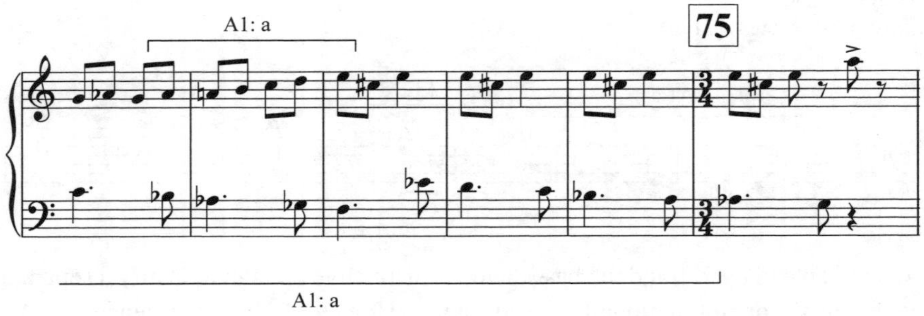

b Shostakovich IV/1: 22$^{1-5}$

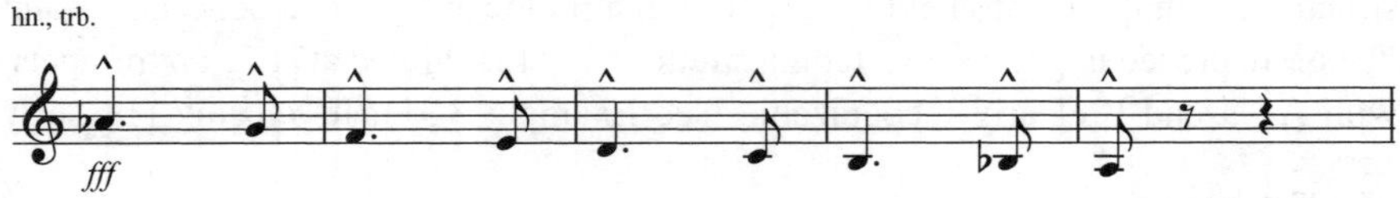

reinforced by the horns' climactic theme from 22 on trombones and tuba, which thus presents consecutively those elements of A1 most associated with maximal tension. A dactylic pedal rooted on the timpani's F♯ announces the start of the stretto: an almost exact augmentation of A1 for the first 12 bars. There are five entries a major or minor second (compound apart from the last entry on F) apart, all taking place over the F♯ pedal. By the end of the fifth entry, immense momentum and tension have accumulated, and the ensuing climax – derived from the introductory figure (I:a) but massively inflated and tearing along at nearly twice the speed – is the loudest so far. Here the connection with A1 is unequivocal: the accented quavers which complete the climax and attempt to bring it to an end at $^{4-1}$79 are clearly derived from the stabbing quavers (A1:d) which first signalled the end of A1 at 5 (Example 3.32). The placing of accented quavers between 79 and 80 is designed to disrupt the steady duple rhythm: the metre change from duple to triple is noticeable only when the expected fall on the second beat of 79^{6} and ^{1}80 is delayed. This unsettling effect will overlap into the next section up to 81, disrupting the waltz at 80.

Section 4: 80 – 84: *Waltz I*

The waltz at 80 posits a radical change of tone. Already problematized as a musical character in the exposition, the waltz as presented here confirms its continuing struggle against A1, and its eventual capitulation with it. Both tonally and rhythmically it is disorientated at first, with no bass grounding and the D

Example 3.32

a Shostakovich IV/1: ^{4}79–^{1}80

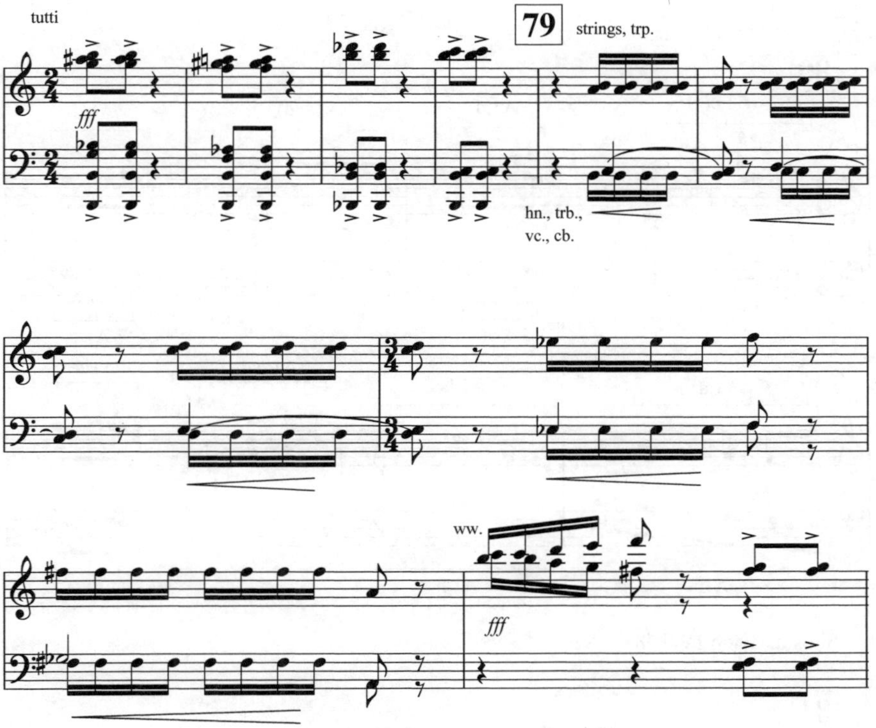

b Shostakovich IV/1: 5$^{1–2}$

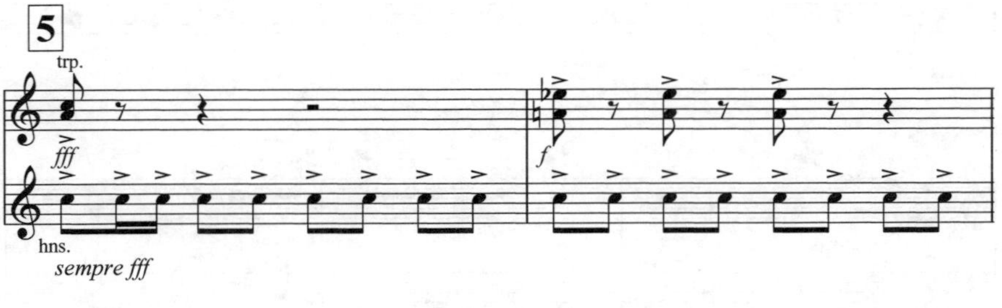

major potential of the first two bars immediately losing its way as A1-derived motifs undercut the new waltz theme (see Example 3.33a). It stabilizes at 81 with a new variant of A1 in C♯ minor; Example 3.33b shows how, as the waltz progresses, its A1 derivation becomes clearer.

C♯ minor is established as the new tonic at 81, in the characteristic flattened

Example 3.33

a Shostakovich IV/1: [80] 1–5

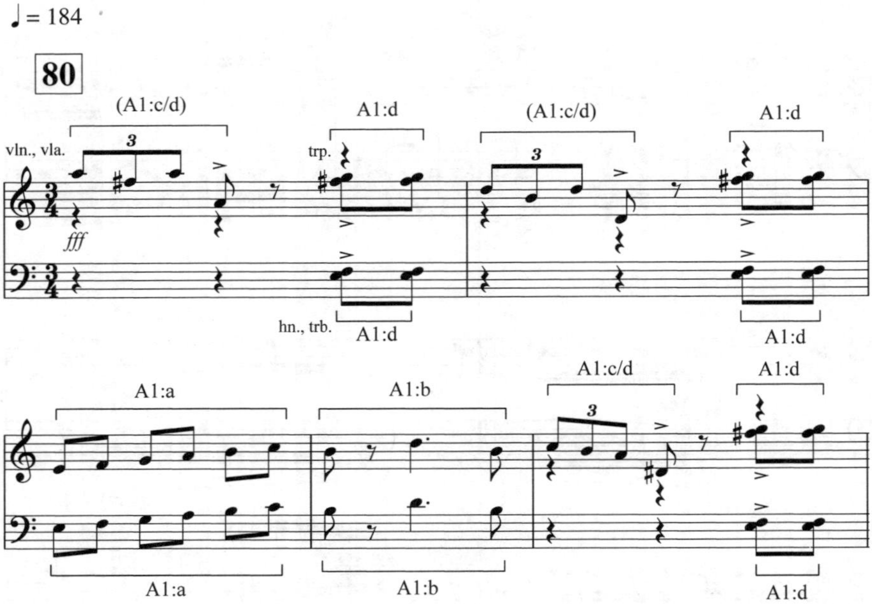

b Shostakovich IV/1: [81] – [82] 3

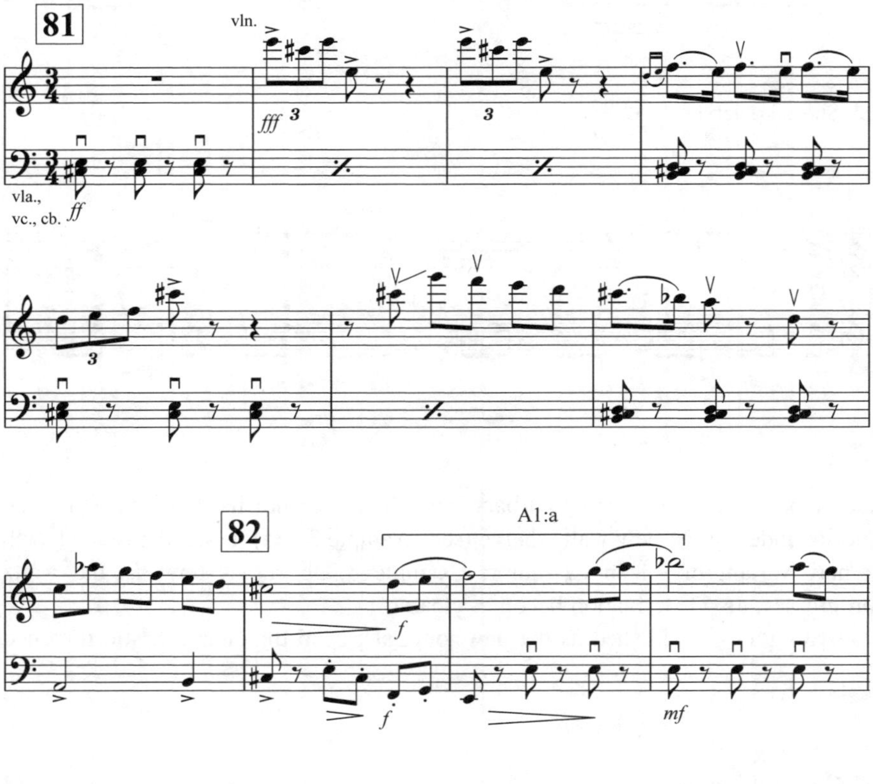

minor mode used by Shostakovich in *Lady Macbeth* (Example 3.34).[22] The Russian modal theorist Aleksandr Dolzhansky dubbed this flattened mode the 'Alexandrian pentachord',[23] and both he and Fanning agree that the Act II passacaglia of *Lady Macbeth* is cast in this mode rather than in D minor, as some scholars have suggested.[24] As an alternative to a straight C♯ minor it has obvious advantages. It gravitates towards the flattened supertonic rather than the dominant or subdominant, and thus is less inclined to initiate a conventional harmonic progression. This restricted movement creates a strongly 'closed' feel, which acts as a check on the otherwise robust tone at 81. Roseberry describes the tone here as a 'biting ländler parody' in the Mahlerian mould, citing the *Poco più mosso subito* passage from the second movement of Mahler's Ninth Symphony as an example (Example 3.35).[25] The aggressively fast tempo recalls Mahler very

Example 3.34

a Shostakovich: *Lady Macbeth*, Act II: 284^{2} – 285^{3}

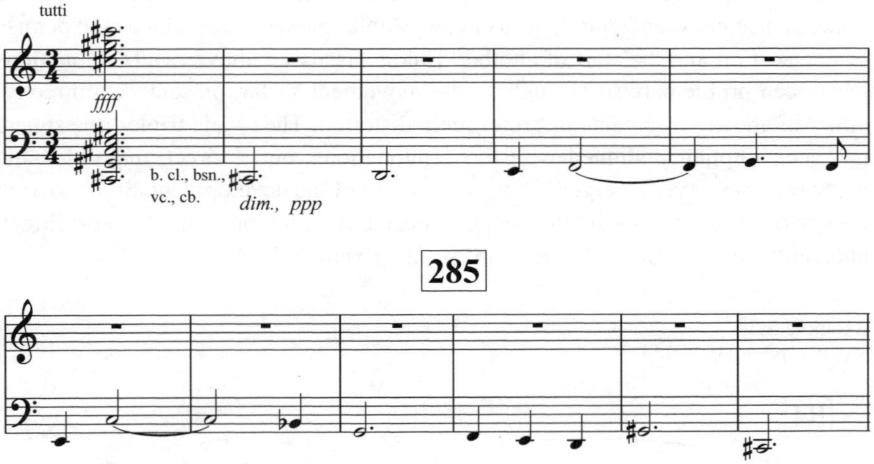

b Alexandrian pentachord

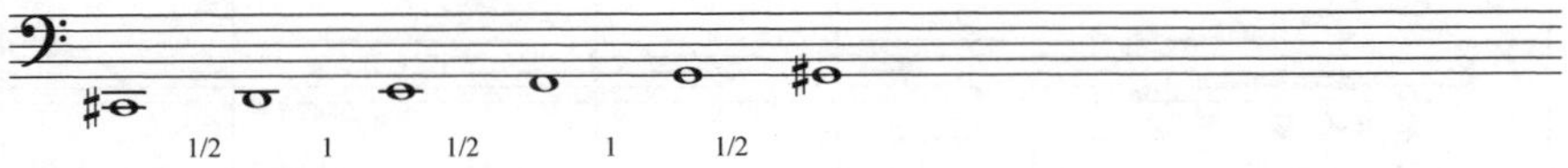

[22] See Fanning, 'Shostakovich in Harmony' in Bartlett, ed., *Shostakovich in Context*, 33–5.

[23] See Ellon D. Carpenter, 'Russian Theorists on Modality in Shostakovich's Music', in Fanning, ed., *Shostakovich Studies*, 91–6.

[24] See Fanning, 'Shostakovich in Harmony', 34–5. The scholars whom Fanning cites are Kröplin (*Frühe sowjetische Oper*, 224) and Koball (*Pathos und Groteske*, 261).

[25] Roseberry, *Ideology*, 415.

Example 3.35
Mahler IX/2: 18$^{33-7}$

Poco più mosso subito (Tempo II)

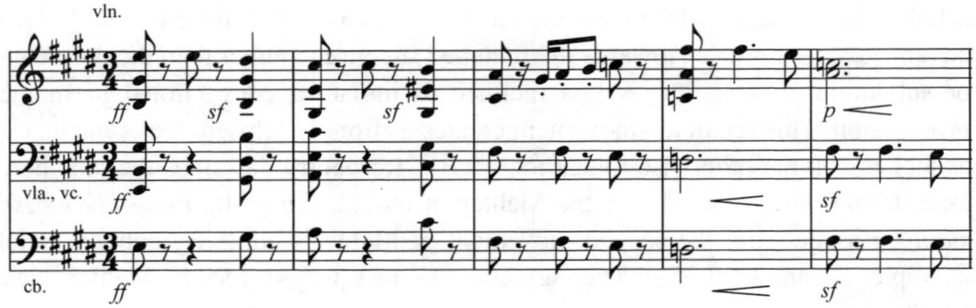

strongly, as does the aggressive stamping accompaniment.[26] Like Mahler's, Shostakovich's waltz effects a transition from grotesque inflection and violence to nonchalance between 82 and 88: as in the Mahler passage, this signals the demise of one section and the start of another. But as discussed above, waltz intonations have been problematized throughout the movement so far, presented 'indirectly' either in ghostly fragments or grotesquely distorted. The whole triple-time sphere has been implicitly aligned with those intonations, but a direct, unproblematic waltz tone has never emerged. Here, at the close of the development, Shostakovich uses two consecutive waltz themes, the second of which presents the most direct, apparently straightforward tone heard so far (Example 3.36).

Example 3.36
Shostakovich IV/1: 84$^{1-4}$

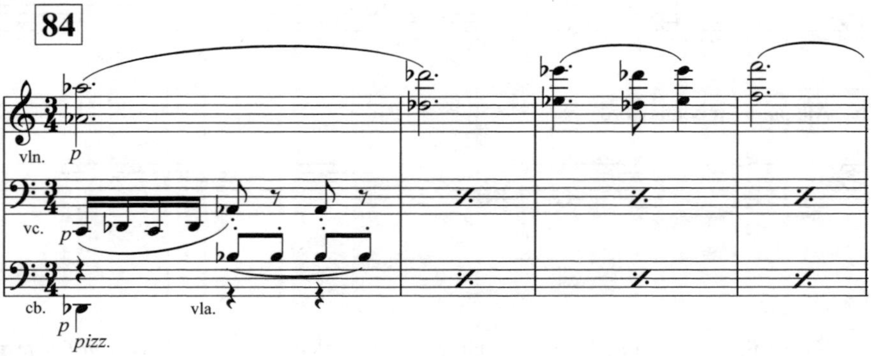

26 For a brief discussion of Shostakovich's use of the 'grotesque' waltz, see Sheinberg, *Irony*, 291–6. She cites this waltz as an example of an 'early instance of waltzing violence' for Shostakovich (p. 296).

Section 5: 84 – 90: *Waltz II*

Whereas the first waltz is basically a transformation of A1, sharing its contours and intervallic structure as well as its aggressive tone, the second is an ironed-out version of B1, stripped of its metrical ambivalence and muted tone and transformed into a barrel-organ waltz. The semiquaver figuration in the bass at 84 dimly recalls the accompaniment of the organ-grinder's waltz in the first tableau of *Petrushka* (Example 3.37).

Such urban *ulichniy* intonations will feature most prominently in the third movement and will be discussed at length in Chapter Five. They are prefigured here, however, in the most bizarre of the development's character variations. Although their tone in the finale is relatively innocent, the discrepancy in the first movement between the waltz's artless presentation and its violent context casts doubt on its sincerity. The sudden diatonicism of B1 at 84 creates a further estranging effect: not only is its initial D♭ major alien to the broad C/A tonal ambit of the first movement, but its serene major diatonicism is wholly unprecedented. The fragile, other-worldly dance fragments of the exposition have presented a false trail. No 'positive', triple-time theme will emerge from either exposition or development: the dance fragments of the exposition at 37 will retain their ghostly character in the recapitulation. The relationship between the waltz at 84 here and the waltz fragments in the exposition is confirmed by the staccato quaver accompaniment to B1 at 86, which recalls the flute and piccolo semiquavers from 37. More intriguingly, the first violins' sudden contraction from wide, sweeping intervals to a narrow, twisting melodic line at ^{5}86 foreshadows the cor anglais's compression of the B2 sequence (between 32 and 36) and the solos leading up to the 'supplication' climax (between 41 and 47) at 97 in the recapitulation (see Examples 3.44 and 3.45 below). This passage will be discussed in due course, but the brief reference to it at ^{5}86 is significant, since it is the development section's only allusion, albeit heavily veiled, to the 'supplication' theme of the exposition climax, which will return in the recapitulation's cor anglais solo between 96 and 99 that is central to the first movement's dramaturgy, as will be seen.

There is no clear hermeneutic conclusion to be drawn from this. As is so often

Example 3.37
Stravinsky: Petrushka: 9$^{3–4}$

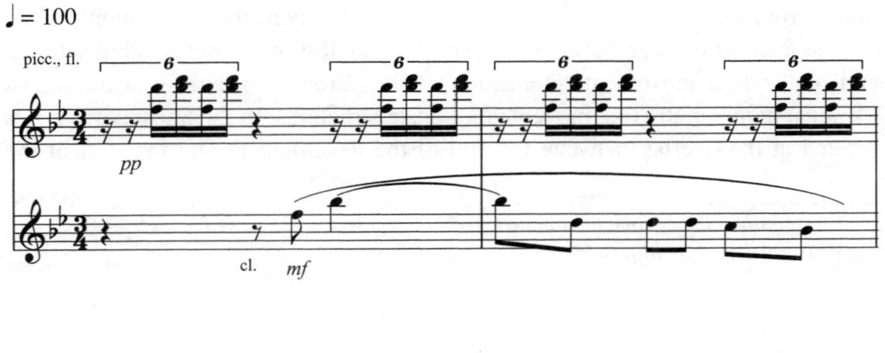

the case with Mahler's use of apparently simple, innocent themes, it is impossible to justify an interpretation of 'negative' or 'positive' for the D♭ major waltz that sounds so disingenuous. Sabinina, for example, interprets it as a moment where 'clarity, peace and harmony are established',[27] and Roseberry describes it as 'deceptive calm'.[28] These are all shades of the same basic response: the D♭ episode is incongruous and thus invites interpretation, while at the same time evading it. The fleeting reference to the final cor anglais solo discussed above is similarly mystifying. All that is verifiable is that this reference confirms the relationship between the 'stable' B1 transformation here and the 'unstable' B2 sequence of the exposition which, as has been discussed, paved the way for the 'supplication' theme of the exposition climax and which will assume comparable prominence in the recapitulation.

Even before the D♭ variant of B1 is complete, therefore, it is beginning to refer outside itself to other key moments in the first movement's dramaturgy. The subsequent association with the waltz intonations of 37 at 86 is an added reference: this waltz is not a self-contained episode, but the repository of those dismembered voices from the exposition. They are still sounding as the development breaks down: the string tremolos at 87 abruptly cut off a new phase of the waltz, which begins to build in intensity at 86^{8}. This ushers in a series of waltz fragments: a scale followed by the first phrase of B1 beneath a *frullato* B♭ pedal, which tails off into echoes of the waltz fragments from the exposition at 37 – 38. The E harp pedal from 36 is here replaced by the *frullato* B♭, though the initial key of B1 from 36 and 88 is the same (B major). All sense of a tonal centre is now suspended: between 89 and 90 an F# bass pedal underpins the B♭ *frullato*. A chorale-like fragment for strings sounds briefly at 89 on two altered diminished chords, and with the *frullato* B♭ still sounding, the diminished string chords are followed up by a glissando shift from C to B major, once again slightly embellished with added seconds (Example 3.38).

Section 6: 90 – 91: *Retransition*

At the start of the retransition at 90, everything is in suspense. There is no familiar material and no sense of any tonal centre; the continued triple metre has lost its definition even before 90, with a fragmented viola line (89^{5-8}) and a string glissando both starting on the second beat. A single A timpani roll, which quickly builds from a C/A dyad to a 12-note brass *fffff* tutti, opens the retransition.

The *frullato* passage between 87 and 89 is, as Roseberry notes, similar to the end of the first movement retransition of the 'Eroica', occurring at an almost identical points in the first movements' sonata structures. In the Shostakovich it is located at the overlap between the end of the development and the start of the

---

27 Sabinina, *Shostakovich-simfonist*, 107.

28 Roseberry, *Ideology*, 415.

Example 3.38
Shostakovich IV/1: [89] – [1][90]

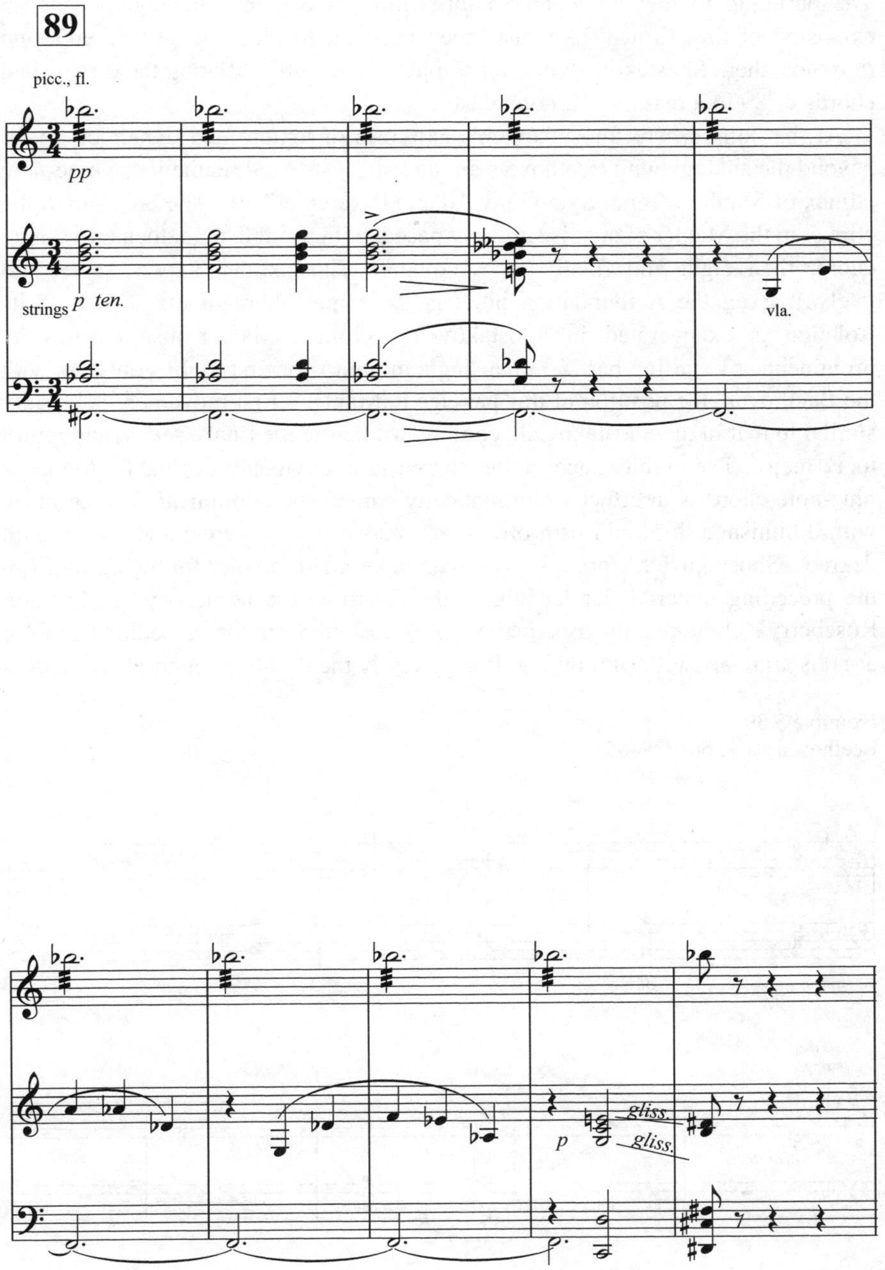

retransition, but the parallel may be extended to encompass 89 – 91, since the diminished chords at 89 can then be compared with Beethoven's (Example 3.39). The build up to the twelve-note chord from 90 can thus be regarded as an extension of the 'Eroica'-like suspended passage. In place of Beethoven's *ppp* tremolos, then, Shostakovich has a *fffff* muted brass tutti, inflating the diminished chords of 89 to a massive 12-note blast.

At the point where Shostakovich's extremes of texture and dynamics go far beyond the analogy with Beethoven, another suggests itself: namely, the nine-note climax of Mahler's Tenth Symphony Adagio (Example 3.40). The build-up to the climax in the Mahler extract is similarly paced, with a single note, then a five-note chord, then eight and finally nine (compare Shostakovich's two, seven and twelve). Even the A foundation pitch is the same; although the degree of its isolation is exaggerated in Shostakovich's climax, Mahler also ensures its prominence by starting bar 203 on a single minim A for first violins only. As with the Beethoven, the position of this passage in Mahler's first movement is broadly similar to that in the Shostakovich, coming just before the final *a tempo* and return to F♯ major. The significance of the shared A is obviously debatable. Mahler's nine-note chord is in effect a chromatically embellished dominant seventh in F♯, with diminished third and fifth on top and added minor second and minor sixth degrees. Shostakovich's brass tutti sounds more alien, neither following on from the preceding material nor leading to the return of the home key of C minor. Roseberry's claim that this is a mediant progression[29] from the preceding C♯ minor at 80 is arguably wishful thinking. It is precisely the desolate sound of its rootless

Example 3.39
Beethoven III/1: bb. 378–85

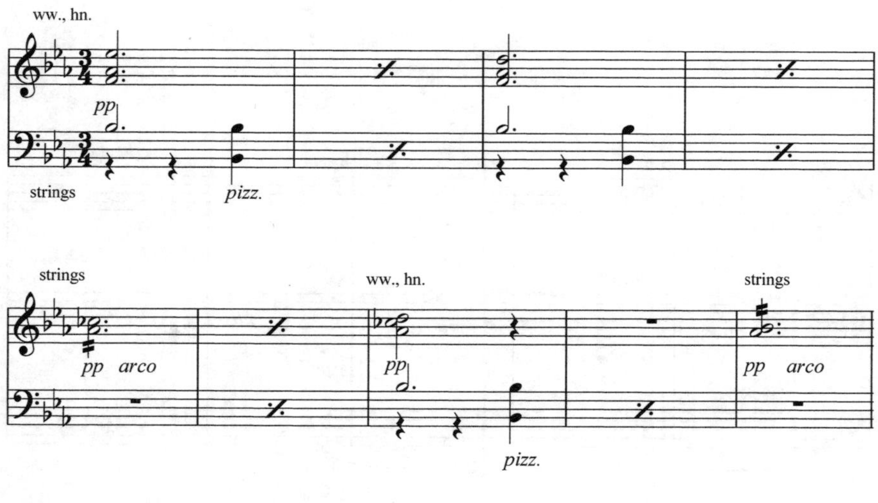

29 Ibid., 416.

Example 3.40
a Shostakovich IV/1: 90 – 91

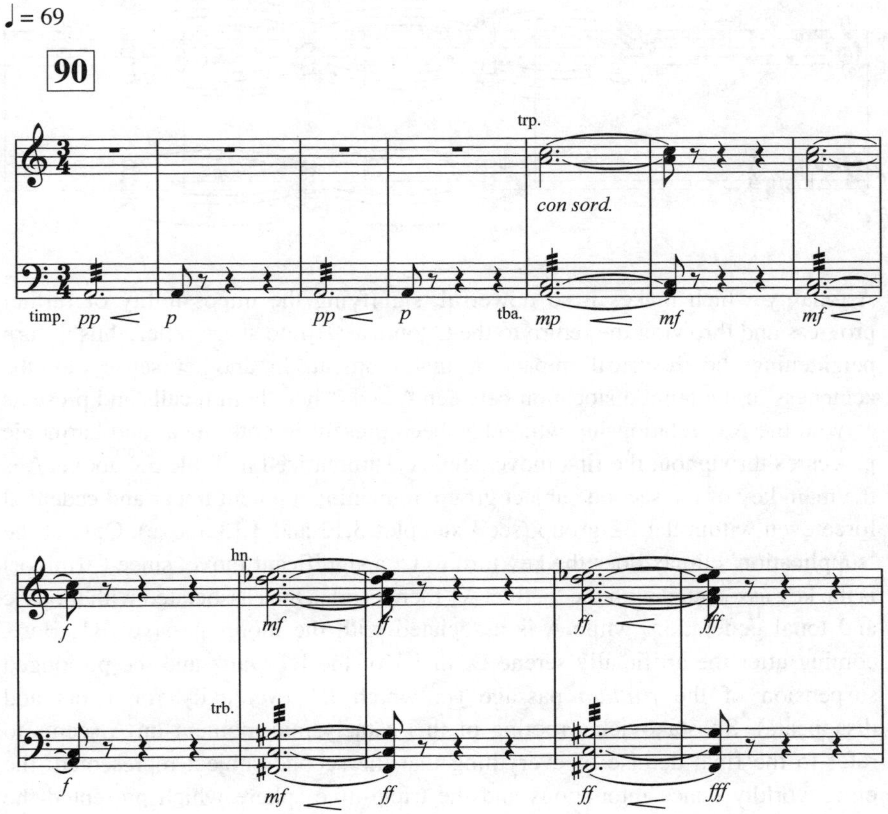

b Mahler X/1: bb. 203–6

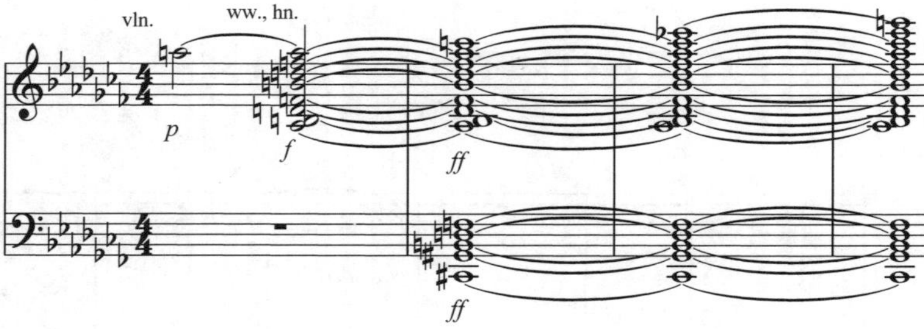

A tonality which makes it so powerful, signifying the impossibility of further progress and throwing the return to the C tonic at 91 into sharp relief, thus in turn heightening the theatrical impact of that moment. In another sense too, the acuteness of the tonal dislocation between A and C here both recalls and presents as void the A/C relationship which has been present in both linear and harmonic processes throughout the first movement. As summarized in Table 3.2 above, A is the main key of the second subject group, remaining a potent linear and cadential force even within the B2 group (see Examples 3.12 and 3.13 above). Only at the 'supplication' climax does the key turn to C: a significant move, since C (minor) is the key associated with the 'active' A1 theme and is thus associated with motivic and tonal generation, while A is associated with the more 'passive' B1. Here, coming after the artificially serene D♭ major of the B1 waltz and the prolonged suspension of the *frullato* passage (in which B1 eventually fragments and disappears), Shostakovich's rooting of this cataclysmic moment on A seems to refer to the final demise of everything that the second subject represented: the other-worldly dance intonations and the triple-time sphere which presented the only real counterforce to A1, as well as its alternative tonal orientation. Shostakovich's evocation of the most terrifying moment in all of Mahler's symphonic output does seem to be a deliberate reference, underlined by the strangeness of the move to A. Where Mahler's agonized dissonance turns suddenly to serene resolution, however, Shostakovich's marks a return to dark menace in the recapitulation. At 91 a piercing woodwind unison heralds the return of the introduction.

As discussed in Chapter One, it was common for Soviet composers to adapt sonata form to suit their lyrical, discursive themes by subjecting them to development in the exposition, often immediately following their first appearance, in a free process of 'developing variation'. Development sections, as a result, could be rather formulaic, with the Myaskovsky–Shebalin type making frequent use of contrapuntal devices such as augmentation, fugue or fugato and stretto. As discussed, late-1920s and 1930s Soviet symphonies which combine themes in their developments were astonishingly rare (Myaskovsky's Eleventh is one of the few that does, and Shebalin's Third, discussed in Chapter One above, is also in a minority in its transformation of themes in the recapitulation). Nowhere in Soviet symphonic literature before 1936 is there anything like the development section of Shostakovich's first movement. His segregation of first and second subject groups is not unusual; nor is his extensive use of contrapuntal techniques. But the highly episodic structure (only the fugato and march run into each other) is unprecedented, as is the extent and importance of the 'character variation' to which his themes are subjected. Also unprecedented is Shostakovich's use of popular idioms such as polka and waltz in the development: the whirlwind fugue is striking, certainly, but well grounded in (if deliberately going far beyond) Soviet symphonic tradition. For a by-then notorious iconoclast, known for his outrageous theatre and ballet scores, to open his development with a polka would perhaps not be especially shocking. But the two waltzes (81 and 84) – one frenzied, the other artificially calm – would probably have been more of a surprise. Their self-containment seems incongruous even in a development section as unorthodox as this one; and the simple diatonic harmonic idiom of the second waltz further alienates it from its context. Shostakovich's development section is like a hall of mirrors: themes are transformed, often grotesquely, into miniature parodies of themselves, and there is no attempt to create links between them: each section is estranged from the next, though they derive their shapes from the same source.

The resulting effect is disorientating: until the recapitulation, key dramaturgical issues mooted in the exposition – the active/passive roles of A1 and B1; the role of the 'supplication' theme and its relationship to A1, B1 and B2; the relative functions of the waltz/march spheres, and that of the fragmented dance intonations – appear to remain in suspense. Instead, throughout the development section, Shostakovich plays with the 'positive'/'negative' A1/B1 roles and questions them, using B1 as well as A1 in the opening polka without disturbing its innocent surface character, and smoothing over the unstable B1 waltz at 84 in a kind of inverted distortion which still produces a slightly grotesque effect. What is more, the waltz is poised on the (artificially stable) knife-edge of D♭ major (enharmonic C♯), which, sooner or later, will inevitably fall to C. The first waltz, based as it is on A1 (and also in C♯), also appears to address the exposition's duple/triple conflict by recasting A1 as a waltz. But the unsteady way in which that particular transformation is achieved – with A1:a, b, c and d disrupting the attempted first entry at 80, and the violence of its lurch to C♯ minor, together with its aggressive tone – seems to negate the idea of A1 as a waltz even as it is so emphatically presented as such (see Example 3.32 above). The recapitulation will continue the first movement's preoccupation with some of these issues, most crucially that of the function of the 'supplication' theme and the transformation of A2 into a strong, independent character. But, as will be seen, there is to be no neat wrapping-up process, with all conflicts resolved; despite the energetic way in which those issues are broached in the exposition, the development and recapitulation reject the very idea of resolution.

Recapitulation

92 – 96: *Introduction – B1*

An extension of the five-bar introduction to eight bars announces the start of the recapitulation. The original semibreves are doubled in value, and the D♭/C clash is developed into an octave rising chromatic scale in minor seconds (Example 3.41). As in the introduction and at 90, brass parts are marked *fortissimo* and *con sordino*, providing a level of intonational continuity with the menacing tone of the retransition and with the preceding climax. Scoring is also much more bass-heavy, with double bass, bassoon and contrabassoon added to the original horns and strings. The result is deliberately overwhelming. No longer merely menacing, the introduction at this point begins the process of assimilating, even resolving, the massive tensions accumulated in the development, which the climax at 90 has confirmed rather than absorbed.

In a very plain sense, all Shostakovich does after this point is present his three exposition themes in reverse order, in declining order of tension. But, as all commentators have noted, that process goes hand in hand with thematic transformation at a highly suggestive – if ambivalent – level. As Koball has observed, this transformation process is so semantically charged that the thematic metamorphoses in the recapitulation do seem to point to 'the existence of a symphonic protagonist'.[30] The presence of such a protagonist is, in a broad sense, an undeniable feature of nearly all Shostakovich's music. Though this instinctive premise seems secure, however, taking it further is fraught with ambiguities, as will be seen.

Dramaturgically, the transformation strategy is immensely effective. The inflated introduction would seem to have overstated itself if it was designed to lead merely to a reprise of the first subject in the home key. Similarly, the second theme

Example 3.41
Shostakovich IV/1: 92$^{1-2}$

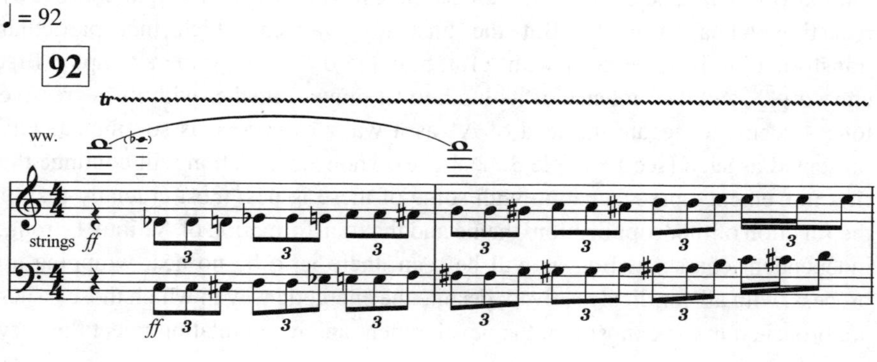

30 Koball, *Pathos und Groteske*, 113.

(A2) could hardly be presented in its original weak, meandering form without feeling like a terrible anticlimax. B1 and B2 are also weak themes, though supporting the B2 sequence which brings about the 'supplication' climax of the exposition. Therefore, apart from A1, all exposition themes pose problems for the recapitulation, since their 'unsatisfactory' presentation in the exposition was calculated to build up tension which has deliberately been left unresolved, or which has been resolved only in a negative sense, as in the rapid engulfing of A2 by A1.

The first theme to be recapitulated is B1, transformed into the heavy, pulsating intonational sphere of A1, now pressed into a compound duple metre. There are important intonational differences between B1 here and the original A1: the theme is presented, as it is at [1], on solo trumpet and trombone, but is marked *con sord.* and *espressivo*. After the initial 9/8 bar, the quaver accompaniment, *ff* at first, but then reduced to *f*, is not accented. As Example 3.42 illustrates, the tonic C minor quickly moves to C♯ at [94], where it continues to F♯ at [95]^{2}, adding to the increased tension preceded by the urgent tone of the high-pitched woodwind interjection at [94], which takes over at [95]. After [95], as the wind figure subsides, any sense of harmonic impetus disappears, as B1 has been stated in full and attention shifted to the woodwind: functional bass movement momentarily evaporates, to be resumed in a long descent to B^{2} at ^{1}[97].

Example 3.42
Shostakovich IV/1: [93] – [97]^{12}: linear summary

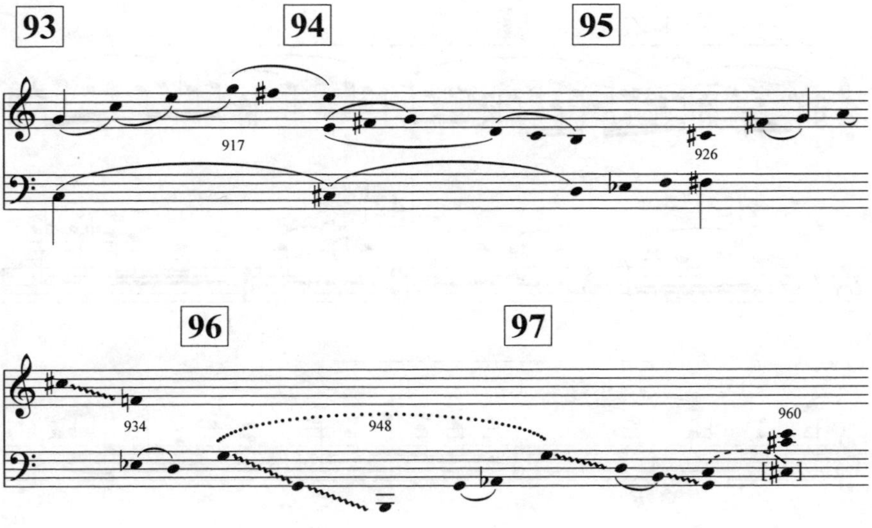

96–99: *B2 – Climax*

The reprise of B2 begins at 96 with a long cor anglais solo, repeating B2 as it appeared at 32–33, a fourth lower. Whereas at 32 B2 signalled a firming-up of the B-group triple metre and a stronger sense of melodic direction, it sounds meandering here. This is largely because of its relationship to the preceding passage: the weak presentation of B1 at 31, as compared with its very strong transformation at 93, has an obvious effect on the relative definition and strength of B2. Metrical focus is also weakened at 96 by the replacement of the triadic bass line that underpinned B2 in the exposition by a bass clarinet descending scale, sinking down from G to B^2 between 96 and 97. This weakens the metrical clarity of B2, and takes it into a darker intonational sphere, confirmed by the switch from a fairly robust presentation on violas and cellos at 32 to the lonely, plaintive sound of the cor anglais. From this point, a sequence of motifs associated with the 'supplication' climax first presented between 41 and 48 is compressed, reaching its apex with the 'supplication' theme (Example 3.43). The first of these motifs occurs at the point where B1 fades out of its second variation beneath a cluster of waltz intonations. Picking up the cue, the E♭ clarinet then presses on towards the first 'plateau' stage of the climax at 42^4. Its derivation is from the first of the B2

Example 3.43
a Shostakovich IV/1: ^{1}41 – 42^6

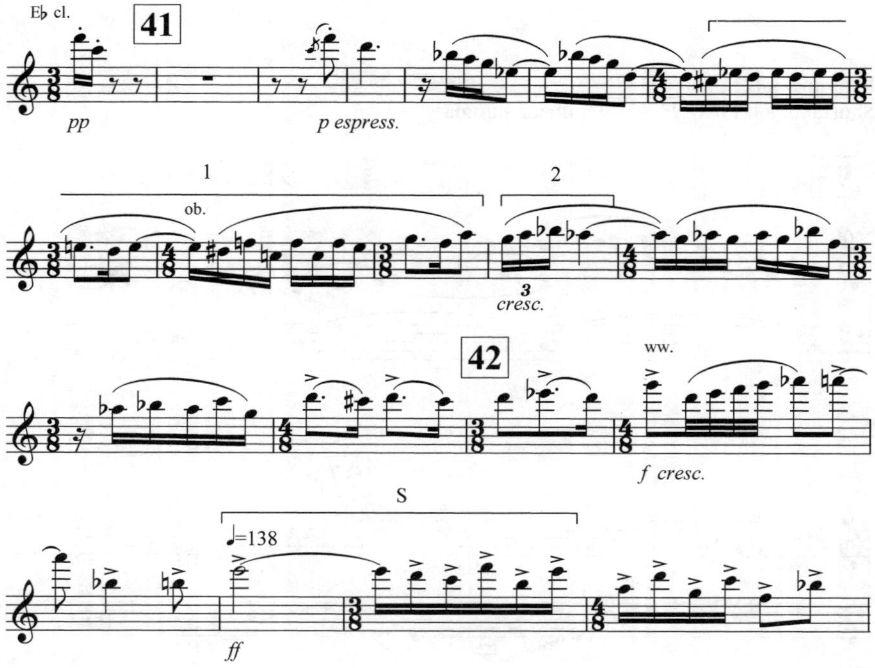

b Shostakovich IV/1: [45]2–6

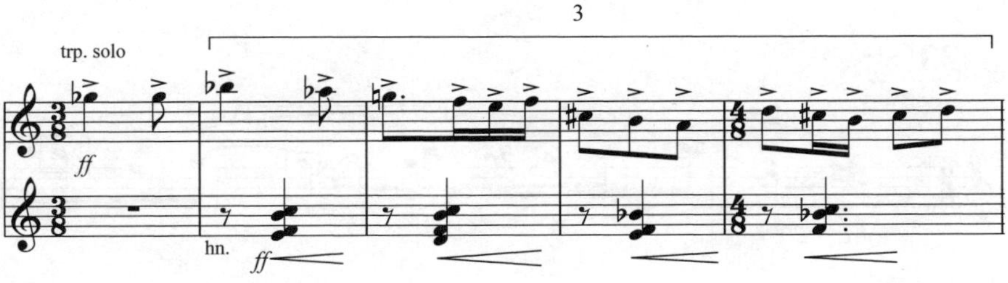

c Shostakovich IV/1: 4[47] – [47]3

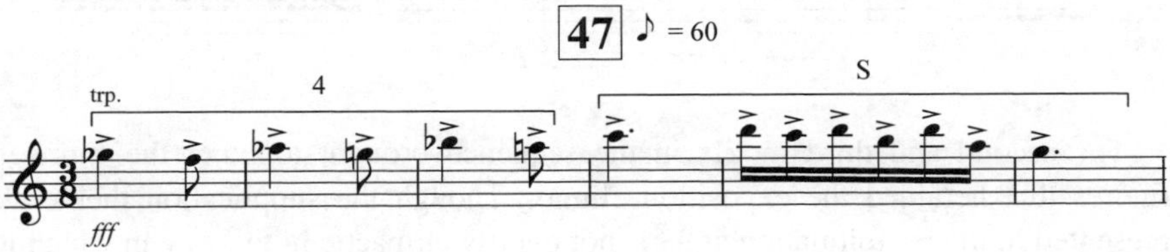

d Shostakovich IV/1: [98] – [98]7

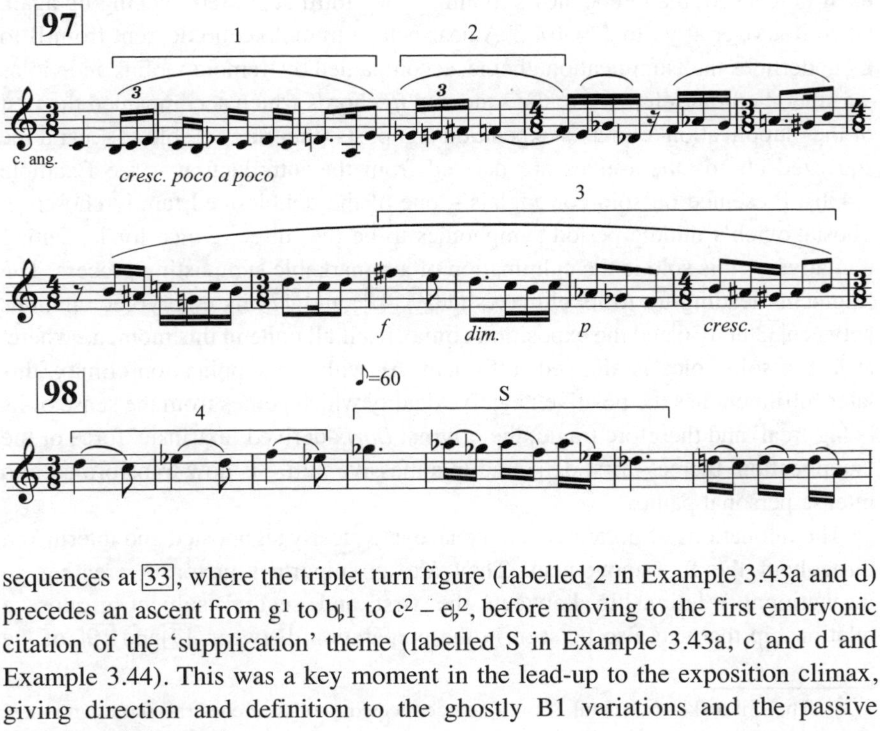

sequences at [33], where the triplet turn figure (labelled 2 in Example 3.43a and d) precedes an ascent from g^1 to b♭1 to c^2 – e♭^{2}, before moving to the first embryonic citation of the 'supplication' theme (labelled S in Example 3.43a, c and d and Example 3.44). This was a key moment in the lead-up to the exposition climax, giving direction and definition to the ghostly B1 variations and the passive interplay of alien voices.

Example 3.44
Shostakovich IV/1: 33[1–9]

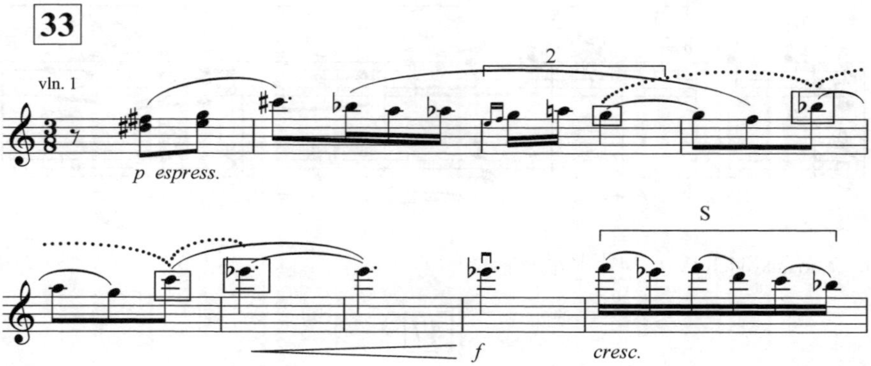

The second and third motifs in the sequence brought together the trumpet figures that heralded the exposition climax. Though the supplication theme as presented in the recapitulation at 98 is not overtly climactic in the way in which it was originally at 47, the force of these associations means that, despite its quiet soloistic presentation, its return here does have a climactic impact. As the theme itself is reached, the tempo slows to almost one-third at ♪ = 60, picking up again when it is over at 99 to ♪ = 108.[31] A near-octave tremolo cello descent from B to C^2 underlines the 'supplication' theme, accompanied by tremolo violins and violas – a smoothed-out reference to the squeezed *fff* chords which accompanied the first of the 'supplication' climax's exposition signposts (the trumpet solo at 45 and the squeezed chords themselves are derived from the introduction – see Example 3.43b). Presented on solo cor anglais – one of the double-reed family chosen in Shostakovich's middle-period symphonies to be the 'direct' voice for lamenting recitatives – this solo is the culmination of a remarkable signposting process. The fragments leading up to its climaxes at 19, 42[4] and 47, its embryonic citations between 33 and 36 and the exposition climax itself all unite in this moment, where, at last, a solo voice is allowed fulfilment. As with the supplication climax, this later fulfilment has the positive/negative duality which comes from the sense of its being 'real' and therefore tragic; the original *Boris*-derived 'extrinsic' force of the 'supplication' theme – first delivered in a massive tutti – is now transformed into intense personal pathos.

The intonations of portent, even menace, are clearly signposted and interlinked throughout the first movement. They are an important factor in creating an intonational relationship between the first and second subject groups, a relationship that can also be seen in the preparation, between 17 and 19, of the

[31] The Sikorski orchestral score, new collected works orchestral score and new collected works piano reduction incorrectly indicate ♩ = 108 here.

trumpet solo that will finally emerge at 45. Example 3.19 above shows the relationship between the triple-time trochees leading up to the climactic superimposition of A1 and A2 at 19 and the trumpet solos prefacing the exposition climax at 47. This long-distance relationship reinforces, if only subconsciously, the impact of the 'supplication' theme at 98. More intriguing is the foreshadowing at 85$^{5-8}$ of the cor anglais's first steps on the climax sequence at 97 (Example 3.45). Adding to this enigma is the fact that the cor anglais line at 97$^{1-5}$ has an equally strong relationship with the E♭ clarinet line at 41$^{4-10}$: a relationship made unequivocal by the cellos' waltz fragment at both 41$^{4-10}$ and 97$^{1-3}$, repeated at 97^{10} – 98 (see Example 3.43a and d).

One thing all that these references confirm is the closeness of the intonational spheres of B1 and B2. Like A1 and A2, they are played off against each another, each reliant on its partner for dramatic purpose. Just as the gentle, wavering triple-metre A2 sphere provided the means whereby A1 could affirm its role as the aggressor in the first subject group, so B1 plays the passive facilitator to B2's more dynamic role. B2 grows out of the shadowy waltz character of B1, which in turn proves to be the long-term initiator of the 'supplication' theme. The dependence of this theme on B1's dance intonations is confirmed very clearly by the 'compression' sequence of 97 – 99. The dance character of that sequence is bolstered further by the link with ^{5}86, which belongs to the intonational sphere of the barrel-organ waltz at 84.

But there is to be no neat ending to this story. As soon as the 'supplication' theme has breathed its last, the very passage from the exposition – the second variation of B1 – which there began the lead-up to the (now fully stated) 'supplication' climax – re-appears in its original form from 40 to 41^{5}. Only the bassoon waltz fragment (41$^{4-5}$) is missing, and the E♭ clarinet cuckoo figure and its subsequent lead-up to the wind unison at 42^{4} is given to first violins; other than

Example 3.45

a Shostakovich IV/1: 85$^{5-8}$

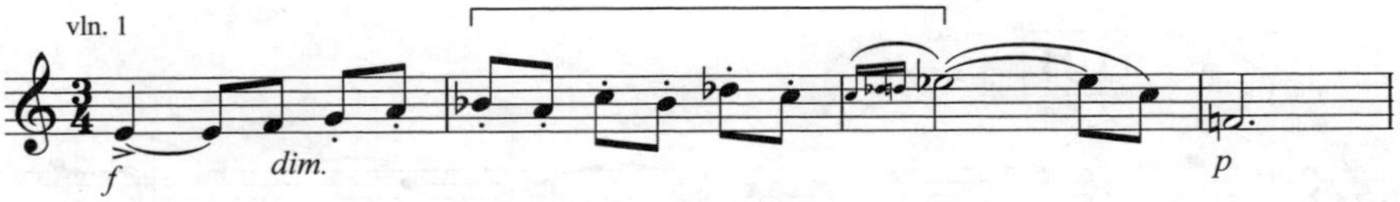

b Shostakovich IV/1: 97$^{1-4}$

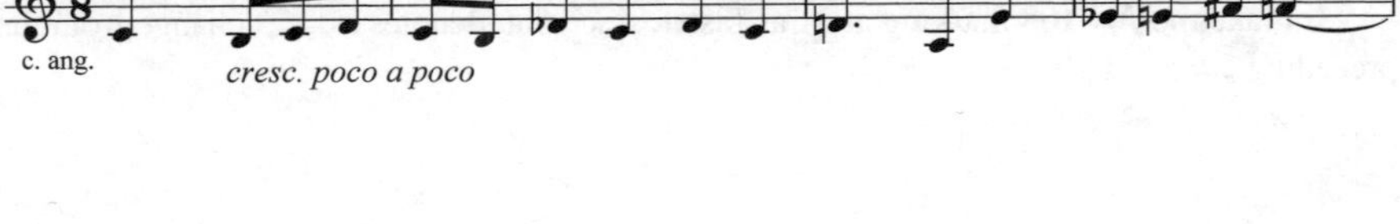

that its presentation is identical. The key – a nominal F major – is not the same as at 40, where it is (nominally) in A, but this is of little or no significance: the only key which has any significant functional role in the recapitulation is the C minor which frames it. As soon as the violin melody – following the clarinet line at 41^{4} – reaches the start of the cor anglais sequence (from the triplet turn at 97), further progress is instantly curtailed. There is to be no further evocation of the climax theme here. Instead, the ghostly waltz fragments are left hanging, asserting their 'otherness' and distancing themselves from any integrated thematic process.

101 – 103 : *A2*

At the slowest tempo yet indicated[32] (apart from the temporary slowing-down at the two 'supplication' climax points), A2 is transformed into a stable quadruple-metre theme in B♭ major (Example 3.46). As with B1, an originally weak lyricism has become strong in the recapitulation. Its dependency on A1 is also refuted: since there is no thematic interaction in the recapitulation, those themes that drew their sustenance from such interaction in the exposition are now given the means to exist independently. A quiet echo of the Mahlerian trumpet triplet theme from ^{4}16 at 102^{4} confirms the neutralization of A2 as it winds down, settling briefly on C minor in preparation for the return of A1.

103 – *End: A1 and Coda*

As the bass rises from C to E♭ in order to strengthen the return to C minor, it halts on D♭. Quiet quaver drum strokes usher in A1, and the tempo drops still further to a ponderous ♪ = 69. A1 returns, clearly in C minor, but lacking bass harmonic reinforcement until 104. The move to C minor is thus achieved subtly, avoiding

Example 3.46
Shostakovich IV/1: ^{1}101

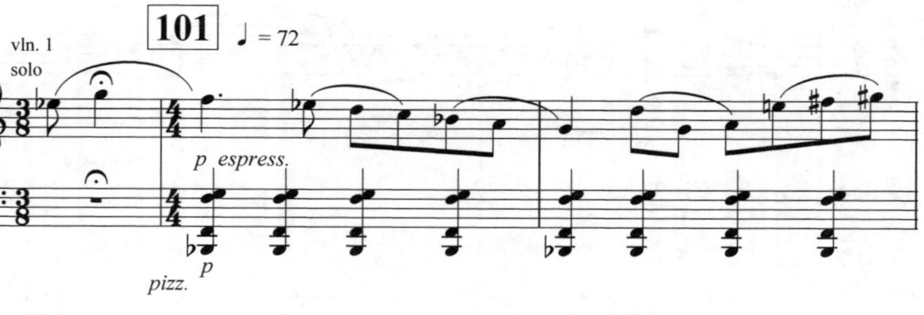

32 I take the ♪ = 108 marking at 31 as faster, since that denotes a ♩ = ♪ change from the preceding ♩ = 54 at 29.

the reassurance of a clear return to the home key. As Longman observes, the transformation of A1 from 'masculine' to 'emasculated' here provides a counterweight to the dramatic recasting of B1 from the 'personal' to the 'collective'.[33] Roseberry's reaction to this startling transformation is to hear it as a 'self-mocking ghost of its original martial identity',[34] while Sabinina hears it as 'mysterious, almost humorous and at the same time sorrowful'.[35] Shostakovich's choice of solo bassoon for the final delivery of his main theme is clearly founded on its ambivalent properties. Its staccato quavers and light drum accompaniment put it into the well-established intonational tradition of benign humour. Yet he has also used a solo bassoon to deliver his 'private' B1 theme, and so it has melancholy associations too. Is the effect sinister, reassuring or grotesque? There is no clear answer. As Taruskin has observed, such a dramatic reversal of an apparently caricatured polarization of 'public' and 'private' (as seen in the exposition) defies easy interpretation. He suggests that the 'irreducible multivalence' of this enigmatic recapitulation is what gives it its strange power: 'There is more to an artwork, one has to think, than there is to a note in a bottle'.[36]

The bassoon's intonational duality ceases to be an issue from [106], when the cor anglais becomes the main focus for the coda, which begins at [107]. A haunting g–d oscillation persists right up to the final bars, beneath which low brass intone quiet C minor chords. The only harmonic movement resembling a cadence is the semitonal slide from D♭ minor to C minor at [107], over which the g–d figure rocks. There is one final rearing-up of violence at [108]: the opening phrase of A1 suddenly cuts through the trance-like atmosphere with a *fff* wind tutti. By way of final reference to the C/A relationship throughout the first movement (and echoing the introduction's fanfare and chords), a *ff* muted brass dominant seventh on A and *fff* C♯–c♯^{2} harp glissandi reiterate the D♭–C cadence figure with sudden vehemence: just as suddenly, it all vanishes, leaving the g–d rocking figure and the quiet C minor chords to finish the movement. In a bizarre final twist, the a–g anacrusis figure of A2 invades the closing bars, recalling the squeezed chords of the introduction (and, by extension, of those at [45] and [98]). The movement ends with the quiet C minor chords overlaid by the cor anglais's hypnotic rocking figure, persisting right up to the penultimate bar.

It would certainly be misconceived to assume that this recapitulation can be easily 'read'. As Taruskin notes, what at first seems to be a straightforward polarizing of public and private proves to be profoundly enigmatic and resistant to any definite interpretation. This, surely, is part of the point. The first movement is intended to end in an atmosphere of uncertainty, and indeed uncertainty is a salient

33 Longman, *Expression and Structure*, 14.

34 Roseberry, *Ideology*, 419.

35 Sabinina, *Shostakovich-simfonist*, 109. Neither Körner nor Kopp offers any interpretative comment on the transformations of the recapitulation.

36 Taruskin, 'Shostakovich and the Inhuman', 493.

dramaturgical feature of the entire symphony. What the recapitulation does do is reverse all the intonational premises of the exposition. What is originally weak becomes strong and vice versa. There is less of a case for arguing that there is a public–private reversal. Although superficially this would seem to be the case, the tone of B1 at 93 is not aggressive or 'negative': it is marked *espressivo*, and though it has acquired an urgency and textural weight it did not have before, the effect is not violently 'collective' in the spirit of A1. Similarly, A1 does not sound 'private' at 103, in spite of its solo presentation: if anything, its 'negative' character remains intact, as is confirmed by the bassoon's grotesque, rather sinister, characterization and the upsurges of violence in the ensuing coda. A2 is still a lyrical theme in the recapitulation, given new definition and independence. The 'supplication' theme is the only one which might convey a public–private reversal, since the cor anglais solo is so unequivocally 'private' in tone – and so extended and laden with intonational significance – that it far outweighs any other theme in the first movement in appearing to be an 'individual' voice. Even in this case, though, there can be no convenient assumptions about 'negative' and 'positive' role-reversals in relation to this intonational transformation. In the exposition, the 'supplication' theme was intertextually associated with the crowd's pleas in *Boris Godunov*. Here, the same association of supplication is given 'private' voice, but the basic level of association is still the same: hence its emotional impact, if not its 'negative' or 'positive' character, is secure.

There can be no doubt that sonata form was the template – albeit loosely constructed – that Shostakovich adopted for the first movement of his artistic 'credo'. This in itself is striking. During the 1935 symphonism conference, Evgenii Braudo quoted Shostakovich's remark (made personally to him) that 'With regard to symphonic composition, Shostakovich said that for him, forms such as sonata, rondo etc. had no essential significance. More essential for him was dialectical conflict [which] … shed new light on the musical-thematic material within the development process.'[37] In view of the strength of Mahler's influence on his creative thinking at the time of the Fourth Symphony's gestation, and the extent to which Mahler is evoked throughout the symphony (as will be discussed in the following two chapters), it would not have been surprising to have seen Shostakovich adopting a much more obviously narrative-based approach to symphonic form (such as that in Mahler's Second Symphony). The fact that he did not may be partly explained by the pitfalls inherent in any obvious narrative musical strategy in 1930s Russia. To begin with, as the 1935 symphonism conference shows, that kind of approach was already drawing harsh criticism from composers either cynical of each other's intentions (cf. Kabalevsky's comments on Myaskovsky's Twelfth Symphony) or weary of the aesthetic shallowness of narrative structures, which they felt were years out of date. Shostakovich had already composed two subtitled symphonies with a loose narrative structure, two

37 *Sovetskaya muzïka*, 1935/5, 45.

operas and numerous film, ballet and theatre scores. The Fourth Symphony was his first major 'abstract' work since his First Symphony and, as has been discussed, it marked the beginning of his serious career as a symphonist. Referring to the Fourth Symphony and the direction his career took after the 'Muddle instead of Music' affair, Shostakovich in his old age reflected to his friend Flora Litvinova that without the extreme level of political pressure brought to bear on him in those years, he would have continued along the lines taken in his Fourth Symphony and written 'just [*prosto*] music'.[38] It was conceived as an abstract work, not a narrative one. But for it to have the kind of theatrical immediacy he wanted, and for it to chime in with the epic spirit of its time – during which those around him were clamouring for a new, neo-Beethovenian kind of symphonism – a dramatization of sonata form was the ideal choice for his opening movement.

That dramatization took a remarkable form. Despite the appearance of diatonic – and hence functional – harmony in the first subject, harmony does not play an especially active or propulsive role in the movement as a whole. The establishment of a home key is emphatic, and an alternative tonal sphere (A) is consistently presented throughout the exposition. But during the development the C/A axis becomes a linear rather than a real tonal force; in the dissonant brass chords just before the retransition, A is presented as starkly divorced from C. Now, at the very end of the recapitulation, A both is referred to as a sudden violent presence, opposing the closing C minor with a dominant seventh, and – finally – reduced to its original motivic state, recalled simply in the final a-g over the tonic C in the closing bars. The whole A tonal area seems to function either as a weakening element of C (as at the close of sections, at [5] and [51]), or as an alternative polarity which is never properly articulated in its own right but which interacts with C minor, the A1/A2 development and the duple-time/triple-time relationship.

If Shostakovich rejected functional harmony as a long-term controlling force in the first movement, he replaced it with a loose tonal and intonational system of relationships that could almost be described as intonationally functional, or even 'symbolic', harmony. The respective associations of C (strong themes with

---

38 Cited in Wilson, Shostakovich, 426. Some care is needed here: the Russian words Shostakovich used were *prosto muzïki*, meaning 'just music', but his use of the abverb *prosto* may also imply 'pure music' in the sense of abstract music. The second meaning seems more likely, as Shostakovich was explaining that, if he had been able to continue his career unimpeded after writing the Fourth Symphony, he would not have had to 'resort to camouflage'. The fact remains that Shostakovich did not say *chistaya muzïka*, which is the conventional Russian term for 'pure music', meaning untexted and non-programmatic music. But that would have made little sense for a composer who gravitated towards opera and song as naturally as he did to string quartet and symphony. My feeling is that Shostakovich used *prosto* instead of *chistaya* simply because he meant that he would have written more non-sub-texted music; he would not have had to resort to quotation or paraphrase to get his 'real' meaning across. Still, in the light of his extensive use of paraphrase in the Fourth Symphony, his remarks to Litvinova remain fairly inscrutable.

relatively clear harmonic identities) and A (less stable) are not so rigorously adhered to that this definition could be applied with complete confidence to the first movement; however, the idea of using key centres symbolically will emerge more strongly in the third movement, which suggests that Shostakovich was concerned with finding a system of long-range tonal planning that could function differently from the processes of functional harmony. The interaction of C and A in the first movement demonstrates that Shostakovich's dramatization of thematic conflict and transformation is not shaped only by motivic proliferation, or even by theatrical gestures, but also by deeper 'internal' processes: the inner and outer structures of this movement are very tightly interwoven. This was an essential part of Shostakovich's affirmative response to his colleagues' discussions about the future of the Soviet symphony: in the Fourth Symphony, it could be argued, the demands of form and content are perfectly balanced without conceding too strongly either to one or the other.

However, the most obvious element in Shostakovich's sonata structure is the thematic material itself. Its characterization is both intensely theatrical and highly unconventional. Shostakovich's deliberate disabling of his themes – A1 immobilized by freezing motivic growth; A2 too weak to exist as a real theme until the recapitulation; B1 crippled by metrical and tonal ambiguity; and B2 dissolving into the embryonic citations of the supplication theme – is extreme, but not in itself unique. Mahler's symphonies are riddled with themes that are subjected to collapse, disintegration or violent negation. What is really unusual about Shostakovich's themes here is that the only 'antidote' to the violent first subject is a theme that is not presented fully until the recapitulation. The 'supplication' theme is the central event of the recapitulation, yet it has not been heard in its entirety until that moment. Its impact is derived from a long-distance planning which has planted the figures associated with it at key points in the exposition's dramaturgy so that it may register as fulfilment. The first phrase of the actual theme has of course been heard already at the climax of the exposition; but the motifs feeding into it and prefacing it are what give it the emotional force it conveys in the recapitulation.

The persistent presence of characters outside the basic thematic structure is also unusual. Although the waltz and puppet fragments are broadly associated with the second subject group, and although they do play a part in the build-up to the supplication theme (and are hence 'positive' characters), their otherness is confirmed in the recapitulation, where they are presented intact. As discussed, these 'voices' point to a sphere which is essentially nostalgic and other-worldly; they represent what 'cannot be' rather than being drawn into a deeper structural role.

Despite the theatricality of this movement and its powerfully suggestive thematic transformations and use of 'external' material, its actual 'meaning' is, of course, elusive. Even to categorize themes as 'positive' and 'negative' is a process entirely at the mercy of subjective responses. As discussed, a key moment such as the exposition climax, though provoking different interpretations, is presented 'negatively' in the sense that it lacks normal thematic motivation and momentum, but 'positively' both in that it is a strong theme and counter-force to A1, and in that it provides the only truly convincing climax of the exposition; all those preceding it are deliberately withdrawn at their crisis points and prevented from achieving fulfilment. The role-reversal of the exposition themes in the recapitulation is far too ambivalent to withstand any single hermeneutic reading, tempting though it may be to construct one. The cor anglais's delivery of the supplication theme is the only moment where any sense of a real 'voice' can be heard; but the character and tone of that voice is not easily defined. It is not the kind of 'direct' lyricism offered by A2 at [101], but seems to represent something far more tragic and less easy to define. For this reason I propose that this theme can be read as a 'voice': perhaps even an authorial voice. Its lyricism sounds hard-won, not incongruous; it is not a neat lyrical theme, but has been planted in the listener's subconsciousness from early on in the movement. In this respect, it is the culmination of the 'plot' of the first movement; the place where the author removes his mask for one brief moment. It is not an example of 'voice' in Abbate's definition, at least as applied to the *Gesang* theme of Mahler's *Todtenfeier*. It does not stand out from the surrounding texture; in fact, it blends with it and is dependent upon it for its growth and climactic impact. But it is an example of allusion to an operatic moment within a symphonic movement, with all the inter-textual associations that carries. And its second, more complete statement in the recapitulation has all the hallmarks of voicing in terms of Shostakovich's later symphonies, where double reed instruments are typically used for long, recitative- or arioso-style lamenting solos.

In terms of the relationship between form and content (as defined by Adorno's theory of material form and Formalist notions of *syuzhet* and *fabula*), this first movement is striking for a number of reasons. First, it announces its sonata form structure in terms of a very blatant aggressive/lyrical duality, and relies on listener's expectations of a lyrical second theme with both themes then being developed separately. It then deliberately fails to fulfil those expectations in a satisfactory way. Although, as discussed, it was common for Soviet symphonies to use contrapuntal techniques in the first movement development, Shostakovich's use of polka and waltz and his extreme treatment of fugato take the principle of thematic transformation to new levels of ambivalence, with the aggressive first subject innocently dance-like, then a furious whirlwind and violent canon, then a manic waltz. Finally, though thematic transformation in the recapitulation would not in itself have been especially striking, the way in which the themes are transformed is far more theatrical – and suggestive – than it is in any of its near contemporaries.

By its stark evocation of textbook sonata dramaturgy, then, the first movement deliberately sets up a form/content dialogue, where 'content' (*syuzhet*) such as the supplication theme is located outside the essential 'form' or *fabula*. The plot – the narrative structure of the movement – thus depends upon, and interacts with, the story – the dramatic conventions of sonata form. In Shostakovich's own manipulation of their interaction, the supplication theme itself is of critical importance. Even if it is not regarded as an authorial voice, its 'free' character – the fluid nature of its presence within the spheres of other themes, its embryonic preparation and its final presentation as a long solo (where even the sudden reduction in tempo at the critical moment denotes its separateness from surrounding material) – mark it out as external to (though dependent on) the basic A/B dramaturgy. The fact that it does not appear in the development at all serves to highlight its separateness. Within this context, its 'inter-textual' significance is added on rather than of primary importance; its hermeneutic impact, like that of other, now de-coded allusions and musical monograms in Shostakovich's music, is thus intrinsic rather than extrinsic. Similarly, the way in which Shostakovich uses the 'outside' voices of the waltz and puppet fragments feeds into the narrative structure (the *syuzhet*) of the movement, so that when the first and second subjects become waltzes in the development, they are notably of a different character from the exposition fragments: tonally relatively simple, metrically secure, and bearing a self-containment and confidence worlds apart from the fractured Mahlerian and Stravinskian allusions of the exposition and recapitulation. Hermeneutically speaking, then, the discomfort of the development waltzes again arises through intrinsic means rather than extrinsic. Their false stability is presented as mask-like, pretending to have grasped the other-worldliness of the exposition intonations and reformed them into stable entities. Tonally, their D♭/C♯ tonics are anything but stable, and the masks quickly fade, leaving the empty 'truth' of the fragmented *frullato* passage and 12-note chord.

Such intrinsic relationships form the essence of the first movement's *syuzhet*, or narrative content. As with any narrative discourse, their potency is dependent on the confines (and hence expectations) of *fabula*, or form. As Adorno noted, musical narrative ultimately 'narrates nothing'[39] in terms of specific meaning. The 'meaning' of this movement is, like that of most symphonic music, undefinable. But it *suggests* narrative in a way that contemporary unprogrammatic Soviet symphonies did not, simply by the intensity of the friction between its form and content. And that itself is significant: its predominantly negative atmosphere, combined with its structural unconventionality, creates an overall impression of darkness, even oppression, which fits only too well with what we know of its social context. As the first movement of an epic symphony, it concludes with a resounding question mark, implying (by contemporary symphonic convention) that brighter things can be expected in the following movements. Instead, Shostakovich's subversion of that convention becomes increasingly radical.

39 Quoted in Nattiez, 'Can One Speak of Narrativity in Music?', 245.

CHAPTER FOUR

Second Movement: Moderato con moto

The Mahler Connection

Sandwiched between the massive structures of the first and third movements, this Moderato is both strikingly short and formally straightforward. Whereas the first movement engages critically with the structural conventions of sonata form, the second movement follows an unproblematic ABAB–coda template that is far less dramatically suggestive. Nevertheless, it does effect a shift away from the uneasy calm of the first movement's coda towards a peculiar ambivalence: half grotesque, half ethereal.

Several commentators have noted that the flowing scalic first theme resembles that of the scherzo from Mahler's 'Resurrection' Symphony.[1] The similarity between the two themes, supported by Mahlerian allusions throughout the movement, is marked enough to support the hypothesis that Shostakovich set out to paraphrase Mahler's scherzo in order to set up a sequence of references to the 'Resurrection' Symphony that would reach its apogee in the finale. Equally important are the differences between the two scherzi, the most striking of which are the relatively static tonal and dramatic processes of the Shostakovich as opposed to Mahler's very active, semi-programmatic structure.

Although Mahler soon withdrew his programme for the Second Symphony (denouncing it as a 'crutch for a cripple, nothing more'[2]), his original description of the scherzo in the Dresden programme is unequivocally dark:

> The spirit of unbelief, of negation, has overpowered him [the hero]. He looks at the flood of apparitions and, having lost the pure mind of a child, he altogether loses the solid hold that love alone can give; he despairs of himself and of God. The world and life become for him a weird apparition; disgust for everything present and future grips him with an iron fist and drives him to the outcry of despair.[3]

---

1 See, for example, Sabinina, *Shostakovich-simfonist*, 110–11; Genrikh Orlov 'V serediniye puti' [In the middle of the journey], in Givi Ordzhonikidze, ed., *Dmitriy Shostakovich*, Moscow: Sovetskiy Kompozitor, 1967, 182; Longman, *Expression and Structure*, 16, Ferruccio Tammaro, *Le sinfonie di Šostakovič*, Turin: G. Giappichelli Editore, 1988, 80. Curiously, neither of the two main German sources (Körner, 'Schostakowitschs Vierte Sinfonie' and Kopp, *Form und Gehalt*) mentions Mahler at all until the discussion of the finale coda. Mikheyeva, however, finds a similarity with the 'Schattenhaft' scherzo of Mahler's Seventh. See Mikheyeva, *Zhizn' Dmitriya Shostakovicha*, 199.

2 Cited in Deryck Cooke, *Gustav Mahler: An Introduction to his Music*, second edition, London: Faber, 1988, 53–4.

3 Constantin Floros, *Gustav Mahler: The Symphonies*, trans. Vernon Wicker, Aldershot:

From Mahler's additional comments to Natalie Bauer-Lechner and Max Marschalk, it is evident that individual alienation was for Mahler the key to understanding the scherzo's shadowy tone. Mahler repeatedly described it in terms of a man watching a ballroom scene 'from a distance through a window', unable to participate. The carefree gaity of the dancers thus represented the 'never-to-be-understood hustle and bustle of life ... a cruel nightmare'.[4] Its links with the *Wunderhorn* song 'Des Antonius von Padua Fischpredigt', where St Antony preaches to the uncomprehending fishes, underline Mahler's intention to portray the 'hustle and bustle of life' in all its complacency as the broad context of the scherzo, while simultaneously focusing more narrowly on the personal anguish of the alienated individual. Sollertinsky, aware of Mahler's own interpretation, viewed it as the first of Mahler's grotesque scherzi (followed by those of the Sixth, Seventh and Ninth Symphonies) which represent Mahler in the role of 'ecstatic preacher' 'crying in the wilderness' like Nietzsche and Dostoevsky: 'the greatest pathos and sharpest irony are, ultimately, created by the combination of frenzied sermon and the sarcasm of awareness of the sermon's complete futility.'[5] The scherzo departs from the song in its insertion of additional sections which look ahead to the finale: the sudden *Vorwärts* passages ([37] – [44] and [49] – [54]) containing the C major third subject group which foreshadows the finale's *Aufersteh'n* theme (Example 4.1).

That remarkable passage will be near-quoted in Shostakovich's finale, as will be seen in the following chapter. And there are good reasons why he might have wanted to save the *Aufersteh'n* allusion for the finale rather than modelling his scherzo too closely on Mahler's, as will be discussed. In the Mahler, the contrast between the *Vorwärts* passages and the 'Des Antonius' themes is too sharp to allow a smooth transition from one to the other: moves are effected by sudden collapse, abrupt ending or violent intrusion. Which form the switch-over takes is dictated by the incoming theme and its relation to its predecessor. The bustling scherzo themes (A and A1), the bombastic *Vorwärts* passages and the sleepy E major *gesangvoll* section ([40] – [43]) can be read as the 'negative' materials of the scherzo, representing (as we know from the song and from Mahler's early programme) the world's busy (or sleepy) complacency. The collapses and ruptures which punctuate the scherzo's progress are thus 'positive', disrupting and opposing that complacency: the sudden climax between [50][9] and [51], described by Adorno as 'the

---

Scolar Press, 1994, 63. For Mahler's programme and comments to Bauer-Lechner and Marschalk on the meaning of the scherzo, see Donald Mitchell, *Gustav Mahler: The Wunderhorn Years*, California: University of California Press, 1975, 183–184, and Floros, *Gustav Mahler*. The source for Mahler's remarks to Marschalk is Alma Mahler's Gustav *Mahler: Briefe 1879–1911*, Berlin: Paul Zsolnay Verlag, 1924, which is listed in Sollertinskiy's bibliography.

4 Quoted in Floros, *Gustav Mahler*.

5 Sollertinskiy, *Gustav Maler*, 29.

Example 4.1

a Mahler II/3: 52^{1} – ^{7}53

Immer noch unmerklich zurückhaltend

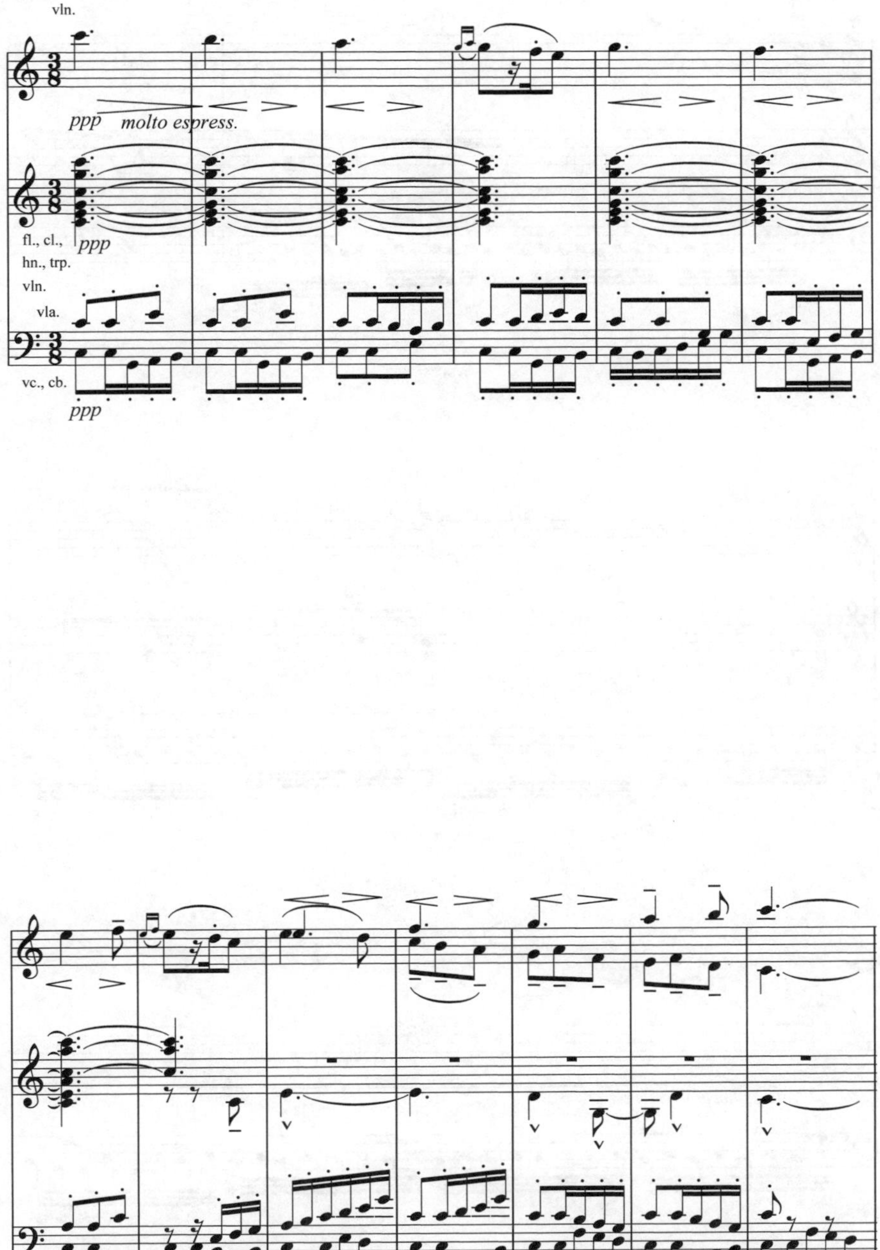

b Mahler II/5: [2]6–11

Sehr zurückhaltend

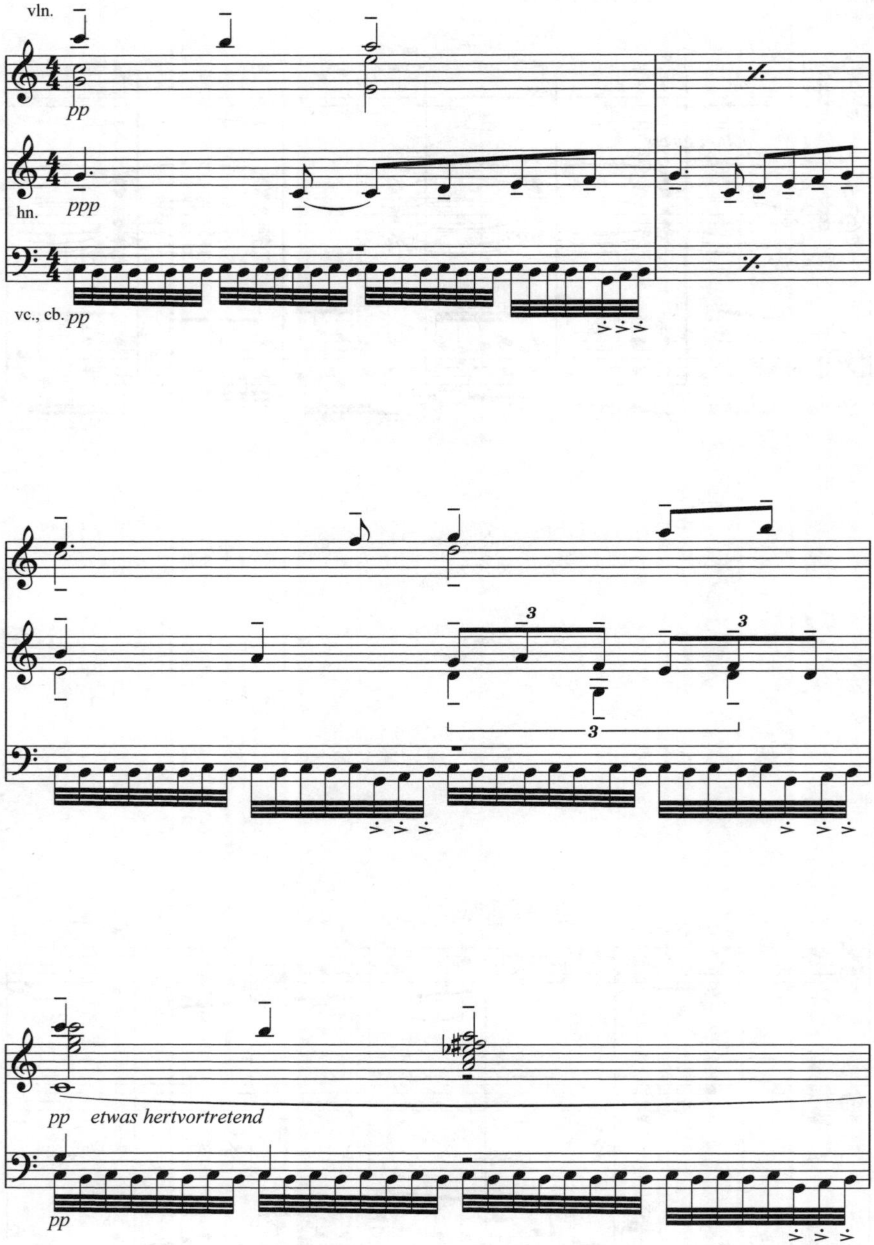

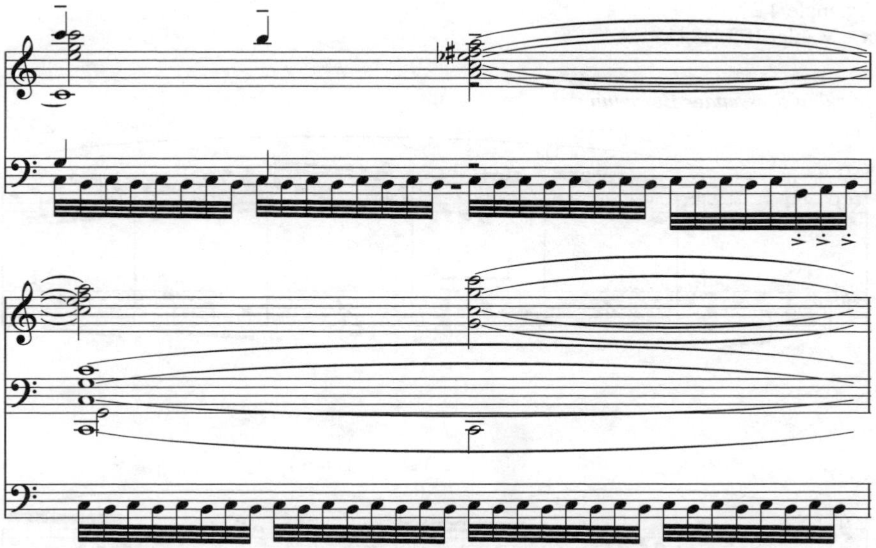

instrumental outcry of one in despair',[6] prefigures the explosive opening of the finale ('Im Tempo des Scherzo's') and its first hint of the *Aufersteh'n* theme, as illustrated in Example 4.1. But this interaction of 'positive' and 'negative' is problematized, since the world Mahler is portraying is only superficially carefree; it is the hero's alienation from it (and its relationship to 'Des Antonius') which challenges its lightweight tone and enables him (and thus the symphony) to attain true fulfilment. Thus a 'negative' musical event, such as a sudden collapse, is 'positive' in a deeper sense, representing truth over artifice. But the *Aufersteh'n* references are positive in both senses, always presented with their essential intonational character intact. They are, as Sollertinsky might have said, instances of a 'direct lyric' asserting itself over the 'indirect lyric' of the 'Des Antonius' themes. Anticipating the redemption of the finale, they stand outside the scherzo's main body of themes, representing hope beyond the despair of the scherzo itself. As shown in Example 4.1, the sustained Cs of the woodwind and strings at II/3: 52 are crucial signposts for the finale's first hint of redemption between 2 and 3, and the basses' C major dance theme (C in Example 4.2d) similarly plants the seeds for the finale's C major bass semiquaver figure starting at 2.

Parallels between Shostakovich's Moderato and Mahler's scherzo go further than the superficial similarity of their opening themes. The striking fluidity of Mahler's 'Des Antonius' themes is mirrored by Shostakovich's. Example 4.2 shows that process in both movements.

6 Adorno, *Mahler*, 7.

Example 4.2
a Mahler II/3: [28]$^{12–31}$:A

In ruhig fliessender Bewegung

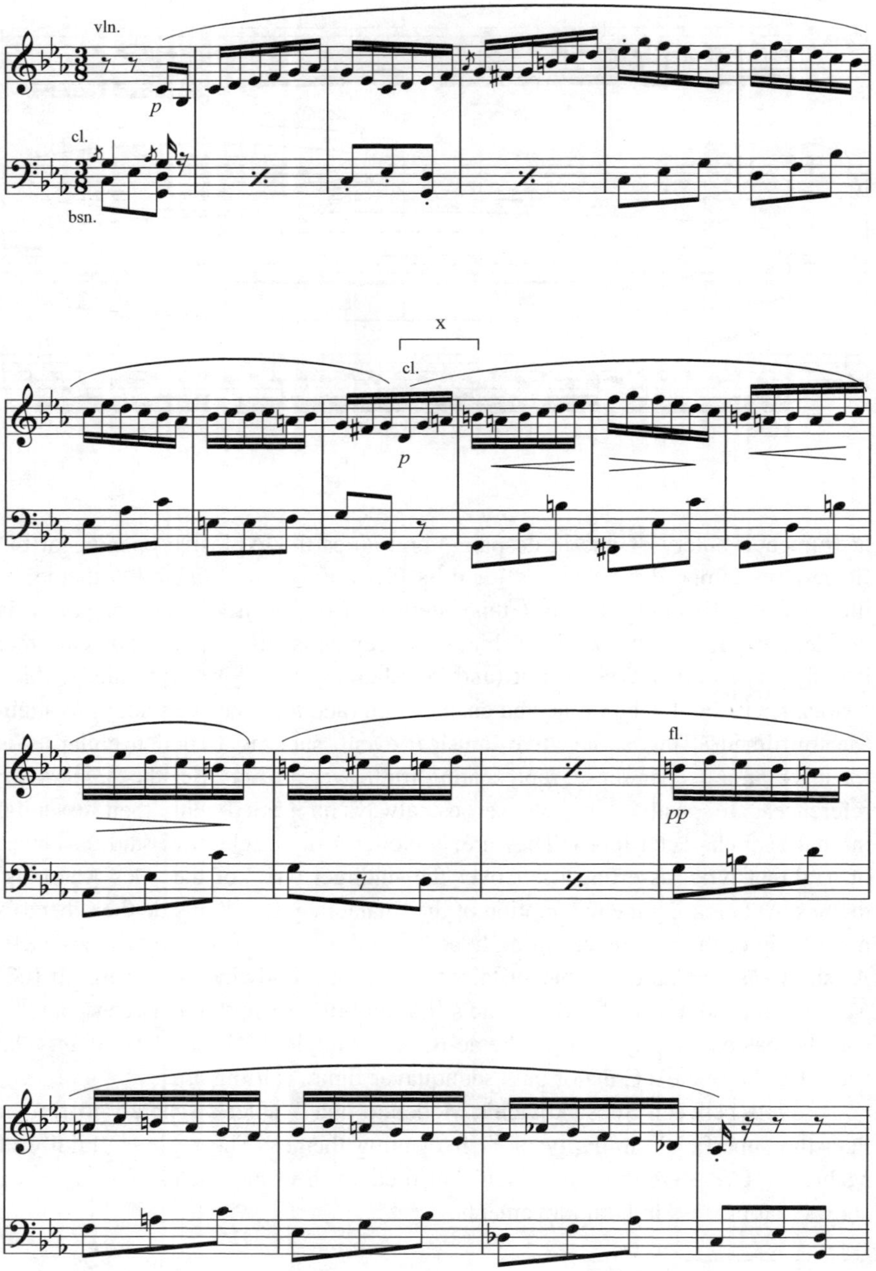

b Mahler II/3: [29]14–18: A1

Immer noch unmerklich zurückhaltend

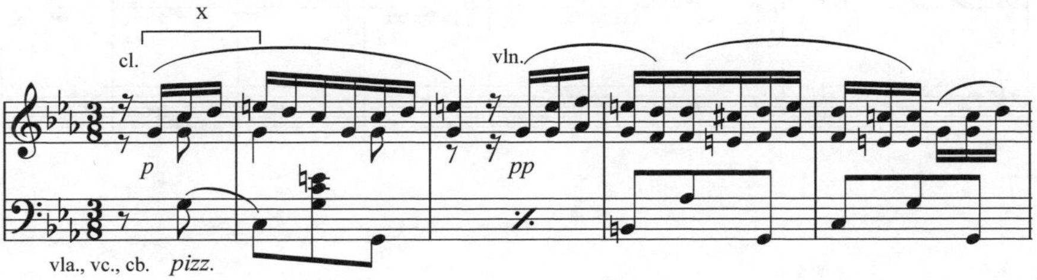

c Mahler II/3: [32]1–4: B

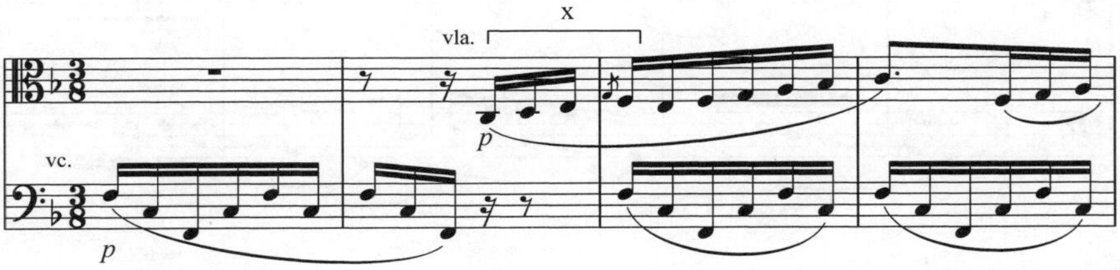

d Mahler II/3: [36]1–4: C

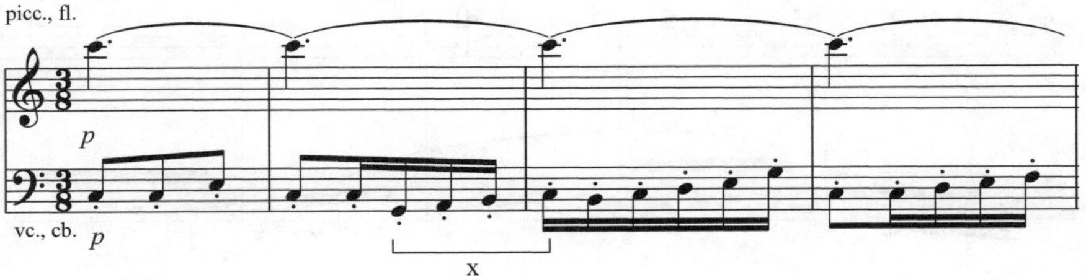

e Shostakovich IV/2: [110] – [111]9: A

♩ = 144

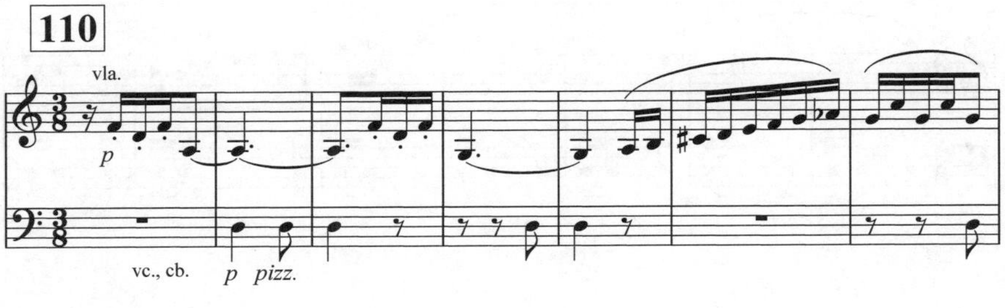

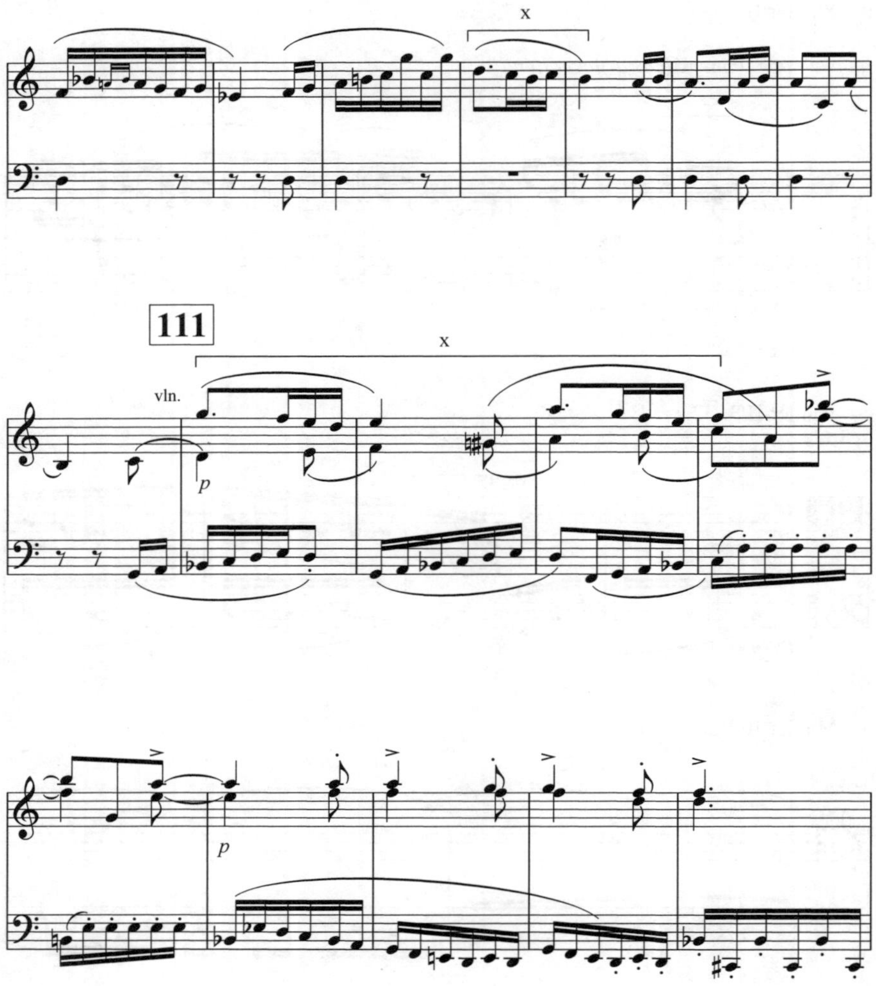

f Shostakovich IV/2: 123 [1–7]: B

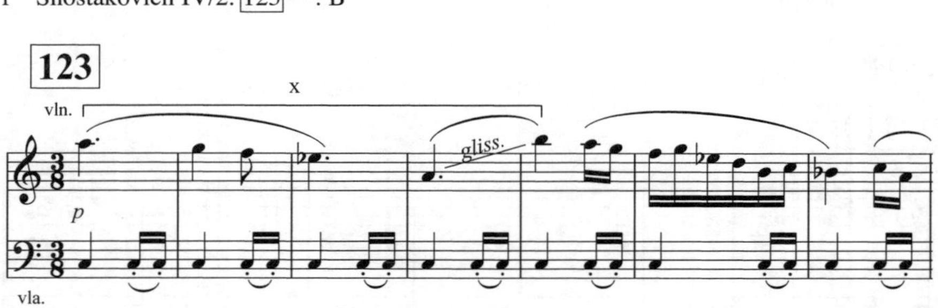

As Example 4.2 demonstrates, all the major-inflected themes in Mahler's scherzo are related, beginning with motif 'x' from the first theme's answering phrase, echoed in A1 and feeding into B and C. A similar process of evolution occurs in the Shostakovich, with themes A and B very closely related, as shown in Example 4.2. The dramaturgy of the two processes is different, however: in the Mahler, the first theme maintains an intonational distinction from other themes owing to the minor–major distinction between them, and this is an important part of the scherzo's dramatic scheme. In the Shostakovich, both themes (A and B) are minor-inflected, and B, though different in colour and contour, is clearly derived from the counter-statement at 111 (see Example 4.2e and f). However, the separation of the first and second thematic groups is clearer in the Shostakovich than in the Mahler, largely because Mahler's second theme (A1) grows more seamlessly out of the first and is similarly scalic in structure, while in the Shostakovich, B is set apart through both structural and textural contrast.

Mahler punctuates his fluid textures with dramatic effects: sudden collapses and interruptions are substituted for elegant transitions. Shostakovich does use similar gestures of collapse, but very sparingly: the resultant static effect is like a pale shadow of Mahler's scherzo. But the type of collapse used in both cases is strikingly similar: a descending chromatic scale, beginning *ff* and falling to *pp* or *p*. In Example 4.3a, c and d, the short chromatic descent is a response to motivic fixation and marks either the resumption of the previous theme or a transition to another; Example 4.3b shows a furious one-bar descent to the return of A after the

Example 4.3
a Mahler II/3: ^{7}32 – 32

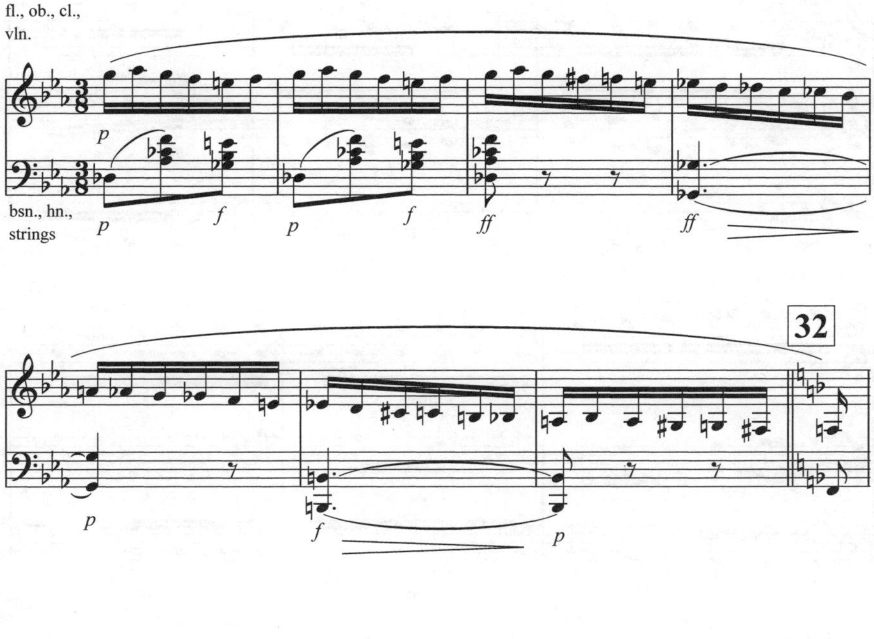

b Mahler II/3: 4[44] – 1[44]

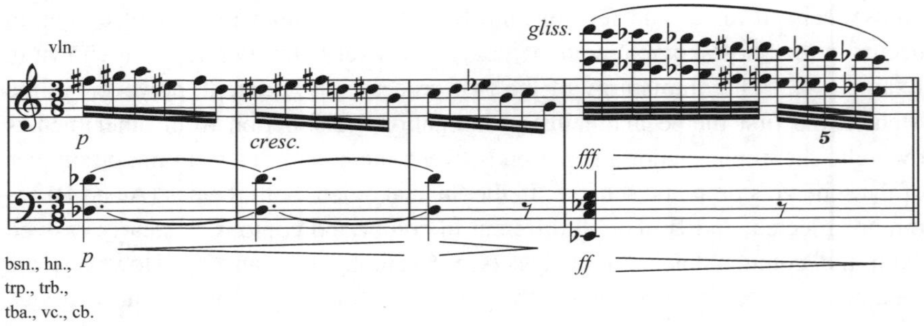

c Shostakovich IV/2: 1[113] – 2[114]

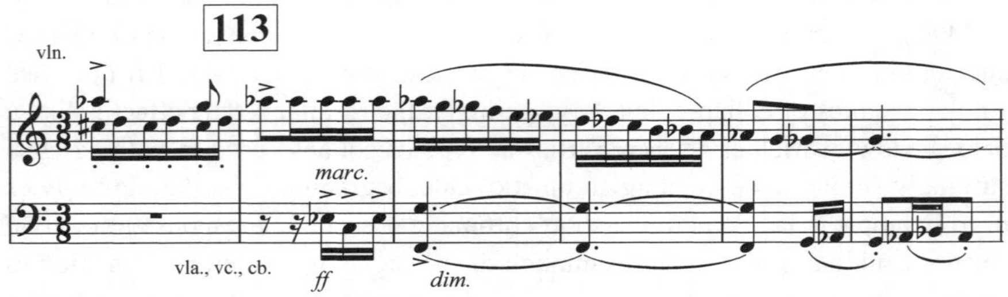

d Shostakovich IV/3: 2[117] – [117]4

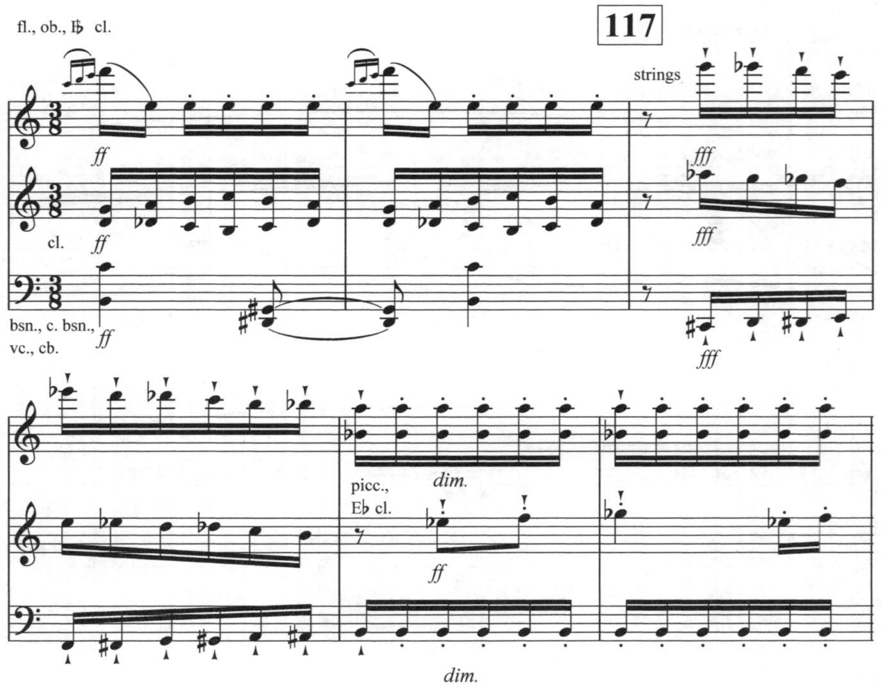

calm repose of the *gesangvoll* episode (40 – 43). The evolutionary nature of thematic relationships in Shostakovich's first subject group is consistently challenged by the rigidity of the paragraphs, which are marked out by each collapse and sudden change-over. There are four 'entries' of the first subject in all: after the first statement of A, each subsequent entry provokes a climax–collapse sequence followed by a return to the first subject in its original key, however briefly (see Table 4.1). This process of dividing fluid thematic textures with sharp transitional effects again recalls Mahler's scherzo, where sections are similarly marked out, punctuated by collapses and sudden closure. Table 4.2 shows this process up to the entry of the third subject group at 36. Finally, the connection between these two movements is rendered unequivocal by Shostakovich's sudden and dramatic paraphrasing of Mahler's introductory timpani and clarinet motifs following the abrupt cut between his first and second subject groups (Example 4.4).

One of the most striking aspects of Shostakovich's Moderato is that despite its obvious allegiance to Mahler, it lacks a comparably overt dramatization of musical characters. Its tone is introverted and subdued, and there is no 'positive' theme to counter its 'negative' mask-like flatness. It is neither lyrical nor dance-like, despite its triple metre; nor is it a scherzo: Shostakovich described it in neutral terms as an 'intermezzo in tempo Allegretto'.[7] Its state of being is passive, not active; dramatic progress is suspended in a static, unreal atmosphere.

The ruptures in Mahler's scherzo have, as discussed, a positive role in the symphony's dramaturgy, questioning the smooth complacency of the flowing first and second themes and clearing ground for the finale's C major 'breakthrough' (to

Table 4.1 Shostakovich IV/2: summary of first subject group: 110 – 123

Figure	Theme	Tonal centre	Notes
110	A	d	Metrically unstable at first.
111			Counter-statement.
112	A	d	Not a proper repeat of A: registrally compressed and shortened. Leads to collapse at 113.
114	A	d	Truncated entry: 2 phrase given cut-off at 122, with Mahler allusions. Short transition to B.

7 Quoted in Fay, *Shostakovich*, 93.

Table 4.2 Mahler II/3: summary of first and second subject groups: 28–36

Figure	Theme	Tonal centre	Notes
28	Introduction	c	*ff* timpani figure and clarinet appoggiaturas.
28^{12}	A	c	Flowing scalic theme.
$^{11}29$		G	Answering phrase.
29^{2}	A	c	
$^{13}30$	A1	C	Waltz-like; E♭ clarinet *mit Humor*. Collapse (chromatic descent).
30^{11}	A	c	Counter-subject.
$^{2}31$	A1	C	Ends with bigger collapse (chromatic descent).
32	B	F	Flowing theme similar to A. Abrupt change-over.
34	A	c	Counter-subject and introductory clarinet appoggiaturas. Fragmentation (*ppp*).
36	C	C	Sudden *ff* switch to rustic bass dance theme, with staccato semiquavers.

use Adorno's term) with the first hint of the *Aufersteh'n* theme. Those in the Shostakovich – the chromatic collapses, abrupt closure and paraphrase (122) and interruption (129) – do not lead anywhere, but are caused by motivic repetition pushing themes to over-exertion. This echoes several abortive climax points in the first movement (IV/1: 27 and 30), where harmonic movement is similarly suspended; from 24 (between the end of the first subject group and the beginning of the second) the tone is obsessive and fixated, and with no sense of either harmonic or thematic momentum the whole dramaturgical process seems in suspense. The static, alienated tone of that section is a particular feature of the Moderato, achieved, as in the first movement, by a combination of thematic and harmonic inertia, as will be seen. Shostakovich's Moderato is the antithesis of Mahler's scherzo, taking its most salient characteristics (flowing themes and chromatic collapses), but deliberately avoiding Mahler's 'positive' seeds of

Example 4.4
a Mahler II/3: 28 1–10

In ruhig fliessender Bewegung

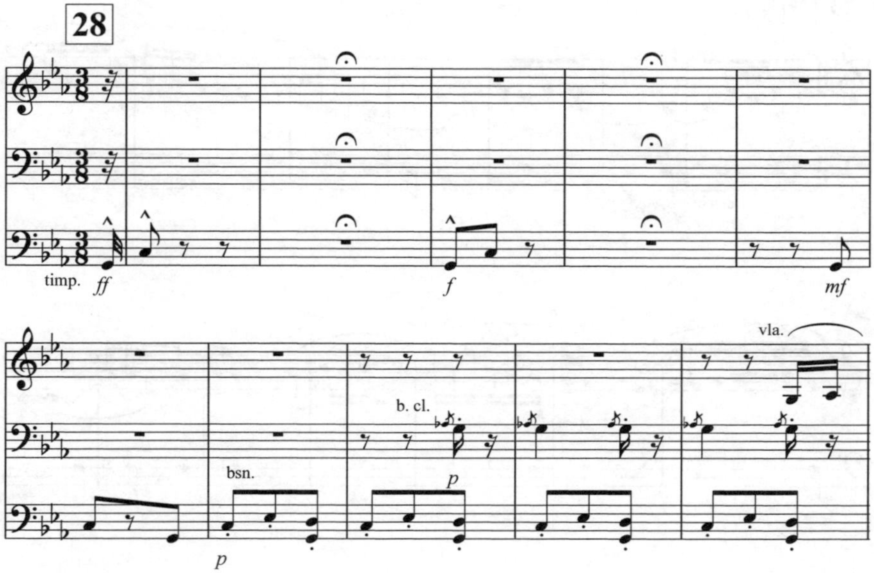

b Shostakovich IV/2: 122 1–5

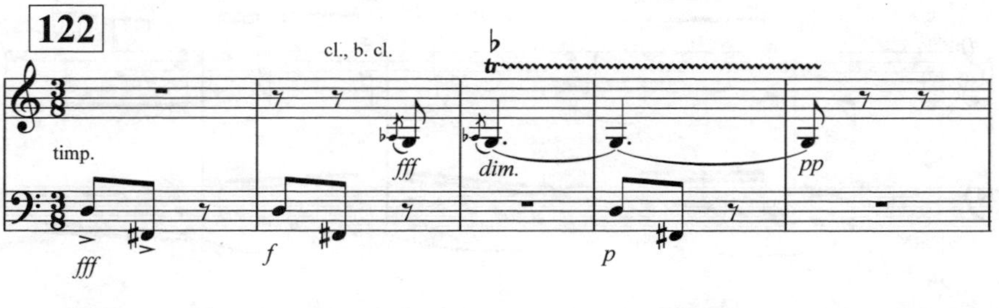

redemption that offer hope of something beyond the bustling triviality of the 'Des Antonius' themes. Those seeds will appear only in Shostakovich's finale, where, however, they will again suggest a deliberate strategy of antithesis to Mahler's Second Symphony.

First Subject Group: 110 – 123: A

The shadowy tone of the first theme, shown in Example 4.5, stems in part from its presentation on violas with pizzicato bass. It is exacerbated by an initial metrical ambiguity: what feels like the opening anacrusis falls not onto the expected first

Example 4.5
Shostakovich IV/2: 110 – 111[9]: A

Moderato con moto ♩ = 144

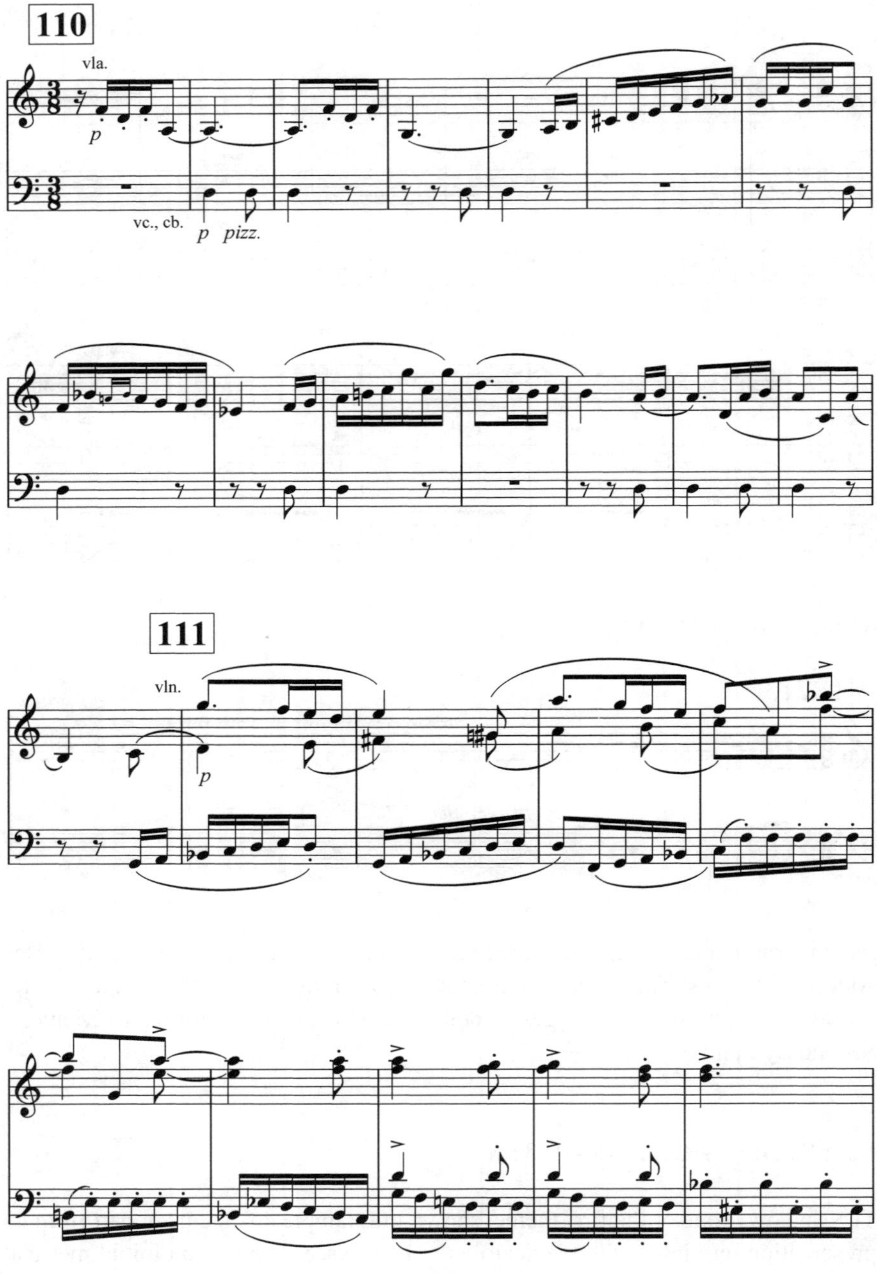

beat, but onto the third beat of the first bar, tied over to the second. The flowing triple metre is thus not established until the sixth or seventh bar. The counter-statement in first violins ([111]) builds on the violins' dotted rhythm in bar 11 and the bass trochees. These trochaic rhythms then dominate the collapse of A at ^{2}[113], suppressing scalic movement in oscillating figuration and reiterated A♭s. As the first of a series of variant entries of A, that at [112] is registrally compressed, quickly turning in on itself and leading to the first fixation–collapse at [113]. The relative tonal clarity of A is also clouded by presenting this variant entirely as a whole-tone scale from A to f^1, with tritones in the bass (Example 4.6). The collapse at [113] (see Example 4.3c) is a one-octave chromatic wedge descent, bringing its $a\flat^1$/F apex back to the tonic D. A truncated opening of theme A leads straight into the second phrase, this time given the grotesque E♭ clarinet characterization familiar from Mahler's scherzo (Example 4.7). This variant of A now begins to fragment; at [116] the process of fixation and intensification begins with oscillating inner parts and an insistent reiterated woodwind figure, beginning with A's opening minor third and expanding to a minor ninth. This prompts a second, more aggressive, collapse: again, a near-octave descent, now *marcato* and *fff* (see Example 4.3d). The collapse is less sudden here than at [113], and is prolonged by a new focus on theme A's minor third, but it is considerably more aggressive. A further incomplete entry

Example 4.6
Shostakovich IV/2: [112]$^{1–6}$

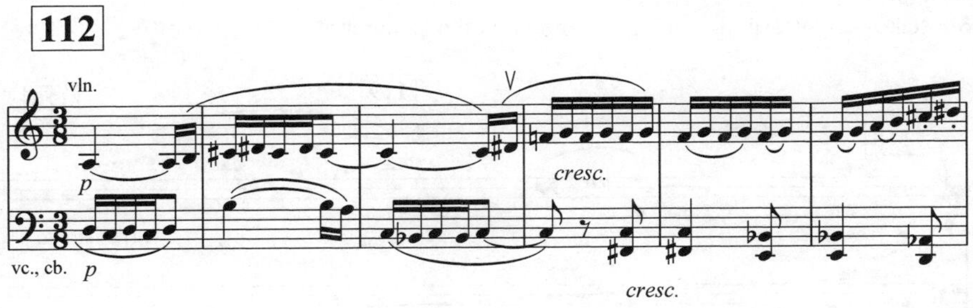

Example 4.7
a Mahler II/3: ^{5}[30] – ^{1}[30]

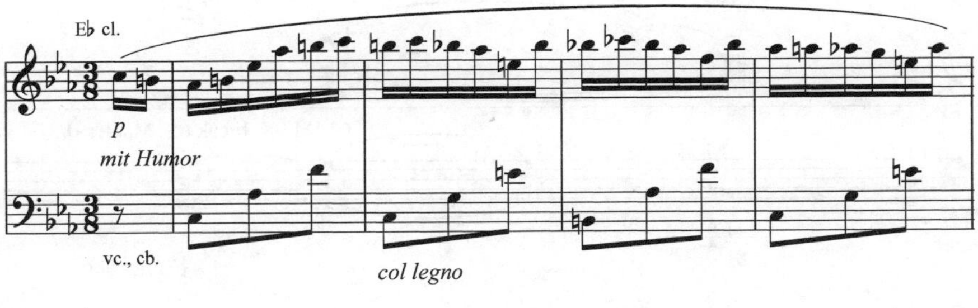

b Shostakovich IV/2: 114$^{1-4}$

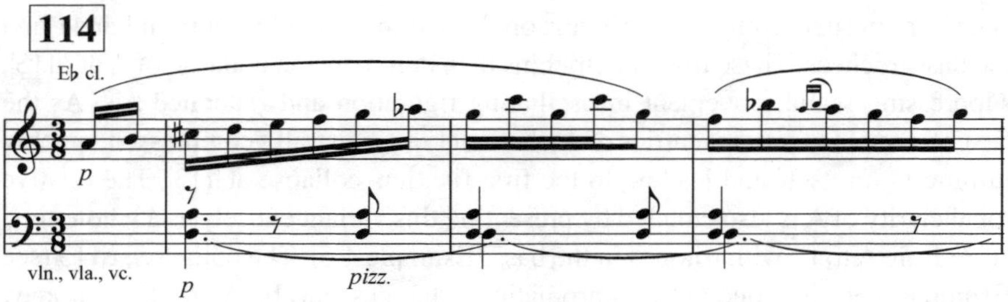

of A at 118 instigates a near-whole-tone bass descent from D to E♭^{1}: A's opening minor third motif transmutes into D♭ major thirds (from 118^6), beneath which the bass descent takes place (Example 4.8). The truncated, compressed variant of A at ^{1}120 on bassoons provides new momentum and marks the start of the basses' ascent from F^1 to C♯ at the final approach to the climax at ^{3}122 (see Example 4.8). Oscillating semiquavers, a dactylic trombone motif and stretto-like entries of A indicate an approaching climax, much in the same way as motivic fixation at ^{2}113 and 116 – 117 prompted the chromatic collapses. An abrupt change of texture marks the basses' C♯ goal, punched out in the strings; woodwind skirls and ascending horn scales push on towards the climax, but its arrival is swiftly

Example 4.8
Shostakovich IV/2: 118 – ^{3}123: linear and motivic summary

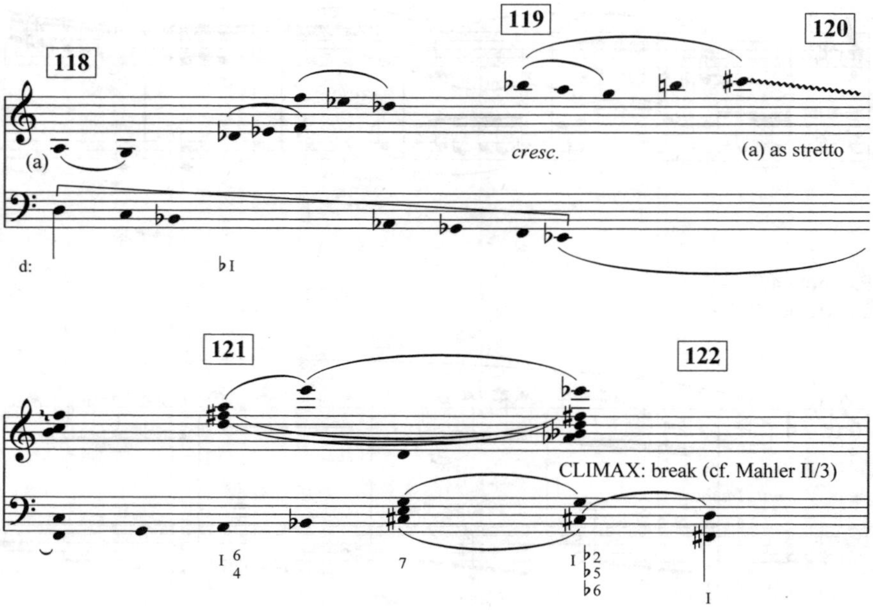

curtailed: clarinet trills answer a violent timpani figure – the second clear reference to Mahler's scherzo (see Example 4.4). Example 4.8 shows that the whole approach to the climactic tutti section between [118] and [122] forms an imperfect arch from D down to E♭^{1}, returning to D, with the climax on C♯: the climax is thus poised on the leading-note, which prevents it from sounding like a fulfilment of the first subject group. The fixation–collapse sequence of the three sections of the Moderato ([110] – [114], [114] – [118], [118] – [123]) intensifies each time, so that the relatively smooth chromatic descent at [113], following only a two-bar motivic reiteration, becomes much more aggressive at [117], after an eight-bar crescendo. The third 'false' entry at [118] degenerates into motivic reiteration almost immediately, with repeated D♭ major tetrachords, horn dactyls, oscillating wind figuration and stretto entries of A; over the basses' C♯ the climax at [122] abruptly breaks off, with the Mahler allusions that follow emphasising its unfinished quality.

Second Subject Group: [123] – [130]: B

The violence of this sudden curtailment leaves an feeling of emptiness: a viola line gropes for a new theme, settling on a dactylic C pedal over which the second theme (B) enters. Its tone is ghostly and desolate, not unlike the second subject (B at [31]) of the first movement, though with a much sharper metrical focus. The static pedal-point – retained for every one of the four entries of theme B, either in its original dactylic form or in oscillating semiquavers – is largely responsible for the eerie effect, though modal ambiguity also plays a significant part. The initial pedal C implies a minor C mode with occasional sharpened fifth, seventh and eighth degrees. However, C as a tonal centre is presented weakly, with A as the starting-pitch for the first two thematic entries, first over the C pedal, then over F at [124]. The C pedal could equally be read as an F $^{6}_{4}$, moving to root position at [124]. As Example 4.9 shows, pedal-points and bass open fifths are a prominent feature of B, and these, along with the steady treading rhythms, form the backbone of its stability. That apparent diatonic stability is disturbed by whole-tone scales and flattened degrees in the bass harmonies: a flattened ninth to the F^{7} chord at [124] and flattened tenth to the E major at [125] (see Example 4.9b). Harmonic support is suspended altogether at [127], where B is presented in parallel fifths, clashing with the overlapping parallel fifths of the canonic fifth entry at [127]^{3} (at two bars' distance). With the addition of the whole-tone scale betwen [126] and [127], the tonal ambit of B is further obscured, becoming far more ambiguous than that of A. The devices Shostakovich uses to cloud the fundamental diatonicism of B create a static, hazy impression: the glissando within the first statement reinforces its ghostly quality. The third statement at [125] sounds more substantial, with a noticeable warming of orchestral texture as horns take over the theme from violins. But its E major is alien to the broad F ambit of this section, and this moment of

Example 4.9

a Shostakovich IV/2: 123 – ^{1}124

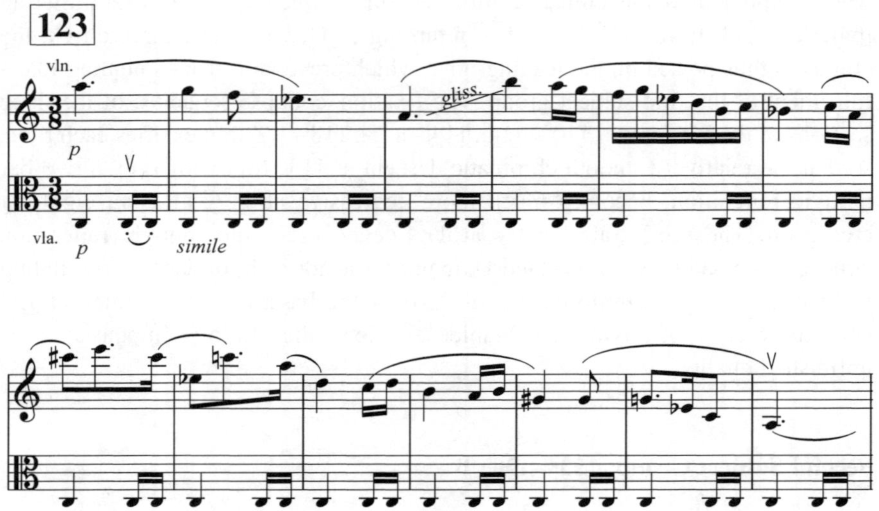

b Shostakovich IV/2: 123 – ^{3}130: linear and motivic summary

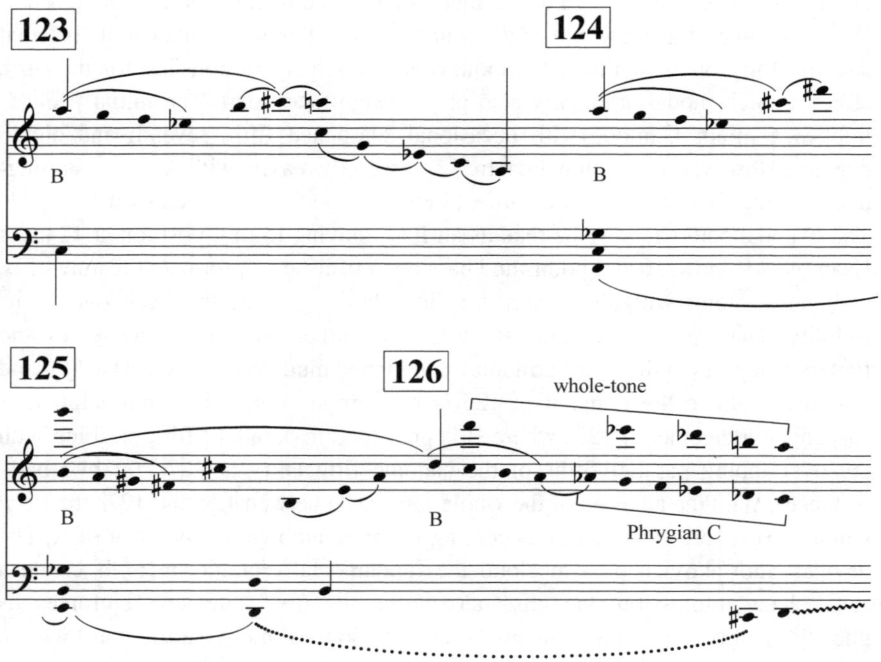

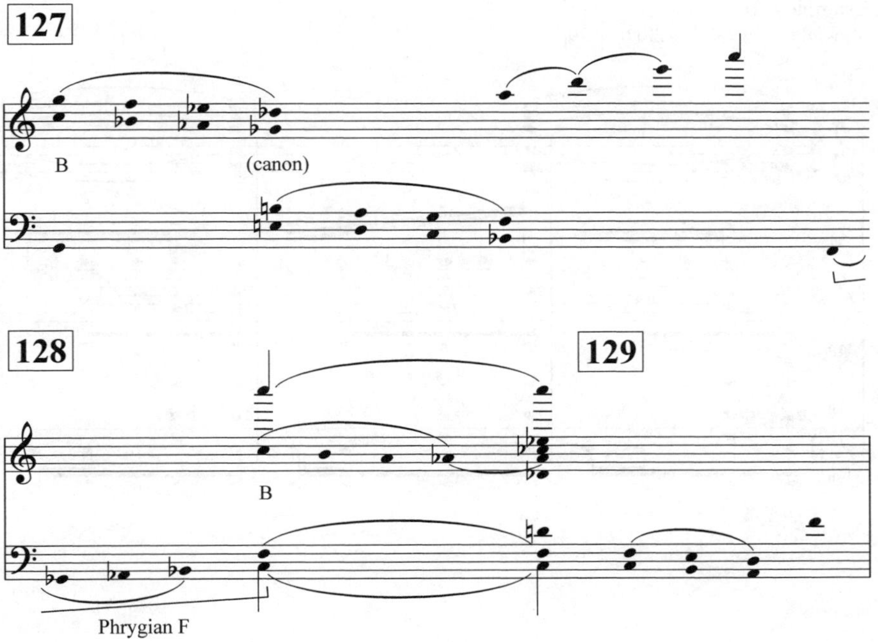

warmth is not only short-lived but also indicative of a new departure both from the tonic and from any diatonic orientation whatever. Almost immediately the mood chills: a descending whole-tone pentachord on flutes (^{3}127 – 127) and oscillating semiquavers introduce the fourth entry, sounding remote on flutes and piccolo in fifths, in dissonant canon with bassoon. Descending whole-tone pentachords overlap in a quasi-stretto between 126 and 128, where an ascending Phrygian F pentachord prefaces the fragmentation of the theme in stretto half-entries, culminating at ^{5}129 with an A♭ minor triad superimposed onto a minor F $^{6}_{4}$, leading the whole section back to the opening F $^{6}_{4}$ at 123. Example 4.9b shows the breakdown of the orderly pattern of the first three entries (which rise by step from A to B as the bass descends from F to E), the ensuing overlapping pentachords that confuse and darken the modal texture, and the Phrygian return to F $^{6}_{4}$.

Like the climaxes of the first subject group, that of the second group (128 – 129) is not a fulfilment of harmonic or thematic processes but rather a fixated reiteration of motifs: a C–F–C bass, an iambic d♭–d♮ semitonal oscillation on horns, an A♭ minor triad on trumpets and a clashing $c\sharp^{2}$–e^{2} string figure. Like the theme A climax at 122, it is violently interrupted by timpani and brass, once again recalling the beginning of Mahler's scherzo, with the opening clarinet appoggiaturas (echoed by Shostakovich at 122) transformed into violent accented semiquavers (Example 4.10). The combination of harmonic inertia and motivic fixation

Example 4.10
Shostakovich IV/2: 128[6] – 129[4]

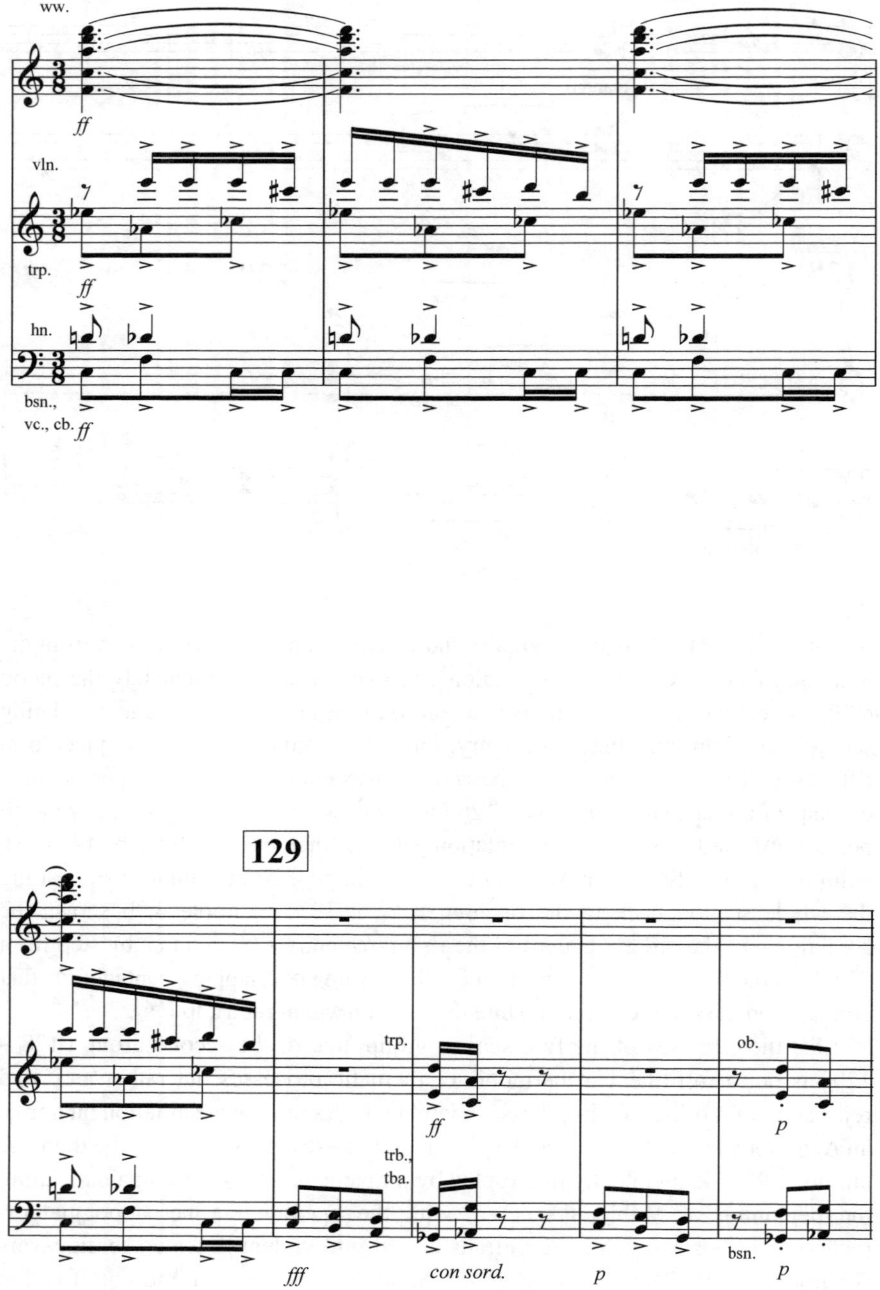

produces a characteristically unsatisfying climax; the allusions to Mahler's abrupt opening bars (and, by extension, to their earlier appearance in the Moderato at 122) register as further negation of a 'normal' climactic moment. Here, it signals a return to the opening theme, now presented as a spidery fugue.

130 – 143 : A as Fugue

The return to the first subject takes the form of a four-voice fugue in D minor initially for strings, with regular tonic–dominant entries between 130 and 134. After that the tonic–dominant axis dissolves, with a disorientating d♭^{2} entry at 134 followed by A♭, then e^1 and B. Woodwinds take over from strings at 139, with burbling stretto entries a major seventh apart (f^1, g♭^{1}, g, A♭) at the distance of a quaver. As shown in Example 4.11, the D minor tonic–dominant entries have F and C as starting-pitches, but by 134 the D minor tonic–dominant relationship is flattened to d♭–A♭ pitch entries (in keys of B♭ and F minor), which appear again in key entries at 136 (C♯, G♯) before piling up with f^2, g♭^{1}, g and A♭. As with the presentation of theme B, a direct, open tone is avoided throughout this section. The secure familiarity of A's return is undermined by its opening entry at 130, where the first two phrases of A are repeated, creating uncertainty as to its continuation. The theme and its modal structure remain intact throughout, though progress beyond the first two phrases is varied: the first entry subsides after the second phrase in order to give room for the second entry, which cuts to the octave

Example 4.11
Shostakovich IV/2: 130 – 139 : fugal entries. Bracketed notes show key of entry.

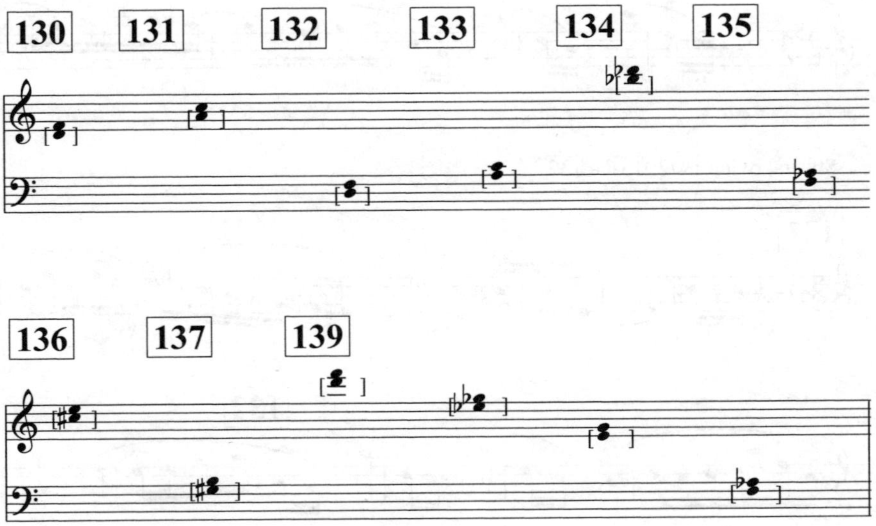

figuration from 114$^{5-7}$ and augments the semiquaver figure at ^{2}115 to echo the counter-statement at 111 as the third entry begins at 132 (see Example 4.12). All subsequent entries up to 136 are modelled on this pattern. After the eighth entry (starting on B) at 137 is completed at 138, repetition of A's opening minor third motif builds to a short climax: the semitonal stretto entries follow in a uniform *piano*, which is maintained until the very end of the fugue section. Any sense of a tonal centre has departed after the first entry group from 130 to 134: from the start of the second group at 136 tension mounts, with entries marked *f* to *fff*. After a brief diminuendo to *p*, this culminates with a crescendo (starting at ^{2}138) through the obsessive repetition of A's minor third and a rising figure in all five voices, characteristically cut off at its peak.

Example 4.12

a Shostakovich IV/2: 111$^{1-3}$

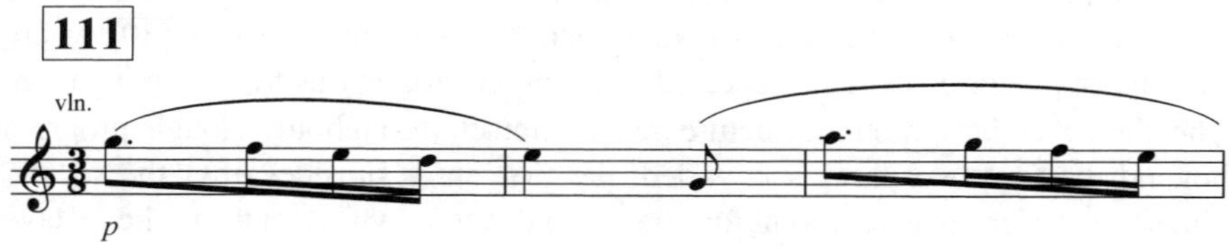

b Shostakovich IV/2: 114^{5} – ^{1}115

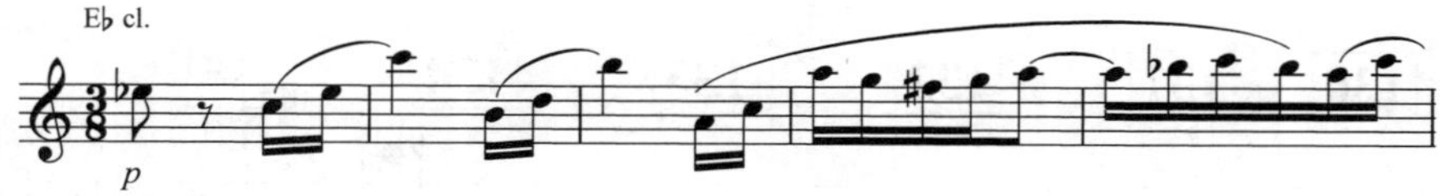

c Shostakovich IV/2: 131 – 132^{2}

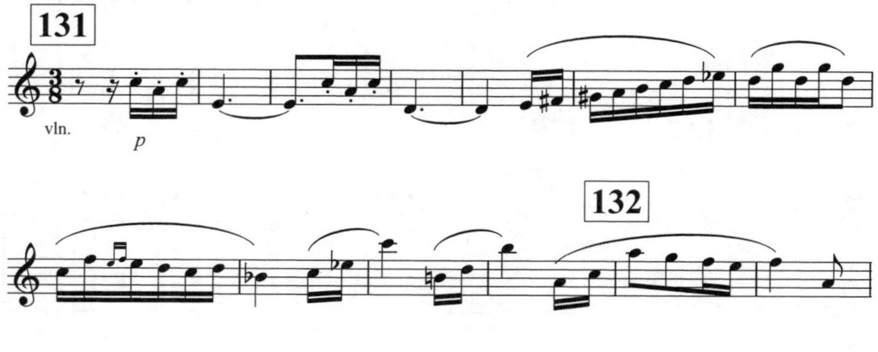

139 – 143: Stretto

The final entry group (139 – 143) is the shortest and most contrapuntally dense section of the fugue, with all four entries complete after just 14 bars: the remainder of the section is given over to strict counterpoint on piccolo, flute and clarinet. Its directionless, burbling tone recalls the passages of dense linear counterpoint from the Second and Third Symphonies, which similarly lack any sense of tonal or rhythmic propulsion. After the four entries are complete, the range of each voice becomes narrower and more chromatic, the unbroken semiquaver movement sounding empty and wandering. A three-bar chromatic 'wedge' crescendo leads straight into the main climax of the Moderato at 143.

Although, as discussed in Chapter Three, fugues were fairly common in Soviet symphonies from this period, Shostakovich's use of fugue was far removed from that of Myaskovsky or Shebalin, both of whom often used fugato in development sections. Whereas in the first movement Shostakovich used fugue as a dramatic technique for sudden acceleration and intensification (as well as for thematic transformation), here he uses it to present the return of the first theme in an unfamiliar, alienating manner, but without losing thematic coherence. After its regular tonic–dominant opening, the fugue quickly loses its tonal bearings, and the compressed dissonance of the stretto, combined with its mechanical woodwind texture, 'estranges' the thematic material still further.

143 – 150: B as Climax

The second theme, initially at its original pitch, now returns in a leaden, monolithic wind peroration, this time in forced co-existence with a strident D pedal and D major woodwind triads. Whereas at 123 there was tonal agreement between the theme and its bass harmonization, here there is none at all: the original F $^6_4$ is replaced by a long D pedal which is unrelated to theme B's a–e♭ contour. The bass's chromatic ascent from D^1 to F^1 begins at 145 as, after two full entries, the rising fourths (a–d^1) pattern breaks and regular entries are replaced by false or incomplete ones. The next (incomplete) entry at 145^6 occurs as the bass begins to gravitate towards C in a process that will culminate in a stifled C minor version of B at 149, just before the sudden turn back to D minor for the coda at 150. Still clashing with the C bass, the entry at 145^6 briefly implies B major, which holds for the next, near-complete entry at 147. At this point, the bass has moved from a C major $^6_3$ to a minor $^6_3$; at the penultimate incomplete entry at 148, it moves to iv$^6_4$, and from there to V^7 before reaching its C minor goal at 149. The final incomplete entry on solo bassoon at 149 orbits forlornly around c, its persistent c♯s always sounding like an attempt to return to d, which it finally achieves as the bass moves to D minor again for the coda at 150 (see Example 4.13). The effect of this uncomfortable return to B – as the climax of the Moderato – is deliberately

Example 4.13
Shostakovich IV/2: 143 – 150: harmonic and thematic summary

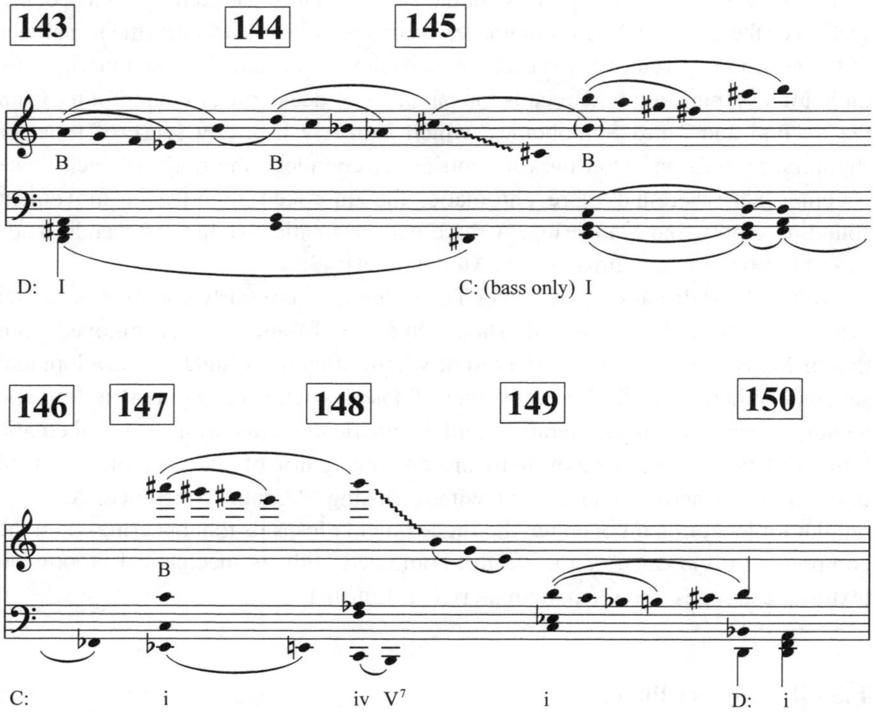

unsatisfying, negating even the gentle ambivalence of its original presentation in favour of something far more purposefully malignant. Replacing its mediant F orbit with the tonic major, while retaining the original key of the first entry, creates an artificial 'tonic' which soon falls victim to an encroaching alternative tonic – C – which then stifles further B entries: after the move to the first $C^6{}_4$, no subsequent entry is complete, and after C minor is reached, the final entry is no more than a subdued echo of B's opening phrase. Yet in other respects – not least in its orchestration (wind tutti, marked *f* with B on unison horns marked *f espress.*) – this section has several hallmarks of a 'breakthrough', asserting a triumphal D (tonic) major, with the first two entries ostensibly tracing a clear I–IV (a–d^1) movement in D. It clears the texture after the contrapuntal waywardness of the previous section and leads straight into the brief coda. But at the same time, its incessant dactylic rhythm, combined with harmonic inertia and the dissonant presence of B, estranges and negates the breakthrough.

To draw comparisons once again with contemporary Soviet symphonies, such a grotesquely inflected delivery of a triumphal moment – as though in a loud, fixated monotone – is an obvious distortion of the 'normal' perorations that frequently characterize 1930s Soviet symphonies, as mentioned in Chapter One (see for example Myaskovsky XI and XII, Kabalevsky I and II, Khrennikov I). Its self-contradictory tone stems from a disjunction between style and tone. Sheinberg's definition of parody – 'incongruity between the object of reference and the referring work'[8] – clearly applies here to some degree, though consequently to view this passage as parodic does not seem appropriate, given its flat, implacable tone. In reality, this passage could be interpreted in countless different ways, many of them shades of the same basic experience: it is clearly an example of double-voicedness of a sort, but of what sort exactly depends on the instincts of the listener. It could be heard as menacing; but could equally be heard simply as a slightly piquant, if rather clumsy, version of the second theme. In the context of the Moderato as a whole, with its constant undermining of fulfilment, either in endings or climaxes, the transformation of B at 143 may be heard as a further example of negation: countering an apparently climactic moment with dissonant harmony and deadened intonation.

³150 – 152: Coda

The coda – a truncated restatement of A in tremolo strings – introduces a new tone, at once magical and grotesque. As Sabinina points out, this coda would be recalled at the very end of Shostakovich's symphonic career in the finale of his Fifteenth Symphony. There are a number of late works which feature unusual percussive effects, the most notable being the finale codas of the Fifteenth Symphony and the Second Cello Concerto, both of which seem to refer directly to the Fourth Symphony's finale coda (see Example 4.14). It is possibly these retrospective associations that influenced Sabinina's sense of this coda as a valedictory 'farewell to beauty'.[9] But in every instance cited above, the tone of these percussive codas is enigmatic rather than visionary or valedictory; in the case of the Fourth Symphony, it serves to cloud a well-defined return to the first subject and to prevent the emergence of a stronger voice. It also reinforces the mask-like tone of the Moderato as a whole by colouring the security of the home key with the alien intonations of castanets, woodblock and side drum struck on its metal rim.

The percussive finale codas of both the Fifteenth Symphony and the Second Cello Concerto have received programmatic interpretation. Yuri Temirkanov heard them as 'ticking away of the hours' in reference to Shostakovich's approaching death. Gennadi Rozhdestvensky heard the lonely tapping sounds very differently: 'For me, and I think for Shostakovich, the association is with prisoners tapping out messages to one another on the hot-water pipes in jail.'[10] Their mysterious, even

8 Sheinberg, *Irony*, 195.

9 Sabinina, *Shostakovich-simfonist*, 111.

10 Quoted in Ian MacDonald, 'Universal because Specific', in Allan B. Ho and Dmitry Feofanov, eds., *Shostakovich Reconsidered*, London: Toccata Press, 1998, 563.

Example 4.14
a Shostakovich IV/2: [150][1–5]

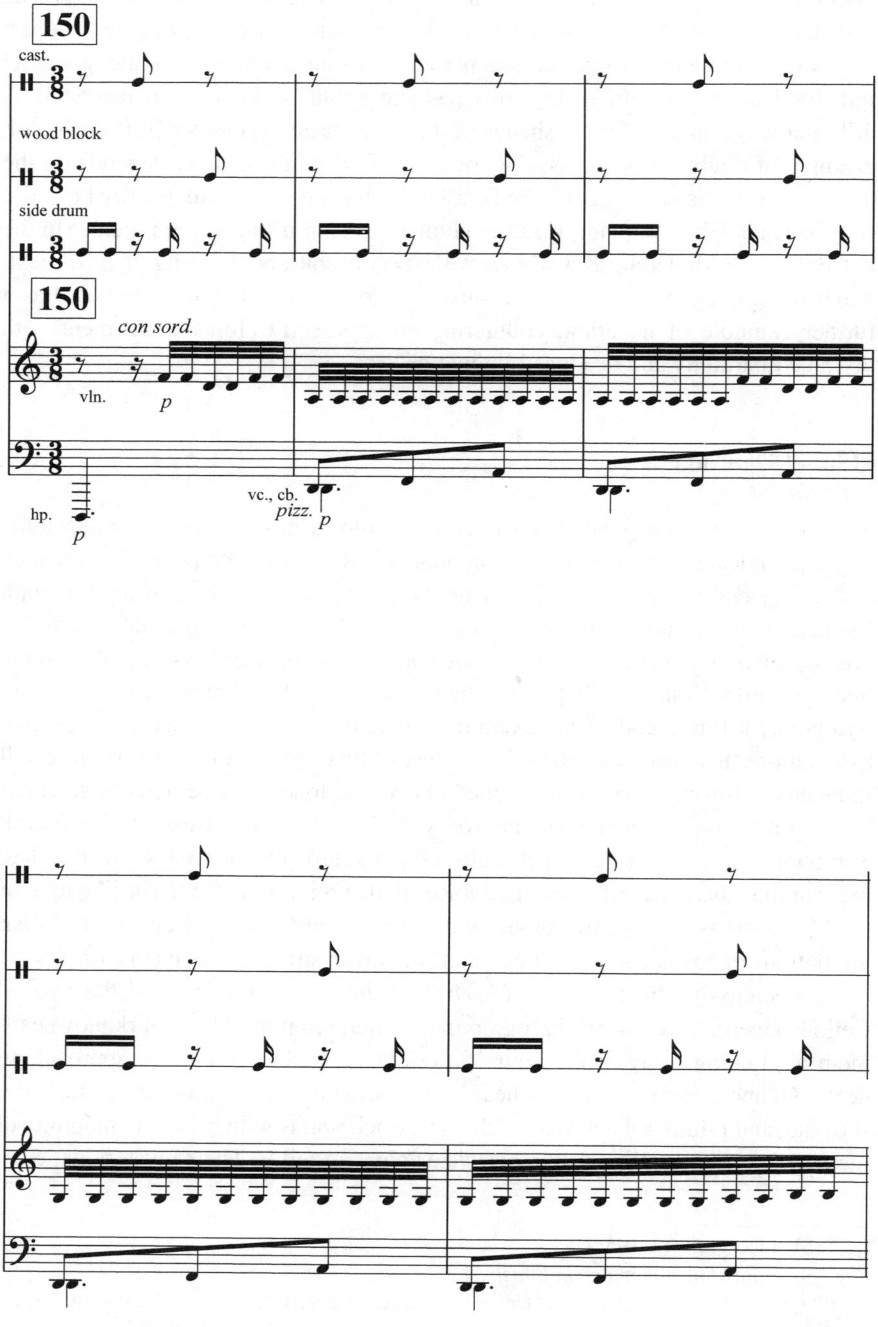

b Shostakovich XV/4: 148 1–4

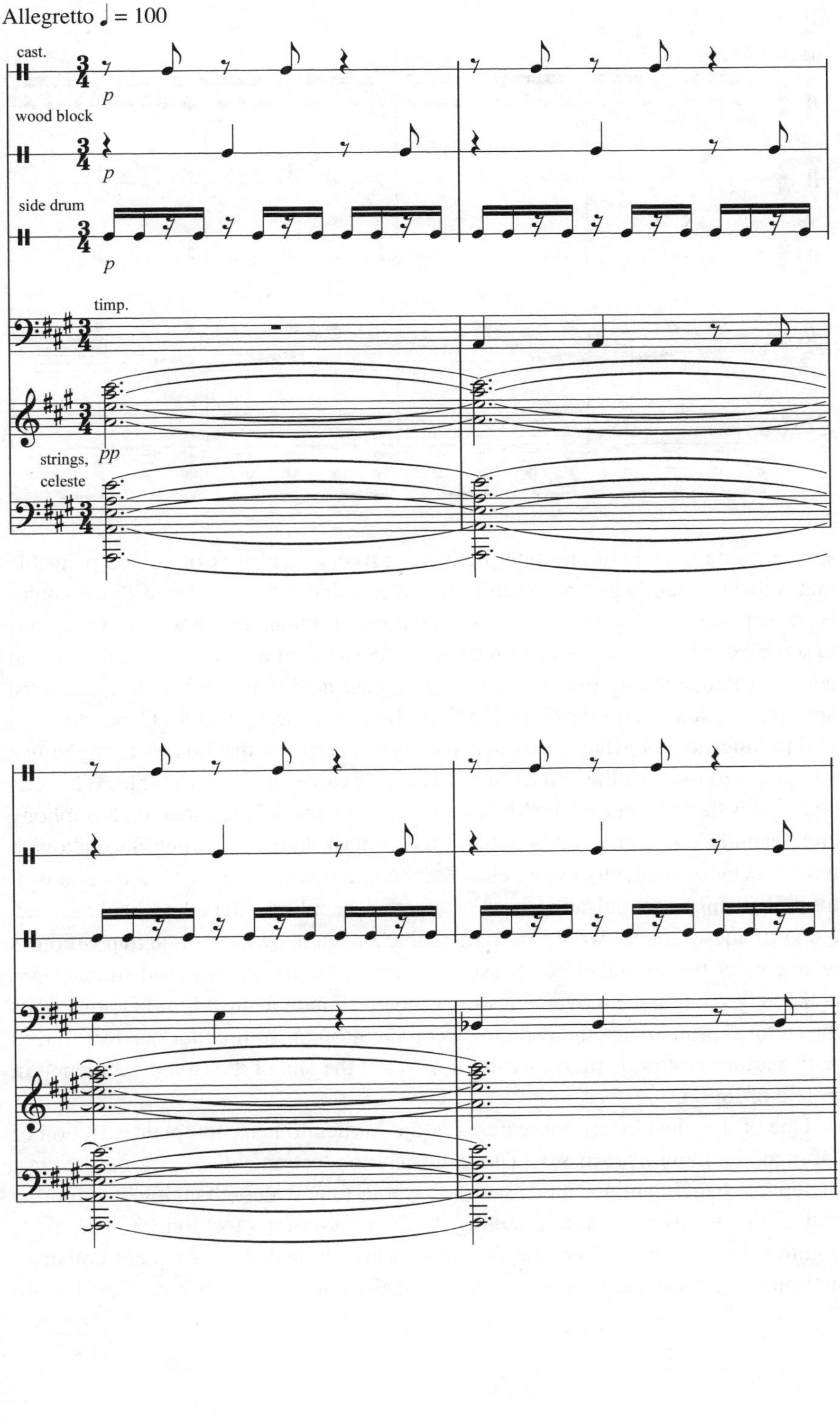

c Shostakovich Cello Concerto II/3: 113 5–8

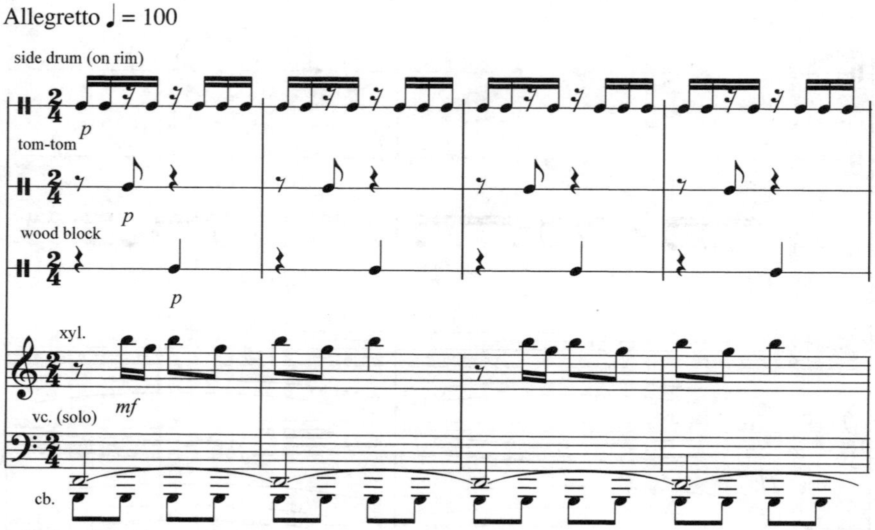

sinister, tone does invite an interpretative response, and it is of course plausible that Shostakovich had some such scenario in mind when he wrote those codas. However, their similarity to the Moderato coda problematizes both interpretations to some extent, as well as raising intriguing questions of its own. Shostakovich had never written anything like this coda before, and he did not repeat the effect until later in his career, with the Fifteenth Symphony and Second Cello Concerto.

The question of what motivated the resurrection of the Fourth Symphony's sound-world towards the end of Shostakovich's career is unanswerable. What can be noted is that the tone of the Moderato coda, like that of the Fifteenth Symphony and Second Cello Concerto, is as definitively mask-like as anything Shostakovich wrote: its automated, clockwork character co-exists with the sinister intonations of tremolo strings and pulsating bass to create a peculiarly dark, mechanical tone. None of these effects would be remarkable on their own; their juxtaposition is what creates the special effect. Most strikingly of all, its newness and strangeness, at the very point in the movement which should sound the most familiar, undercuts the 'return' principle of the coda to sweep the ground from under our feet. Faced with another grotesque mask, we are left – as at the end of the first movement – in a state of limbo.

One of the most important features of the Moderato is its complete rejection of 'normal' harmonic processes. Those norms are 'estranged' by various means, including changing minor-mode scales to whole-tone scales, changing bass fourths and fifths to tritones and retaining bass pedal-points for longer than feels comfortable. 'Normal' thematic progress is also impeded by frequent collapses and sudden cut-offs; climaxes are neither tonally nor motivically motivated but are fixations on single motifs (as at 3[122], [128] – [129], [138] – [139]) that are then violently curtailed. The whole movement is thus controlled by processes of estrangement and negation. There is no sense in which the 'positive' aspects of Mahler's scherzo can find equivalence here; the 'positive' meaning of the 'negative' ruptures in the scherzo is transmuted into mechanical reflection, and stripped of healing potential.

An 'Intertextual' Reading?

That Shostakovich's Moderato is related to Mahler's scherzo seems clear. But what conclusions may be drawn from that association? The most obvious answer is that Shostakovich chose to create a shadowy version of the 'Resurrection' scherzo as preparation for the 'anti-utopian'finale which was to follow.[11] In Mahler's scherzo, the germ of the finale's *Aufersteh'n* theme is signposted in a new passage, as though reaching beyond the world represented in the scherzo to something higher. Shostakovich's Moderato is tightly self-contained: though briefly alluding to the 'Resurrection' scherzo at [122], that allusion merely confirms its relationship to it rather than indicates any special significance (such as that suggested by the allusion to *Boris Godunov* in the first movement). The programmatic aspects of the 'Resurrection' scherzo are not echoed in the Moderato, however; Shostakovich does not emulate Mahler's tone of bustling complacency. Rejecting both 1930s Soviet symphonic models (folk-like and lyrical for slower movements, jaunty scherzis for faster ones) and – by virtue of alluding to them – rejecting Mahler's dance-like characters, Shostakovich created a movement that had no strong character, but that was instead a shadowy mask. The effect is disorientating, both for a listener used to Myaskovsky, Shebalin, Kabalevsky and others, and for a listener who recognises its Mahlerian model. The effect of the Moderato's intertextual relationship with the 'Resurrection' scherzo is thus to highlight its ambivalence to the point of negativity.

---

11 For a discussion of Shostakovich's music as 'anti-utopian' see Mark Aranovskiy, ed., *Russkaya muzïka i XX vek* [Russian music and the twentieth century], Moscow: National Institute for the Study of the Arts, 1997, Chapter 6, 213–49.

CHAPTER FIVE

Third Movement: Largo–Allegro

During the period of maximal Soviet control of the arts – the late 1920s to the mid-1950s – the finale was, at least in terms of its official reception, the most important movement in a Soviet symphony. Just how much emphasis was placed on it can perhaps be seen from the reception in 1937 of Shostakovich's Fifth Symphony, an unremittingly dark work until the very end, when a brash surge to a D major conclusion sealed Shostakovich's subsequent rehabilitation: Soviet discussions of his later symphonies would persistently account for even his most ambivalent of finales in an optimistic light. As discussed in Chapter One, the Fourth Symphony's final coda, ending in a *morendo* C minor, has been judged by scholars and journalists alike to have been the main factor in sealing the symphony's fate. And, as will be discussed in this chapter, there has been a sprinkling of supposition about the timing of that coda's composition in relation to the *Pravda* attacks on Shostakovich, which came after he had begun the finale, though it is not known where he was up to at the time the attacks took place. But in truth, as discussed in Chapter One, what set the Fourth Symphony apart from its contemporaries was not its minor-mode coda, nor its three-movement design, nor even its deployment of urban popular music. Rather, it was its indirect, masked tone and lack of what Sollertinsky described as a 'direct lyric'. Compared with symphonies by Shebalin, Myaskovsky, Kabalevsky and even Popov, Shostakovich's Fourth stands out for its almost total avoidance of a straightforward tone of the kind found in any of the most common types of Soviet symphonic themes: either lyrical, heroic, lively or grandiose. The fractured first movement, riven with sudden ruptures and over-inflated crescendi arising from nowhere and ending abruptly, contains only one theme other than its violent first subject which sounds 'direct' – the 'supplication' theme – and that is heard in its entirety only in the recapitulation ([97] – [99]): it does not figure at all in the development. The other two themes, A2 and B, are crippled by uneven metre and phrase structure; neither sounds strong enough to balance the first subject, so that balance has to be brought in 'from outside', with an allusion to *Boris Godunov* which even then cannot be integrated properly into the thematic structure of the movement but evolves gradually throughout the exposition and recapitulation. In the second movement too, the lyrical second theme is too confined by its harmonically static presentation to breathe freely: it is another mask, its lyricism estranged and stilted. The combined effect of the first two movements is to undermine completely the listener's expectations of what – in contemporary Soviet terms – would be considered 'normal' symphonic dramaturgy. Thus, while in purely dynamic, physical terms there is at this point a clear need for a firm, fast tempo, and in dramatic terms a need for resolution, the signposts which would normally indicate that convention are subverted or absent.

The Idea of a Finale

The stage is set for some sort of resolution. But what kind of resolution there can be when the norms of Soviet symphonic dramaturgy have been so radically undercut is by no means clear. To refer to Michael Talbot's finale terminology,[1] a 'summative' finale is the obvious choice: it would address the dramaturgical issues of the first movement and tie up the symphony as a whole. A 'relaxant' finale is out of the question: there are too many loose ends in the preceding dramaturgy. Similarly, a 'valedictory' finale would be a dramatic non-sequitur: although the first movement contains stretches of energetic, even frenzied, motion (as in the fugato), its overall tempo is only allegretto, with numerous directions to reduce the tempo at key points. The 'intermezzo' second movement 'in tempo Allegretto' is also too muted in tone to justify a prolonged slow finale. In addition, the recapitulation and coda of the first movement are powerfully valedictory in their own right, and even the brief second movement coda – especially in view of its latent association with the end of the Fifteenth Symphony – has valedictory qualities. The finale coda will share the ghostly, ambivalent tone of the preceding movements, but will not answer their questions: there is to be no summing-up of any kind.

The finales of Soviet symphonies contemporaneous with the Fourth tended to be either relaxant or summative, since the valedictory type was problematised by the risk of assumption of a level of narrative, which made subdued endings ideologically suspicious.[2] Soviet finales were therefore normally positive in tone: Myaskovsky's Sixteenth and Khrennikov's First are the only significant Soviet symphonies written between 1929 and 1937 to end with anything other than an exultant peroration, and in both cases the finales are 'optimistic' in mood, with subdued, but not tragic, codas.[3] The three-movement design of Shostakovich's Fourth Symphony is in itself not particularly unusual, as discussed in Chapter One: the First Symphonies of Shebalin, Popov and Khrennikov (1925, 1934 and 1935 respectively) each have only three movements. Shebalin's Second (1929) has only

1 Michael Talbot, *The Finale in Western Instrumental Music*, Oxford: Oxford University Press, 2001.

2 Despite Kuznetsov's suggestion that a symphony could end in a 'depressed, slow vein' at the 1935 symphonism conference, no Soviet symphony of the 1930s – with the notable exception of Shostakovich's Fourth – had a finale coda that fits Kuznetsov's description. See Chapter One, p. 22.

3 Myaskovsky's Sixteenth is in any case semi-programmatic: the funeral march was allegedly composed in response to the *Maxim Gorky* airship crash, and the finale takes Myaskovsky's song 'The Planes are Flying' as its main theme.

two (though the first movement is in two distinct sections: an Andante followed by an Allegro), and his 'Lenin' Symphony (1931) has three movements. For Myaskovsky, a three-movement design was almost standard. In all these instances, the balance of slow and fast tempi is very obviously considered: the middle movement is always slow, while the outer movements may be Allegro or Moderato, but never both Moderato. Shostakovich's decision to follow an Allegretto first movement and Moderato scherzo with a Largo suggests a trajectory of decreasing tempo and dramatic tension. But following the Largo is a very fast Allegro (the prototype for Shostakovich's later whirlwind scherzi), with a metronome marking of 𝅗𝅥. = 84. In the ensuing divertimento, tempi fluctuate between ♩ = 184 and ♩ = 100. The first coda almost reverts to the original Allegro tempo, at 𝅗𝅥. = 100; the second coda is half that speed at 𝅗𝅥. = 50.[4] Overall, then, the balance of the finale is fast, with the opening funeral march acting as a compressed slow movement destined to play a cyclical role in the codas. Table 5.1 shows the tempo changes.

To return to Talbot's finale archetypes, it is not unusual to find what he describes as either 'divided' or 'hybrid' finales: a Romantic development of the Baroque and Classical 'double finale', which comprises distinct thematic areas not motivically connected and notably different in tone. Talbot's example of a Classical double finale is that of Haydn's 'Farewell' Symphony (1772), which follows a self-contained 'relaxant' sonata structure (Presto) with a 'valedictory'

Table 5.1 Shostakovich: IV/3 Tempo changes

Figure	Theme	Tempo, MM	Notes
152	A	Largo ♩ = 69	Funeral march
167	B	Allegro 𝅗𝅥. = 84	Scherzo
191	C	♩ = 126	Waltzes
202	C	♩ = 160	Polka
212	C	♩ = 184	Waltz/song
219	C	♩ = 100	Galop
238	–	𝅗𝅥. = 100	Coda I
246	A	𝅗𝅥. = 50	Coda II

4 Both the 1982 and 2003 collected works scores have 𝅗𝅥. = 50; the 1962 Sikorski edition has ♩. = 50, which is clearly a misprint.

Adagio. To illustrate the 'divided finale' Talbot cites Mendelssohn's 'Scottish' Symphony, whose two main themes, in A minor and A major respectively, remain distinct entities throughout.[5] The problematizing of the finale coda is a key factor in Talbot's discussion of hybrid finales, and here he turns to Mahler – most significantly to the finale of his First Symphony. Summarizing James Buhler, Talbot points to the apparently anomalous 'false coda' at I/4 [33], which has troubled commentators from Richard Strauss to Henry-Louis de La Grange. Following Adorno, Buhler views this passage as a *Durchbruch* deliberately instigated prematurely in order to show, in Mahler's own words, 'a struggle in which victory is furthest from the protagonist just when he believes it closest'.[6] Its function in the overall dramaturgy of the finale is thus viewed by Buhler as an immanent critique of sonata form, throwing doubt on the inevitability of a final summation by achieving it before time and then subjecting it to renewed questioning. Talbot's interpretation of the peculiar dramaturgy is that the F minor and D major components of this movement are self-contained enough – if not equally weighted – to constitute a divided finale. The result is ultimately 'summative', implying a final resolution weighted towards the coda.[7]

Shostakovich's finale does not fit into any of Talbot's primary archetypes, though its constituent parts can individually be categorised as summative, relaxant and valedictory, with the framing funeral march ultimately bestowing a valedictory (in the darkest sense possible) conclusion upon the preceding summative coda. The extended divertimento, though episodic and decidedly 'un-symphonic', is dominated by the easy-going tone characteristic of the relaxant finale. To dub the finale 'divided', however, implies disjunction between parts – even self-containment – that is belied by the extent of motivic unity between the scherzo and divertimento; the funeral march also brings about the transition from the brash summative first coda to the second, valedictory, one. Talbot's definition of the 'hybrid' finale crucially acknowledges the distinction between formal design and expressive content: a finale may be summative in weight but relaxant or valedictory in tone. Shostakovich's finale is clearly weighty, and both the opening Largo and the violent Allegro have the seriousness of purpose which could point to a summative character. But the divertimento relaxes that pressure, and though there are strong thematic links between it and the Allegro, its overall tone remains relatively lightweight.

The episodic form of the finale causes further problems for the creation of a summative tone. Thematic development is minimal outside the scherzo section ([167] – [191]): though there are long-range connections between the themes, these are generally dramaturgical (as in the return of the funeral march in the coda) rather than structural in the strict sense. Similarly, the disparity of tone between

5 See Talbot, *The Finale*, 131–2.

6 Buhler, '"Breakthrough" as Critique of Form', 126.

7 Talbot, *The Finale*, 136–9.

one section and another inhibits the sense of progress which is an inherent part of a summative finale. This is why Orlov has described Shostakovich's finale type as 'synthetic' rather than summative, meaning that it draws together contradictory elements and eschews the uniform tone typical of contemporary Soviet symphonies.[8] However, this feature of Shostakovich's finale partially echoes another summative type identified by Talbot: the 'pot-pourri' finale, exemplified in Talbot's study by the finale of Brahms's First Symphony. By means of subtle deviations from an otherwise standard sonata template, Brahms's finale is able to draw on unusual resources to attain the heights of a true summation. An unusually long introduction (93 bars) presents material which then feeds into the development and recapitulation in crucial and sometimes very dramatic ways.[9] And though Shostakovich's finale has no equivalent seed-bed of introductory material, both its opening funeral march and the scherzo following play vital roles in the unfolding drama. In this sense, then, Talbot's definition of the pot-pourri finale has some relevance for Shostakovich's finale even if ultimately summation is denied it.

Inasmuch as Shostakovich, like any other Soviet composer in the 1930s, was aware of the expectations associated with a symphonic finale, his creation of the ultimate hybrid finale may be seen as a deliberate avoidance of an optimistic conclusion (which would have rung decidedly hollow) without going straight for a valedictory ending which would inevitably have required some kind of programmatic justification. It sets out to be different, to thwart listeners' expectations at every turn and to avoid evoking an obvious dramaturgical archetype such as the *Bildungsroman* (the dramatic trajectory of the Fifth Symphony, at least as applied after its première in 1937). Shostakovich's finale may be episodic and at least 50 per cent 'relaxant', but the funeral march which opens and closes it – especially in its final incarnation in the second coda – is powerful enough to absorb the lighter middle section, and hence to convince beyond any doubt of its seriousness of purpose. In this respect, the Fourth Symphony finale is summative in intent and weight even if its devastated ending seems to contradict that affirmatory label.

The summative finale was, of course, a primarily Romantic preoccupation with roots in Beethoven. Paul Bekker described the phenomenon as *Finalsymphonie*: he credited Schubert, Bruckner and Mahler with moving the symphonic centre of gravity away from the first movement to the finale.[10] Sollertinsky, who in his 1932

8 Orlov, 'V serediniye puti', 185.

9 The most striking instances are the reappearance of the horn theme at the climax of the development at b. 285 and the brief chorale phrase (from bb. 47–51) in the coda (bb. 407–416). For Talbot's analysis, see *The Finale*, 98–99.

10 Bekker's grouping of Brahms, Mendelssohn and Schumann (central Germans) as 'unsymphonic' in opposition to the Austrian trio of Schubert, Bruckner and Mahler is unconvincing. See Talbot, *The Finale*, 170–71 for a concise critique of Bekker's arguments.

monograph similarly described Mahler's orientation towards the finale as the centre of the symphonic drama, would probably have agreed with Bekker to some extent. But as his 1943 lecture 'Historical Types of Symphonic Dramaturgy' makes clear, Sollertinsky was measured in his praise for Bekker, who was a favourite (as was Romain Rolland) of the ASM and RAPM alike during the 1920s. Sollertinsky's symphonic categories, as discussed in Chapter Two, are quite different from Bekker's: the 'Beethovenian' type is 'Shakespearian' and 'dialogical'; the 'monological' type is represented by the epic narratives of Liszt, Strauss and Berlioz, among others; while the third type is represented by Mahler and Chaikovsky, who resist either classification. Sollertinsky notes perceptively that, while both Mahler and Chaikovsky remained close to Beethoven in spirit, their troubled relationship with fate and with their fellow men pushed them to the limits of epic tragedy and pathos.[11] It is at this point that he goes on to describe the 'direct lyric' and 'indirect lyric' employed by both composers and developed further by Shostakovich, as discussed in Chapter Two.

Sollertinsky's notion of direct and indirect lyric provides an extremely useful conceptual tool for discussing Shostakovich's music, as has been seen in relation to the first movement in Chapter Three. That the music of Mahler, and possibly Chaikovsky too, was Shostakovich's chief reference-point when he composed the Fourth Symphony is very clear. In terms both of dramatic structure and ambivalence of tone, Mahler is the most obvious role-model for Shostakovich's critique of the heroic, epic language and dramaturgy of 1930s Soviet symphonism. In this critical spirit, the weighting of his symphony towards the finale echoes the summative archetype employed by Mahler and Chaikovsky, with all the narrative implications that conveyed. Those implications were, as discussed, problematized in the Soviet Union both by the assumption of ideological content and (at least for Shostakovich) the harshness of Soviet reality itself. In recognizing both the dangers of an obvious dramaturgy (if negative) and the moral imperatives of communication with his Soviet listeners, Shostakovich's finale could not be wholly summative, relaxant or valedictory, which is possibly why he avoided a narrative-style trajectory in favour of a sequence of fairly self-contained episodes. But if Shostakovich was deliberately subverting the possibility of reading his symphony like a novel, there is no doubt that the material he used had immense intonational and hermeneutic richness. From funeral march to whirlwind waltz-scherzo, to his evocation of an urban musical sound-scape, to paraphrases of Mahler, Stravinsky and Chaikovsky, to the first raucous coda and, finally, to the desolation of the second, hardly a single theme is 'innocent': nearly all are loaded with semantic weight. This finale was intended to say 'something' in the best traditions of its summative ancestors.

11 Sollertinskiy, 'Historical Types of Symphonic Dramaturgy', translated in Roseberry, *Ideology*, 522–39.

Funeral march: Largo

The funeral march topos used by Shostakovich here has clear enough precedents, among them the funeral march from Mahler's First Symphony, the song 'Die zwei blauen Augen' from his *Lieder eines fahrenden Gesellen* (which that movement quotes) and the *Marcia funebre* of Beethoven's 'Eroica'.[12] As Table 5.2 and Table

Table 5.2 Shostakovich: IV/3: summary of first subject group

Figure	Theme	Tonal centre/mode	Notes
152	A	c Dorian	Dotted rhythms. 'Closed' feel, with prominent minor 3rd.
153	A1	f → c	Important rising major 7th figure, initiating a more 'open' feel, with 5ths and octaves (154).
155	A1	Suspended	Development of A1.
156	A	c Dorian	G–A♭ oscillation more dominant: re-statement left incomplete.
157	Bridge	c ♭5th	March-like bridge theme undermines c Dorian and leads to C major climax.
159	B	C major	Fanfare intonations with strong C major in brass. Climax.
161	Bridge	c	*Otkrïtnost*: 'Closed' feel with tightly oscillating minor 2nds prominent. Begins to open out into major but closes again with return of c/A1.
163	A1	c	Extention of A1: opens out at 164 with perfect 4ths and 5ths.
165	A	c Dorian	G–A♭ oscillation takes over and A disintegrates.

12 Volkov notes a specific similarity between the Mahler song and Shostakovich's

5.3 show, Shostakovich's funeral march shares with his models a minor-key opening theme, characterized by dotted rhythms and a rising minor third. This is balanced by a major-key middle section, characterized (in both the Mahler and the Beethoven) by triadic themes and gentle triplet accompaniment, and in the Shostakovich by semiquaver figuration. However, in spite of the

Table 5.3 Funeral march templates in Beethoven III/2, Mahler I/3 and Mahler, 'Die zwei blauen Augen'

a Beethoven: III/2: *Marcia funebre: Adagio assai*

Bar	Theme	Key	Notes
1	A	c	Prominent rising minor 3rd; minimal movement or accompaniment. Persistent triplet drum-stroke figure. Dotted rhythm.
16	A1	E♭	Lyrical theme.
30	A	f → c	
36	A1	E♭	
50	A	f → c	
69	B	C	*Maggiore*: triadic theme with triplet accompaniment.
104	A	c →	*Minore*.
114		f →	Fugue.
173	A	c	
181	A1	E♭	
195	A	f → c	
209	B var.	→ D♭	Coda.
238	A	c	Coda.

funeral march (*Shostakovich and Stalin*, 165). The funeral march from Mahler's First Symphony, with its tonic–dominant accompaniment and growling double bass delivery, is a more obvious model but Volkov is attracted to the song as model chiefly by the presence of a text: 'Nun hab' ich ewig Leid und Grämmen!' [Sorrow and grief are now with me for ever], with all the obvious programmatic resonances that brings to the Fourth Symphony. However, such a clear use of the funeral march trope scarcely needs a text to make its broader meaning plain.

b Mahler I/3: *Marcia funebre: Adagio assai*

Bar	Theme	Key	Notes
1	A	d	Rising minor 3rd prominent; tonic–dominant timpani. Dotted rhythms.
6	B	A	*Mit Parodie*: *klezmer* band parody.
8^3	A	d	
10	C	G	*sehr einfach*: triplet accompaniment at first.
13	A	e♭	
15	B	B♭	
16	A/B	d	
17	A	d	Coda.

c Mahler: 'Die zwei blauen Augen': *Mit geheimnisvoll schwermütigem Ausdruck*

Bar	Theme	Key	Notes
1	A	e	Rising minor 3rd dotted rhythm.
17	A1	C	Major–minor fluctuation.
37	B	F	Triadic theme, with triplet accompaniment.
65	A	f	Echo of opening (2 bars).

minor–major–minor template shared by all, only Beethoven's slow movement is cast in a clear ABA pattern, although this can be obscured by other materials outside it such as the variant of theme B at the start of the coda. Mahler's *klezmer* second theme plays a far more significant role than does his G major third theme, recurring three times and eventually merging with the funeral march just before the coda. 'Die zwei blauen Augen' is also problematic: its structure is binary rather than ternary, though it could be argued that the return of the opening bars of the funeral march at the end carries sufficient dramatic weight to count as a real return, thus at least gesturing towards a ternary framework.

The clearest parallels here are between Mahler's *maggiore* sections and Beethoven's; the ABA design of Shostakovich's funeral march differs from theirs, and his C major middle section is not self-contained as are the other *maggiore* sections. But the *minore–maggiore–minore* form does suggest a template derived from either these or other similar sources. The Shostakovich, Beethoven and Mahler I marches all employ prominent second and third themes ('Die zwei blauen Augen' has only two, with the second theme corresponding to the role of the third, *maggiore* themes of the other examples); Shostakovich's A1 shares (to a lesser extent) Beethoven's lyrical 'open' tone at bar 16 (A1 in Table 5.3a), and also shares the motivic continuity of theme A1 from Mahler's 'Die zwei blauen Augen' themes. In each of these examples, second themes are extensions of the first, repeating and developing the opening motif; Shostakovich's climax theme at 160 opens out fully into C major, with semiquaver figuration in wind and strings that can be viewed as a strident echo of Beethoven's *maggiore* and Mahler's gentle theme C (see Example 5.1). The modal contours of Shostakovich's themes are wide-ranging, and their identification in Table 5.1 as Dorian is really no more than an approximate label which rarely holds for the duration of the themes so analysed. It is more useful to observe simply that the funeral march section from

Example 5.1
a(i) Beethoven III/2: bb. 1–4: A

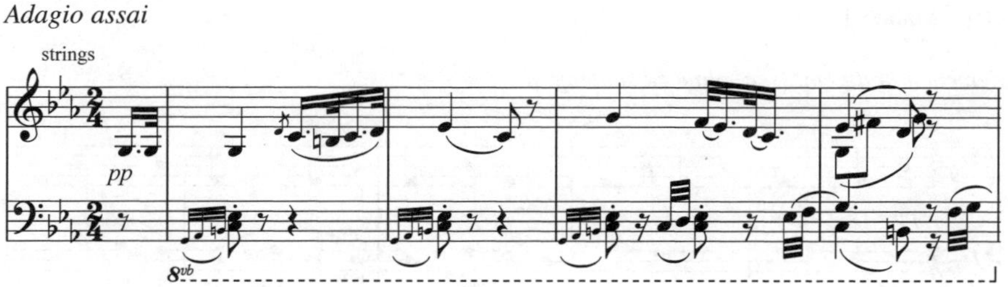

a(ii) Beethoven III/2: bb. 36–9: A1

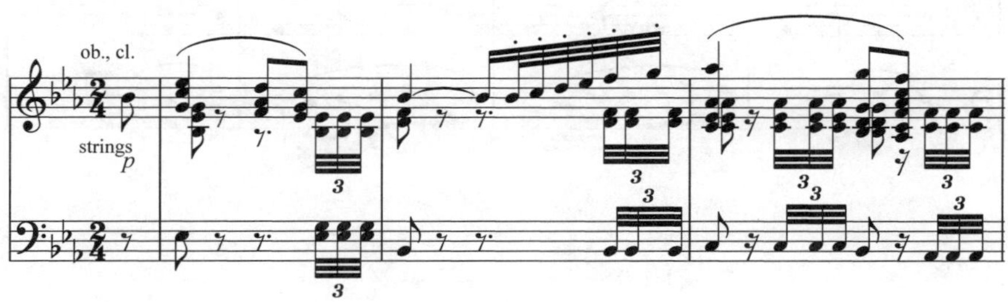

a(iii) Beethoven III/3: bb. 69–72: B

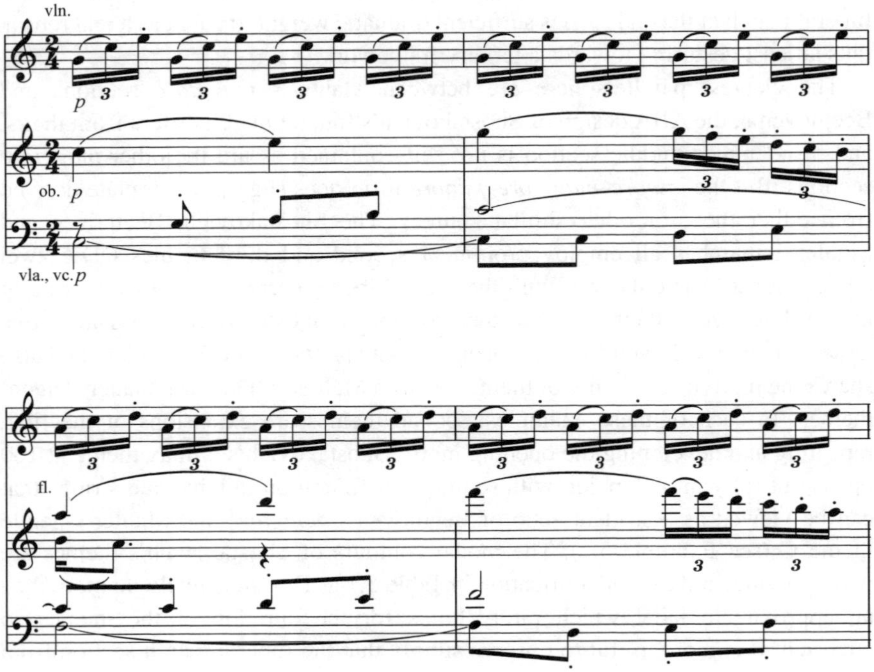

b(i) Mahler I/3: [1]1–9: A

Feierlich und gemessen, ohne zu schleppen

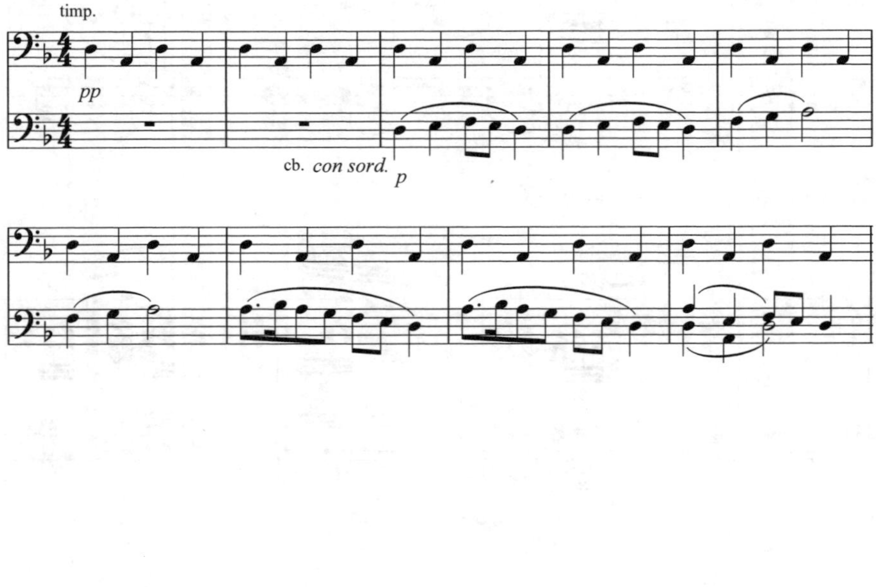

b(ii) Mahler I/3: [1]5 – 5[1–4]: B

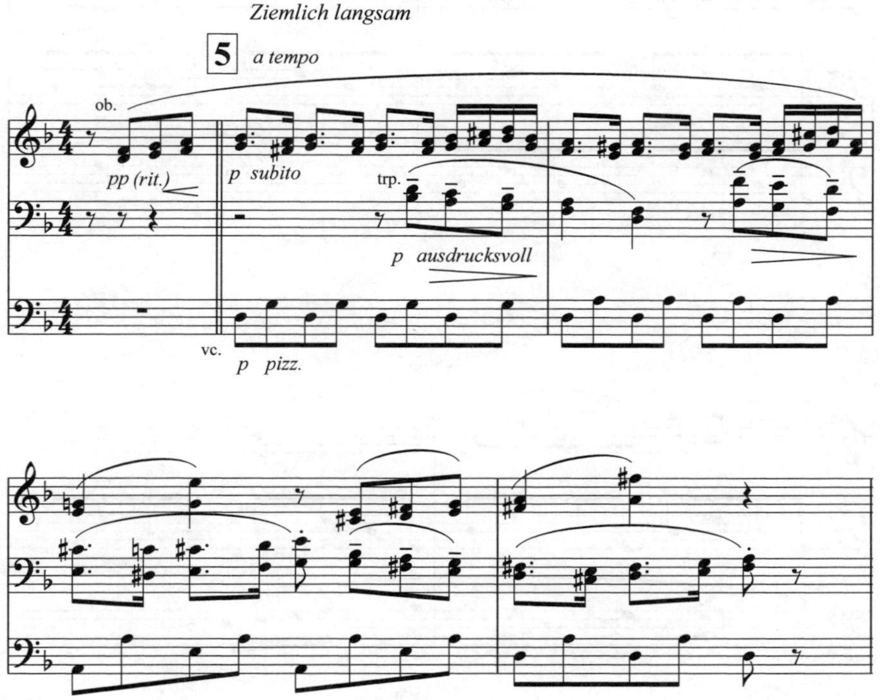

b(iii) Mahler I/3: 10[1–7]: C

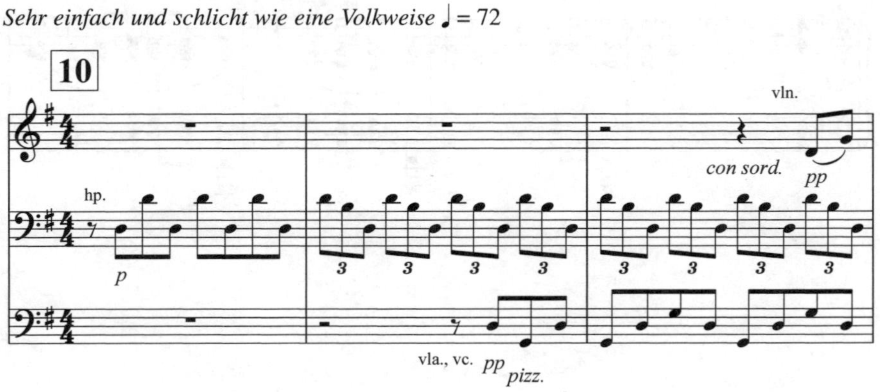

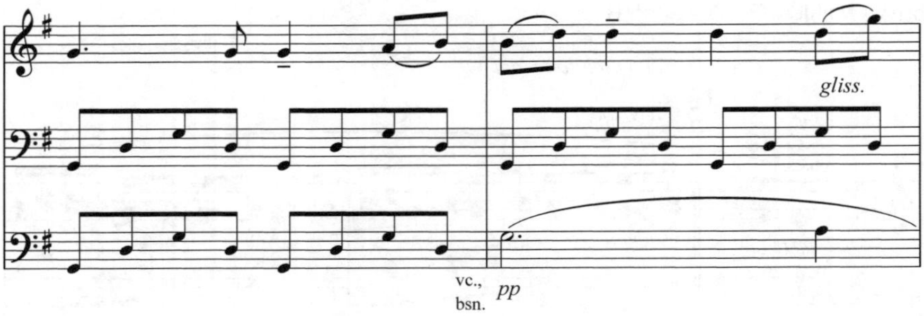

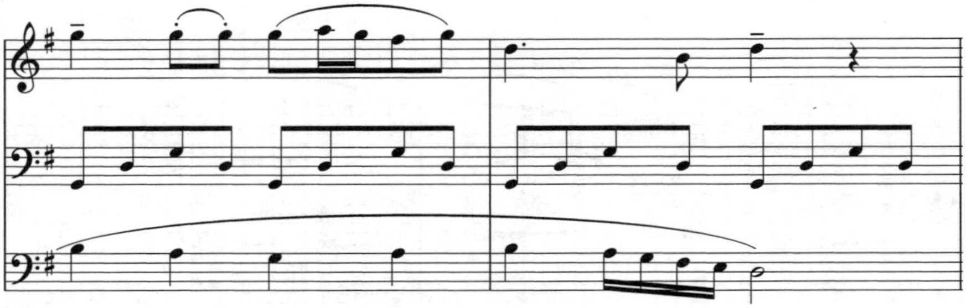

c(i) Mahler: ‘Die zwei blaue Augen’: bb. 1–4: A

Alla marcia

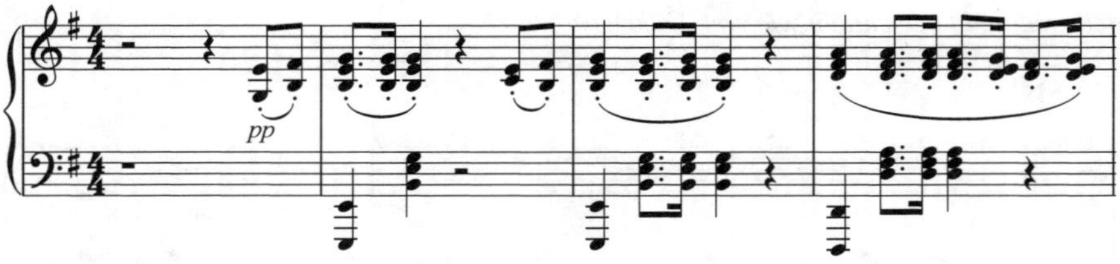

c(ii) Mahler: 'Die zwei blaue Augen': bb. 17–21: A1

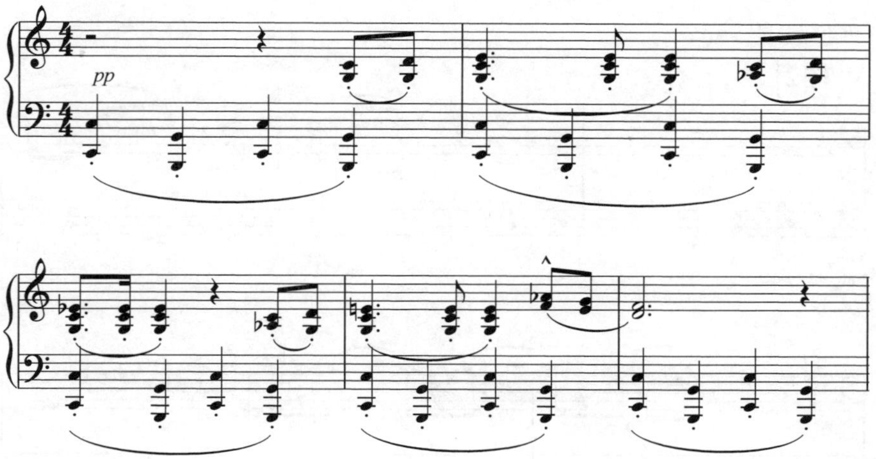

c(iii) Mahler: 'Die zwei blaue Augen': bb. 39–43

Leise, bis zum Schluss

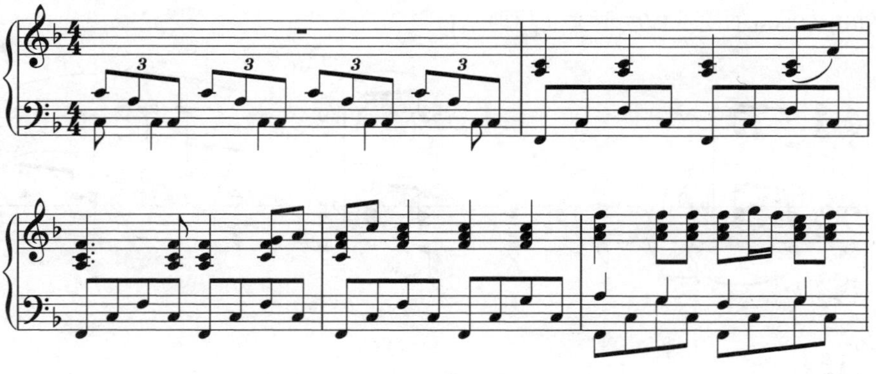

d(i) Shostakovich IV/3: 152 1–6: A

Largo ♩ = 69

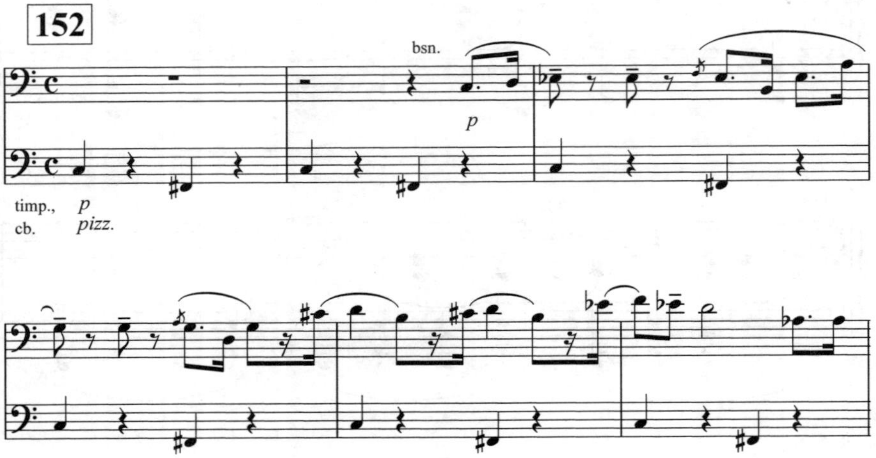

d(ii) Shostakovich IV/3: 153 3 – 154 2: A1

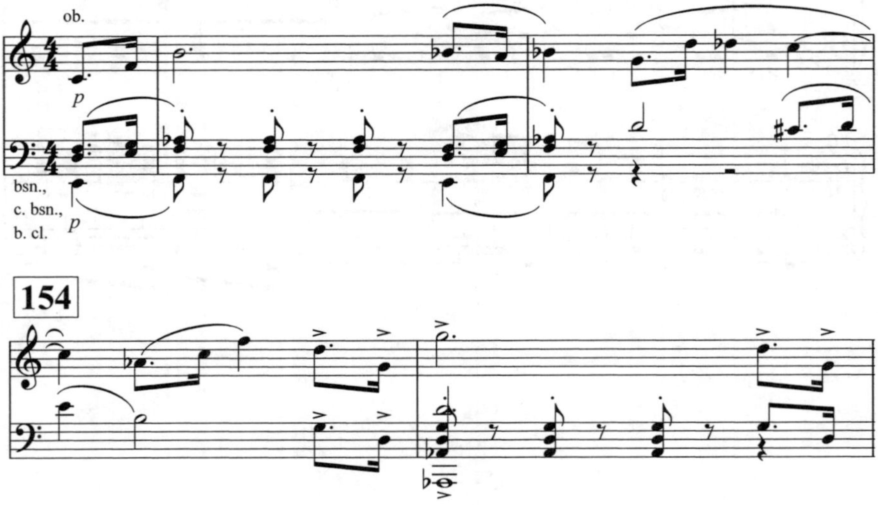

d(iii) Shostakovich IV/3: 160 $^{1–3}$: climax of A

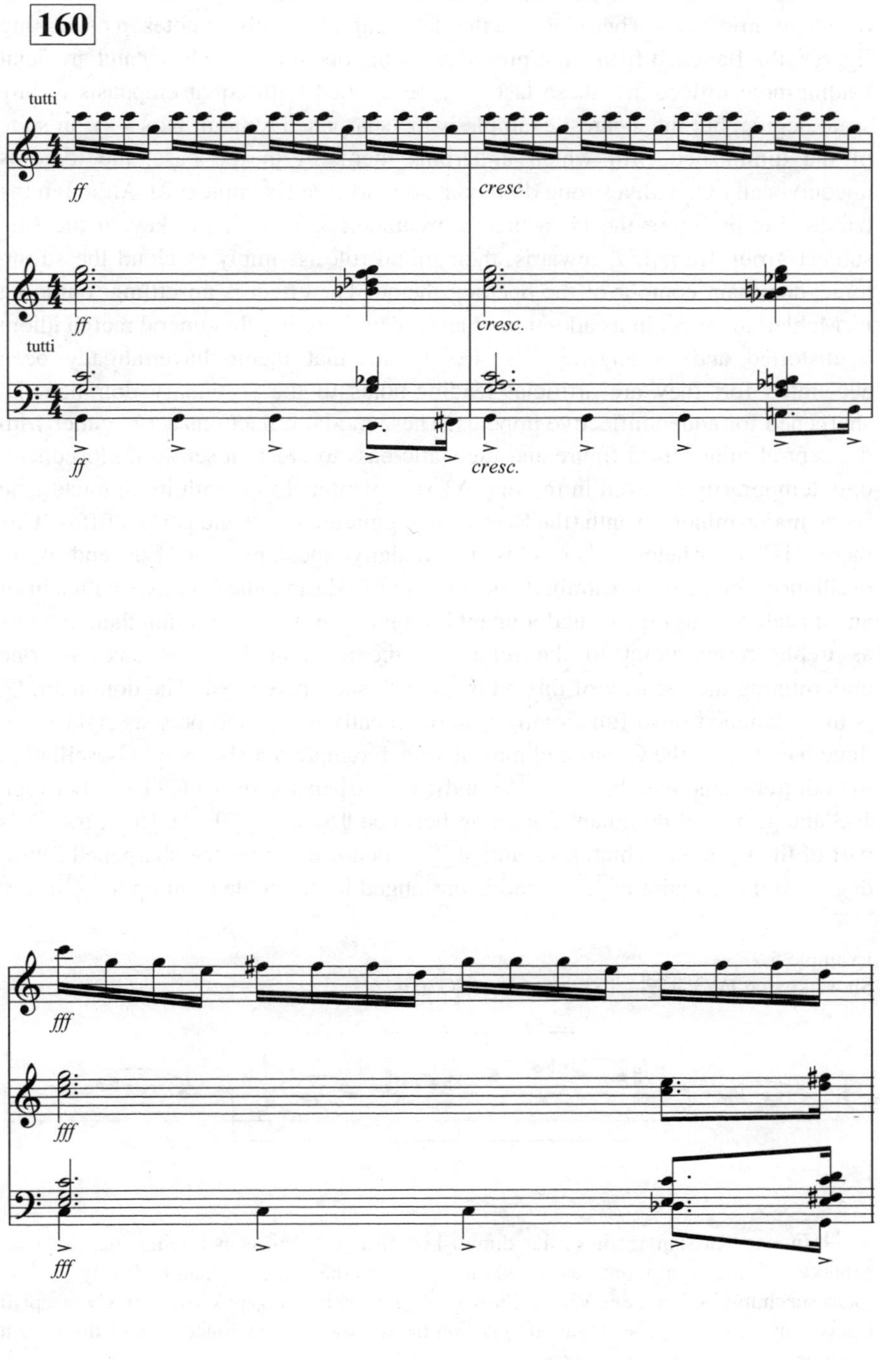

152 to 167, with the exception of the central climax, operates entirely within the sphere of the minor mode, and that within that sphere Shostakovich uses a number of salient inflections. These include the flattening of neighbour notes in oscillating figures, the flattened fifth (first presented in the opening C–F♯ bass) and artificial leading-note inflections; these last may be applied with equal emphasis to any scale degree, but the clearest example is the sharpened tonic in bars 4–5. In spite of the diminished fifth which underpins theme A in the bass, the tonic is unequivocally C, with a strong dominant support (see Example 5.2). Although the basses' F♯s prefigure the G♭ which helps undermine the home key in the first subject group from 157 onwards, their initial role is simply to cloud the strong tonic–dominant contour of the opening theme. The effect is unsettling: outdoing its Mahlerian model in its adoption of an 'eccentric lyric', the funeral march idiom is distorted and estranged.[13] The C♯s within that theme have already been accounted for: they are artificial leading-notes to the secondary dominant D, sharpened for added inflective impetus. These modal inflections act together with the central minor third figure and the static bass to create a sense of closedness, only temporarily relieved in the first A1 statement at 153^{3}, with its characteristic rising major-minor seventh (the B♮ is an appoggiatura to B♭) and perfect fifths. This theme is nevertheless also 'closed', modally speaking: the E/F and A♭–G oscillations in the bass restrain it and temporarily disable the C/G axis with a brief and unstable focus on the subdominant F minor. The A♭–G figuration then features as treble counterpoint to the return of theme A at 156, its anxious tone undermining the security of this return, which soon peters out. The dominant, G, is then flattened (also functioning enharmonically as F♯) and persists right up to three bars before the C major climax at 160. Example 5.3 shows A♭–G oscillation in both treble and bass between 153 and 157, suspension of the C/G axis between 153 and 156, and dominant flattening between 157 and 159. At 157^{2}, the G♭ is part of the E♭ minor which lasts until 158, when it becomes the sharpened fourth degree to the C major at 159^{1}, and is prolonged in the treble right up to 160.

Example 5.2
Shostakovich IV/3: 152 – 153, showing C/G axis

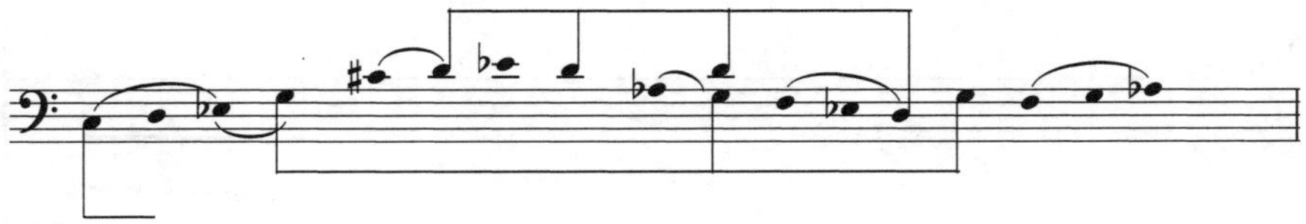

[13] In one Russian reading, the diminished fifth is seen as betraying the '*balagan* subtext' of the symphony as a whole, placing the funeral march firmly in the 'petrushechnnïy' sphere. See Vera Val'kova, 'Tragicheskiy balagan: k voprosu o kontseptsii Chetvërtoy simfonii' [The tragic *balagan*: on the question of the conception of the Fourth Symphony], *Muzïkal'naya akademiya*, 1997/4, 81.

Example 5.3
Shostakovich IV/3: 152 – 160: summary of linear and harmonic processes

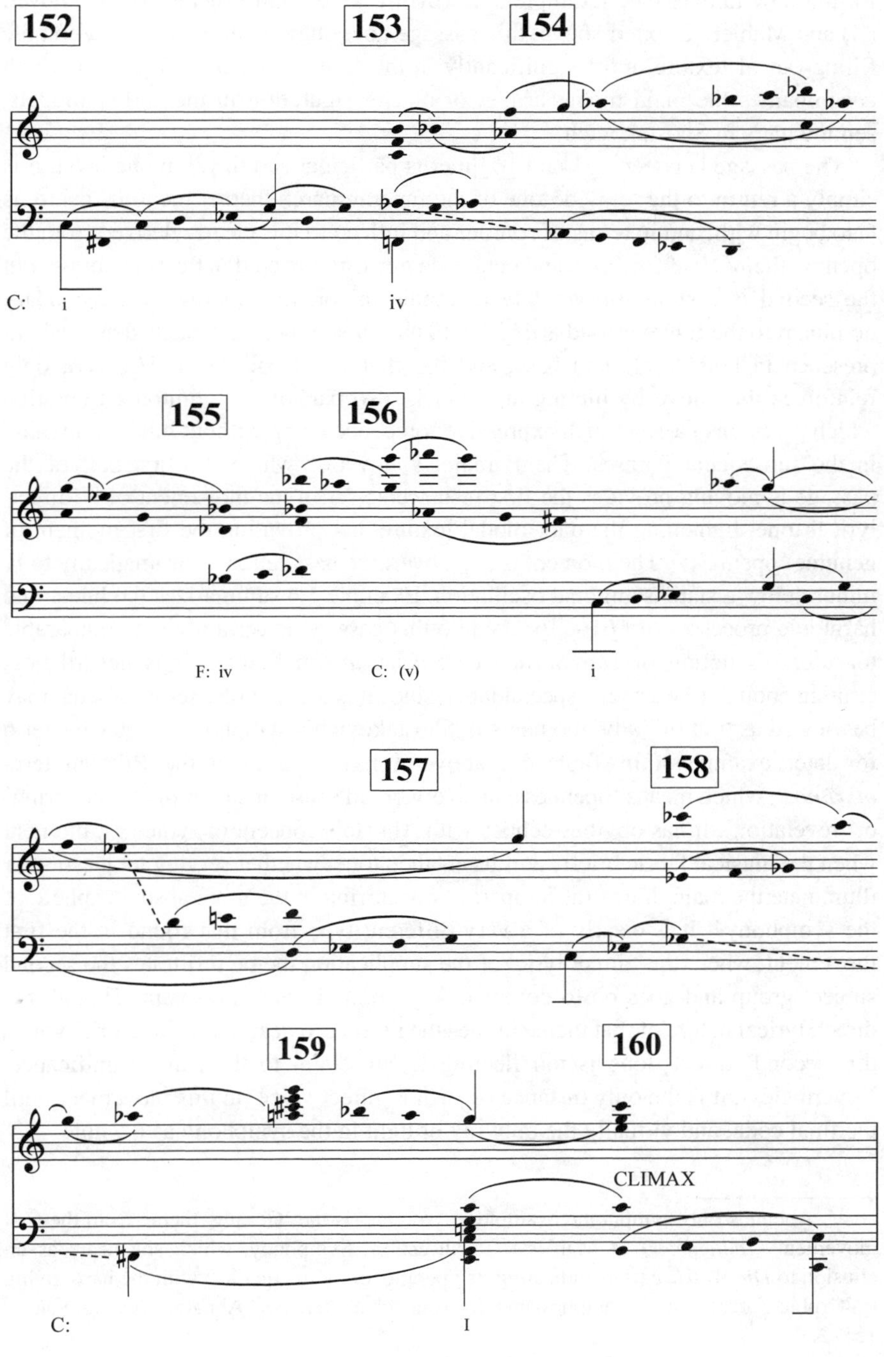

The C major section from 159 to 161 is a climactic extension of the first group, turning minor inflections to major and inverting its dotted rising minor third to form a new fanfare (see Example 5.1d (iii)). Like the third themes of Beethoven (B) and Mahler (C) cited above, this passage does share with its models a notable filling-out of texture, most significantly in the form of a repeated pattern which accompanies the main theme: triplet or quaver figuration in the earlier models, semiquavers in Shostakovich.

The passage between 161 and 163 merits particular scrutiny. On one level, it is simply a return to the 'closed' tone of the funeral march theme: the tonal centre is C to begin with, and in terms of contour and inflection it is clearly derived from the opening theme. Its fifth, sixth and octave degrees are lowered in the first phrase, but the second is a straightforward F♯ harmonic minor, functioning as a secondary dominant to the E major triad at 162$^{2-3}$. F♯ has already been established as a salient presence in both treble and bass, and the flattened C octave at 161^{1} not only reinforces this move by hinting at B but is also part of the semitonal figuration which gives this passage such expressive force, occurring without modal flattening in the subsequent phrases. The E major $^{6}_{4}$ towards which the first half of the passage is moving provides the first instance so far in the movement of a 'direct' lyrical tone, lightening the dark modal texture and providing the first moment of genuine 'openness'. The moment is soon over: the bass retreats chromatically to E♭ minor below a static semitonal oscillation. Example 5.4 summarizes the linear and harmonic processes of 161 – 163. While this passage is certainly not comparable to Adorno's notion of *Durchbruch* or *Suspension* in Mahler, it is nevertheless striking enough to warrant a special label, since it is the first of a series of what may be viewed as 'out of body' moments in Shostakovich's symphonies (see Chapter 6 for later examples). In Table 5.2 above, I have suggested the Russian term *otkrïtnost*, which means 'openness' in a very broad sense; it can imply 'uncovering' or 'revelation'. It has obvious echoes with Abbate's concept of 'voice': a moment when the musical fabric briefly admits an alien tone, whether serving to question or illuminate the main drama (as in opera) or occurring in the more abstract sphere of the symphony.[14] It is clearly of a very different type from that found in the first movement, where the 'direct lyric' of the supplication theme infiltrates the second subject group and goes on to dominate key points in the movement. Though the direct, lyrical nature of that theme invites the listener to hear it as an authorial voice, this second 'direct' tone is too fleeting to lay claim to the same significance. Nevertheless, it is the only instance of such a 'direct voice' in this movement until the final coda, and virtually the only ray of light in the symphony as a whole.

14 Abbate's only symphonic example of 'voicing' is the 'Gesang' theme from the first movement (*Todtenfeier*) of Mahler's 'Resurrection' Symphony, which she hears as an allusion to *Die Walküre* (thus indicating its operatic, or 'song' quality) with the harp giving it 'Orphic force', further emphasising its song character. See Abbate, *Unsung Voices*, 151–2.

Example 5.4
Shostakovich IV/3: 161 – 163: linear and harmonic summary

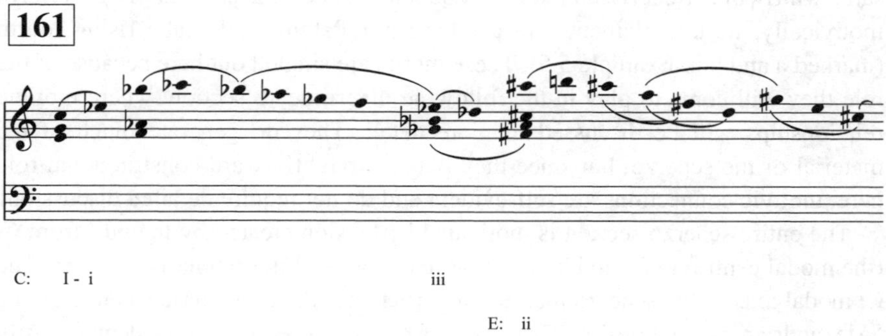

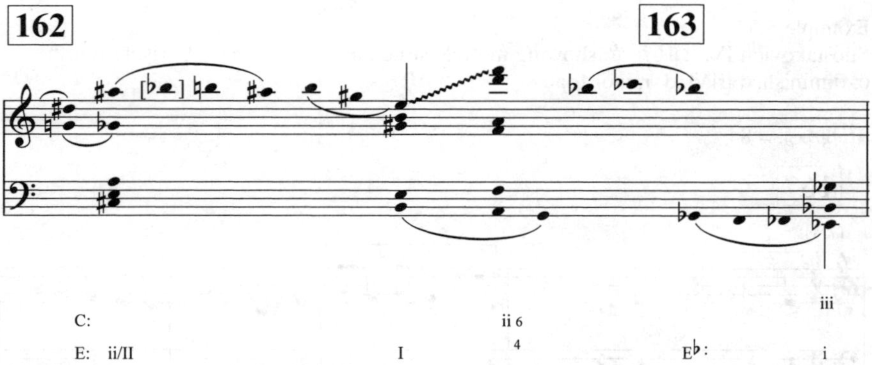

The return to the funeral march is short-lived; after the restatement of A1 at 163, only half of the opening theme follows it before disintegrating beneath an onslaught of A♭–G oscillation. Fragments of the scherzo theme immediately supplant the march, thus avoiding a rigid break between the first and second sections.

167 – 191: Scherzo: Allegro

If the second movement drew its inspiration from the 'Resurrection' Symphony's flowing, dance-like scherzo, and the funeral march from Mahler's First Symphony, then this scherzo has no such precedent. It is firmly in the mould of Shostakovich's later violent scherzi, most notably that of the Tenth Symphony. Sabinina called it a 'toccata scherzo',[15] thereby linking it with the scherzo of the

15 Sabinina, *Shostakovich-simfonist*, 112.

wartime Eighth Symphony. This finale scherzo does not have the *perpetuum mobile* aggression of its later counterpart, although its very fast tempo creates the same whirlwind effect (Example 5.5). The scherzo theme is particularly generative motivically: its key elements are a falling minor third and scalic rising fourth (marked a and b in Example 5.5). These motifs are singled out here because of the role they will come to play in the following divertimento section, where motivic relationships will be discussed in more detail. They do generate much of the material of the scherzo, but since they play a straightforward constructional role here, motivic connections are self-evident and do not require detailed discussion.

The entire scherzo section is motivated by tension created by the pull from C♯ (the modal centre) to D, and by the dual intonations of these polarised forces. The C♯ modal axis of the scherzo theme is a particularly dark one, based as it is on the 'Alexandrian pentachord',[16] (Example 5.6). The flattened second degree easily

Example 5.5
Shostakovich IV/3: 167$^{1-9}$, showing motivic structure a: minor third, b: rising fourth, c: diminished triad, d: minor triad

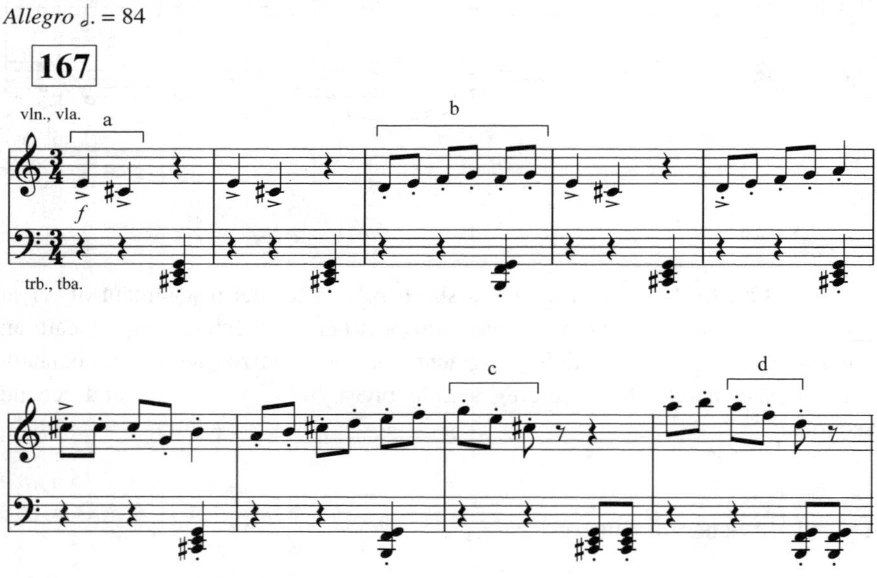

Example 5.6
Alexandrian pentachord, transposed to C♯

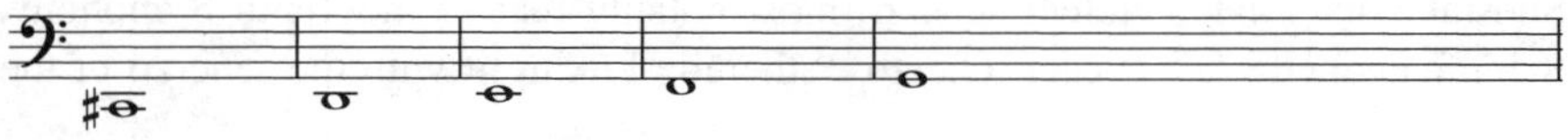

16 Carpenter, 'Russian Theorists', 91–6.

leads to misunderstandings, with C♯ easily read as the leading-note to D. Longman, Darby and Ferruccio Tammaro, for example, view this section as being in D minor,[17] though the sense of C♯ as tonic at the outset is very strong, and there is only a fleeting moment (motif d at ^{6}[168]) when a D minor triad briefly suggests a possible D tonic. The powerful pull from C♯ to D inherent in the scherzo theme itself produces an extremely ‘closed’, rigid effect; unless the flattened mode changes, there is very little room for manoeuvre. This happens fairly quickly, with a move towards G minor ([168]) with D major (^{4}[169], b.121) as the temporary goal (see Example 5.7a). These first 21 bars contain the basic seeds of the scherzo’s development: a strong C♯ mode outlines a violent, aggressive theme, with C♯ minor challenged by a constant pull towards a diatonic D major peroration (which finally comes at [184]). A move to G minor at [168], building on the minor triad of motif d, also has longer-term significance: this chord will eventually dissipate the accumulated tonal energies in an insistent reiteration of its initial triadic formulation (see Example 5.7b).

Example 5.7a demonstrates that, while this section gives the impression of constantly striving towards a goal (hinted at briefly but strikingly by the D major chord at ^{4}[169] and later becoming the key of the climax theme at [182]), an impression reinforced by the continuous movement of repeated ascending scales and motifs, bass movement is minimal, and ultimately the trajectory is flatwards from C♯ to C♮. The abruptness of the cadence at [173] underlines its artificiality; C minor is not the true goal, but the relative emphasis of the cadence allows the music to draw breath before resuming its apparent climb upwards. But between [173] and [180], despite the continual process of ascent, retreat and ascent, no further harmonic goal is reached; the ascent to d^1 in the treble and D^1 in the bass at [174] echoes the D^6_3 at ^{1}[169] but is merely a reiteration of the first motif of the scherzo theme, which is then repeated for 90 bars with no sense of harmonic movement at all. Momentum here is poised on a knife-edge: if tempo and drive are allowed to flag even slightly in performance the effect will be deadening. Longman’s comment that this passage causes ‘the stagnation rather than the kinetic release of the energy achieved at [173]’[18] is fairly made. Is the desired effect here accumulation of energy or its suspension? The line between one and the other is dangerously thin. Every crotchet is accented, and every new entry marked *ff*, though there is no attempt to exceed this level: what is required here in performance is sustained force, not dramatic growth.

A sudden change of texture and theme at [180] announces a new turn of direction. This is a turning-point in the scherzo’s dramaturgy: from this point onwards, the fourths of the forthcoming climax theme begin to feature as the bass switch from C♯ to D (and so to D major) begins in earnest (see Example 5.7a).

---

17 Longman, *Expression and Structure*, 18; Darby, ‘Problems of Context’, 326; and Tammaro, *Le sinfonie di Šostakovič*, 81.

18 Longman, *Expression and Structure*, 19.

Example 5.7
a Shostakovich IV/3: 167 – 191 : summary of motivic, linear and harmonic process

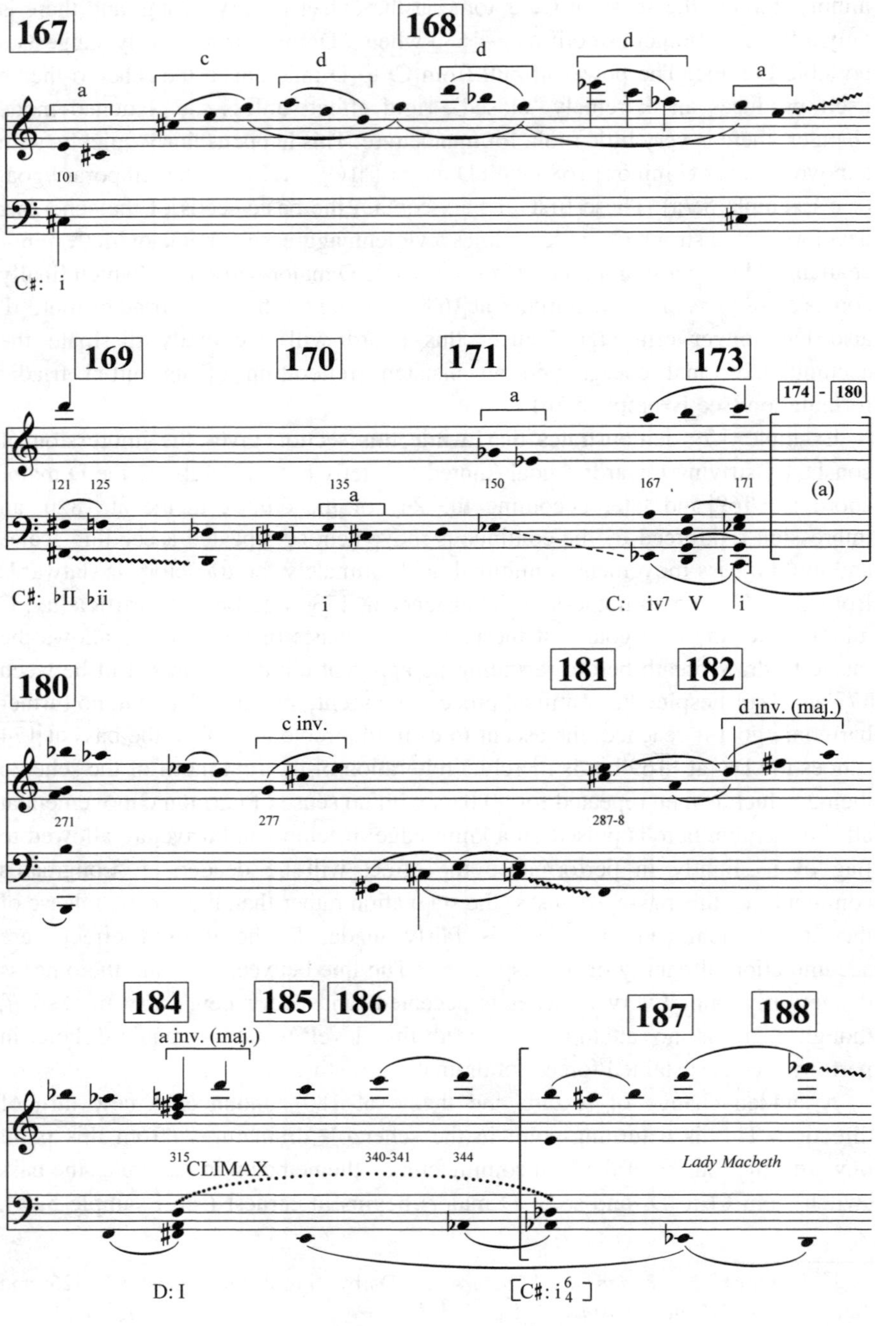

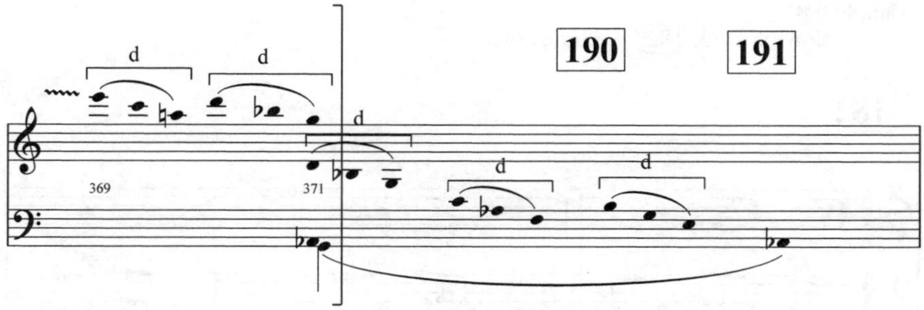

b Shostakovich IV/3: 189$^{1–3}$

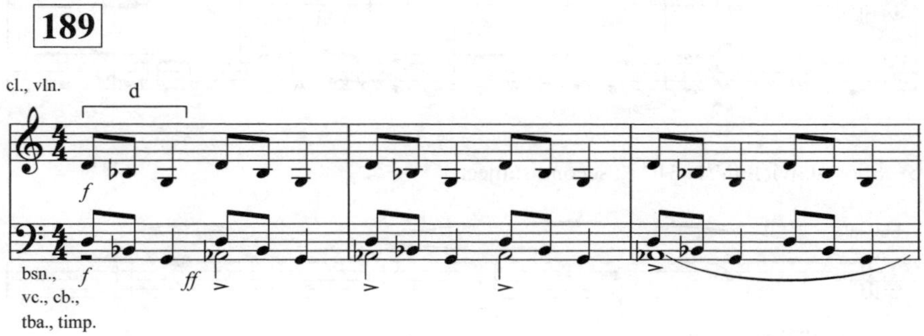

Although the scherzo theme maintains a powerful presence, it is gradually undermined by the rising fourths of the climax theme (Example 5.8a). The climax theme itself is, as Sabinina and Körner have noted,[19] a transformation of the first movement's second subject (Example 5.8b), with similar triadic outlines within a rising octave. As the approach to the climax theme begins from 182, a D major arpeggiation comes to rest on a $^6{}_3$ D major chord at 184, echoing that at ^{4}169. After this goal has been reached, and the D major climax theme heard in its entirety (184 – 185), the bass again moves flatwards from F♯ down to D (see Example 5.7a). The wrench away from D major is violent: between F♯ and E♭, a move to A♭ in the bass at 186^5 (b. 344) instigates the first of a series of *Lady Macbeth* paraphrases from the molestation of Aksinya in Act I, scene 2 and the violent sex scene in scene 3 (Example 5.9). The intonations of violence here are very clear, tearing apart remnants of the climax theme with the semitonal oscillations and minor third of motif a, the diminished triadic outline of b, the off-beat rhythmic blows of c (forcing the climax theme into compressed reiteration) and the diminished fourth of d. Through the C♯ minor $^6{}_4$ at 186^8 (enharmonic A♭/

[19] Sabinina, *Shostakovich-simfonist*, 112; Körner, 'Schostakowitschs Vierte Sinfonie', 219.

Example 5.8
a Shostakovich IV/3: 182 1–7: climax theme

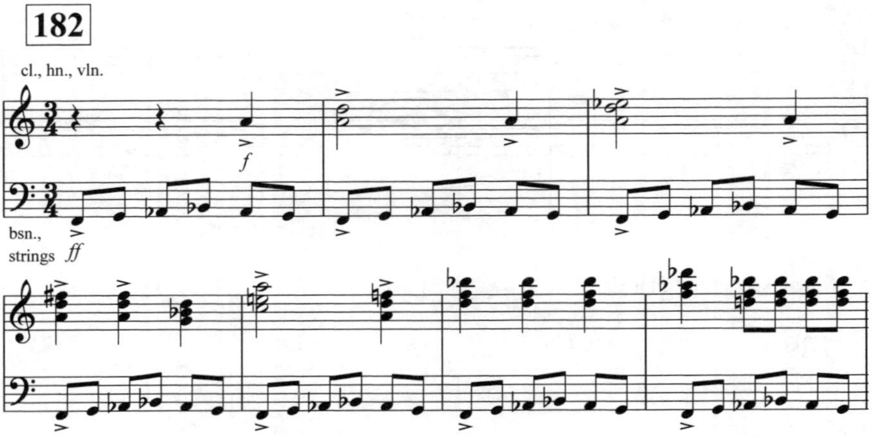

b Shostakovich IV/1: 31 3–9: second subject

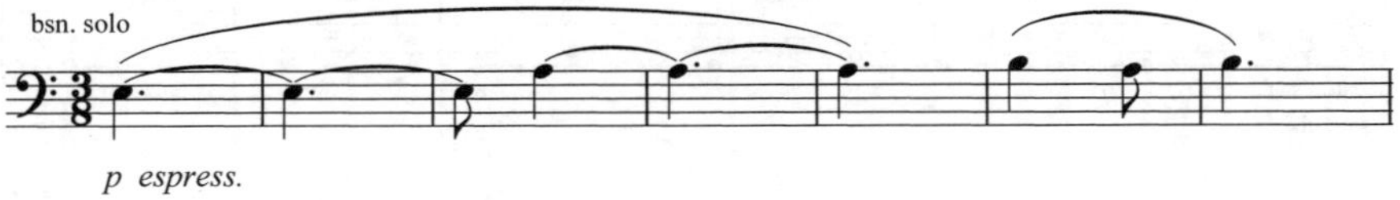

D♭) (b. 347) which supports the first of the *Lady Macbeth* paraphrases, that pull back to C♯/D♭ can be seen to exert a strong influence on motivic events, here reflecting in tonal terms the stress induced by the negation of the triumphal D major climax. The 'galop' triadic figuration dissipates the scherzo's energy over 26 bars, sinking to E by 190 (see Example 5.7): the a♭^{2} from 188 is echoed in the bass on horns, clouding an otherwise clear G minor between ^{2}189 and ^{2}190, and continues into the next section in harmony with the bass clarinet, blurring the piccolo's B♭ minor broken chord at 191.

The whole scherzo section demonstrates Shostakovich's 'symbolic' use of tonal forces and its interaction with motivic, intonational and even inter-textual content. His evocation of the flattened C♯ minor mode, so powerfully used in *Lady Macbeth*, is uniformly dark, and the closed, semitonal character of the mode itself means that movement away from it – especially to a major mode – sounds artificial. What is especially notable here is that, instead of using a sudden switch to D major (as though to emphasise its falseness), Shostakovich paces the arrival of D major and the triumphal theme over a long time-span, allowing it to register as a convincing moment and thus making its swift and violent rejection (with the sequence of *Lady Macbeth* allusions) all the more powerful.

Example 5.9

a Shostakovich IV/3: 186^{7} – 188^{2}: motivic structure (a, b, c, d)

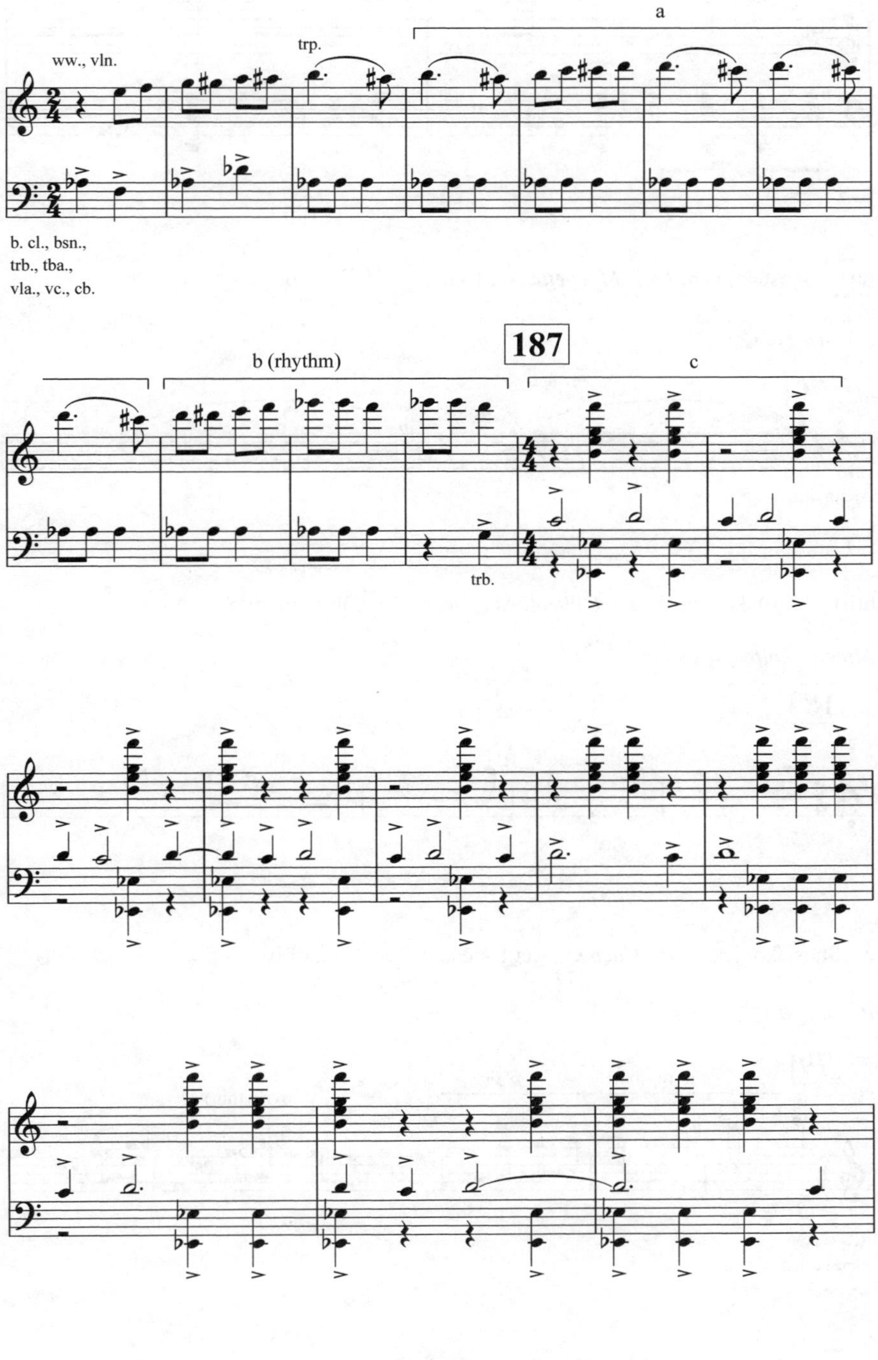

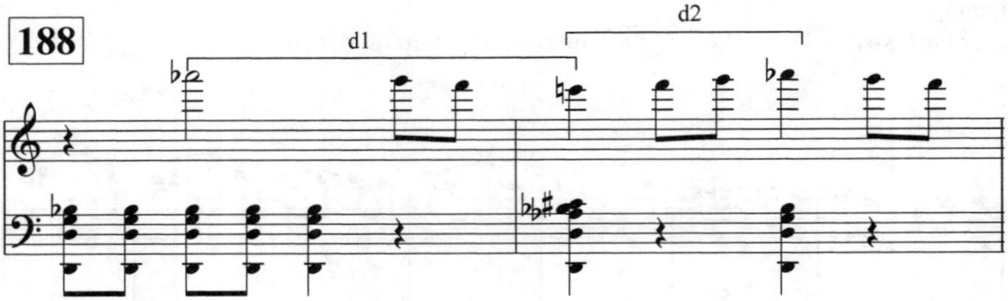

b(i) Shostakovich: *Lady Macbeth*, Act I scene 1, 70$^{1-2}$: motif a

Allegro 𝅗𝅥 = 12

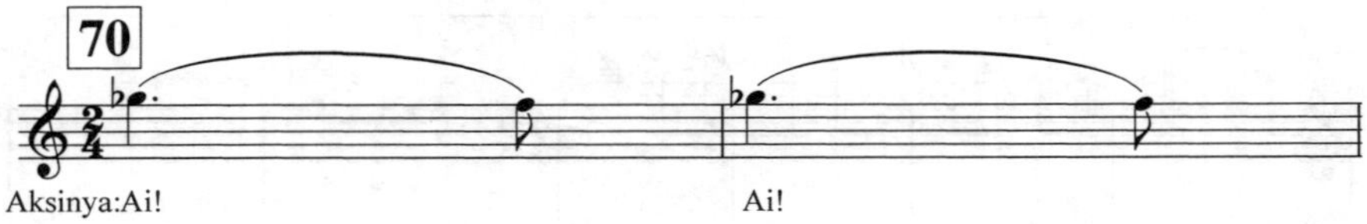

b(ii) Shostakovich: *Lady Macbeth*, Act I scene 3, 183$^{1-5}$: motif a

Allegro molto 𝅗𝅥 = 138

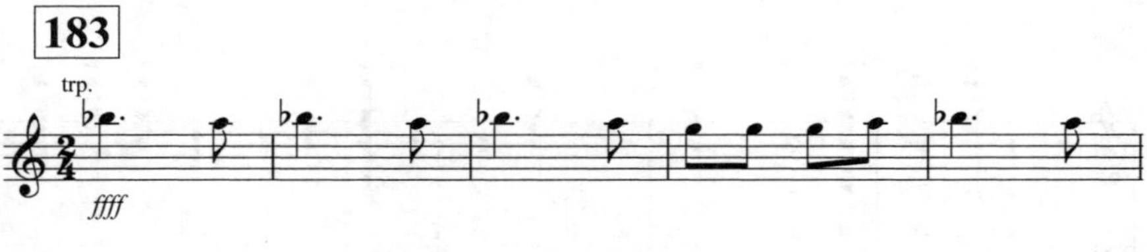

c Shostakovich: *Lady Macbeth*, Act I scene 2, 79$^{1-6}$: motif b

Presto 𝅗𝅥 = 132

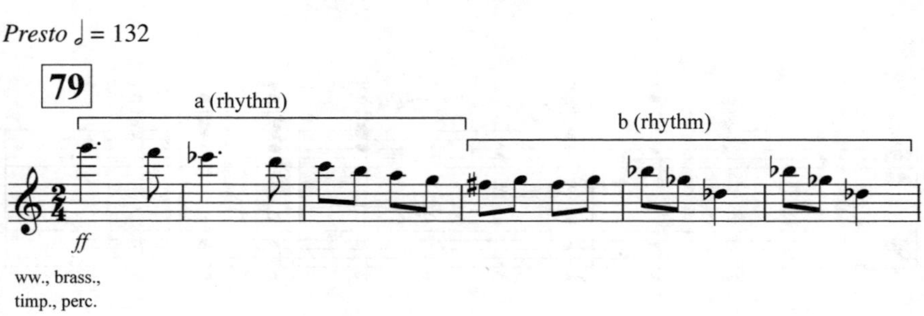

d Shostakovich: *Lady Macbeth*, Act I scene 2, 188$^{1-4}$: motif c

Allegro molto

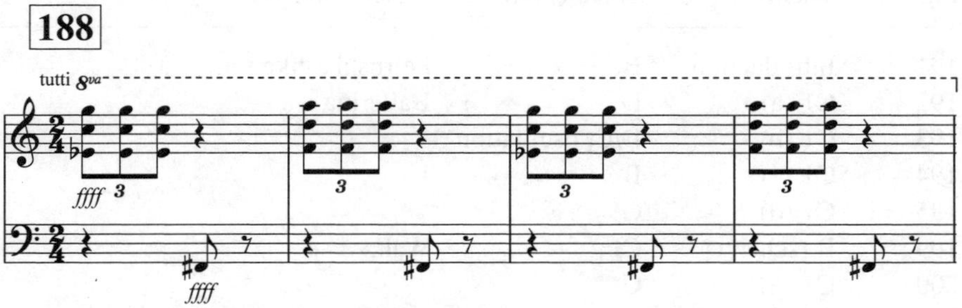

e(i) Shostakovich: *Lady Macbeth*, Act I scene 2, 88$^{2-5}$: motif d1

Presto 𝅗𝅥 = 132

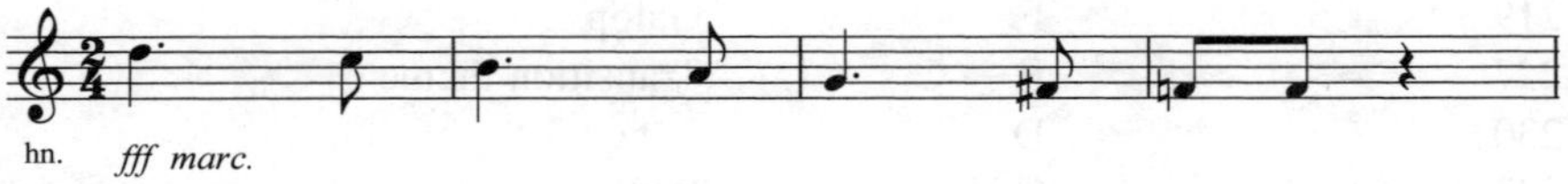

e(ii) Shostakovich: *Lady Macbeth*, Act I scene 3, 185$^{5-9}$: motif d2

Allegro 𝅗𝅥 = 104

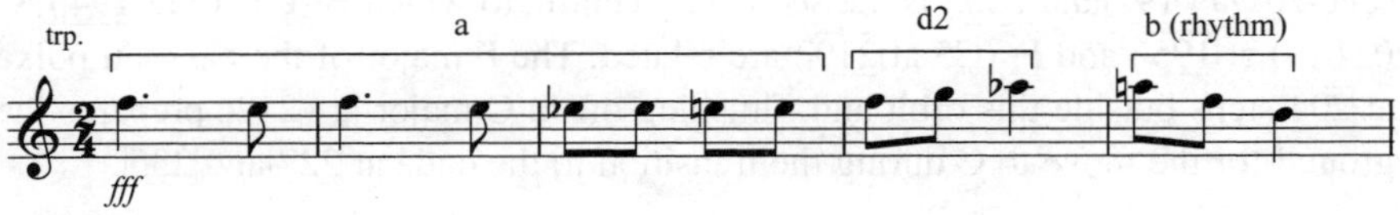

Divertimento

With the abruptness of a cinematic cut, the finale enters the longest of its three main sections. Its sequence of episodes represents a considerable range of urban popular genres: Petrushka and his *balagan*, complete with ballerina waltz (191–202), a Keystone Kops 'chase' polka for bassoon solo (202–212), a barrel-organ waltz (212–217), an operetta-galop (219), containing fragments of a march tune (224) and a popular song (230). These are the six basic elements of the divertimento's urban sound-scape. Its division into sections and sub-sections is not entirely straightforward, however, and commentators have disagreed on a number of boundaries.[20]

Table 5.4 shows that the scherzo theme (B) is always associated with the tonal centre of C♯; only the barrel-organ waltz at 212 shares this tonal centre of gravity, while the other divertimento themes orbit around it, repeating the processes of the

[20] See Longman, *Expression and Structure*, 18; Sabinina, *Shostakovich-simfonist*, 112–13; Fanning, 'Shostakovich: "The Present-Day Master of the C-major Key"', 121–2 and Kopp, *Form und Gehalt*, 174–84.

Table 5.4 Shostakovich IV/3: sectional divisions between 191 and 235

Figure	Theme	Tonal centre	Description
191	Introduction	B♭ → b♮	Petrushka-like tone
192	C1 (a)	D	Ballerina waltz
193	C1 (b)	D/C♯ oscillation	
194	C1 (c)	B	
195	C1 (d)	G	
199	B (scherzo)	C♯	Waltz
200	C1 (d)	G	
202	C2	F → E → F	Polka
212	C3	C♯	Barrel-organ waltz
217	C4/B	C♯	Waltz
219	C5	F♯	Galop
227	–	F → C	Transition theme
230	C6	D	Song
233	B/C7	C♯	Waltz
235	–	C♮	Transition to coda

scherzo: D (192 and 230) is the secondary centre, to which B (C1 (c) at 194), G (C1 (d) at 195) and F♯ (C5 at 219) are related. The F major of the bassoon polka at 204 steps outside this orbit and, finishing off in C major at ^{2}212, prepares the ground for the move to C during the transition to the coda at 227 and 235.

191 – 202: *Petrushechnïy Waltz (C1)*

The opening 'Petrushka' section has received particular scrutiny in Vera Valkova's discussion of the Fourth Symphony. She sees this passage as confirmation of her interpretation of the puppet-like intonations from the first movement as belonging to the mythologization of the *balagan* tradition which flourished in the first two decades of the twentieth century (as represented by Stravinsky's *Petrushka*, Bulgakov's *Master i Margarita* and Aleksandr Blok's *Balaganchik*).[21] Valkova's reading of the Fourth Symphony as a 'tragicheskiy balagan' [tragic puppet-show] is certainly given weight by this passage, in which the puppet-booth intonations of Petrushka (as familiarized by Stravinsky, at least) are unequivocal. And she is surely right to perceive these intonations in the context of this cultural tradition: the old Petrushka shows loved by Stravinsky, Alexandre Benois and Blok appealed to a *fin de siècle* nostalgia for Old Russia, childhood and hence innocence; in their adult hands the character of Petrushka was no longer the abusive, violent hero his

21 See Val'kova, 'Tragicheskiy balagan'.

audiences knew and loved, but a pathetic, tormented figure, suffering at the hands of those around him.[22] The puppet characterization of Shostakovich's finale is certainly of this idealized type: in fact, the cultural reference point here is Stravinsky's *Petrushka*.[23] It is not the first instance of Shostakovich's evocation of *Petrushka* in a symphony: the opening bars of his First Symphony come straight out of Stravinsky's sound-world (Example 5.10). The first movement of the First Symphony contains numerous *Petrushka*-derived themes, of which the two most obvious are the cheeky woodwind acciaccaturas of the introduction and the second subject's ballerina waltz (Example 5.11).

There is, then, nothing unusual or unique about Shostakovich's symphonic evocation of Petrushka. What is unusual, once again, is its tone in the Fourth Symphony, which once again suggests a masking of the 'direct' lyric. The cut to the balagan at 191 sounds distant at first: the barrel-organ has just started cranking up, summoning the audience to a new show. The A♭ pedal clouding the scene, carried over from the previous section, is an unobtrusive but effective 'estranging' device. With the entry of the ballerina waltz, Shostakovich returns to one of the

Example 5.10
a Shostakovich I/1: bb. 1–3

Allegro ♩ = 152

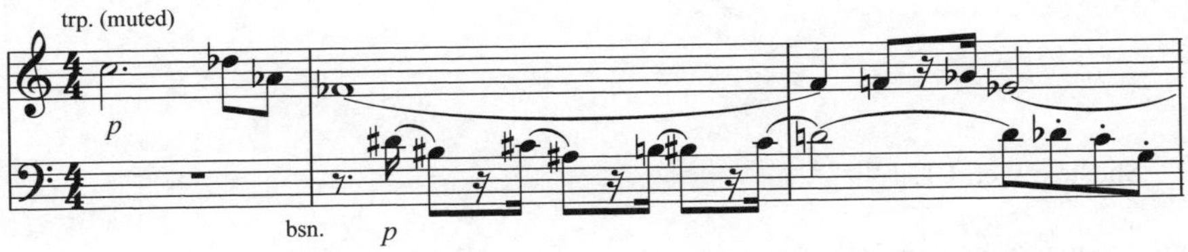

b Stravinsky: Petrushka, Fourth Tableau: [125]7–8

Allegro ♩ = 175

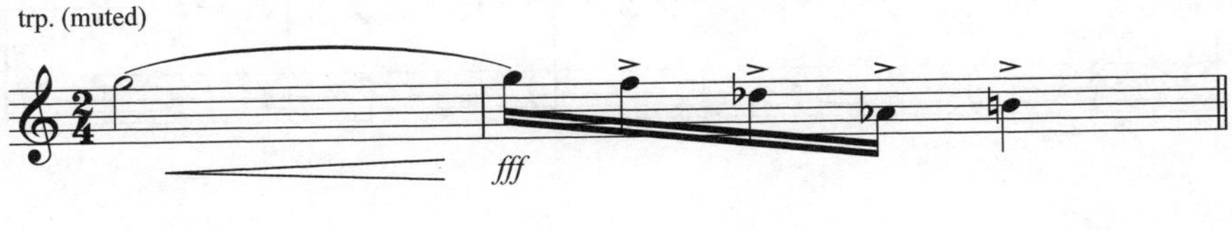

22 For details of the history of Petrushka in Russia and the State's appropriation of him as a mouthpiece for Soviet propaganda, see Catriona Kelly, *Petrushka: The Russian Carnival Puppet Theatre*, Cambridge: Cambridge University Press, 1990. For a superb account of the evolution of the Russian Pierrot-Petrushka figure in modernist art, most notably in Meyerhold's theatre, see J. Douglas Clayton, *Pierrot in Petrograd: The Commedia dell-Arte/Balagan in Twentieth-Century Russian Theatre and Drama*, Montreal and Kingston: McGill-Queen's University Press, 1993.

23 See also Bobrovskiy, 'Posle pervogo ispolneniya Chetvërtoy', 263.

Example 5.11

a Shostakovich I/1: 5[1–4]

♩ = 208

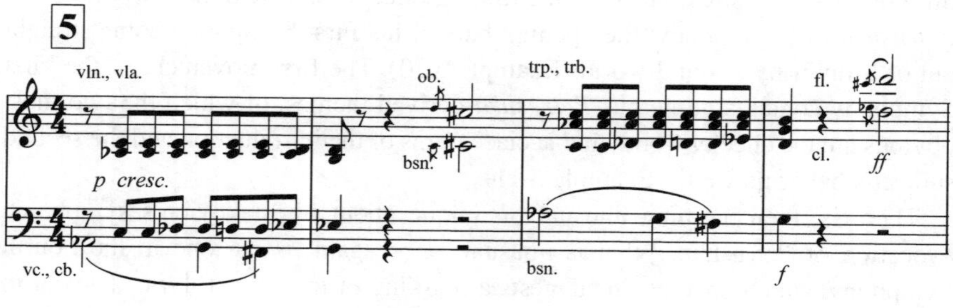

b Stravinsky: *Petrushka*: [4–1] 33

Lento ♩ = 50

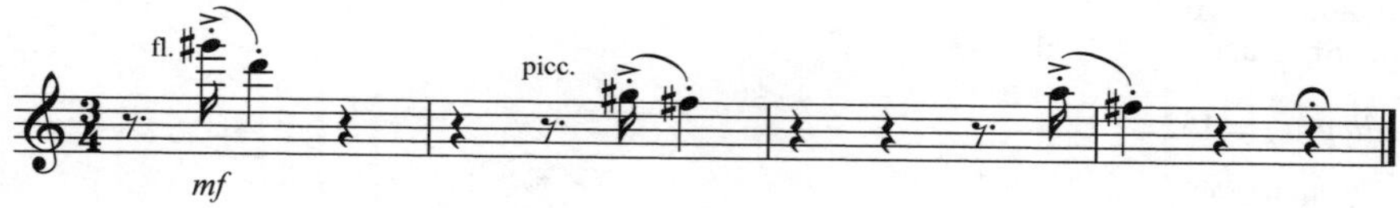

c Shostakovich I/1: 13[1–7]

Allegro non troppo ♩ = 160

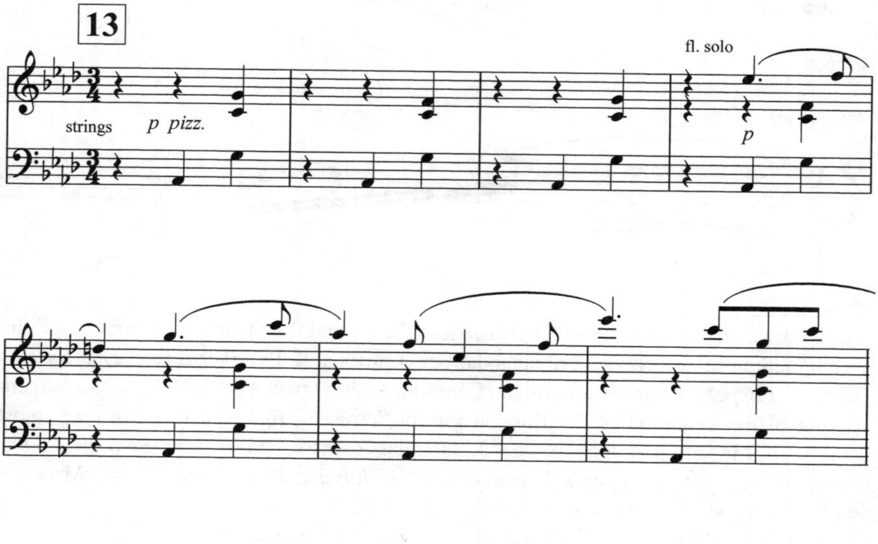

d Stravinsky: Petrushka: 71 $^{4–8}$

Lento cantabile ♩ = 72

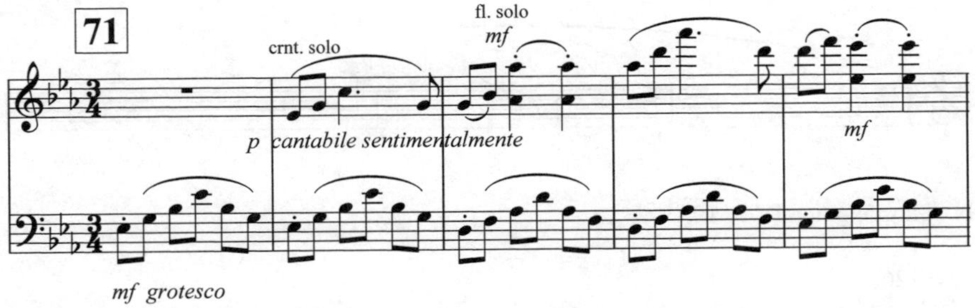

most haunting passages of the first movement (Example 5.12). In both instances, the harp's pedal-point sits on top of the theme (at 192 it lies below as well), which creates a hazy, unreal effect far less robust than a static bass pedal. This whole section brings together the *petrushechnïye* fragments from the first movement: the flute and piccolo intonations which sounded at a loss at 37 are heard here in their proper place. The fourth theme (C1 (d)) at 195 picks up a later fragment from this first movement passage (Example 5.13). As in the first movement, none of the finale's *petrushechnïye* themes are ironically inflected: they are presented 'innocently', though not 'authentically'; their harmonic orientation is not quite straightforward enough for that. They form part of a longer divertimento sequence built from popular idioms such as waltz, hurdy-gurdy music, urban popular songs and dances. Whether critics such as Sollertinsky would have viewed Shostakovich's use of such music as another manifestation of his 'indirect lyric' is of course unverifiable, but likely given that Sollertinsky cited the circus-like finale of the Sixth Symphony as a prime example of Shostakovich's 'Chaplinesque' use of masks, either lyrical or humorous. As though underlining the mask-like, unreal quality of the *petrushechnïye* waltzes, Shostakovich blurs their relatively simple

Example 5.12
Shostakovich IV/1: 36 $^{1–7}$

♩ = 108

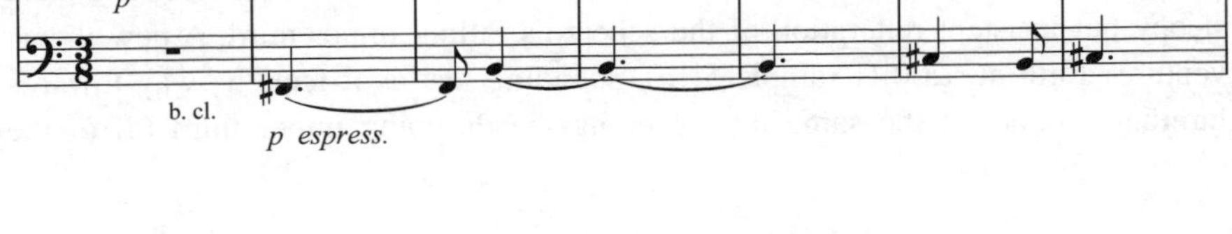

Example 5.13

a Shostakovich IV/1: 37$^{3-5}$

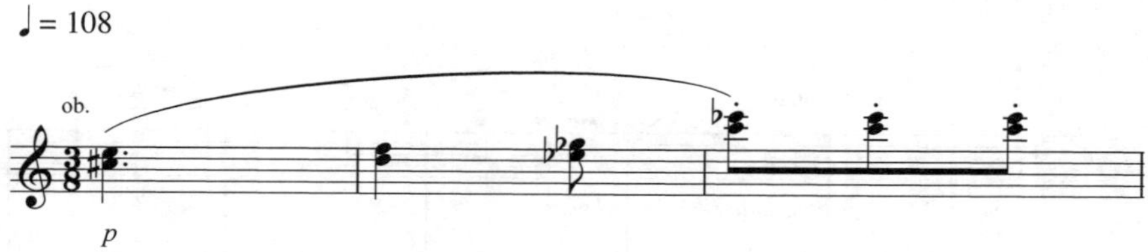

b Shostakovich IV/3: 195$^{1-2}$

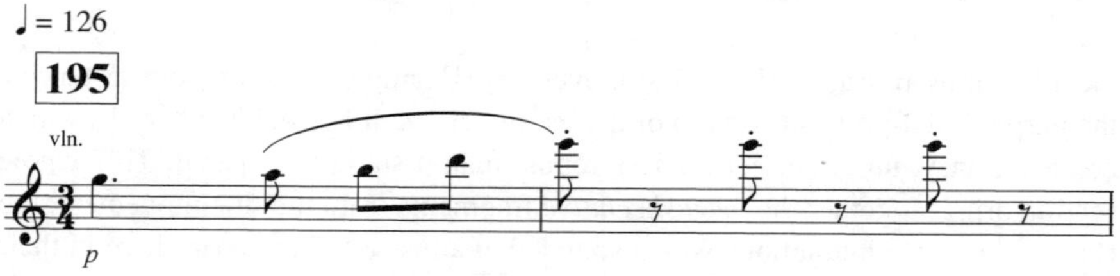

diatonic contours with semitonal oscillations from D to C♯, once again echoing the continuing preoccupation with D and C♯ as competing tonal centres. C♯ continues to represent the intonations and tonal orbit of the violent, 'negative' scherzo, as becomes clear by 198^{5}, with D major and its related keys (B minor and G major) occupying the lyrical, 'positive' sphere of the *petrushechnïye* dances (Example 5.14).

Example 5.14 demonstrates that the D–C♯ oscillation begins at 193, again creating a clouded effect that is reinforced during a move to the relative minor at 194, when the D–C♯ oscillation moves to the treble. It is suspended entirely between 195 and 198, when a more direct tone and harmonic focus emerges, though even here not every detail is predictable: the violas' chromatic flattening of f^{2}♯ and e^{2} at 195$^{5-7}$ distorts the smooth contours of the violin and cello lines. To add to its pungency, the viola part is marked both pizzicato and *f*, while the outer lines are arco and *p*: it is clearly intended to disturb equilibrium. After the flourish and sequence of chords at 198, the diminished triad figure (c) (see Example 5.5a above) from the scherzo theme enters, to be echoed by a drowsy transformation of that theme at 199 (Example 5.15). This offers a further parallel with 36 – 37 in the first movement, where the strings reinforce the harp's move from e^{1} to c♯1 at 36$^{7-8}$. It is the first perceptible infiltration of the divertimento by the scherzo theme, and its effect on the 'positive' tone of the waltz is pronounced. A 16-bar C♯ pedal begins as the diminished triad sounds, pulling away from the *petrushechnïy* sphere with disorientating piccolo flourishes (dim echoes of the piccolo semiquavers at 37) and sleepy but insistent reiteration of the scherzo's falling minor third. A new theme ventures forth at ^{4}200 (Example 5.16), sounding lost as it feels its way towards familiar ground, at the same time echoing the drooping minor third (a) of the

Example 5.14
Shostakovich IV/3: [191] – [201]: motivic, linear and harmonic summary

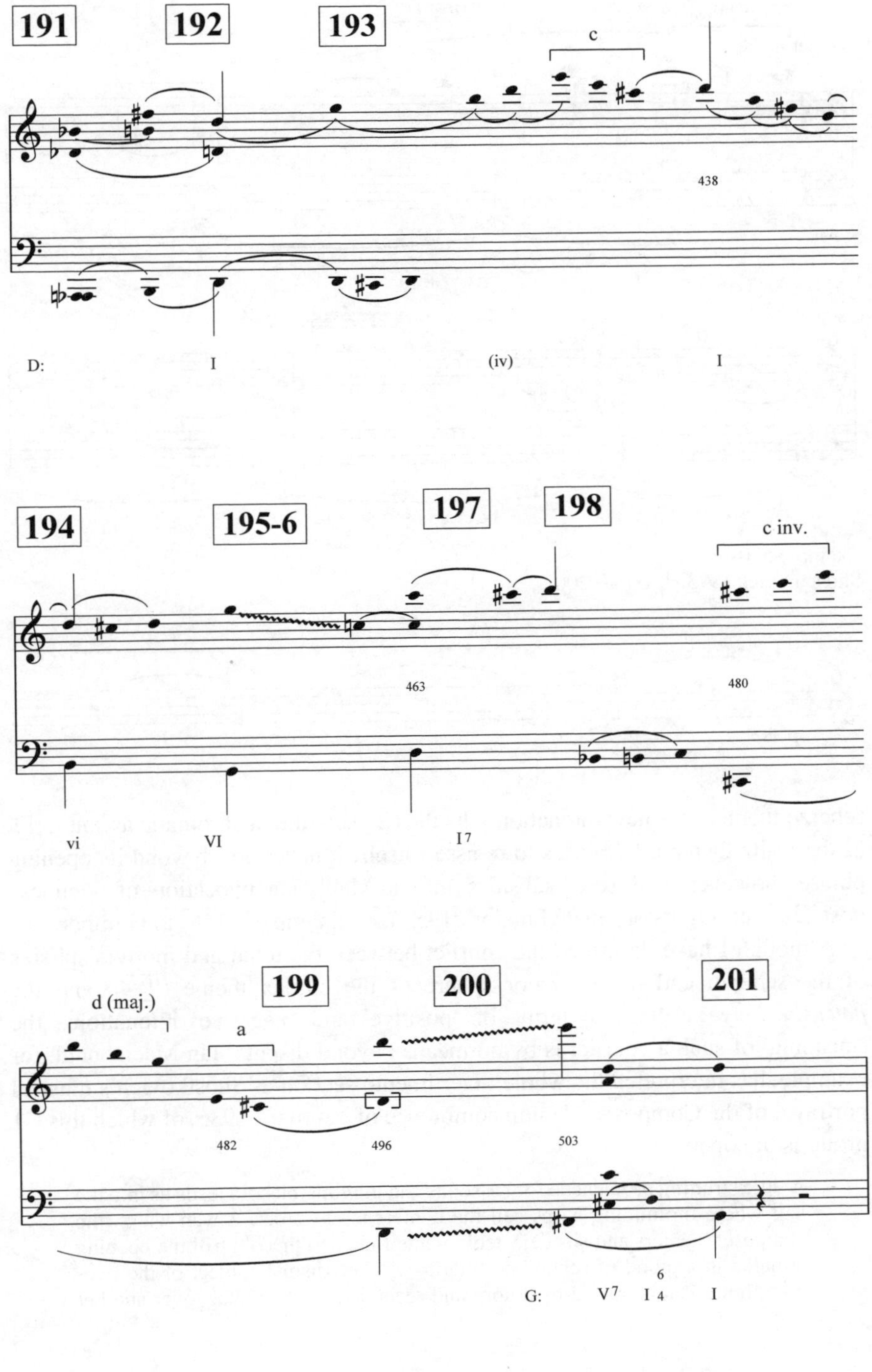

Example 5.15
Shostakovich IV/3: 198^{4} – ^{2}199

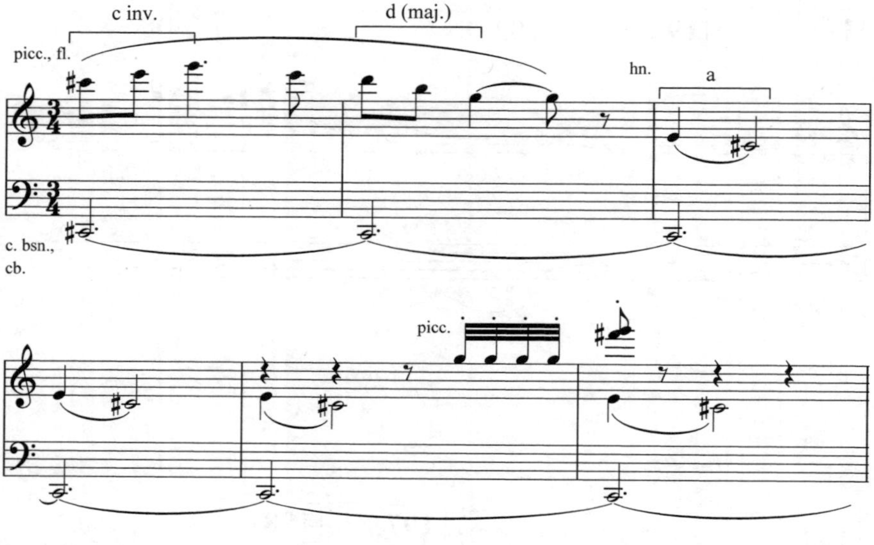

Example 5.16
Shostakovich IV/3: ^{4}200 – ^{2}200

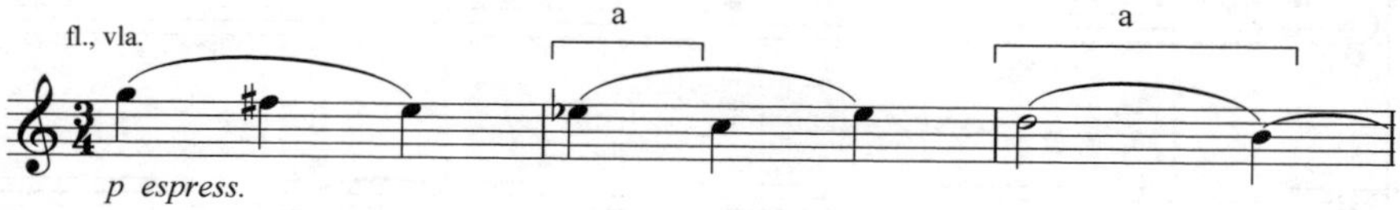

scherzo theme. This new intonation jolts the C♯ pedal into a chromatic ascent to F♯, as the waltz theme C1 (d) tries to re-assert itself. It never gets beyond its opening phrase, however, and soon subsides into a Mahlerian evocation of Viennese nostalgia, turning its original G major (195) (see Example 5.14b) to G minor.

Although I have described the conflict between the tonal and motivic spheres of the scherzo and the D major sphere of the climax theme (184) and the *petrushechnïye* waltzes in terms of 'positive' and 'negative' intonations, the 'meaning' of such a conflict is by no means beyond dispute. Ian MacDonald, for example, has interpreted the whole divertimento section as Shostkovich's musical portrayal of the Composers' Union conference of February 1936, of which this C1 group is the opening:

> A little strutting promenade for bassoons and giggling piccolo leads us into the hall where thrumming harps call the conference to order. A wan waltz (the composer?) enters and sits dejectedly while flute and piccolo trill the opening remarks in a mood of schoolboy hilarity … The dismal subject of the two-note figure is now raised by a horn and seconded by the violas, over another

> brooding pedal-point. For a moment, the music freezes, as though lost in thought – then perks up and resumes waltzing in sentimental mode.[24]

A problem with MacDonald's reading (apart from the fact that we know Shostakovich never attended the conference) is that his attribution of personal characterisation to a given theme is not borne out for the course of the section. In short, it is not a systematic reading, but a merely convenient one: what, for example, might be made of the 'wan waltz' in its third incarnation at [195], where it is no longer wan but decidedly jaunty? And what of the transformation of the scherzo theme – the 'two-note figure' which, according to MacDonald's established code, represents officialdom, crude brutality, and even Stalin himself? These details might well, in a 'programmatic' reading, suggest some level of semantic content. But, MacDonald's account apart, it is near-impossible to project any sort of concrete scenario upon them: the myriad of shades and nuances create a constant intonational haze in which nothing is consistent. And this, surely, is the whole point. The succession of puppet characters and themes passes through as though heard and seen from a distance: their presentation is indirect. Their links with the first movement merit consideration: where they were a ghostly, insubstantial presence there, they are real and tangible here. But the other-worldly nostalgic tone of their appearance in the first movement remains potent in the finale: the veiled, sleepy waltz at [200], for example, echoes that of the first movement at [38], with its shared chromatic bass movement and inability to progress further than the first phrase.

My own instincts about this section are that the 'masked' tone of the *petrushechnïye* themes creates an impression of distance which is less ironic than nostalgic. Rather in the spirit of the Petersburg Silver Age depictions of the Russian fairground and *commedia dell'arte* characters (such as those by Blok in *Balaganchik* and Meyerhold's 1906 production of it, together with Benois's set for Stravinsky's *Petrushka*), the characters and music of the *balagan* are represented by Shostakovich as Russia's past: idealized and sentimentalized precisely because the *balagan* tradition, like Old Russia itself, was dying. That is not to say that this section should be read tragically; its tone is not at all tragic. On the contrary, unlike many of the Silver Age interpretations of the character of Petrushka as a tragic hero, Shostakovich's evocation of the *balagan* has the multivalence of Stravinsky's: cheeky, wistful, cheerful and mournful by turns. If there is tragedy not far beneath the surface of this urban sound-scape, then it is less likely to be of the Romantic Silver Age kind than to be related in some way to the brutalization of Soviet life and culture under Stalin in the 1930s. It may even be that the tonal and motivic conflict which besets the whole divertimento section (the pull to C♯ which operates throughout is, in the end, negated only by an abrupt, and almost certainly angrily satirical, paraphrase of the C major 'Gloria' coda from

24 MacDonald, *The New Shostakovich*, 115.

Stravinsky's *Oedipus rex*) is, on however subconscious a level, a metaphor for the constant and oppressive threat of violence in Stalinist culture.

202 – 212: *Polka (C2)*[25]

The polka theme is motivically dependent on the scherzo theme, founded on inversions of its descending minor third (a) and triad (d) (Example 5.17). As Table 5.5 illustrates, the tonal centre of the main theme (C2) oscillates between E and F, with the central part of the theme an E major arpeggio which, via an unceremonious flattening of the C♯ of E:ii, briskly finishes off in F (Example 5.18). Each of the polka's four appearances is more or less identical to the others, with variations in texture only. The third entry is slightly destabilized by intrusive up-beats, off-beats and glissando echoes, effects all intended to sound like wrong entries. The most off-putting of all is the out-of-synch effect at ^{8}208, where the woodwinds' descending pairs are reversed by the violins. The episode at 208^{4} continues this lop-sided tone, with an off-beat piccolo disturbing the four-square duple metre and a clumsy trombone theme (a variant of C2 and partially derived from the scherzo's minor third motif (a)) which sounds in the wrong metre, with short-breathed phrases in a monotonous falling–rising–falling pattern (Example 5.19). After a brief detour to B♭ as tonal centre, the fourth entry of the bassoon from 211 rounds off in C major via B♭–B♮–C .

This 'chase' sequence carries far less cultural baggage than the preceding section: the intonations are 'new' Russia, not old, and the tone is absurd or humorous rather than poignant or innocent. There is a disjunction between part

Table 5.5 Shostakovich IV/3: structure of polka

Figure	Theme	Key
202	C2 (1)	e–F
204	4-bar refrain	d
204^{6}	C2 (2)	e–F
206	4-bar refrain	d
206^{4}	C2 (3)	e–F
208	4-bar refrain	d
208^{4}	trombone episode	→ e♭ → c
211	C2 (4)	e–F → C

25 Neither old nor new collected works scores have the metronome mark of ♩ = 160 here that is found in the Sikorski score. However, if the previous metronome mark of ♩ = 126 at 191 is adhered to, then not only the 'chase' polka, but the following waltz at 212 will drag.

Example 5.17
Shostakovich IV/3: 202^{4} – 203^{5}

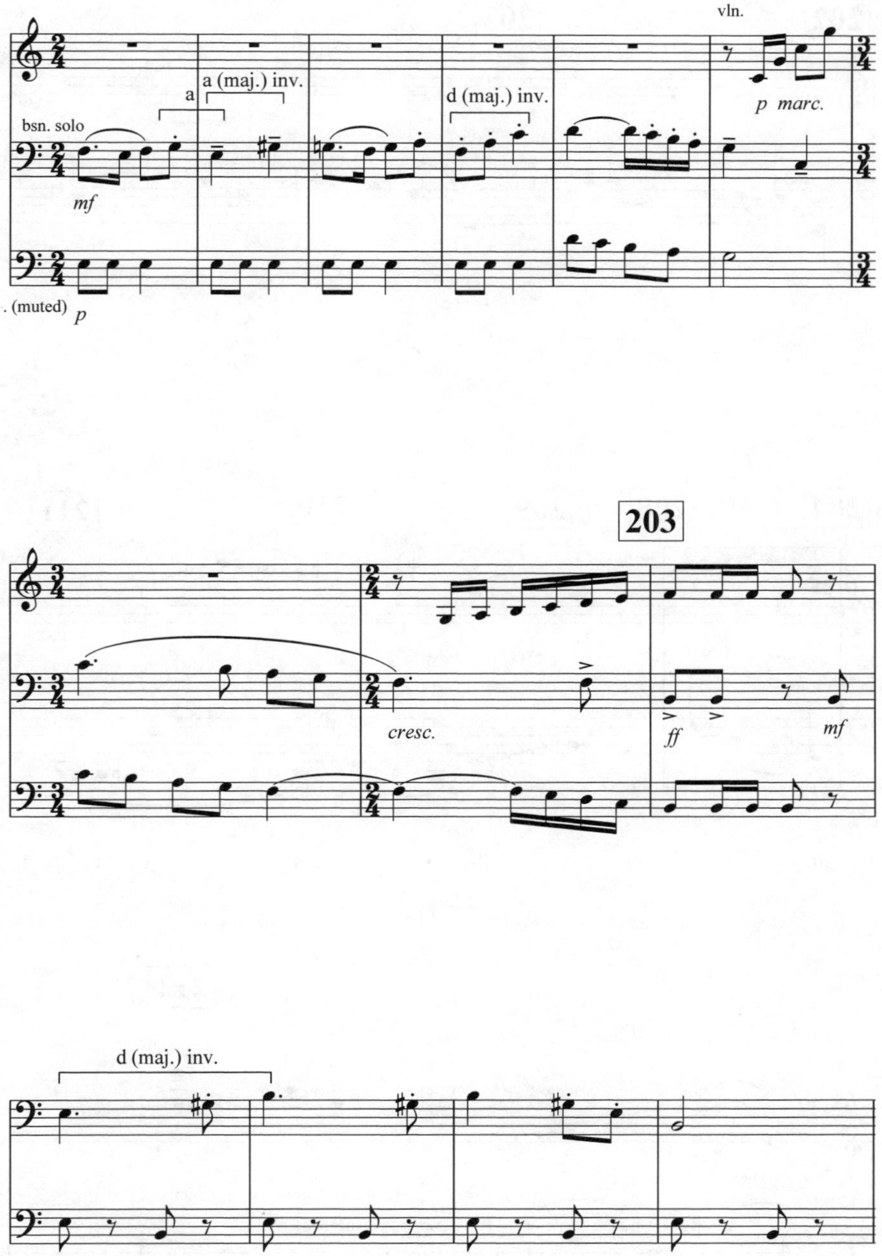

Example 5.18
Shostakovich IV/3: 202 – 212: motivic, linear and harmonic summary

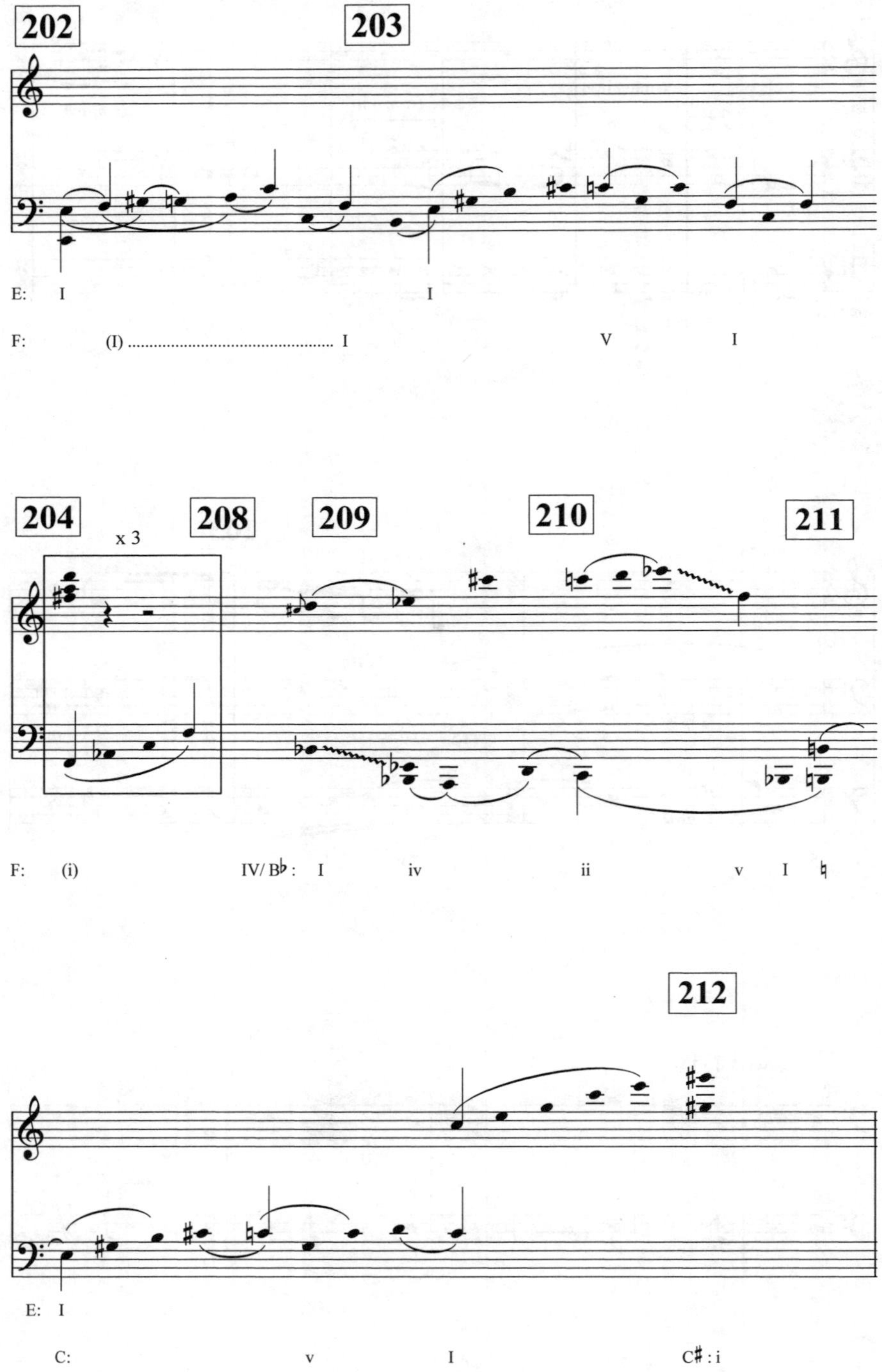

Example 5.19
Shostakovich IV/3: $\boxed{208}^{5} - {}^{1}\boxed{209}$, showing motivic relationship to the scherzo

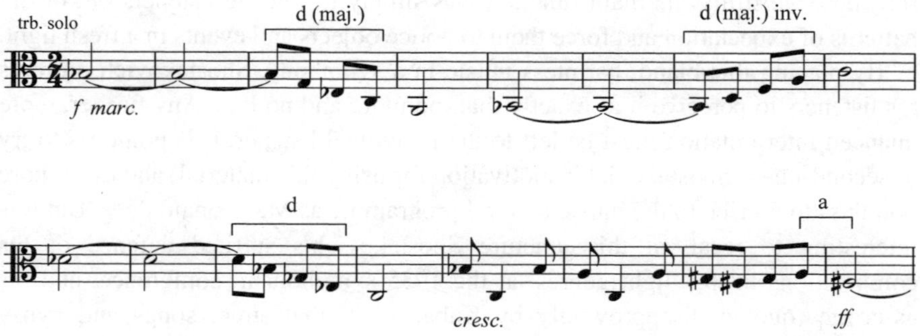

and whole here, though: the sheer emotional emptiness of the theme is unprecedented in Shostakovich's 'serious' orchestral work up to the Fourth Symphony. Where similarly mindlessly jolly themes appear in his incidental scores, the intention is invariably satirical. The ballet scores in particular are littered with galops and polkas, many of which are clearly throwaway filler items. But there are some notable exceptions, of which the quirky polka from *The Golden Age* is probably the most famous.[26] The object of satire – Western politicians discussing disarmament and world peace – was indicated in the polka's subtitle, 'Once Upon a Time in Geneva … (Angel of Peace)' (Example 5.20). In contrast to the polka from *The Golden Age*, the Fourth Symphony's bassoon polka is not presented in a blatantly unusual way: apart from its quirky harmonic side-slips, there are no grotesque inflections such as extra wide leaps or 'wrong' notes. What is unusual, though, is its four-squareness and banal character in a symphonic context. Merely removing this music from its natural cultural framework (namely, American Keystone Kops films showing in Soviet cinemas) invites the listener to perceive it in a new light: a classic Meyerholdian technique. Although, as

Example 5.20
Shostakovich, *The Golden Age*, Polka: $\boxed{45}^{6-10}$

Allegretto ♩ = 84

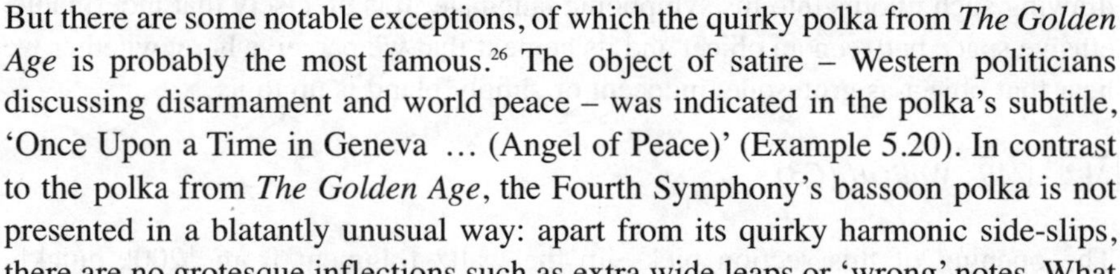

26 Sheinberg cites this polka as an example of Shostakovich's 'wrong-note' musical satire (Sheinberg, *Irony*, 116).

discussed in Chapter Two, for Meyerhold the purpose of estrangement (*ostraneniye*) was primarily critical, it was not necessarily intended to inspire ridicule or hostility: its main function was simply to jolt the listeners out of old patterns of expectation and force them to notice objects and events in a fresh light.

By placing this bland, harmless music in a symphony, Shostakovich prompts his listeners to perceive it as exactly that: no more and no less. Any further, more nuanced interpretation must be left to the individual listener. It is pointless to try to second-guess Shostakovich's motivation for using this material, and even more pointless to ascribe to the music a literal programme as MacDonald does. But it is interesting to recall at this juncture Shostakovich's spirited defence of his compositions in the 'light genres' at the 1935 symphonism conference, and his assertion (quoted disapprovingly by Kabalevsky) that street songs and gypsy romances were all appropriate material for a new musical language.[27] While the bassoon polka does not quite fit into this category, Shostakovich's words imply acceptance of light music in general rather than a tendency to use it only for satirical purposes. But, as with Mahler, the presentation of popular idioms in an otherwise 'serious' work is never straightforward, and that very complexity may well have been the factor which most attracted Shostakovich to the idea of drawing such idioms into his symphonic language. It is precisely that indefinable, elusive space between an object and its context that we perceive here: whether we hear that object as grotesque, innocent or simply bland is up to us.

212 – 219: *Waltz II (C3)*

The opening of this section picks up the waltz fragment from ^{4}200, quickly dispelling both the duple metre and C tonic of the polka. As in the polka, though, its main intervals and rhythms derive from the scherzo theme: the minor third of motif a, the rising fourth (here inverted and diminished) of motif b, the diminished triad of motif c (sometimes arpeggiated) and the minor triad of motif d (here generally major). As at ^{7}199 – 199^{5}, the waltz's opening phrase confirms its relationship to the scherzo by pitch as well, with E–C♯ a central motif here as for motif a of the scherzo theme. The transition from polka (C major) back to waltz (beginning in C♯ minor) is made via a brief reference to the last incursion of C♯ at 198^{5}: the clarinet entry at 212 echoes the four-bar fragment at ^{4}200. The relationship between the new waltz section and the old is confirmed by the flute's introductory $g\sharp^{1}$–$g\sharp^{2}$ flourish (see Example 5.21a). Whereas the waltz themes of C1 (b, c and d) retained a strong basic shape, this waltz is delivered in fragments: some overlapping, others divided by reiteration of a single element or extension of one phrase. Example 5.22 lists the five main phrases in order of appearance and brackets scherzo motifs. Two of these phrases, c and d have a strong cadential feel,

[27] *Sovetskaya muzïka*, 1935/4, 38.

Example 5.21

a Shostakovich IV/3: 212$^{1-5}$, showing motivic relationship to scherzo

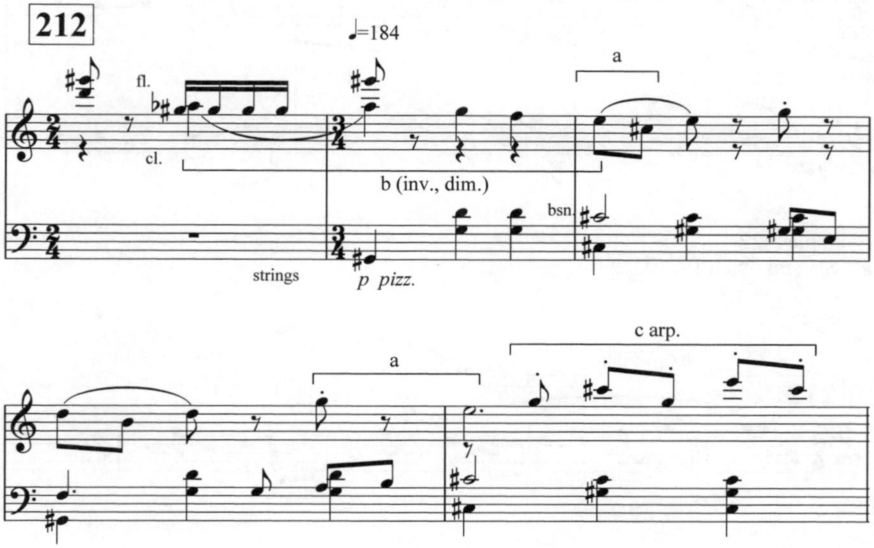

b Shostakovich IV/3: ^{1}199 – ^{1}200, motifs a, b, c bracketed

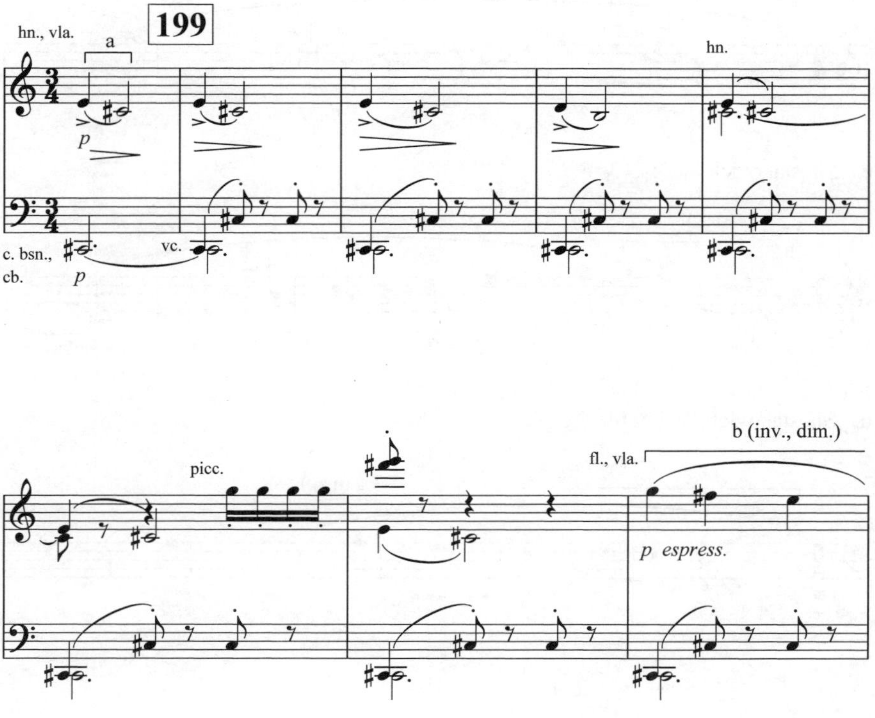

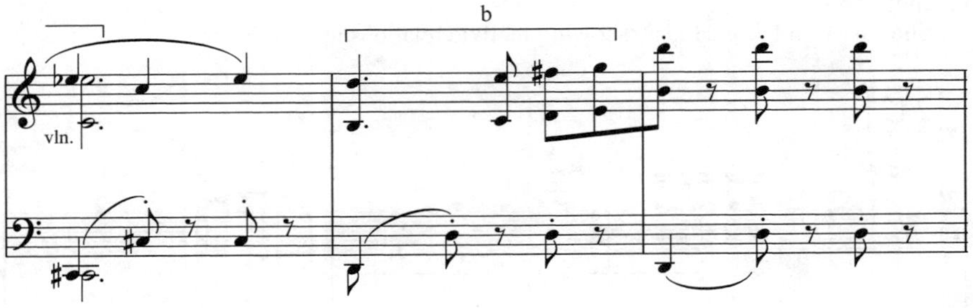

Example 5.22

a Shostakovich IV/3: 212$^{1-5}$

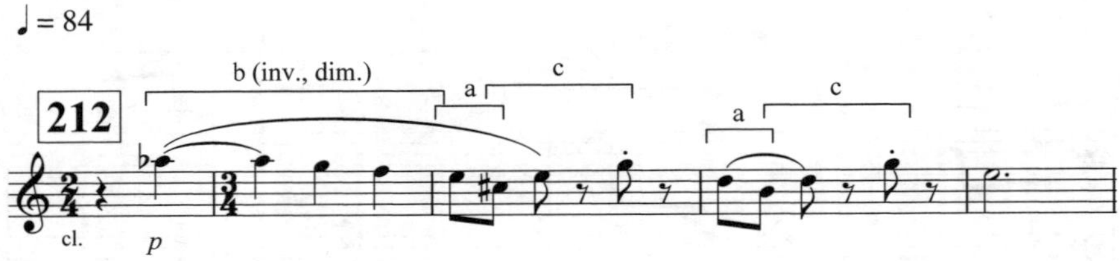

b Shostakovich IV/3: ^{4}213 – 213

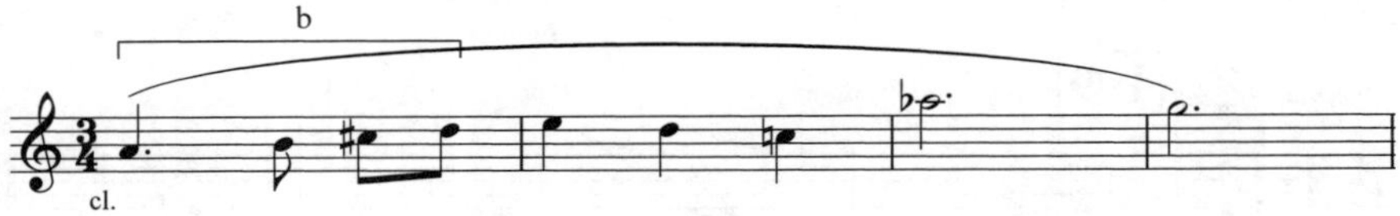

c Shostakovich IV/3: 213$^{4-8}$

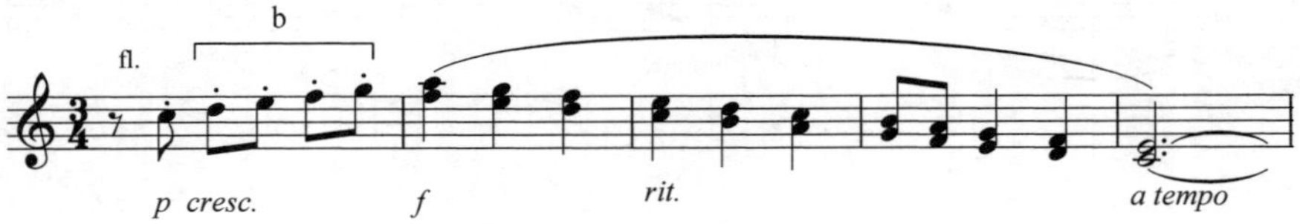

d Shostakovich IV/3: 214$^{5-8}$

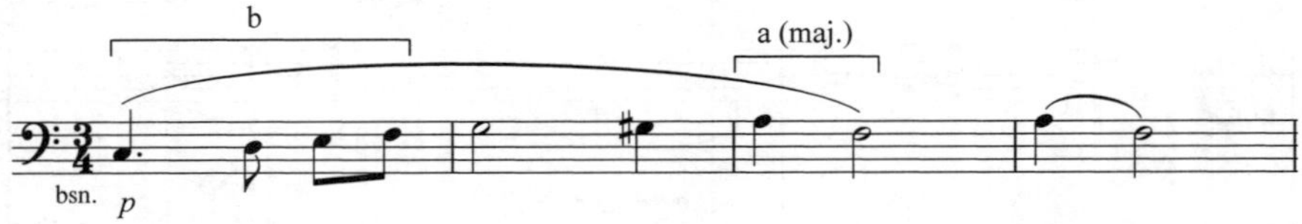

while b sounds like an answering phrase; a is clearly an opening phrase, as confirmed by its more forceful repetition between 213 and 214 (Example 5.23). Example 5.22d is actually a near-quotation from the well-known 1925 Irving Berlin song 'Always' (Example 5.24).[28] The other phrases are derived from the Berlin quotation, some sounding like opening phrases, others like middle and closing phrases. Though they are presented in a mixed-up order that suggests they are all variations on the opening theme (Example 5.22a), they are in fact variations not on that theme as presented at 212 but as heard in its 'closing' phrase at 214$^{5–12}$. As already observed, the scherzo's motivic and tonal influence upon the C3 group is particularly strong, with C♯ introduced as the tonic straight away. Motifs a, b and

Example 5.23
Shostakovich IV/3: 213$^{6–15}$: reiteration of a: motifs a and b bracketed

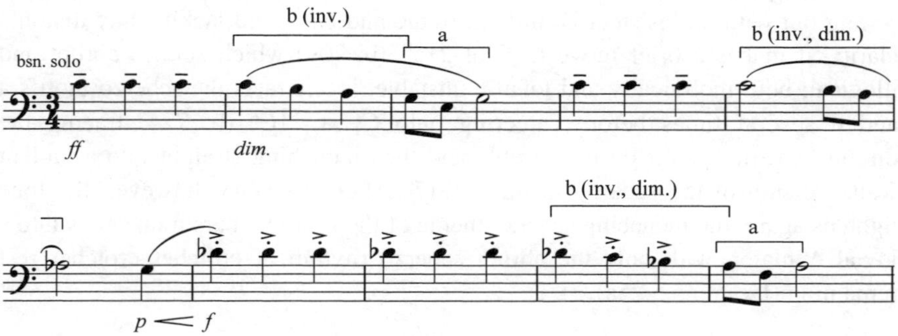

Example 5.24
Irving Berlin: 'Always', chorus: bb. 1–8

moderate tempo

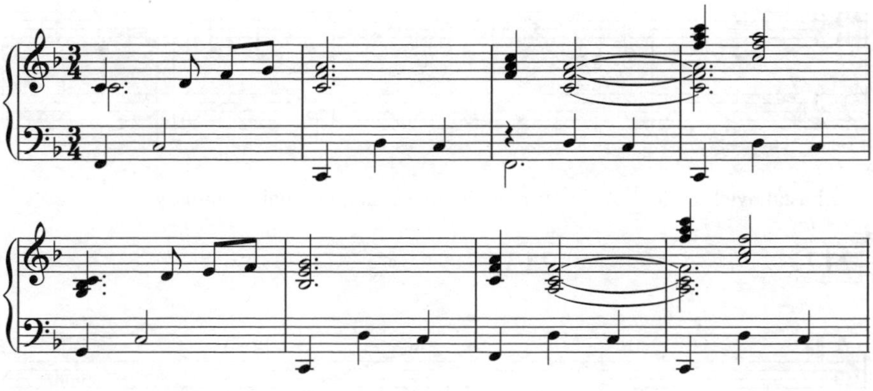

I'll be loving you, always / with a love that's true, always.

28 I am grateful to David Fanning for this reference.

c from the scherzo theme feature strongly in the 'opening' and 'closing' phrases of the waltz theme, suggesting a dependency on the scherzo which is confirmed as the waltz progresses. The dramatization of C♯ as aggressor initially broached in the scherzo section continues, with both C♯ and G♯ used enharmonically in C major and F major contexts. As Example 5.25b shows, G♯ is used as a pivot; initially a strong dominant support for C♯, it becomes part of a iv $^{6}{}_{3}$–V–I C major cadence at 213$^{5–8}$ (see Example 5.22, phrase c). The bassoons' D♭s immediately oppose that C major, using the A♭ again as its dominant; all the time as the phrases of the song recall (but also seem to neutralize) the scherzo's motifs a and c in short iambic major thirds and major triads. As the bassoon reaches the final phrase in F major at 214^{5}, D♭ has become merely a jocular flattened sixth inflection to the dominant in the bass (b. 697). However, the tone darkens as the pull back to C♯ intensifies from 215, preparing the ground for the scherzo variant at 217 (C4). Once again setting out with an insistent D♭ in both treble and bass, and lacking any diatonic clarity, it makes a brief move to C at 215^{7} (b. 709) which sounds abrupt and illogical; both motivically and tonally unstable, it reiterates the scherzo motifs a and d several times before careering onto C♯ at 216^{6} (b. 724) tracing the diminished triad motif c in the treble and then launching straight into a violent waltz version of the scherzo theme at 217. After this entry, however, the tone lightens again: the menacing scherzo theme of the first few bars transmutes into a jovial A major, with only the abrupt scherzo rhythm of crotchet–crotchet–rest remaining (Example 5.25a).

Example 5.25
a Shostakovich IV/3: 217$^{1–5}$ (C4), showing theme in harmonic reduction

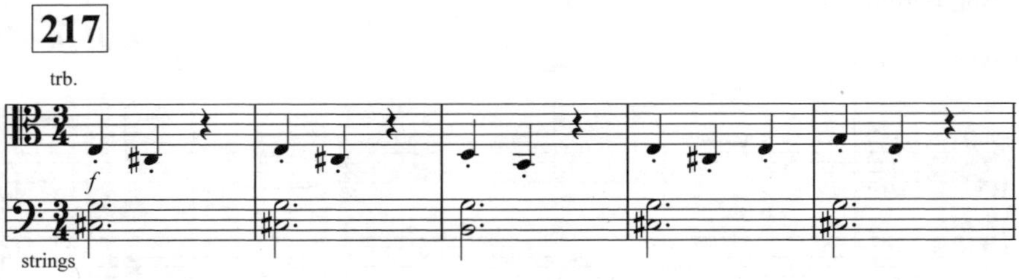

b Shostakovich IV/3: 212 – 219: motivic, linear and harmonic summary

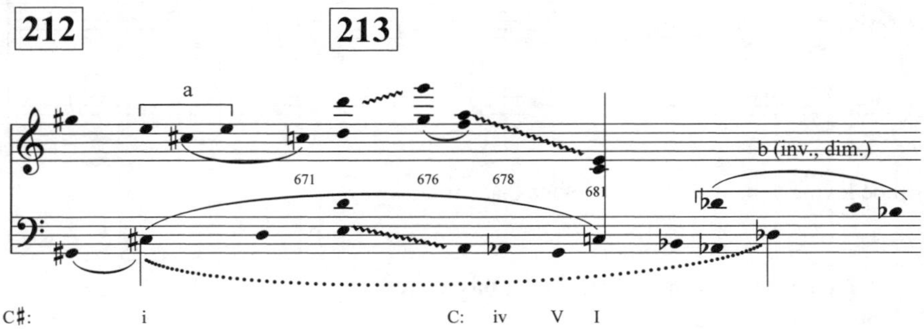

214

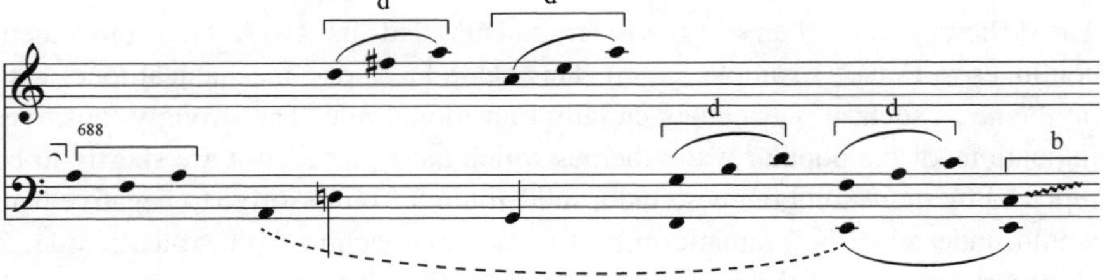

215

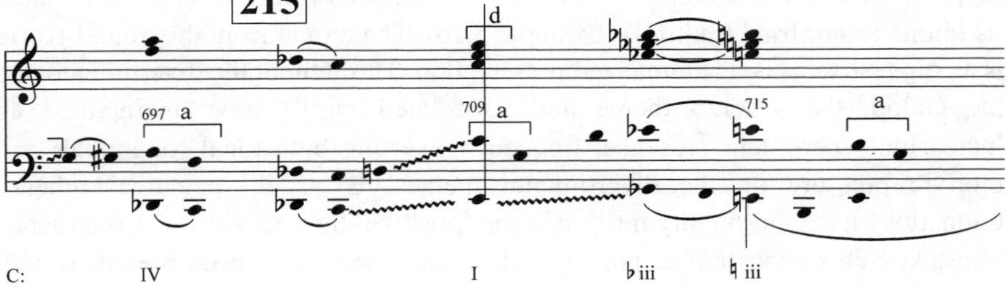

216

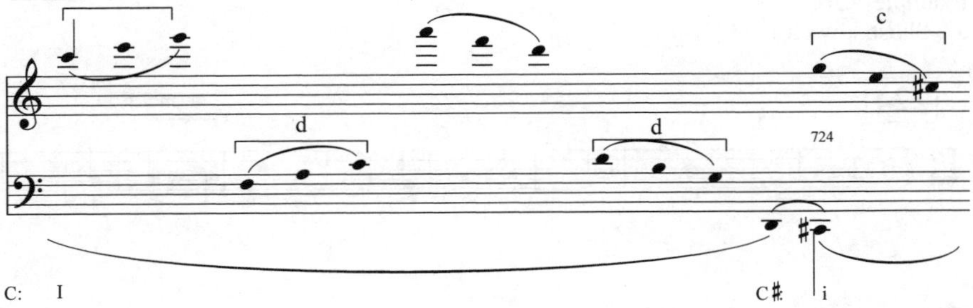

217

219

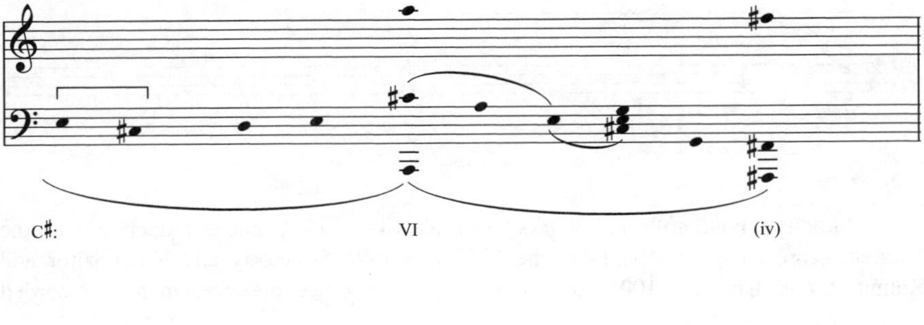

219 – 227: *Galop (C5)*[29]

The scherzo-waltz theme quickly fragments and its C♯–A bass movement continues to F♯ (see Example 5.25b). This galop has a dry, mechanical tone, with no theme as such: it plays an essentially transitional role. The strongly 'positive' intonations of the popular waltz themes which have preceded it are shortly to be replaced by more sombre ones, and a sudden lurch from positive to negative here would undermine the dramatic impact of the approaching light-to-dark coda. It also marks a return to the static oscillating bass figuration from the funeral march in place of the more conventional diatonic movement of the divertimento, thus instigating a more tightly 'closed' tone: the first sign that the end is in sight.

A march fragment at 224 seems to glance back at the merry fairground soundscape of C1 and C3, echoing the scherzo's falling minor third (motif a) and, later, its falling minor triad (motif d) (Example 5.26). The retreat from this sound-world is as suggestive as is its dramatized presentation. Throughout the divertimento and the Galop, the scherzo theme and its related motifs have maintained an increasingly persistent presence, frequently exerting both tonal (or modal) and motivic pressure on the divertimento themes. By 224, 'negative' scherzo intonations have thoroughly infiltrated the 'positive' light music waltz fragments. Shostakovich's evocation of popular culture has throughout been presented with one eye on this moment: innocence is shortly to be replaced by bitter experience.

Example 5.26

a Shostakovich IV/3: 224$^{1-9}$

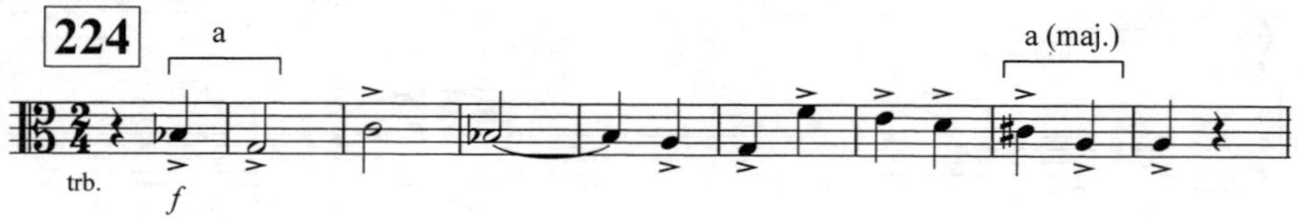

b Shostakovich IV/3: 226$^{1-2}$

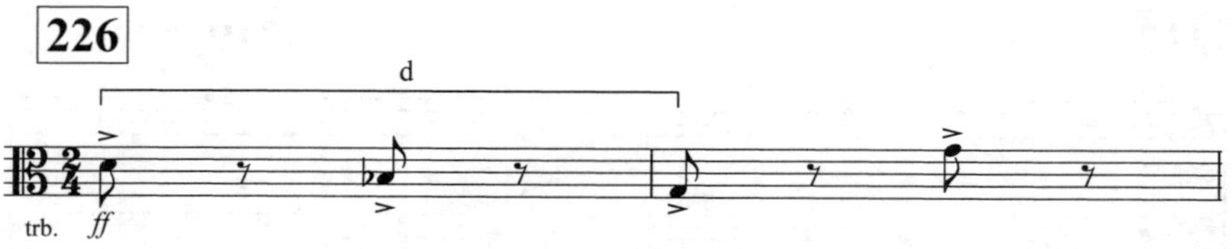

[29] Although both collected works, Shostakovich's 1946 piano reduction and the Sikorski score have ♩ = 100 here, the 1962 and 1976 Sovetskiy and Kompozitor and Kalmus scores have 𝅗𝅥 = 100, which is closer to the tempo observed in most recorded performances.

227 – 230: *Transition Theme*

Following a move from F♯ to F♮ in the bass, this new theme is heard over a bass C, with added seconds and sixths clouding its basic C major orientation. Its tone is completely new: the 'closed' minor mode of the galop is replaced by major-key openness, and its tight oscillations by expansive fourths and major thirds. Although at this point the analogy with Mahler's 'Resurrection' Symphony has not yet been implied, when this theme returns at 235, it is very pointedly made (see Example 5. 29 below), with a strong allusion – almost a quotation – to the delayed C major cadence a few minutes into the 'Resurrection' finale. Shostakovich's transition theme at 227 is not itself a quotation or paraphrase of a Mahler theme, but its later context at 235 – 238 does suggest a relationship with Mahler's finale at this earlier juncture, namely with the rising fourths and fifths of Mahler's prominent horn call figure (Example 5.27a). Towards the end of the 'Resurrection' finale, the *Auferstehʼn* trombone theme first heard at 5, opening with a rising fourth, is echoed over the new tonic D♭ (Examples 5.27a and b); and it is this moment that Shostakovich's transition theme seems to echo (Example 5.27c). Shostakovich's theme does not fragment or dissipate; it comes to rest on its oscillating major second figure, and transmutes into a new theme at 230 (C6),

Example 5.27
a Mahler II/5: ^{1}5 – 5^{4}

Langsam

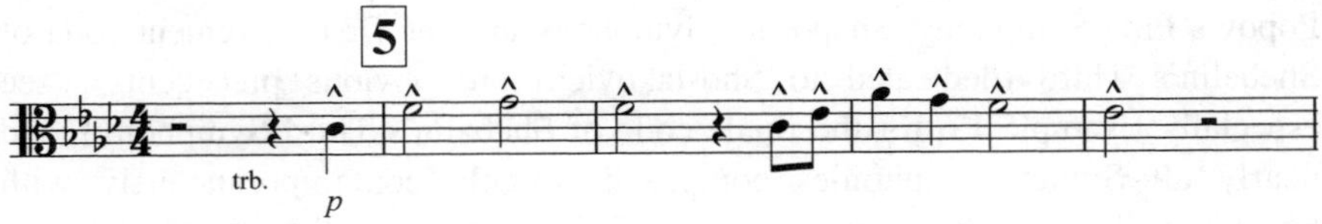

b Mahler II/5: 34$^{7–10}$

Langsam

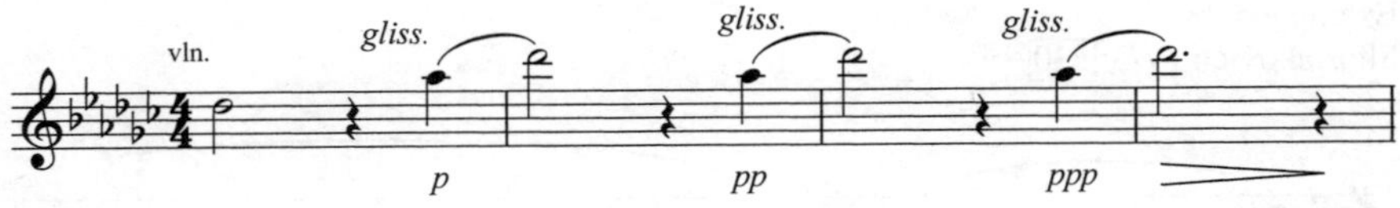

c Shostakovich IV/3: 227$^{1–8}$

♩ = 100

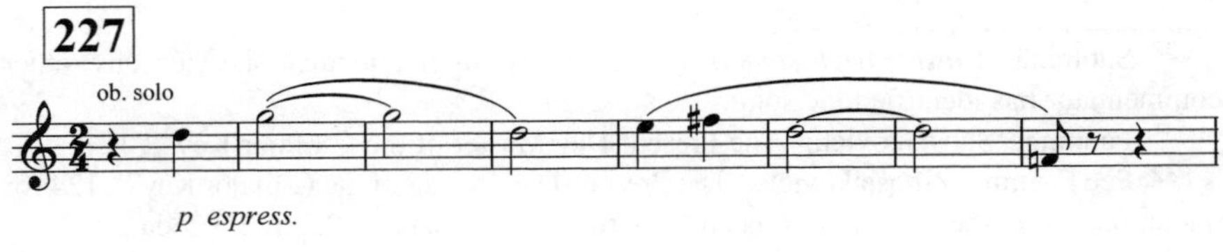

which Sabinina decribed as similar to a popular song of the 1930s.[30] It has its own distinctive identity: melancholy and world-weary (Example 5.28). Now reincarnated as a *petrushechnïy* waltz, the scherzo theme returns out of the blue at 233 (C7). Its repetition is more or less exact until 234^{5}, when it turns aside from the G minor triad (from 168), and moves instead to an 11-bar C♯ pedal, over which the scherzo dissipates in descending quaver figuration. The C♯ pedal is dislodged by the subsequent transition passage (and Mahler semi-quotation) to C major, starting at 235.

235 – 238: *Transition to Coda*

The re-appearance of the transition theme from 227 now appears in a new light, over a long bass passage which brings about the definitive bass move to C at 237. Fanning has noted the allusion to Mahler's 'Resurrection' finale here: the relationship between the two is most obvious in the basses' sudden turn to C major in the Shostakovich.[31] Where Mahler's tone is radiant, with strings, two harps, four horns, woodwind and brass, however, Shostakovich's is less substantial, with violins and violas muted (see Example 5.29).

238 – 246: *Coda I*

With the 'open' tone of C major now established, the scene is set for a glorious C major coda. As Fanning has noted, there was no shortage of models: those of Popov's First Symphony, Shaporin's Symphony and the first movement coda of Shebalin's Third (dedicated to Shostakovich) are obvious precedents[32] (see especially Example 1.6 for the finale coda of Shebalin's Third Symphony), and nearly all Soviet symphonies composed roughly contemporaneously with Shostakovich's Fourth end with a climactic peroration, as discussed in Chapter One.

Example 5.28
Shostakovich IV/3: 230$^{2–8}$

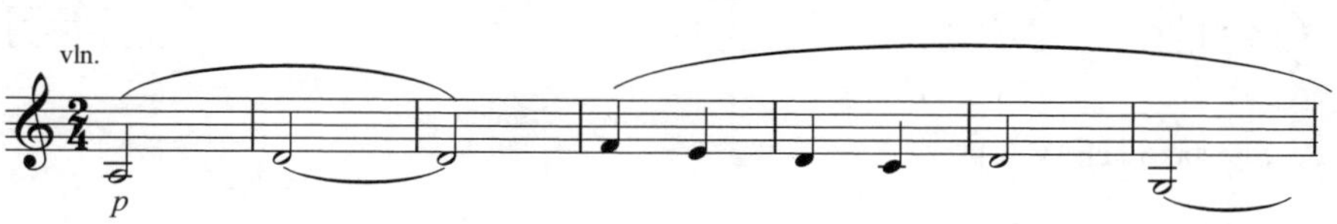

[30] Sabinina, *Shostakovich-simfonist*, 113. Frustratingly, neither she nor any other commentator has identified the song.

[31] Fanning, 'Shostakovich: "The Present-Day Master of the C-Major Key"', 121.

[32] See Fanning, 'Shostakovich: "The Present-Day Master of the C-major Key"', 124 for quotations from Shebalin III/1 coda and a harmonic summary of Popov I/3 coda.

Example 5.29
a Mahler II/5: [2]6–11

Sehr zurückhaltend

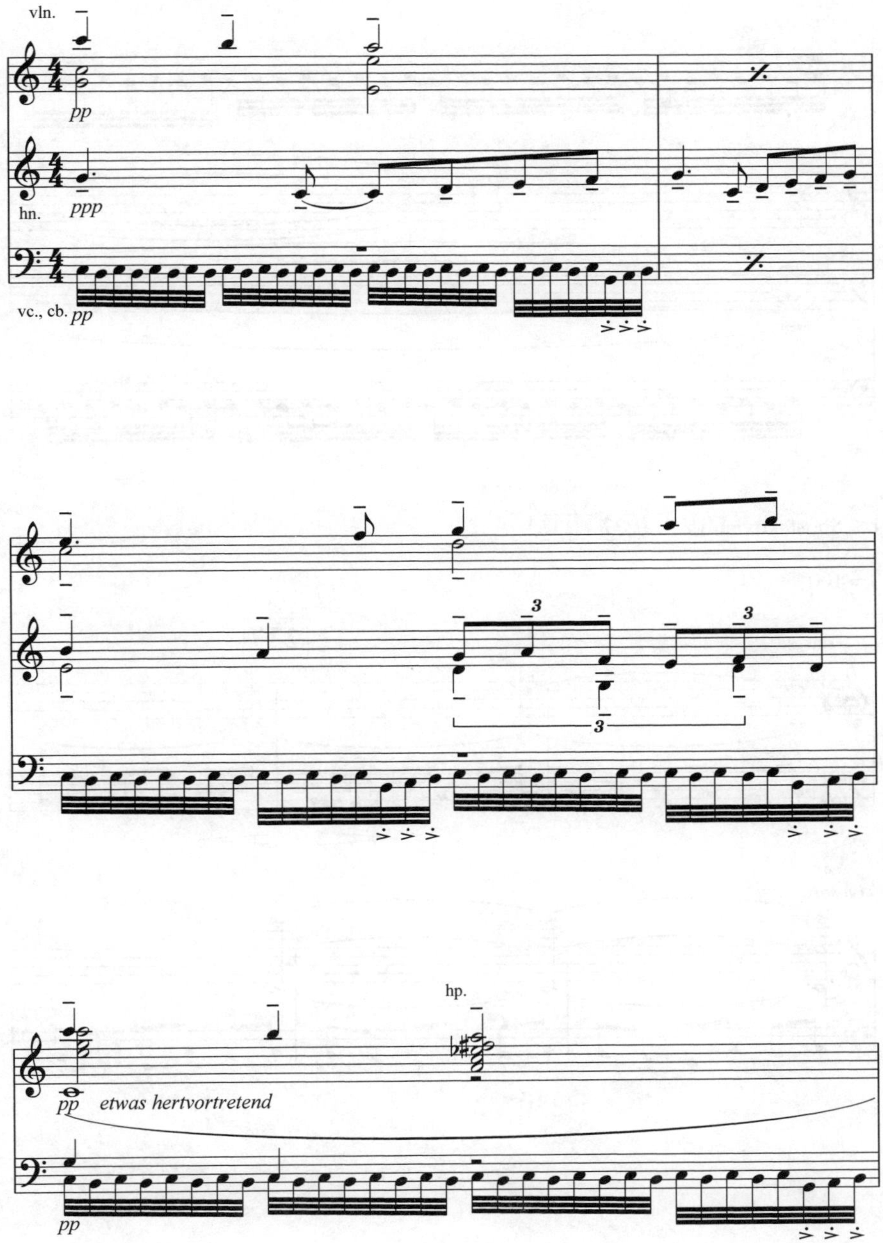

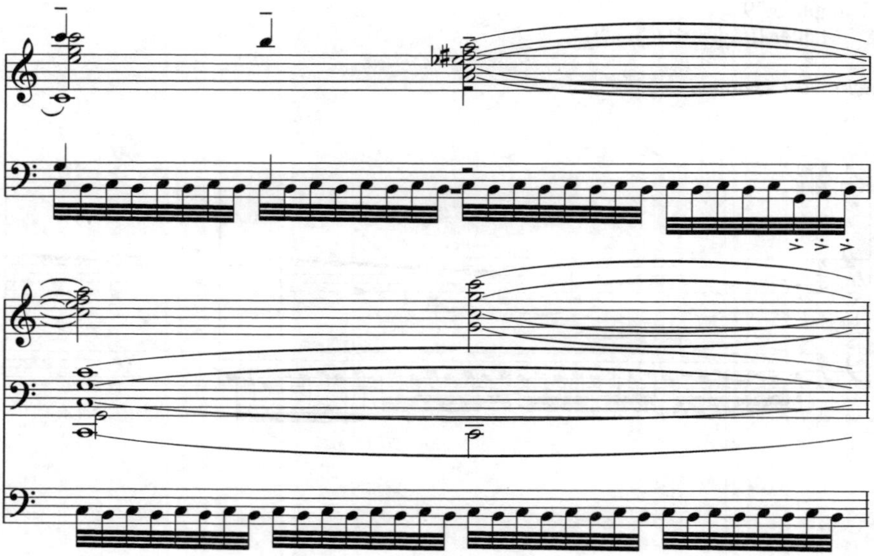

b Shostakovich IV/3: 2[237] – [237]4

♩ = 100

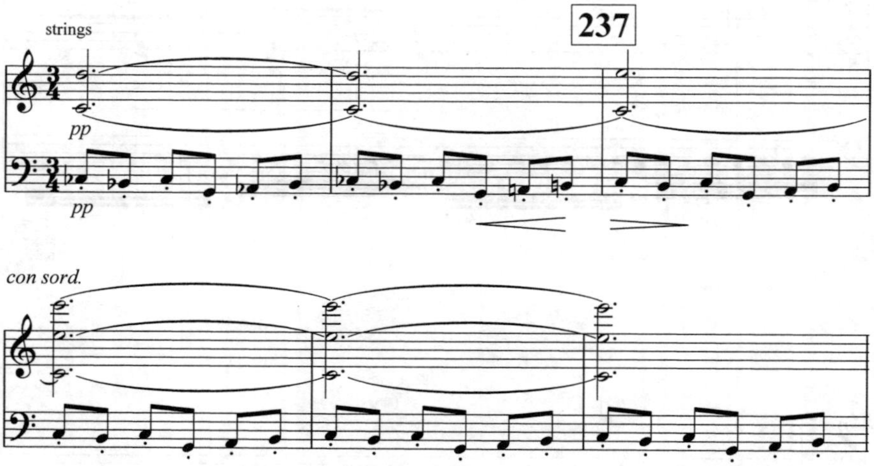

What happens next is extraordinary. The celestial C major starts to crumble, falling to D♭ (C♯) ^{10}238. Following a ten-bar timpani C major dominant–tonic crescendo, the finale launches straight into a raucous coda: a paraphrase of Stravinsky's 'Gloria' chorus from *Oedipus rex* (Example 5.30b). As Fanning has observed, Stravinsky's chorus is resonant with dramatic irony, since the listener knows what the crowds who so acclaim Jocasta do not: that it is her actions which have angered the gods and reduced the people to such dire straits.[33] So there is already one level of ironic disjuction operating in the 'Gloria' paraphrase. The second level arises from context: the music of the coda is new, unprepared except for its C major key and, most importantly, massively overstated. This is no straightforwardly 'summative' coda, but a violent parody of one. The coda theme is repeated, *fortissimo*, four times in all: halfway through the third statement the secondary theme of the funeral march blares out in unison woodwind. Following the next 'Gloria' statement, the funeral march theme takes over the coda in the bass, augmented and inflated to massive proportions, and stated almost in its entirety, below violent, agonized counterpoint.

246: *Coda II*[34]

Almost as suddenly as it arrived, the 'Gloria' coda fades (*fff* to *ppp* in just four bars). Now in C minor and marked *piano*, the funeral march's secondary theme re-enters over a hushed C pedal, ushered in by a low-voiced chorale. At 250 the transition theme re-enters, in F♯ minor on solo violin, and the bass pedal shifts from its steady crotchet pulse to a syncopated rhythm: a very pointed reference to the coda of Chaikovsky's 'Pathétique' Symphony, which, as shown in Example 1.6, was also used by Shebalin in the coda of his Third Symphony (Example 5.31). Following another reference to the transition theme at 254 – now in C minor – the celeste begins its sequence of C minor broken chords. At this point the 'Pathétique' bass all but stops (it continues on the timpani almost to the end of the movement) and a long sustained C minor chord takes over, coloured only by celeste and final echoes of the transition theme. The distinctive sound of the celeste, and in particular the a^1–d^2 fourth of its final notes, inevitably calls to mind Mahler's valedictory final movement of *Das Lied von der Erde*, 'Der Abschied'.[35]

It is not surprising that the dual coda of this symphony has attracted hermeneutic interpretation: indeed, the only surprise is that it has taken so long for

---

33 Ibid.

34 The collected works editions have the metronome indication of 𝅗𝅥. = 50; the Sikorski score has ♩. = 50, which is clearly incorrect.

35 Körner ('Schostakowitschs Vierte Sinfonie', 222), Fanning ('Shostakovich: "The Present-Day Master of the C-major Key"', 126) and Taruskin ('Shostakovich and the Inhuman', 493) all note the similarity in tone between Shostakovich's coda and the ending of *Das Lied*.

Example 5.30

a Shostakovich IV/3: 238 1–5

𝅗𝅥 = 100

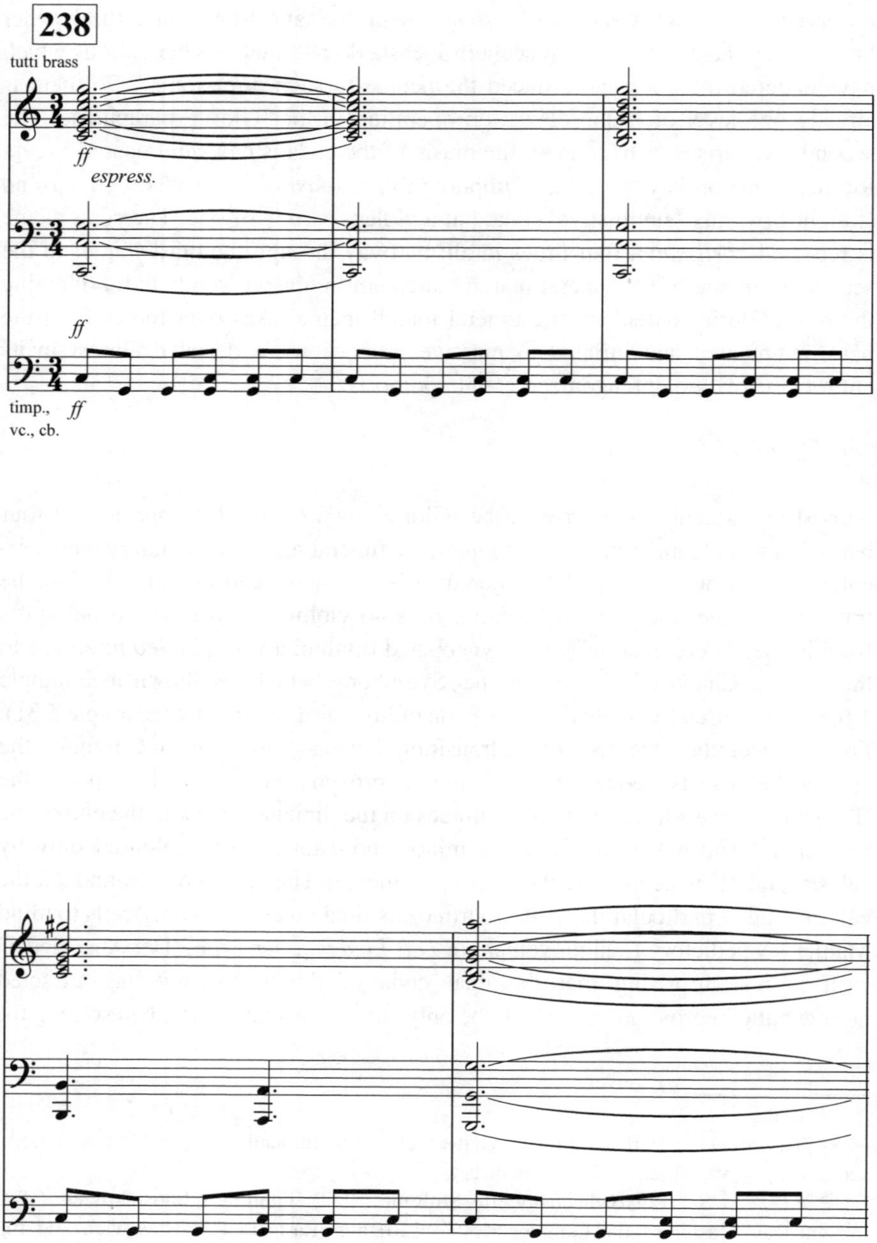

Example 5.30
b Stravinsky: *Oedipus rex*, Act I, 'Gloria' chorus: 93[1–4]

𝅗𝅥 = 69

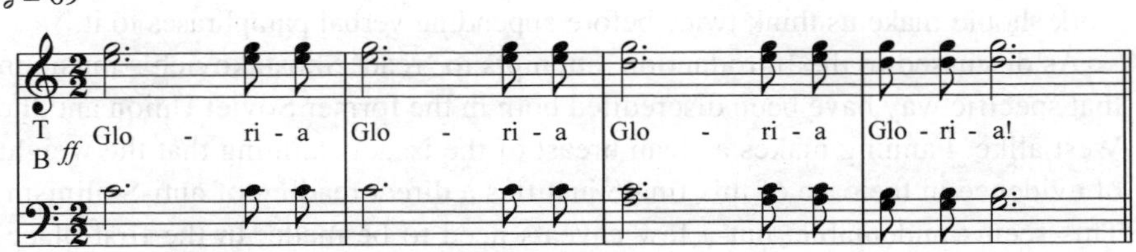

Example 5.31
a Shostakovich IV/3: 250[1–4]

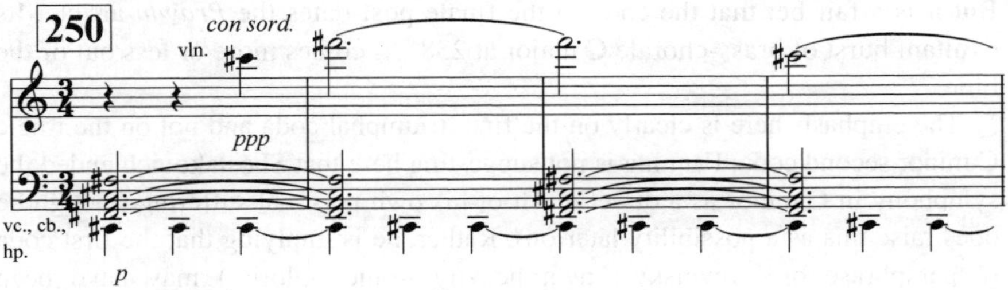

b Chaikovsky VI/4: M[1–4]

Andante giusto 𝅗𝅥 = 76

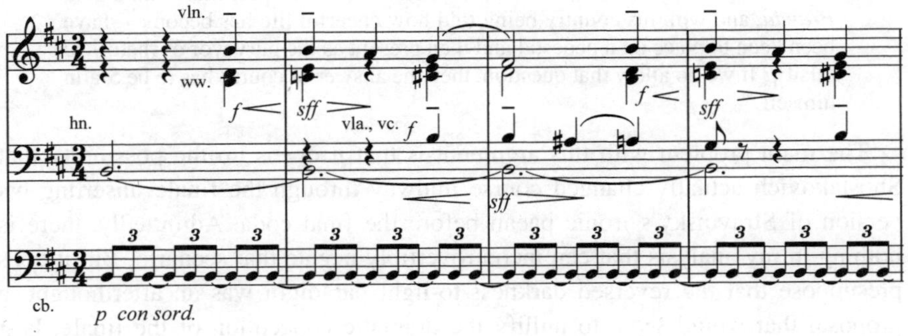

such a suggestive sequence of paraphrases to attract the attention of a commentator who has been able to identify them all.[36] As Taruskin observes, this is real message-in-a-bottle stuff, positively asking to be interpreted.[37] Both

---

36 Fanning, 'Shostakovich: "The Present-Day Master of the C-major Key"', 121–6. Despite Volkov's recent claim that the finale quotes the final movement of Stravinsky's *Firebird*, I have not been able to identify the citation. See Volkov, *Shostakovich and Stalin*, 166.

37 Taruskin, 'Shostakovich and the Inhuman', 493.

Taruskin and Fanning have noted that the coda was almost certainly composed post-denunciation, although Taruskin deliberately resists the temptation to draw the obvious conclusions, his point being that the 'irreducible multivalence' of this work should make us think twice before appending verbal paraphrases to it.[38]

As discussed in the Introduction, attempts to 'read' Shostakovich's music in that specific way have been discredited both in the former Soviet Union and the West alike. Fanning makes a clean breast of the issue, claiming that the weight of evidence in the case of this finale justifies a direct reading of anti-Stalinism. This seems undeniable, but a few caveats need to be made. In the first place, Fanning, like Taruskin, makes the observation that the coda was composed in the aftermath of Shostakovich's denunciation: 'Where exactly [Shostakovich] was in the composition of the Symphony when the storm broke is not known. But it is a fair bet that the coda to the finale post-dates the *Pravda* article. Its exultant burst of brass-chorale C major at 238 … comes more or less out of the blue.'[39]

The emphasis here is clearly on the first, triumphal coda and not on the tragic C minor second coda; Fanning is not suggesting here that Shostakovich ended the symphony in C minor as a direct result of his own personal suffering (though he does raise this as a possibility later on). Rather, he is implying that the first coda (a paraphrase of Stravinsky's own heavily ironic 'Gloria') may have been prompted by Shostakovich's desire, post-denunciation, to express satirical contempt for the Stalin regime:

> Who would be the likeliest object of public acclamation in Russia in 1936?; whom might Shostakovich – in the aftermath of his personal mauling in *Pravda*, and with his country being told how cheerful life has become – have been keen to place on a pedestal and then present as the purveyor of rhetorical falsity? If we do allow that question, then the answer of course has to be Stalin himself.[40]

The main problem with this argument is that it opens up the possibility that Shostakovich actually changed course midway through the finale, inserting his version of Stravinsky's ironic paean before the final coda. Admittedly, there is nothing in my analysis that can incontrovertibly negate that scenario. But it does presuppose that the reversed darkness-to-light paradigm was an afterthought, a proposal that would seem to nullify the dramatic conception of the finale. Is it

---

38 Ibid. This view is echoed in Hakobian's recent study, where he concludes that the Fourth Symphony's 'symbolism of mysterious, meaningful associations' constitute, in Tynianov's phrase, a 'domashnyaya semantik' [domestic semantic]: in other words, a hermeneutic layer than is perceptible only to the composer and his closest friends. Hakobian desribes the symphony as 'unknowable'. See Hakobian, *Dmitriy Shostakovich*, 155.

39 Fanning, 'Shostakovich: "The Present-Day Master of the C-major Key"', 120–21.

40 Ibid., 127.

really plausible that Shostakovich might have planned a finale that moved from funeral march to violent scherzo, to divertimento, to end merely with a repeat of the funeral march? Without the first 'apotheosis' coda, the second coda would lose all its impact; without an apotheosis, its pointed rejection becomes meaningless. And considering the fairly systematic nature of the references to Mahler in the Moderato through to the finale, a planned structure that deliberately referenced the 'Resurrection' Symphony but then subverted those references is surely more plausible. Crowning those allusions with a musical depiction of public acclamation which is well known to be ironic, and which then turns in on itself, repeating the funeral march and quoting from Chaikovsky's 'Pathétique' Symphony would seem an extremely apt ending. Indeed, given the state of political events in Russia at the time, it would seem all too appropriate, regardless of Shostakovich's own political position.

At this point, mention must be made of the sole dated fragment from the finale piano draft, shown in Example 5.32. Yakubov presents it at the end of his transcription of Manuscript F (the finale), page 4, system 15a. The seven-bar fragment appears upside-down and is cancelled with a wavy line drawn through it, on the page of draft that extends from bar 651 to bar 936 of the finale as we know it. To the far right of the cancelled bars is a date, which Yakubov reports as 16 II 1936 (though the year 1936 is all but illegible on the reduced size of the facsimile). Yakubov suggests that this is the earliest of all the finale drafts, and the date in itself would seem to confirm this. However, we do not have all the facts available here to make a conclusive guess at the intended position of the fragment in the finale: there are pages missing from the drafts and so we cannot tell if this page began as the continuation of another. To add to the confusion, the fragment itself does not seem to belong anywhere in the published score. Though it is almost certainly a mid-movement fragment rather than an opening, its thematic contours (rising fourth and falling minor third figure in the treble) seem to be a conflation

Example 5.32
Yakubov: transcription of Manuscript F, page 4, system 15a

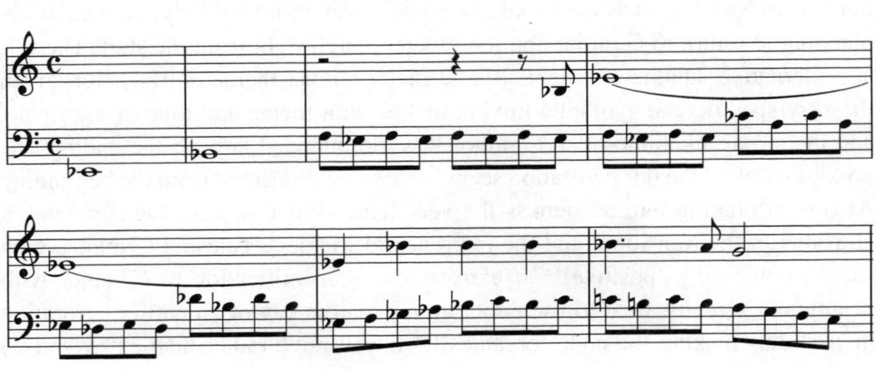

of the rising fourth and descending minor third motifs that figure in several key places in the finale: the 'Resurrection' rising fourths between 227 and 230, the song-theme's rising fourths between 230 and 233 and the rising fourth and descending dotted minor third of the triumphant D major theme between 184 and 186. The E♭ (minor) key of the fragment would seem to preclude it from a place between the C-centred 227 and 230, and its oscillating bass firmly rules it out of inclusion between 184 and 186. That leaves us with the possibility that it belongs in the song section between 230 and 233, where its oscillating accompaniment and rising fourths are entirely in place. But its 4/4 time does not fit there, nor does its emphasis on E♭ or its combination of oscillating and scalic bass movement. In short, the fragment does not fit in convincingly anywhere in the finale; it is not even possible to guess whether its tempo is slow or fast, though the descending dotted minor third figure in the treble does, if anything, indicate a fast tempo.

The facsimile of the finale draft contains a number of such fragments. Part 1 of Manuscript F has four, of five, five, two and three bars' length; page 2 contains two, of five and ten bars' length, and page 3 has two crossed-out bars, though all of these clearly belong to the music on either side, and were not false starts, as the ones on page 1 seem to be. It seems safe only to say that this fragment and its tantalizing date indicate only that Shostakovich was working on the finale at the time of the *Pravda* denunciations (which we knew already); that its mid-movement appearance would suggest that work on the finale was already well underway; but that the fact that it was comprehensively scrapped may well indicate that Shostakovich began work on the finale *again* after *Pravda*'s second attack on him on 6 February. The fragment could just as easily be cited as proof that Shostakovich was near the end of the finale on 16 February 1936 as that he had not started it in its published form at all; without further manuscript evidence, it cannot be used conclusively to support either view.

Nevertheless, the idea that Shostakovich had not planned the ending at the time he started work on the finale in its published form does not seem plausible. In any case, the symbolic use of C minor (funeral march) and the C♯ mode of the scherzo, both of which interact in various ways with the major keys of climax, urban popular music and the 'Gloria' coda, makes the hypothesis that the dual coda was not part of Shostakovich's original conception even more unlikely; he was surely planning to return to C minor and the funeral march right from the start. There is an 'alternative' apotheosis theme: the D major climax theme of 184. But, given the very specific and symbolic linking of key with theme and tone in the finale, and the strong likelihood that C minor was the intended key for the ending, the possibility of a D major peroration seems deliberately rejected from the beginning. Also worth taking into account is the very real, 'direct' tone of the *Aufersteh'n* allusions in the transition, and the reference to Mahler's celestial C major: with such a powerfully 'positive' – if extroversive – identification of C major with beauty and serenity, then to use either an alternative key or an earlier peroration theme (thus making the coda 'organically' introversive rather than extroversive) seems a singularly crass proposition. Shostakovich's references to Mahler are too painfully real for 'introversive' integration, and too fragile to be followed by a peroration such as that at [184]: like the wistful dance intonations of the first movement, the allusions to the 'Resurrection' Symphony hang in the air, out of reach: they hold out the possibility of a radiant C major coda which is then bitterly negated, with a return to the opening funeral march and further 'extroversive' allusions, this time to Chaikovsky's 'Pathétique'.

If the hypothesis that the 'Gloria' coda was composed in response to Shostakovich's post-*Pravda* trauma is discounted (and, as discussed above, the dated fragment does not demonstrate convincingly that Shostakovich had begun the finale in its published form at the time of the attacks), then Fanning is still surely right to perceive an anti-authoritarian intention behind the symphony's ending. But he does maintain a level of distance from his interpretation of the coda; quoting Inna Barsova's comments on 'planes of meaning' in the Fifth Symphony, he concludes that the Fourth operates along similar lines. The darkness-to-light paradigm subverted in the second coda suggests one level: Shostakovich's ironic response to official pronouncements urging composers to 'leave to future generations memorials of our glorious, never-to-be-forgotten epoch'.[41] On another level, there is Shostakovich's personal situation to consider: referring to the ominous phrase from 'Sumbur vmesto muzïki' which warns that 'Shostakovich's game of ingenious trickery ... may end badly', Fanning writes:

> Here too we might think that Shostakovich, working on his coda within weeks of that article, was determined to show musically just how badly things might indeed end – maybe for him, maybe for the Russian People, maybe even one day for his political tormentors, and maybe for none of these, but just as an existential principle.[42]

Ultimately, as Fanning is careful to point out, our choice of reading is a personal matter and, just as crucially, one of reception and not intention. But any suggestion that the finale structure was altered by the *Pravda* events is clearly problematic. Still, what is left after this possibility has been discounted adds up to quite a lot. The 'Resurrection' paraphrase which supports the transition theme (a major theme in the closing pages of the symphony) has a tragic impact because it refers to past hopes and ideals, now twisted and defiled. The *Oedipus* paraphrase is fitting because Shostakovich needs an apotheosis in order to subvert it and the ironic associations of Stravinsky's chorus provide Shostakovich with a ready-made ambivalence. The return of the funeral march theme overrides the 'Gloria' chorus – the 'direct' voice beginning to assert itself over the grotesque mask – and returns the finale to a 'real' ending which juxtaposes intonations of hope and faith in eternal life (the now-faint 'Resurrection' – related transition theme, together with references to one of Mahler's most beautiful symphonic codas: the 'ewig'

41 Ibid., 130.
42 Ibid.

close of *Das Lied*) with those of tragedy: Chaikovsky's 'Pathétique'. Like irony, tragedy depends on context for its impact. Without those references to eternal life and beauty, the tragic coda which contains them would be considerably less so. To conclude, then: the coda of this finale seems to refer so painfully to the destruction of humanity and of human values in Stalin's Russia that a more 'personal' interpretation seems almost inappropriate. It is, above all, this crushing of hope that the coda most powerfully evokes.

CHAPTER SIX

Conclusion

Introduction

The Fourth Symphony was, in Shostakovich's own words, the 'credo of [his] creative work'. It was conceived at a time when the future of Soviet symphonism was being vigorously debated and was perceived as being in a state of crisis. The chief reason for this was a general feeling in Soviet musicology during the later 1920s and 1930s that the symphony, as an abstract art form, was not only the genre that could best demonstrate Soviet musical sophistication at a time when Western symphonism was allegedly in decline, but also the one which proved most resistant to the expectation that all art should imply social 'content'. Beethoven's symphonies were repeatedly cited as models for the kind of 'organic', sophisticated yet accessible and 'revolutionary' symphonies many critics and composers had in mind. But, despite all the exhortations directed at composers during the RAPM years and beyond, a new 'Beethovenian' symphonist had failed to materialize. Rather, RAPM's stranglehold on cultural life had negatively affected composers' creativity, as apparent in symphonies written even after 1932. Older figures such as Myaskovsky (b. 1881) and Shcherbachëv (b. 1889) found it hard to shake off the effects of years of RAPM censure, and only one among Myaskovsky's symphonies written during the 1930s (the Thirteenth Symphony, 1933) ventures beyond the conservative style that he had established in the late 1920s. Those less talented, such as Shebalin and Kabalevsky, arguably suffered less from RAPM interference and were able to compose more or less consistently in their academic, rather conventional fashion throughout their careers. It was the youngest and most talented composers, above all Shostakovich and Popov, who emerged from the RAPM years with strong individual voices.

As discussed in Chapter One, at the 1935 'Discussion about Soviet Symphonism' some of the works we might today regard as models of socialist realist symphonism – Knipper's Fourth ('Poem about the Komsomol Fighter') and Myaskovsky's Twelfth ('Collective Farm') – were openly criticized. Throughout the 1920s Shostakovich had contrived to keep a foot in both the progressive and proletarian camps, more or less successfully placating the latter largely through his collaborations in film and theatre. And, as discussed, it was his experience in these media that he proposed to bring to his 'serious' creative work. At the same time, his Fourth Symphony was to bear the fruit of his fascination with Mahler: his mastery of the Soviet 'light genres' would take on the role played by military marches and dances in Mahler's symphonies. In the absence of any firm guidelines pertaining to the tone and structure of future Soviet symphonies, Shostakovich could well have hoped that the aesthetic foundations for acceptance of this radical approach to symphonic language had been laid through Sollertinsky's advocacy of Mahler's music. As discussed in Chapter One, the notion that composers should now start writing in a 'socialist realist' style was not forcefully broached at the time when Shostakovich was writing his Fourth Symphony. Further, remarks (unchallenged) such as those by Kuznetsov on possible 'depressed' symphonic endings do suggest that optimism was not regarded as a compulsory ingredient for the future that Soviet symphonism composers were so passionately discussing.

With regard to the political situation at the time of the Fourth's composition, it seems plausible that Bukharin's and Radek's strong advocacy for a genuine as opposed to 'socialist' realism in art – though ultimately doomed – could have been widely influential. Although their critical attitude to tendentious art was contradicted by Zhdanov's own speech, their Congress speeches in 1934 were sufficiently well received by writers to have given cause for some encouragement. Sollertinsky's own continued advocacy of Mahler as a 'democratic' fellow traveller can be placed in the same context of that liberal interpretation of Marxist-Leninist aesthetics: RAPM-style symphonies, like the tendentious proletarian literature criticized by Bukharin, were viewed by liberal figures such as Sollertinsky as un-Marxist and artistically redundant. In addition, the appearance of reform in the shape of the 1936 Stalin Constitution that Bukharin and Radek themselves had drafted may have kept alive a flicker of hope in the darkening years of the mid-1930s. Some of this blend of caution and hope can be seen in the 1935 symphonism conference: with general opinion divided and the spectre of socialist realism still seemingly at arm's length, Sollertinsky's circumspection contrasts oddly with Shostakovich's bold remarks about light music. Asafiev's work had already laid the foundations for Rïzhkin's thesis of inherently 'dialectical' symphonism, and it was this concept, combined with Sollertinsky's claims for Mahler's symphonies as 'democratic', that laid the potential foundations for a new aesthetics of Soviet symphonism, and thus for the acceptance of Shostakovich's new symphony.

One view expressed repeatedly at the 1935 discussions was that composers needed to find a way of creating 'content' in the symphony without resorting to textual means, which were widely regarded as primitive. Following on from the belief (primarily voiced by Asafiev, Sollertinsky and Rïzhkin) that a symphony must be 'organic', the importance of thematic and motivic coherence was strongly implied. The song-symphony was judged by many prominent composers and critics to be a facile attempt at inserting ideological content into a symphony with no such attempt at organic unity; moreover, Knipper's own musical language was regarded (especially by Shostakovich and Shebalin) as crudely simplistic. Programmatic (but untexted) works did not necessarily fare any better: Myaskovsky's Twelfth was declared to be less satisfactory purely as a piece of music than his Sixth, regardless of its alleged content. Though there was no consensus reached, composers voiced general agreement over the need to forge a new kind of symphonism – perhaps using popular materials, so long as they were not too trivial – which would be comprehensible to a broad spectrum of listeners and yet able to bear comparison with the greatest works of nineteenth-century symphonic literature. As discussed, there was opposition to Shostakovich's suggestion that gypsy songs and 'street' [*ulichnaya*] music should be used in the creation of this new language; Rïzhkin's concern was that Shostakovich may have been advocating turning the symphony into the kind of mixture of polka, march and galop that he felt had been taken to extremes in *The Bolt*. But Sollertinsky's work on Mahler had already laid ideological and aesthetic grounds for the notion of 'democratic' symphonism, which by definition used the kind of materials Shostakovich was advocating. Given the overtly Mahlerian character of the Fourth Symphony, it seems plausible that Shostakovich and Sollertinsky shared a vision for the future of Soviet symphonism, with each depending on the other for exemplification in theory and practice.[1]

Though Sollertinsky's 1932 monograph had been well received, and Mahler's symphonies were regularly performed in Leningrad during the 1930s,[2] Mahler had not attained the kind of Beethovenian status that would have made him a safe role-model for Soviet composers. As seen in Chapter One, in the conclusion to his Mahler book Sollertinsky felt that he had to emphasize that Mahler – a petit-bourgeois 'fellow traveller' – could *not* be such a role-model, even as he was clearly putting him forward as one. The reasons for this, as discussed, may have been Mahler's reputation as an individualistic, even neurotic, figure; the quasi-religious content of the Second, Third, Fourth and Eighth Symphonies may also have been an obstacle to his complete acceptance in Soviet Russia.[3] In addition, there was the sheer length and complexity of Mahler's symphonies. It is hardly surprising that he never became a favourite of RAPM (as Beethoven was) when familiarity with symphonies was achieved through piano four-hand performances; many of Mahler's would have taken well over an hour – as well as considerable skill – to play. Only the formation in the 1920s of the Bruckner–Mahler society in Leningrad gave devotees of Mahler's symphonies a prime opportunity for deeper aquaintance.[4]

1 Shebalin confirmed that 'Shostakovich as a symphonist owed much that was positive to [Sollertinskiy].' See Mikheyeva, *I.I. Sollertinskiy*, 112–13.

2 Between 1931 and 1936, Mahler's Second Symphony was performed three times and the Fourth four times, with occasional performances of *Das Lied von der Erde* (1931–32, 1935–36), the Fifth (1932–33, 1933–34), the Seventh (1931–32) and the Ninth (1931–32, 1932–33). See Mikheyeva, *Pamyati*, 245.

3 When Bruno Walter visited Moscow and Leningrad in 1926, he noted that the directors of the Bolshoi had refused to perform Mahler's Fourth Symphony on the grounds that 'in new Russia one ought not to sing of heaven and angels'. Quoted in Schwarz, *Music and Musical Life*, 45.

4 Sollertinskiy was a regular attender of these meetings. The conductor Nikolay Mal'ko reported that he demonstrated incredible familiarity with Mahler's symphonies (especially

Even in 1935, when *Lieder eines fahrenden Gesellen*, *Kindertotenlieder* and the Second Symphony were performed in Leningrad, Sollertinsky voiced support for Mahler only briefly and rather cautiously.[5] This gives the distinct impression that his efforts to have Mahler granted 'acceptable' status had not been wholly successful. But equally, the fact that Mahler's music was still performed and discussed in 1935–36 indicates that they had not failed either. Sollertinsky himself would have played a central role in organizing these concerts; he had been artistic advisor to the Leningrad Philharmonic since 1929, gave frequent pre-concert lectures and wrote the Philharmonic's programme notes.[6] Despite the hostility directed at him in the press after the 'Muddle instead of Music' affair, Sollertinsky kept his Philharmonic post, and even began lecturing in the history of Western music, aesthetics and drama at the Leningrad Conservatoire in mid-1936.[7] His position in Leningrad's musical life remained strong and influential throughout the 1930s, with the three-month hiatus in his critical activities immediately after the 'Muddle instead of Music' debates being the only real dent in his career.

Attempting to draw a picture of Leningrad's musical life at the time of the Fourth's aborted première is fraught with difficulties. While I have argued here and in Chapter One that Shostakovich could justly have expected his symphony to be performed, the fact remains that by December 1936 the political situation looked ugly, with the first of the three great show-trials having already taken place in August that year, and the second scheduled for January–February 1937. It may be the case that, while purges seemed mostly confined to the Party, the art world did not feel unduly threatened. But changes in the political climate could occur so rapidly that it is not possible to guess how Shostakovich – at least as a composer – might have responded to the *Pravda* attacks of January–February 1936, except to note that he continued to work on the Fourth Symphony, and that he was hopeful its première would go ahead as planned.

The Fourth Symphony made no obvious concessions to the charge of 'formalism' directed at *Lady Macbeth*, as voiced in the 'Muddle instead of Music' article. Its musical language is even closely related to that of *Lady Macbeth*, as several commentators have noted,[8] even alluding to it in places. Still, Shostakovich

---

for a non-musician), and would conduct as they were played on the piano, giving information about details of orchestration and dynamics as he did so. See Nikolai Malko, *A Certain Art*, New York: William Morrow, 1966, 145, and Mikheyeva, *I.I. Sollertinskiy*, 38.

5 The circumspect nature of Sollertinskiy's speech at the 1935 discussions was so uncharacteristic that it drew comment from the composer Viktor Beliy (*Sovetskaya muzïka*, 1935/5, 35).

6 Programme notes for Philharmonic concerts were sometimes published as booklets of between 30 and 60 pages. See Mikheyeva, *Pamyati*, 272–85 for a list of Sollertinskiy's publications, including published Philharmonic programme notes.

7 Mikheyeva, *I.I. Sollertinskiy*, 110–11.

8 Sabinina, *Shostakovich-simfonist*, 106; Darby, 'Problems of Context', 292, and Tammaro, *Le Sinfonie di Šostakovič*, 72.

may well have put most of the criticisms in the *Pravda* articles down to the plot of *Lady Macbeth*, and in particular to the sexual content singled out by the anonymous author of the article. His ballet *The Limpid Stream*, the subject of February's *Pravda* attack, had previously been regarded even by Sollertinsky as a creative failure. Fay suggests that Shostakovich accepted the commission purely on financial grounds, and indeed there was much adverse criticism of the banality of the plot at the time of its première. Sollertinsky's negative review, for example, complained that Shostakovich's music for *The Limpid Stream* was 'inferior to the remarkably masterful score of *The Golden Age*'.[9] It seems likely that Shostakovich, having put his best creative efforts into a completely abstract symphony, would have expected it to be well received. As the 1935 discussions show, the Fourth Symphony fulfilled many of the qualities judged desirable in a Soviet symphony. Its musical language was clear and expressive; it was not formulaic, drily modernistic or academic; it did not use popular idioms trivially, but in a highly suggestive and expressive way; it was tightly constructed, with the qualities of 'dialectical' process (in terms of the extensive interaction of themes in the first movement, and that between tonal, thematic and intonational relationships in the first and third movements) that Asafiev and others regarded as the essence of true symphonism; and it suggested 'content' without relying on a programme or subtitle. Whatever the potential problems arising from the nature of that 'content' (one wonders what a critic who recognized the allusions to Musorgsky, Mahler, Stravinsky and Chaikovsky would have made of it), it magnificently fulfilled Aleksey Ogolevtsev's demand at the 1935 discussions for composers to 'leave to future generations memorials of our glorious, never-to-be-forgotten epoch',[10] even if not in the way Ogolevtsev might have had in mind.

Shostakovich's 'New Way'?

The Fourth Symphony was unique in many ways. As discussed, it was radically different from its contemporaries, chiefly in its approach to thematic transformation and relationships, the nature of its materials (as compared with the lyrical, cheerful or folky themes used by Myaskovsky, Kabalevsky and Shebalin) and the first movement's strikingly dramatized treatment of classic sonata form dramaturgy. Though other Soviet composers did use established forms, they tended to avoid using them in such an overtly 'textbook' way. It was rare for them to write allegro themes as four-square as the first subject of Shostakovich IV/1; usually they aimed for something more subtle. Several 1930s Soviet symphonies (including Myaskovsky XI, XII, XV) began with long, searching introductions,

9 Fay, *Shostakovich*, 82.

10 *Sovetskaya muzïka*, 1935/6, 39. See also Fanning, 'Shostakovich: "The Present-Day Master of the C-major Key"', 130.

often with a soloistic character; Kabalevsky II and Khrennikov I give their first themes to a solo wind instrument, and invariably opening themes would evolve into something fuller as they went along. Shostakovich's first subject, on the other hand, is given a strong, complete statement straight away, with nothing left to do but to repeat, fragment and disappear. Many contemporary Soviet sonata expositions, as discussed in Chapter One, introduced their themes less aggressively because the first statement often led to a gradual development and growth (see especially Myaskovsky XI/1, XII/1, XV/1, Kabalevsky II/1, Khachaturian I/1, Popov I/1). Shostakovich's first subject is deliberately overstated so that its over-exertion and collapse leave a question-mark in the mind of the listener only a few minutes into the first movement; after that, there will be no clear-cut theme until the climax at 47 and in the subsequent development. Hence, though Shostakovich's announcement of his 'first subject' is exaggerated, its purpose is to undermine, not reinforce, the textbook sonata structure it seems at first to evoke.

Shostakovich's way of engaging with formal conventions (*fabula* in Formalist terminology) in the Fourth Symphony was, then, to assert them aggressively in order to counter them with equally aggressive narrative strategies (the *syuzhet*). One such strategy was his use of thematic transformation that, as discussed, was especially dramatic – if ultimately highly ambivalent – in the Fourth Symphony's first movement. Another was his use of allusion: the first movement's allusion to the supplication theme from *Boris Godunov* took the form of gradual evolution through both first and second subject groups. Despite the impact of its climactic appearance at 47, its latent expressive force is fully realized only in the recapitulation, where all the exposition signposts leading up to that statement are linked in a continuous solo line leading to the final, complete appearance of the theme. Formalist terminology relating to motifs – for example, Tomashevsky's 'bound' and 'free' motifs, where bound motifs relate to the story and free to the plot – can be applied to the roles of both the supplication theme and the waltz intonations: they act as 'free' motifs, appearing at key moments in the deeper 'plot' of the movement, whereas the main themes constitute its 'story' and are therefore 'bound' motifs. The fact that the supplication theme, with its *Boris*-linked inter-textual significance, occupies the central role in both exposition and recapitulation gives it immense expressive force. Further, the long-range planting of the motivic seeds leading up to the 'supplication' theme's final statement in the recapitulation suggests that it was intended to play a crucial role from the start: a theme which interacts with, but does not clearly belong to, either of the two main subject groups. Such motivic 'planting' of a theme is a strong example of Shostakovich's conscious exploitation of a formal structure to deliver an overarching narrative strategy.

The hermeneutic role of allusion and paraphrase in the second and third movements relies, like the 'supplication' theme, on 'inter-textual' meaning derived from the programmatic (or verbal) content of the original sources. The Moderato, as discussed, is an echo of Mahler's 'Resurrection' scherzo, intentionally flattening Mahler's sharp characterization to produce a mask-like shadow of its model. Thus frozen in a state of limbo, the Moderato is a numb sequel to the ambivalent recapitulation and coda of the first movement, continuing its twilight, static mood. The significance of Shostakovich's re-casting of the Mahlerian scherzo is dependent on further allusions to the 'Resurrection' symphony in the finale; the Moderato anticipates Shostakovich's rejection of C major redemption in a profoundly 'negative' allusion to Stravinsky's ironic 'Gloria' chorus before repeating the funeral march in C minor. The subsequent allusion to Chaikovsky's 'Pathétique' has obvious tragic import; likewise, the closing allusions to *Das Lied von der Erde* – replacing its ethereal C major with a numb C minor – seem to signify a tragic loss of hope and purity.

Shostakovich would not present such a suggestive sequence of allusions or quotations again until the Eighth Quartet (1960) and the Fifteenth Symphony (1971). In the first of these, Shostakovich himself declared the work to be autobiographical, and claimed to have quoted a number of works. Some have obvious meaning, such as the revolutionary song 'Tormented by Grievous Bondage', Katerina's doomed appeal to Sergey from the last act of *Lady Macbeth*, and Shostakovich's own DSCH motif (D-E♭-C-B, or D-Es-C-H in German). Others have less clear significance, such as the allusions to Beethoven's Quartets No. 14 Op. 131 and No. 16 Op. 135 (the 'Muss es sein?' introductory motif).[11] The quotation from *William Tell* in the Fifteenth Symphony's first movement is notoriously ambiguous; Shostakovich's own (intentionally misleading?) explanation that the first movement depicted events in a toyshop does nothing to shed light on its possible significance.[12] Apart from Sabinina's connection of the supplication theme with *Boris Godunov*, no mention has been made of the allusions in the Fourth Symphony until the late 1990s,[13] though it is hard to imagine his contemporaries did not notice them. Shebalin, for one, had alluded to the ending of the 'Pathétique' in his own Third Symphony, and would surely not have missed Shostakovich's employment of exactly the same closing device. Sollertinsky, too, must have been aware of, if not actually party to, Shostakovich's Mahlerian allegorizing. And orchestral musicians (if only cellos and basses) would surely have recognised the 'Pathétique' in the symphony's closing pages. Though these issues are food for speculation only, the thought that no-one recognized the

11 For a detailed discussion of the quotations in the Eighth Quartet, see David Fanning, *Shostakovich: String Quartet No. 8*, Aldershot: Ashgate, 2004, 51–6.

12 Fay, *Shostakovich*, 272. My personal view is that Shostakovich was simply making fun of his own penchant for anapest rhythms and their inevitable association with the galloping theme from *William Tell*.

13 Taruskin mentions the *Oedipus* and *Das Lied references* ('Shostakovich and the Inhuman', 493); Fanning also brings in the 'Pathétique' (Fanning, 'Shostakovich: "The Present-Day Master of the C-major Key"', 126).

Mahler–Stravinsky–Chaikovsky sequence until 2001 does not seem plausible.[14] But they add fuel to speculation over why Shostakovich might have been worried about his symphony's possible reception, even if we discount – as we surely must – Volkov's contrived notion that he feared Asafiev might have publicly 'interpreted' references and so drawn attention to the symphony's supposed 'hidden' meaning.

Though it is hardly surprising that Shostakovich chose not to enlighten his prospective audience about the presence of such loaded musical allusions, he did continue to use allusion sporadically throughout his career. His Fifth Symphony's reference to the first of his Four Romances on poems by Pushkin Op. 46, 'Vozrozhdenie' [Rebirth], has been noted many times.[15] Later, in the Tenth Symphony and Eighth Quartet, Shostakovich asserted his musical 'other' in more directly personal terms, through the use of his DSCH monogram and, in the case of the symphony, that of a recent female muse-figure, Elmira Nazirova.[16] But whether loaded with meaning or apparently meaningless, Shostakovich's use of quotation and paraphrase remained an important part of his compositional technique, and the Fourth Symphony was the first major work to use them to such dramatic, and suggestive, effect.

Adornian terms such as 'breakthrough', 'suspension' and 'fulfilment' can, as discussed, be applied to Shostakovich's music as a way of describing the interaction of *fabula* and *syuzhet*, or, as Adorno put it, the work's 'material form'. All of these concepts operate more distinctly in the Fifth Symphony, which, given its higher degree of formal regularity, is hardly surprising. Suspension, in particular, becomes a category that interacts with allusion, as in the reference to 'Vozrozhdenie' just before the return of the opening theme at the end (see Example 6.1b below). The music at this point feels as though it is resting for a moment, reflecting and allowing itself to be 'real' before grimly doing its duty. In the Tenth Symphony, the third movement's 'ELMIRA' horn call has a similarly disconnected feel, sounding 'like a soul in search of a body', as one commentator has described it.[17] And in the middle-period 'war' symphonies (and nearly all the string quartets), Shostakovich's solo writing attained new levels of immediacy though recitative-style phrasing and rhythms. Whether the out-of-body feel of Shostakovich's 'suspended' passages comes from allusion, musical signatures or recitative, 'suspension' is a generally useful term for discussing such passages in his music.

---

14 The reason why the Chaikovsky reference has been missed in Russian and Western scholarship until very recently may be because the ending of the 'Pathétique' is usually played so quietly that the basses' pulsating rhythm is barely heard. I only noticed it myself in 2000 in a performance where the ending did not fade out so quickly.

15 For musical examples, see Taruskin, 'Shostakovich and the Inhuman', 532–4.

16 See Nelly Kravetz, 'A New Insight into the Tenth Symphony of Dmitry Shostakovich', in Bartlett ed., *Shostakovich in Context*, 159–74.

17 Fanning, *The Breath of the Symphonist*, 53.

Another term I have suggested for a passage in the finale is *otkrïtnost*, or 'openness'. In this context, it describes the change from oscillating, semitonal figuration, which is thus *zakrïtïy*, or 'closed' in tone), to the sudden brightness of major triads ([162]). Oscillating semitones do not always signify this 'closed' tone in Shostakovich: the 'Vozrozhdenie' passage of the Fifth's finale, for example, features oscillating tones and semitones at their most radiant ([120] – [121]). But at least in the Fourth Symphony, it is nearly always the case that a 'negative' characterization features scales and semitonal oscillation, whereas a 'positive' tone is invariably created by triadic shapes that can quickly move to the major. At [162] the suddenness of that move to the major is sharply poignant, and it is very quickly withdrawn in a striking prefiguration of the close of the 'Vozrozhdenie' passage (Example 6.1).

Adorno's two other main Mahlerian categories, breakthrough and fulfilment, are also pertinent features of Shostakovich's mature style. The coda of his Fifth Symphony, for example, can be regarded as a classic case of premature (and hence unconvincing?) breakthrough and 'reversed' fulfilment, turning abruptly from minor to major at the culmination of a still threatening theme, and colouring it with the trumpets and trombones' extended ♭7–♭6–5 against D major (Example 6.2).[18] In a similar vein, the climax of the Fourth Symphony's second movement ([143]) is estranged by tonal means, negated by fixated harmonies and incessantly repeated anapest rhythms. The Fourth Symphony's finale also fails to achieve a real breakthough; rejecting the hinted-at C major suggested by the 'Resurrection' paraphrase between [235] and [238], it launches straight into an alternative C major 'fulfilment' (the 'Gloria' paraphrase) which sounds unprepared and therefore false. At other times, Shostakovich deliberately negates a potentially 'real' breakthrough: the Fourth Symphony's finale has a strong candidate for a climax theme ([182]) that breaks off at its peak with the *Lady Macbeth* sequence (from [186]) and then quickly dissipates, leading into the central divertimento section (see Example 5.8a). More convincingly, the second subject of the Fifth Symphony finale holds out the possibility of a truly uplifting ending. From its first appearance at [108], in its heroic build-up to [110] and even in its guise as the transcendently lyrical horn solo at [112]², this theme has a far more convincingly positive tone than the opening theme as it appears in the coda (see Example 6.3). At [111] it is brutally curtailed and replaced by a recollection of the opening theme before its lyrical transformation. As this lyrical passage subsides, the 'Vozrozhdenie' quotation

18 The ending of Sibelius's Second Symphony could be cited as a counter-example; the turn to D major is equally sudden, and the swirling coda theme also sounds darkly ominous until the very last moment. Moreover, it is by no means safe to assume that the audience who had wept in the slow movement of Shostakovich's Fifth found the coda unconvincing; at least one report states that many were on their feet cheering even before the end (see Taruskin, 'Shostakovich and the Inhuman', 522–3). My suggestion that the Fifth Symphony's coda is a 'reversed' breakthough/fulfilment is, therefore, only a personal view.

Example 6.1
a Shostakovich IV/3: [162] – [163]²

Largo ♩ = 69

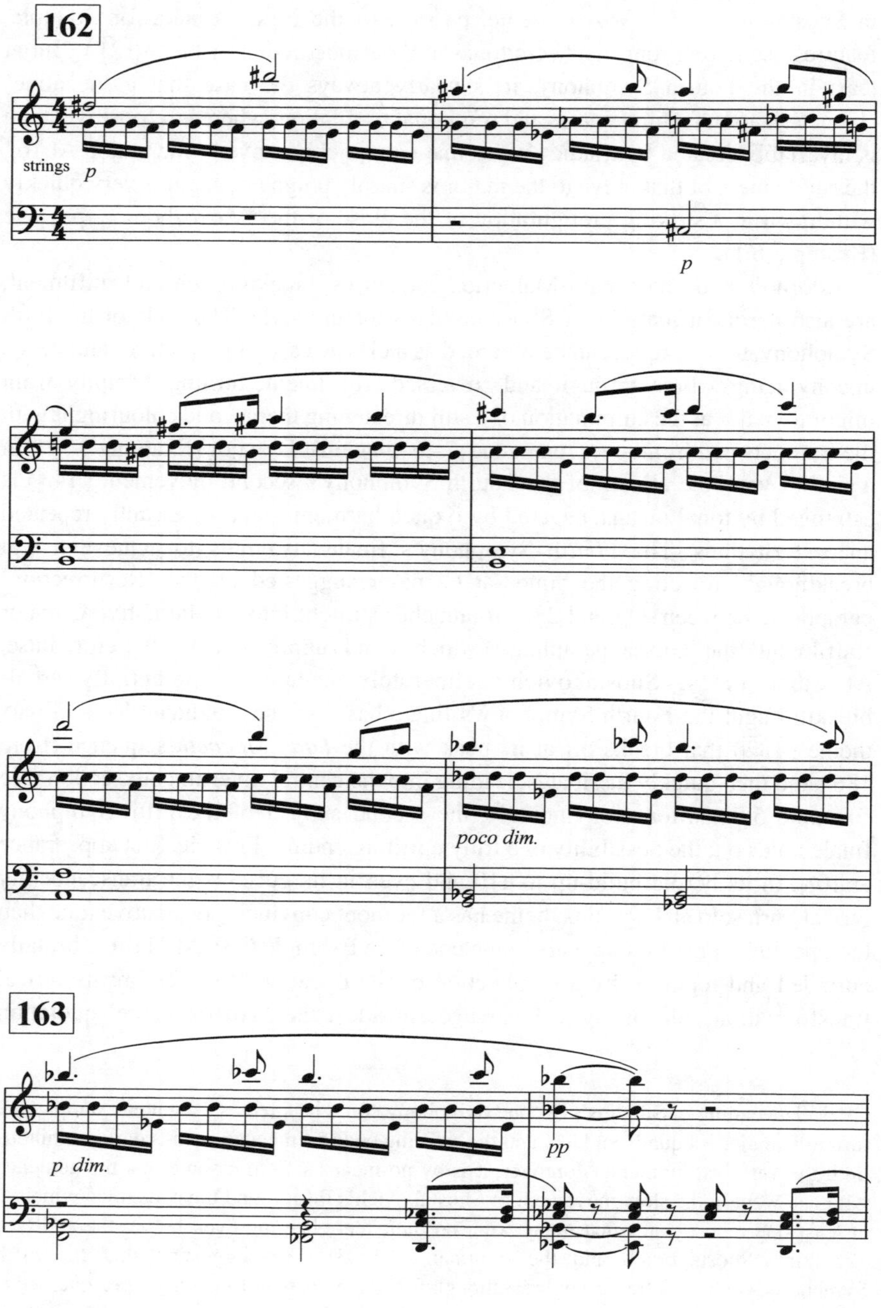

b Shostakovich V/4: $\boxed{120}^{1-13}$

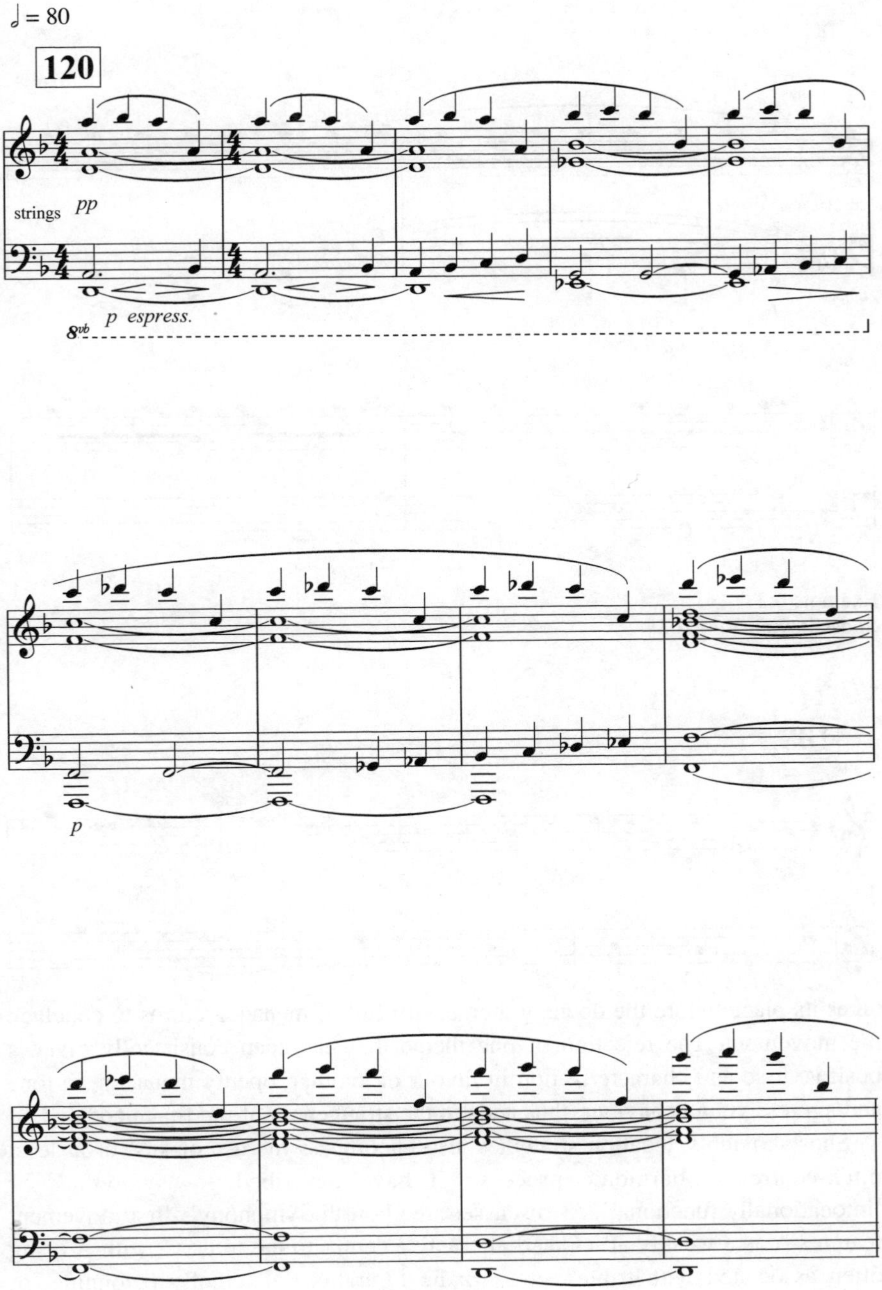

Example 6.2
Shostakovich V/4: $\boxed{133}^{5-8}$

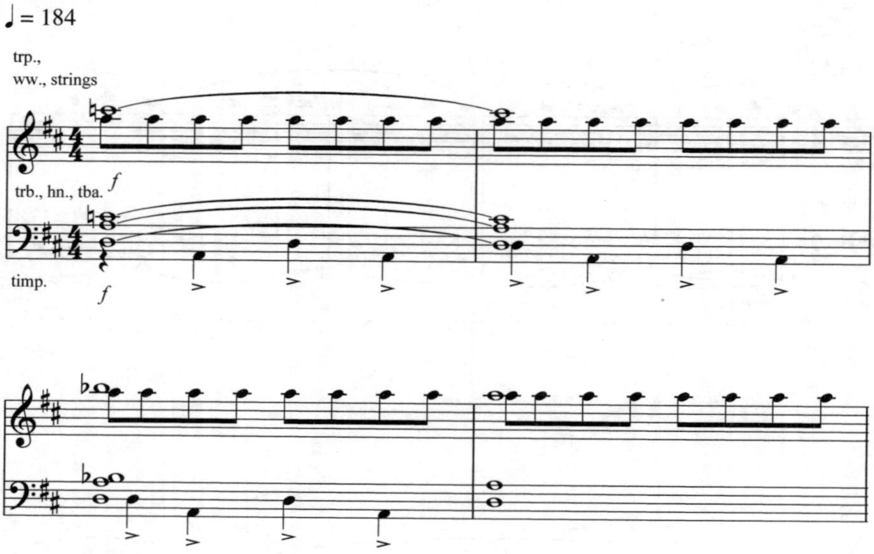

Example 6.3
Shostakovich V/4: $\boxed{108}^{1-7}$

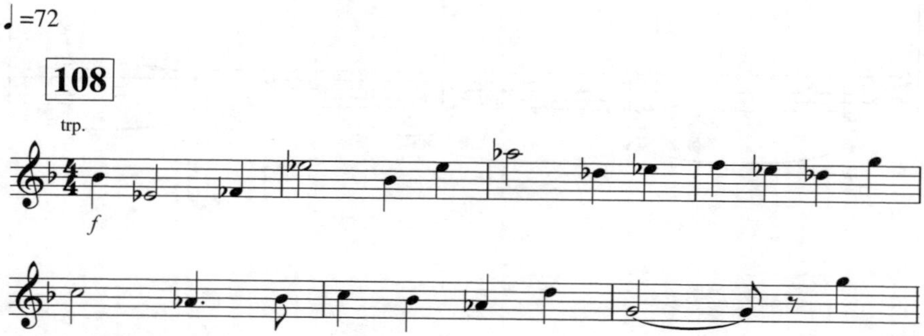

takes its place before the opening theme, still full of menace, returns to conclude the movement. The rejection of one theme that has been consistently given a positive tone and characterization in favour of another, openly menacing in tone and aggressive in behaviour, thus adds to the strangeness of the finale coda.

Shostakovich's negation strategies also encompass his use of key, or at least pitch-centre, in harmonic processes I have described as 'symbolic', or 'intonationally functional'. As discussed, the Fourth Symphony's first movement features A as a weakly articulated alternative centre to the tonic C, with A being often associated with triple-metre, triadic figuration, all chiefly belonging, or relating, to the second subject sphere. That sphere is where all the puppet- and dance-like characters are presented in their eerily disembodied form, as though hovering over the body of the movement like departed spirits from another time and place. After the waltz intonations are either brutalized or artificially smoothed over in the development ([80] – [87]), the whole sphere of A with its attendant intonations is articulated with destructive violence in the sequence of dissonant clusters between [90] and [91]. Similarly, in the finale, C♯ (flattened minor mode) takes on the role of aggressor/negator: it poses a threat to the superficial diatonic innocence of the divertimento, continually pulling its major-mode orientation back towards the minor (see especially [198]^{5} and [217]). As I have suggested in Chapter Three, the relationships between key centre and tone (or intonation) in the Fourth Symphony imply – albeit to varying degrees – a symbolic use of tonality rather than a functional one, and strongly suggest that Shostakovich planned the symphony's structure more carefully than some Western commentators have maintained. By devising such a system of relationships between harmony, themes, characters (use of musical types such as dances, scherzi, marches, triumphal codas and so on) and actual allusion or paraphrase, Shostakovich created a symphony whose dramaturgical structure penetrated its deepest fabric: one that masterfully – and very deliberately – balanced 'form' and 'content'. Its theatricality and heightened expressivity should have guaranteed that Shostakovich's colleagues could not have accused him of 'formalism' – though of course, the same could be said for *Lady Macbeth*, which was trumpeted as both musically brilliant and socially relevant before the *Pravda* articles appeared.[19] Following on directly from *Lady Macbeth*'s triumph, the Fourth Symphony displays many of the same preoccupations: use of light idioms, extreme expressive effects and immense orchestral forces, an often symbolic use of keys and themes to suggest meaning,[20] a dramatic relationship between diatonic and modal writing, and a strong use of musical types (in *Lady Macbeth*, Shostakovich evokes 'high' musical forms such as passacaglia for serious passages and 'low' genres such as operetta as sardonic commentary on superficial characters and emotions). Similarities between *Lady Macbeth* and the Fourth Symphony point not to Shostakovich's defiance of Party guidelines when he composed the symphony, but to the pre-*Pravda* approval of such techniques; and, as discussed, he may well have put the real motivation for those criticisms down to the opera's sexual content rather than to its language. *Pravda*'s musical criticisms were so vague – referring to 'fidgety, screaming, neurotic music'[21] – that Shostakovich could hardly have taken them seriously; he

19 See Fay, 'From *Lady Macbeth to Katerina*: Shostakovich's Versions and Revisions', in Fanning, ed., *Shostakovich Studies*, 160, and Taruskin, 'Shostakovich and the Inhuman', 504–5.

20 In opera, of course, such relationships are usually referred to as leitmotifs. Shostakovich – probably irritated by critics' desire to pinpoint meaning too crudely in *Lady Macbeth* – claimed that there was no use of leitmotif in his opera. However, see Fanning, 'Leitmotif in *Lady Macbeth*', in Fanning, ed., *Shostakovich Studies*, 137–59.

21 Treitler et al., eds, *Strunk's Source Readings in Music History*, 1399.

had to hope that, in the smaller-scale, abstract (and therefore less potentially controversial) genre of the symphony, his musical language would be better received.

Like any musical work, the Fourth Symphony does not 'narrate' anything that can be verbally expressed. But the musical fabric itself does 'narrate' in the sense that its relationship with the formal structures and norms of musical language that contain it is an especially fraught one. As with the Formalists' claim that Pushkin wrote *Evgeny Onegin* not to tell the story of Onegin but to comment on the human condition through the workings of the *syuzhet* or plot, so the disturbed nature of the Fourth Symphony's language and structure communicates with an intensity which becomes the 'content', or *syuzhet* of the work itself, over and above any extroversive (or historical) significance it seems to possess. As I hope to have shown, the dialogue between 'form' and 'content' in this work encompasses every facet of the compositional process, from the long-range planning of motivic and thematic growth and transformation, and the carefully worked-out relationship between tonality, theme and intonation or characterization, to the more direct semantic techniques of allusion and paraphrase. With such means at his disposal, I believe that Shostakovich intended the Fourth Symphony to show that an abstract symphony could engage with musical language and form to become far more than the sum of its parts: to communicate, however abstractly, something vital about his own society and what it means to be a human being.

Bibliography

Books

Abbate, Carolyn, *Unsung Voices: Opera and Musical Narrative in the Nineteenth Century*, Princeton: Princeton University Press, 1991.

Adorno, Theodor W., *Philosophy of Modern Music*, trans. Anne H. Mitchell and Wesley V. Bloomster, London: Sheed and Ward, 1973.

———, *Mahler: A Musical Physiognomy*, trans. Edmund Jephcott, Chicago and London: University of Chicago Press, 1992.

Agawu, V. Kofi, *Playing with Signs: A Semiotic Interpretation of Classical Music*, Princeton: Princeton University Press, 1991.

Allen, Graham, *Intertextuality*, London: Routledge, 2000.

Any, Carol, *Boris Eikhenbaum: Voices of a Russian Formalist*, Stanford, California: Stanford University Press, 1994.

Apetyan, Zarui A., *Gavriil Popov: iz literaturnogo naslediya. Stranitsï biografii* [Gavriil Popov: from a literary legacy. Pages from a biography], Moscow: Sovetskiy Kompozitor, 1986.

Aranovsky, Mark, ed., *Russkaya muzïka i XX vek* [Russian music and the twentieth century], Moscow: National Institute for the Study of the Arts, 1997.

Artizov, Andrey, and Naumov, Oleg, eds, *Vlast' i khudozhestvennaya intelligentsiya 1917-1953 gg*. [The regime and the artistic intelligentsia 1917–1953], Moscow: 'Demokratiya', 1999.

Bahr, Ehrhard, and Kunzer, Ruth Goldschmidt, *Georg Lukács*, New York: Frederick Ungar Publishing Co., Inc., 1972.

———, *Image, Music, Text*, trans. Stephen Heath, London: Fontana, 1977.

———, trans. Michael Holquist and Caryl Emerson, *The Dialogic Imagination*, ed. Michael Holquist, Austin: University of Texas Press, 1981.

———, *Problems of Dostoyevsky's Poetics*, trans. Caryl Emerson, Manchester: University of Manchester Press, 1984.

———, ed. Vadim Liapunov and Michael Holquist, *Art and Answerability*, trans. Vadim Lapunov, Austin: University of Texas Press, 1990.

Bartlett, Rosamund, ed., *Shostakovich in Context*, Oxford: Oxford University Press, 2000.

Berlin, Isaiah, *Russian Thinkers*, Harmondsworth: Penguin, 1978.

Bernandt, G.B., Yampolsky, I.M., and Kiseleva, T.E., *Kto pisal o muzïke* [Writers on music], vols 1–4, Moscow: Sovetskiy Kompozitor, 1989.

Bernard-Donals, Michael F., *Mikhail Bakhtin: Between Phenomenology and Marxism*, Cambridge: Cambridge University Press, 1994.

Blium, Arlen V., *Sovetskaya tsenzura v epokhu total'nogo terrora 1929–1953* [Soviet censorship in the epoch of totalitarian terror 1929–1953], St Petersburg: Akademicheskiy Proyekt, 2000.

Bobïkina, Irina. A., ed., *Dmitriy Shostakovich v pis'makh i dokumentakh* [Dmitri Shostakovich through letters and documents], Moscow: Glinka State Central Museum of Musical Culture, 2000.

Bogdanov-Berezovsky, Valerian M., ed., *V pervie godi sovetskogo muzïkal'nogo stroitel'stva: stat'i, vospominaniya, materiali* [In the first years of Soviet musical development: articles, reminiscences, materials], Leningrad: Sovetskiy Kompozitor, 1959.

Bonds, Mark Evan, *After Beethoven: Imperatives of Originality in the Symphony*, Cambridge, Massachusetts.: Harvard University Press, 1996.

Brandist, Craig, *Carnival Culture and the Soviet Modernist Novel*, London: Macmillan Press Ltd, 1996.

———, and Tihanov, Galin, eds, *Materializing Bakhtin: The Bakhtin Circle and Social Theory*, Basingstoke: Macmillan Press Ltd, 2000.

———, and Shepherd, David, eds, *The Bakhtin Circle: In the Master's Absence*, Manchester: Manchester University Press, 2004.

Braun, Edward, *Meyerhold on Theatre*, London: Methuen, 1969.

———, *Meyerhold: A Revolution in Theatre*, Iowa City: University of Iowa Press, 1995.

Brown, Edward J., *Mayakovsky – A Poet in the Revolution*, Princeton: Princeton University Press, 1973.

———, *Russian Literature Since the Revolution*, revised edition. Cambridge, Massachusetts: Harvard University Press, 1982.

Brown, Malcolm Hamrick, ed., *A Shostakovich Casebook*, Bloomington and Indianapolis: Indiana University Press, 2004.

———, and Wiley, Roland J., eds, *Slavonic and Western Music: Essays for Gerald Abraham*, Ann Arbor: University of Michigan Research Press, 1985.

Channon, John, ed., *Politics, Society and Stalinism in the USSR*, Basingstoke: Macmillan Press, 1998.

Chung, Hilary, ed., *In the Party Spirit: Socialist Realism and Literary Practice in the Soviet Union, East Germany and China*, Amsterdam: Rodoni, 1994.

Clark, Katerina, *The Soviet Novel: History as Ritual*, Chicago and London: University of Chicago Press, 1981.

———, *Petersburg, Crucible of Cultural Revolution*, Cambridge, Massachusetts: Harvard University Press, 1995.

Clayton, J. Douglas, *Pierrot in Petrograd: The Commedia dell'Arte/Balagan in Twentieth-Century Russian Theatre and Drama*, Montreal and Kingston: McGill-Queen's University Press, 1993.

Cohen, Stephen F., *Bukharin and the Bolshevik Revolution: A Political Biography 1888–1938*, London: Wildwood House, 1974.

Conquest, Robert, *The Great Terror*, London: Macmillan, 1968.

Cooke, Deryck, *Gustav Mahler: An Introduction to his Music*, second edition, London: Faber, 1988.

Danilevich, Lev, *Dmitriy Shostakovich*, Moscow: Sovetskiy Kompozitor, 1980.

Darby, Joseph E., 'Dmitri Shostakovich's Second, Third and Fourth Symphonies: Problems of Context, Analysis and Interpretation', PhD diss., City University of New York, 1999.

Davies, Sarah, *Popular Opinion in Stalin's Russia: Terror, Propaganda and Dissent, 1934-1941*, Cambridge: Cambridge University Press, 1997.

Eaton, Katherine Bliss, *The Theater of Meyerhold and Brecht*, Westport, Connecticut: Greenwood Press, 1985.

Eco, Umberto, *The Role of the Reader*, Bloomington: Indiana University Press, 1979.

———, *Semiotics and the Philosophy of Language*, Bloomington: Indiana University Press, 1986.

———, *The Open Work*, Cambridge, Massachusetts: Harvard University Press, 1989.

Edmunds, Neil, *The Soviet Proletarian Musical Movement*, Bern: Peter Lang, 2000.

———, ed., *Soviet Music and Society under Lenin and Stalin: The Baton and Sickle*, London and New York: RoutledgeCurzon, 2004.

Emerson, Caryl, *Boris Godunov: Transpositions of a Russian Theme*, Bloomington: Indiana University Press, 1983.

———, *The First Hundred Years of Mikhail Bakhtin*, Princeton: Princeton University Press, 1997.

Erlich, Victor, *Russian Formalism: History-Doctrine*, New Haven and London: Yale University Press, 1965.

———, ed., *Twentieth-Century Russian Literary Criticism*, New Haven and London: Yale University Press, 1975.

Ermolaev, Herman, *Censorship in Soviet Literature 1917–1991*, Lanham, Maryland: Rowman & Littlefield Publishers, Inc., 1997.

Fanning, David, *The Breath of the Symphonist: Shostakovich's Tenth*, London: Royal Musical Association, 1988.

———, *Shostakovich: String Quartet No. 8*. Aldershot: Ashgate, 2004.

———, ed., *Shostakovich Studies*, Cambridge: Cambridge University Press, 1995.

Fay, Laurel, *Shostakovich: A Life*, Oxford: Oxford University Press, 2000.

Fitzpatrick, Sheila, *The Cultural Front: Power and Culture in Revolutionary Russia*, New York: Cornell University Press, 1992.

———, *Everyday Stalinism*, Oxford: Oxford University Press, 1999.

———, ed., *Cultural Revolution in Russia 1928–1931*, Bloomington: Indiana University Press, 1978.

Floros, Constantin, *Gustav Mahler: The Symphonies*, trans. Vernon Wicker, Aldershot: Scolar Press, 1994.

Freeborn, Richard, *The Russian Revolutionary Novel*, Cambridge: Cambridge University Press, 1982.

Garrard, John and Carol, *Inside the Soviet Writers' Union*, London: The Free Press, 1990.

Garros, Véronique, Korenevskaya, Natalia, and Lahusen, Thomas, eds, *Intimacy and Terror: Soviet Diaries of the 1930s*, New York: The New Press, 1995.

Glikman, Isaak, ed., *Pis'ma k drugu: Dmitriy Shostakovich–Isaaku Glikmanu* [Letters to a friend: Dmitriy Shostakovich to Isaac Glikman], Moscow: DSCH and St Petersburg: Kompozitor, 1993.

Glikman, Isaak, Story of a Friendship, trans. Anthony Phillips, London: Faber, 2001.

Golub, Spencer, *Evreinov – The Theatre of Paradox and Transformation*, Ann Arbor: University of Michigan Research Press, 1984.

Grigoriev, L., and Platek, Ya., *Dmitry Shostakovich about Himself and his Times*, Moscow: Progress, 1980.

Groys, Boris, *The Total Art of Stalinism: Avant-Garde, Aesthetic Dictatorship and Beyond*, Princeton: Princeton University Press, 1992.

Günther, Hans, ed., *The Culture of the Stalin Period*, London: Macmillan, 1990.

Haas, David, *Leningrad's Modernists: Studies in Composition and Musical Thought, 1917–1932*, New York: Peter Lang, 1998.

Hakobian, Levon, *Music of the Soviet Age, 1917–1987*, Stockholm: Melos, 1998.

————, *Dmitriy Shostakovich: opït fenomenologii tvorchestva* [Dmitriy Shostakovich: an attempt [to analyse] the phenomenology of his creatve activity], St Petersburg: Dmitriy Bulanin, 2004.

Hayward, Max, and Labedz, Leopold, *Literature and Revolution in Soviet Russia 1917–62*, London: Oxford University Press, 1963.

Hefling, Stephen, ed., *Mahler Studies*, Cambridge: Cambridge University Press, 1997.

Hingley, Ronald, *Russia: A Concise History*, revised edition, London: Thames and Hudson, 1991.

Hirschkop, Ken, *Mikhail Bakhtin: An Aesthetic for Democracy*, Oxford: Oxford University Press, 1999.

Ho, Allan B., and Feofanov, Dmitry, eds, *Shostakovich Reconsidered*, London: Toccata Press, 1998.

Hulme, Derek C. Dmitri *Shostakovich: A Catalogue, Bibliography and Discography*, second edition. Oxford: Clarendon Press, 1991.

Jackson, Timothy L., *Tchaikovsky: Symphony No. 6 (Pathétique)*, Cambridge: Cambridge University Press, 1999.

Kadarkay, Arpad, ed., *The Lukács Reader*, Oxford: Blackwell Publishers Ltd, 1995.

Kay, Norman, *Shostakovich*, London, Oxford: Oxford University Press, 1971.

Kelly, Catriona, *Petrushka: The Russian Carnival Puppet Theatre*, Cambridge: Cambridge University Press, 1990.

———, and Shepherd, David, *Constructing Russian Culture in the Age of Revolution: 1881–1940*, Oxford: Oxford University Press, 1998.

———, eds, *Russian Cultural Studies: An Introduction*, Oxford: Oxford University Press, 1998.

Khentova, Sof'ya, *Shostakovich v Petrograde-Leningrade* [Shostakovich in Petrograd-Leningrad], Leningrad: Lenizdat, 1979.

———, *Shostakovich: zhizn' i tvorchestvo* [Shostakovich: life and works], Leningrad: Sovetskiy Kompozitor, 1985.

———, *V mire Shostakovicha* [In Shostakovich's world], Moscow: Kompozitor, 1996.

Kiralyfalvi, Béla, *The Aesthetics of Georgy Lukács*, Princeton: Princeton University Press, 1975.

Koball, Michael, *Pathos und Groteske: Die deutsche Tradition im symphonischen Schaffen von Dmitri Schostakowitsch*, Berlin: Verlag Ernst Kuhn, 1997.

Kopp, Karen, *Form und Gehalt der Symphonien des Dmitrij Schostakowitsch*, Bonn: Verlag für Systematische Muzikwissenschaft, 1990.

Kotkin, Stephen, *Magnetic Mountain: Stalinism as a Civilisation*, Berkeley: University of California Press, 1995.

Kovnatskaya, Lyudmila G., ed., *Shostakovich: mezhdu mgnoveniem i Vechnost'iyu. Dokumentï. Materialï. Stat'i* [Shostakovich: between a moment and eternity. Documents, materials, articles], St Petersburg: Kompozitor, 2000.

Kramer, Lawrence, *Franz Schubert: Sexuality, Subjectivity, Song*, Cambridge: Cambridge University Press, 1998.

———, *Musical Meaning: Toward a Critical History*, Berkeley: University of California Press, 2002.

Kröplin, Ekhart, *Frühe sowjetische Oper*, Berlin: Henschelverlag, 1985.

Krylova, S., and Lebedinskiy, L., *Rabochiye o literature, teatr i muzïke* [Workers on literature, theatre and music], Leningrad: Priboy, 1926.

Lahusen, Thomas, and Dobrenko, Evgeny, *Socialist Realism without Shores*, Durham, North Carolina, and London: Duke University Press, 1997.

Layton, Robert, ed., *A Companion to the Symphony*, London: Simon and Schuster, 1993.

Leach, Robert, *Vsevolod Meyerhold*, London: Cambridge University Press, 1989.

Lemon, Lee T., and Reis, Marion J., *Russian Formalist Criticism: Four Essays*, Lincoln, Nebraska: University of Nebraska Press, 1965.

Longman, Richard M., *Expression and Structure: Processes of Integration in the Large-Scale Instrumental Music of Dmitri Shostakovich*, London: Garland Publishing Inc., 1989.

Lukács, Georg, *The Meaning of Contemporary Realism*, trans. John and Necke Mander, London: Merlin Press, 1963.

———, *Writer and Critic*, trans. Arthur Kahn, London: Merlin Press, 1970.

———, *Studies in European Realism*, trans. Edith Bone, London: Merlin Press, 1972.

Lunacharsky, Anatoly, *On Literature and Art*, trans. Avril Pyman and Fainna Glagoleva, Moscow: Progress Publishers, 1973.

MacDonald, Ian, *The New Shostakovich*, Oxford: Oxford University Press, 1990.

MacFadyen, David, *Songs for Fat People: Affect, Emotion and Celebrity in the Russian Popular Song, 1900–1955*, Montreal and Kingston: McGill-Queen's University Press, 2002.

McQuere, Gordon, ed., *Russian Theoretical Thought in Music*, Ann Arbor: University of Michigan Research Press, 1983.

Maksimenkov, Leonid, *Sumbur vmesto muzïki: Stalinskaya kul'turnaya revolutsiya 1936–1938* [Muddle instead of music: the Stalinist cultural revolution 1936–1938], Moscow: Yuridicheskaya Kniga, 1997.

Malko, Nikolai, *A Certain Art*, New York: William Morrow, 1966.

Markov, Vladimir, *Russian Futurism: A History*, London: Macgibbon and Kee Ltd, 1969.

Marples, David, *Motherland: Russia in the Twentieth Century*, London: Pearson Education Limited, 2002.

Martynov, Ivan, *Dmitri Shostakovich: The Man and his Work*, trans. T. Guralsky, New York: Greenwood Press, 1947.

Matejka, Ladislav, and Pomorska, Krystyna, *Readings in Russian Poetics: Formalist and Structuralist Views*, Cambridge, Massachusetts: The MIT Press, 1971.

Mazel', Lev, *Etiudï o Shostakoviche: stat'i i zametki o tvorchestve* [Shostakovich studies: articles and writings on his work], Moscow: Sovetskiy Kompozitor, 1986.

Mikheyeva, Lyudmila, *Pamyati I.I. Sollertinskogo: vospominaniya, materialï, issledovaniya* [In memory of I.I. Sollertinskiy: reminiscences, materials, works], Leningrad: Sovetskiy Kompozitor, 1974.

———, *I.I. Sollertinskiy: zhizn' i naslediye* [I.I. Sollertinskiy: life and legacy], Leningrad: Sovetskiy Kompozitor, 1988.

———, *Zhizn' Dmitriya Shostakovicha* [Life of Dmitriy Shostakovich], Moscow: 'Terra', 1997.

Mitchell, Donald, *Gustav Mahler: The Wunderhorn Years*, California: University of California Press, 1975.

Moshevich, Sofia, *Dmitri Shostakovich, Pianist*, Montreal and Kingston, McGill-Queen's University Press, 2004.

Nelson, Amy, *Music for the Revolution: Musicians and Power in Early Soviet Russia*, University Park, Pennysylvania: Pennysylvania University Press, 2004.

Nestyev, Israel V., *Prokofiev*, Stanford, California: Stanford University Press, 1961.

Norris, Christopher, ed., *Shostakovich: The Man and his Music*, London: Lawrence and Wishart, 1982.

Nove, Alec, ed., *The Stalin Phenomenon*, London: Weidenfeld and Nicolson, 1993.

O'Connor, Timothy, *The Politics of Soviet Culture: Anatolii Lunacharsky*, Ann Arbor: University of Michigan Research Press, 1983.

Olkhovsky, Andrey V., *Music under the Soviets: The Agony of an Art*, London: Routledge and Kegan Paul, 1955.

Ordzhonikidze, Givi, ed., *Dmitriy Shostakovich*, Moscow: Sovetskiy Kompozitor, 1967.

Ottaway, Hugh, *Shostakovich's Symphonies*, London: BBC, 1978.

Paperno, Irina, and Grossman, Joan Delaney, eds, *Creating Life: The Aesthetic Utopia of Russian Modernism*, Stanford, California: Stanford University Press, 1994.

Peterson, Ronald E., *A History of Russian Symbolism*, Amsterdam: John Benjamins Publishing Company, 1993.

Pike, Christopher, ed., *The Futurists, the Formalists and the Marxist Critique*, London: Ink Links, 1979.

Polyakova, Lyudmila, *Soviet Music*, Moscow: Foreign Languages Publishing House, 1961.

Pople, Anthony, ed., *Theory, Analysis and Meaning in Music*, Cambridge: Cambridge University Press, 1994.

Popova, I.E., *Aram Khachaturian: stat'i i vospominaniya* [Aram Khachaturian: articles and reminiscences], Moscow: Sovietskiy Kompozitor, 1980.

Proffer, Carl R., ed., *Modern Russian Poets on Poetry*, Ann Arbor: Ardis, 1976.

Pushkin, Aleksandr, *Boris Godunov*, trans. Philip L. Barbour, Westport, Connecticut: Greenwood Press, 1953.

Pyman, Avril, *A History of Russian Symbolism*, London: Cambridge University Press, 1994.

Rabinovich, David, *Dmitri Shostakovich – Composer*, trans. George Hanna, London: Lawrence and Wishart, 1959.

Razhnikov, V,. *Kirill Kondrashin rasskazïvaet o muzïke i zhizni* [Kirill Kondrashin talks about music and life], Moscow: Sovetskiy Kompozitor, 1989.

Roseberry, Eric, *Ideology, Style, Content and Thematic Process in the Symphonies, Cello Concertos and String Quartets of Shostakovich*, New York and London: Garland Publishing Inc., 1989.

Rudnitsky, Konstantin, *Meyerhold the Director*, trans. George Petrov, Ann Arbor: Ardis, 1981.

Russell, Robert, and Barratt, Andrew, *Russian Theatre in the Age of Modernism*, London: Macmillan Press, 1990.

Sabinina, Marina, *Shostakovich-simfonist: dramaturgiya, estetika, stil'* [Shostakovich-symphonist: dramaturgy, aesthetics, style], Moscow: Muzïka, 1976.

Samuels, Robert, *Mahler's Sixth Symphony: A Study in Musical Semiotics*, Cambridge: Cambridge University Press, 1995.

Scher, Steven Paul, ed., *Music and Text: Critical Inquiries*, Cambridge: Cambridge University Press, 1992.

Schmidt, Paul, ed., *Meyerhold at Work*, Manchester: Carcanet New Press, 1981.

Schoenberg, Arnold, *Style and Idea*, London: Faber, 1975.

Schwarz, Boris, *Music and Musical Life in Soviet Russia, 1917–1981*, enlarged edition, Bloomington: Indiana University Press, 1983.

Scott, H.G., ed., *Problems of Soviet Literature*, Westport, Connecticut: Greenwood Press, 1979.

Scriven, Michael, and Tate, Dennis, *European Socialist Realism*, Oxford: Berg Publishers, 1988.

Shakhnazarova, Nelli G., *Paradoksï sovetskoy muzïkal'noy kul'turï. 30-e godï* [Paradoxes of Soviet musical culture in the 1930s], Moscow: 'Indrik', 2001.

Shalin, Dmitri N., *Russian Culture at the Crossroads: Paradoxes of Postcommunist Consciousness*, Boulder, Colorado: Westview Press, Inc., 1996.

Shebalina, A.M., ed., *Pamyati V. Ya. Shebalina: vospominaniya, materiali* [In memory of V.Ya. Shebalin. Reminiscences, materials], Moscow: Sovetskiy Kompozitor, 1984.

———, *V.Ya. Shebalin: godï zhizni i tvorchestva* [V.Ya. Shebalin: life and works], Moscow: Sovetskiy Kompozitor, 1990.

Sheinberg, Esti, *Irony, Satire, Parody and the Grotesque in the Music of Shostakovich: A Theory of Musical Incongruities*, Aldershot: Ashgate, 2000.

Shukman, Ann, *Bakhtin School Papers*, Oxford: RPT Publications, 1988.

Skurko, Ye.R., and Chigareva, Ye.I., eds, *V.P. Bobrovskiy: stat'i, issledovaniya* [V.P. Bobrovskiy: articles and works], Moscow: Sovetskiy Kompozitor, 1990.

Slonim, Marc, *Soviet Russian Literature: Writers and Problems 1917–1967*, Oxford: Oxford University Press, 1964.

Sollertinskiy, Dmitri and Lyudmila, *Pages from the Life of Dmitri Shostakovich*, trans.G. Hobbs and C. Midgley, London: Robert Hale, 1981.

Sollertinskiy, Ivan I., *Gustav Maler*, Leningrad: Muzgiz, 1932.

———, *Izbranniye stat'i o muzïke* [Collected articles on music], Leningrad-Moscow: Muzgiz, 1946.

———, *Istoricheskiye etyudï* [Historical studies], Leningrad: Muzgiz, 1963.

———, *Kriticheskiye stat'i* [Critical articles], Leningrad: Muzgiz, 1963.

Starr, S. Frederick, *Red and Hot: The Fate of Jazz in the Soviet Union 1917–1980*, Oxford: Oxford University Press, 1985.

Steiner, Wendy, ed., *The Sign in Music and Literature*, Austin: University of Texas Press, 1981.

Stetina, Edmund, *Die Vierte Symphonie von Dmitrij Šostakovič: Ein zurückbehaltenes Bekenntnis*, Aachen: Shaker-Verlag, 1997.

Straus, Joseph N., *Remaking the Past: Musical Modernism and the Influence of the Tonal Tradition*, Cambridge, Massachusetts: Harvard University Press, 1990.

Struve, Gleb, *Russian Literature under Lenin and Stalin 1917–1953*, Norman, Oklahoma: University of Oklahoma Press, 1971.

Talbot, Michael, *The Finale in Western Instrumental Music*, Oxford: Oxford University Press, 2001.

Tammaro, Ferruccio, *Le sinfonie di Šostakovič*, Turin: G. Giappichelli Editore, 1988.

Taruskin, Richard, *Musorgsky: Eight Essays and an Epilogue*, Princeton: Princeton University Press, 1993.

———, *Defining Russia Musically*, Princeton: Princeton University Press, 1997.

Terras, Victor, ed., *Handbook of Russian Literature*, New Haven and London: Yale University Press, 1985.

Thurston, Robert W., *Life and Terror in Stalin's Russia 1934–1941*, New Haven and London: Yale University Press, 1996.

Treitler, Leo, et al., eds, *Strunk's Source Readings in Music History*, New York: Norton, 1997.

Tull, James Robert, 'B.V. Asaf'ev's Musical Form as a Process: Translation and Commentary', PhD diss., Ohio State University, 1977.

Vaughan James, C., *Soviet Socialist Realism: Origins and Theory*, London: Macmillan Press, 1973.

Volkov, Solomon, *Testimony: The Memoirs of Dimitri Shostakovich as Related to and Edited by Solomon Volkov*, London: Faber, 1981.

———, *Shostakovich and Stalin*, London: Little, Brown, 2004.

Werth, Alexander, *Musical Uproar in Moscow*, London: Turnstile Press, 1949.

Wilson, Elizabeth, *Shostakovich: A Life Remembered*, London: Faber, 1994.

Articles

Atovmyan, Levon, 'Iz vospominaniy' [From a reminiscence], *Muzïkal'naya akademiya*, 1997/4, 67–77.

Barber, John, 'The Establishment of Intellectual Orthodoxy in the U.S.S.R. 1928–1934', *Past and Present*, 83, 1979, 141–64.

Bobrovskiy, Viktor, 'Posle pervogo ispolneniya Chetvërtoy' [After the first performance of the Fourth], in Skurko and Chigareva, eds, *V.P. Bobrovskiy: stat'i, issledovaniya*, 262–70.

———, 'Rol' simmetrii v protsesse formoobrazovaniya Shostakovicha' [The role of symmetry in Shostakovich's formal processes], in Skurko and Chigareva, eds, *V.P. Bobrovskiy: stat'i, issledovaniya*, 192–205.

Bogdanov-Berezovskiy, Valerian M., 'K probleme sovetskogo simfonizma' [On the problem of Soviet symphonism], *Sovetskaya muzïka*, 1934/6, 29–44.

Brooks, Jeffrey, 'Socialist Realism in *Pravda*: Read All About It!', *Slavic Review*, 53, 1994, 953–71.

Brown, Malcolm H., 'The Soviet Russian Concepts of "Intonatsia" and "Musical Imagery"', *The Musical Quarterly*, 30/4, 1974, 557–67.

Buhler, James, '"Breakthrough" as Critique of Form: The Finale of Mahler's First Symphony', *19th-Century Music*, 20/2, 1996–97, 125–43.

Burke, Richard N., 'Film, Narrative, and Shostakovich's Last Quartet', *The Musical Quarterly*, 83/3, 1991, 413–29.

Carpenter, Ellon E., 'Russian Theorists on Modality in Shostakovich's Music', in Fanning, ed., *Shostakovich Studies*, 76–112.

Cone, Edward T., 'Schubert's Promissory Note: An Exercise in Musical Hermeneutics', *19th-Century Music*, 5/3, 1982, 233–41.

Dearling, Robert, 'The First Twelve Symphonies: Portrait of the Artist as Citizen-Composer', in Christopher Norris, ed., *Shostakovich: The Man and his Music*, London: Lawrence and Wishart, 1982, 47–80.

Dobrenko, Evgeny, 'The Disaster of Middlebrow Taste, or, Who "Invented" Socialist Realism?', *South Atlantic Quarterly*, 94/3, 1995, 773-806.

Eisen, Samuel D., 'Whose Lenin is it Anyway? Viktor Shklovsky, Boris Eikhenbaum and the Formalist-Marxist Debate in Soviet Cultural Politics', *The Russian Review*, 55, 1996, 65–79.

Fairclough, Pauline, 'Mahler Reconstructed: Sollertinsky and the Soviet Symphony', *The Musical Quarterly*, 85/2, 2001, 367–90.

———, 'The "Perestroyka" of Soviet Symphonism: Shostakovich in 1935', *Music and Letters*, 83/2, 2002, 259–73.

Fanning, David, 'The Soviet Symphony', in Robert Layton, ed., *A Companion to the Symphony*, London: Simon and Schuster, 1993, 292–326.

———, 'Leitmotif in *Lady Macbeth*, in Fanning, ed., *Shostakovich Studies*, 137–59.

———, 'Shostakovich in Harmony', in Bartlett, ed., *Shostakovich in Context*, 31–42.

———, 'Shostakovich: "The Present-Day Master of the C-major Key"', *Acta Musicologica*, 73, 2001, 101–40.

Fay, Laurel, 'Shostakovich versus Volkov: Whose *Testimony*?' *The Russian Review*, 39, 1980, 484–93.

Frolova-Walker, Marina, 'National in Form, Socialist in Content: Musical nation-building in the Soviet Republics', *Journal of the American Musicological Society*, 51/2, 1998, 331–71.

Graham, Gordon, 'Lukács and Realism after Marx', *The British Journal of Aesthetics*, 38/2, 1998, 198–208.

Haas, David, 'Boris Asaf'ev and Soviet Symphonic Theory', *The Musical Quarterly*, 76/3, 1992, 410–32.

Heller, Leonid, 'A World of Prettiness: Socialist Realism and its Aesthetic Categories', *South Atlantic Quarterly*, 94/3, 1995, 687–713.

Jha, Prabhakara, 'Lukács, Bakhtin and the Sociology of the Novel', *Diogenes*, 129, 1985, 63–90.

Johnson, Julian, 'Analysis in Adorno's Aesthetics of Music', *Music Analysis*, 24/2–3, 1995, 295–313.

Kiralyfalvi, Béla, 'Georg Lukács or Bertolt Brecht?', *The British Journal of Aesthetics*, 25, 1985, 340–48.

Körner, Klaus, 'Schostakowitschs Vierte Sinfonie', *Archiv für Musikwissenschaft*, 31/2–3, 1974, 116-136, 214–36.

Korsyn, Kevin, 'Towards a New Poetics of Musical Influence', *Music Analysis*, 10/1–2, 1991, 3–72.

Kramer, Lawrence, 'Haydn's Chaos, Schenker's Order; or, Hermeneutics and Musical Analysis: Can they Mix?', *19th-Century Music*, 16/1, 1992, 3–17.

McCreless, Patrick, 'The Cycle of Structure and the Cycle of Meaning: The Piano Trio in E minor, Op. 67', in Fanning, ed., *Shostakovich Studies*, 113–36.

Maus, Fred Everett, 'Music as Narrative', *Indiana Theory Review*, 12, 1991, 1–34.

Micznik, Vera, 'Mahler and "The Power of Genre"', *Journal of Musicology*, 12/1, 1994, 117–51.

———, 'The Farewell Story of Mahler's Ninth Symphony', *19th-Century Music*, 20, 1996–97, 144–66.

———, 'Music and Narrative Revisited: Degrees of Narrativity in Beethoven and Mahler', *Journal of the Royal Musical Association*, 126/2, 2001, 193–249.

Nattiez, Jean-Jacques, 'Can One Speak of Narrativity in Music?', *Journal of the Royal Musical Association*, 115/2, 1990, 240–58.

Newcomb, Anthony, 'Once More "Between Absolute and Program Music": Schumann's Second Symphony', *19th-Century Music*, 7/3, 1984, 233–48.

Orlov, Genrikh, 'V serediniye puti' [In the middle of the journey], in Ordzhonikidze, ed., *Dmitri Shostakovich*, 166–88.

Ottaway, Hugh, 'Looking Again at Shostakovich 4', *Tempo*, 115, 1975, 14–24.

Rothstein, Robert A., 'The Quiet Rehabilitation of the Brick Factory: Early Soviet Popular Music and its Critics', *Slavic Review*, 39/3, 1980, 373–88.

Shnitke, Al'fred, 'Zametki ob orkestrovoy polifonii v chetvërtoy simfonii D.D. Shostakovicha' [Notes on the orchestral polyphony of Shostakovich's Fourth Symphony], *Muzïka i sovremennost'* [Contemporary music], 1966/4, 127–61.

Shostakovich, Dmitri, 'Dumï o proydennom puti' [Thoughts about paths I have taken], *Sovetskaya muzïka*, 1956/9, 14.

Sollertinskiy, Ivan, 'Problema simfonizma v sovetskoy muzïke' [The problem of symphonism in Soviet music], *Zhizn' iskusstva* [Life of art], 46, 1929, 1–3.

Souster, Tim, 'Shostakovich at the Crossroads', *Tempo*, 78, 1966, 2–9.

Spiridonova, Lidia, 'Gorky and Stalin', *The Russian Review*, 54, 1995, 413–23.

Straus, Joseph N., 'The "Anxiety of Influence" in Twentieth-Century Music', *Journal of Musicology*, 9/4, 1991, 430–47.

Taruskin, Richard, 'Interpreting Shostakovich's Fifth Symphony', in Fanning, ed., *Shostakovich Studies*, 17–56.

———, 'Shostakovich and the Inhuman', in Taruskin, *Defining Russia Musically*, 468–544.

Val'kova, Vera, 'Tragicheskiy balagan: k voprosu o kontseptsii Chetvërtoy simfonii' [The tragic *balagan*: on the question of the conception of the Fourth Symphony]', *Muzïkal'naya akademiya*, 1997/4, 78–84.

Whitesell, Lloyd, 'Men with a Past: Music and the "Anxiety of Influence"', *19th-Century Music*, 18/2, 1994, 152–67.

Yakubov, Manashir, 'The "Original" Fourth Symphony', *DSCH Journal*, 15, 2001, 60–62.

Scores

Beethoven, L. van, Symphony No. 3 'Eroica' Op. 55, New York: Dover, 1997.

Berlin, Irving, *The Songs of Irving Berlin: Ballads*, Milwaukee: Hal Leonard Corp., 1991.

Kabalevskiy, Dmitriy, Symphony No. 1 Op. 18, Moscow: Muzgiz, 1934.

———, Symphony No. 2 Op. 19, New York: Leeds Music Corp., 1945.

Khrennikov, Tikhon, Symphony No. 1 Op. 4, New York: Leeds Music Corp., 1945.

Mahler, Gustav, Symphony No. 1, New York: Dover, 1987.

———, Symphony No. 2, New York: Dover, 1987.

———, Symphony No. 6, New York: Dover, 1991.

———, Symphony No. 9, New York: Dover, 1993.

———, Symphony No. 10: *A Performing Version of the Draft for the Tenth Symphony, prepared by Deryck Cooke*, London: Faber, 1976.

———, *Lieder eines fahrenden Gesellen*, ed. Colin Matthews, London: Josef Weinberger Ltd, 1977.

———, *Fünfzehn Lieder, Humoresken und Balladen aus Des Knaben Wunderhorn*, Vienna: Universal Edition, 1994.

Musorgskiy, Modest, *Boris Godunov*, Moscow: Muzgiz, 1959.

Myaskovskiy, Nikolay, Symphony No. 11 Op. 34, Moscow: Muzgiz 1934.

———, Symphony No. 12 Op. 35, Moscow: Muzgiz, 1932.

———, Symphony No. 15 Op. 38, Moscow: Muzgiz, 1937.

———, Symphony No. 16 Op. 39, Moscow: Voks, 1947.

Popov, Gavriil, Symphony No. 1 Op. 7, unpublished score, personal collection of David Fanning.

Shcherbachëv, Vladimir, Symphony No. 3, Moscow: Muzgiz, 1935.

Shebalin, Vissarion, 'Lenin' Dramatic Symphony Op. 16, Moscow: Muzgiz, 1960.

———, Symphony No. 3 Op. 17, Moscow: VOKS, 1946.

Shostakovich, Dmitriy, Symphony No. 1 Op. 10, vol. 1 of the collected works, Moscow: Muzïka, 1987.

———, Suite from *The Golden Age* Op. 22, Moscow: Muzïka, 1987.

———, *Lady Macbeth of the Mtsensk District* Op. 29, Hamburg: Sikorski, 1979.

———, Symphony No. 4 Op. 43 for two pianos. Moscow: DSCH Publishers, 2000.

———, Symphony No. 4 Op. 43. Moscow: DSCH Publishers, 2003.

———, autograph manuscript of the two-piano reduction. Glinka State Museum of Musical Culture, fond. 32, ed. xr. 98; facsimile up to [139] in the Centre Chostakovich archive, Paris.

———, Symphony No. 4 Op. 43, Hamburg: Sikorski, 1962.

———, Symphony No. 4 Op. 43, Moscow: Muzïka, 1982.

———, Symphony No. 4 Op. 43, New York: Kalmus, n.d.

———, Symphony No. 5 Op. 47, London: Eulenburg, 1966.

———, Cello Concerto No. 2 Op. 126, London: Boosey and Hawkes, 1968.
———, Symphony No. 15 Op. 141, Hamburg: Sikorski, 1972.

Videos

Larry Weinstein (director), *The War Symphonies: Shostakovich against Stalin*, Oley, Pennsylvania: Bullfrog Films, 1997.

Index